ERIC MENDELSOHN
Architect 1887–1953

ERIC MENDELSOHN
Architect 1887–1953

Edited by Regina Stephan

With essays by Charlotte Benton, Ita Heinze-Greenberg, Kathleen James, Hans R. Morgenthaler, and Regina Stephan

THE MONACELLI PRESS

Contents

Foreword

My father, Eric Mendelsohn, was what I would call a well-rounded human being. He was an innovator and a renaissance man. He was not only an architect, for he knew so much about all aspects of art, economics, politics, music, and philosophy—not just superficially, but earnestly—as if he had studied these disciplines all his life.

He was wise at predicting the future, exhibiting uncanny foresight regarding political events and wartime issues. He was, however, not a very social person. He preferred to be alone in his study or office, working late into the night, always accompanied by the music of Bach or Beethoven. Since he shared a birthday, March 21, with Bach, he always felt a strong connection with this beloved composer, and many of his famous sketches were born listening to music.

Eric was a very definite and positive person, strong in his opinions and strong in his beliefs—he knew no concessions. Fortunately, he was blessed with a great sense of humor, which provided balance to his personality. As his daughter, I found him intimidating, and yet I was full of admiration for him. We shared similar appetites and he loved playing with me, both at home and in the world.

Since my mother, Louise, died nineteen years ago, I have taken on the duties of promoting the works of my father. I find that he deserves as much honor and admiration today as he did in the 1920s.

Esther Mendelsohn-Joseph

Preface

There are three very closely related things with which I would like to preface this book: an explanation of its origin, a clarification of points that may at first be confusing, and an expression of gratitude for help and support.

This book grew out of the realization that despite the significance of Eric Mendelsohn for the architecture of the twentieth century, his life and work are radically underrepresented on the international book market. While in recent years a number of younger architectural historians have published studies on individual themes and phases of his work, they have done so in a form less accessible to the broader public, that of the scholarly dissertation. Thus the resolve grew to bring together the work of these scholars in a single book, along with the work of Charlotte Benton, who has studied the architecture of the 1920s and 1930s in Great Britain for a number of years, and in so doing to make the results of their research more widely available. Charlotte Benton (Cambridge, England), Ita Heinze-Greenberg (Haifa, Israel), Kathleen James (Berkeley, California), and Hans R. Morgenthaler (Denver, Colorado) responded with extraordinary enthusiasm and spontaneously expressed their willingness to contribute to the book. The close professional cooperation and the selfless exchange of information and material in the service of a common goal were particularly stimulating and made it possible to establish points of contact between the individual themes, even when the authors focused entirely on their own areas of research. In its present form, therefore, this publication consists of a collection of essays by five different authors, representing a wide range of styles and scholarly approaches. The contributions also reflect the different universities and institutions where the authors work or teach, manifesting a broad spectrum of architectural-historical research. This, I think, represents one, if not the only, appropriate response to the personality and architecture of Eric Mendelsohn, whose life and work exemplify the political, technical, artistic, and economic developments of the twentieth century.

Born in 1887 in the small East Prussian town of Allenstein, the fifth child of middle-class parents, it was by no means a given that Mendelsohn would develop into a cosmopolitan architect who would live and work around the world. Yet this development manifested itself amazingly early: already as a young man, Mendelsohn enjoyed a close friendship with Einstein's collaborator Erwin Finlay-Freundlich, who would later arrange the commission for the Einstein Tower in Potsdam. In the early 1920s Mendelsohn lectured abroad on his own architecture, and in 1920 the first monograph devoted to his work was published.

With exceptional tenacity he established an international network of clients and colleagues with whom he worked closely, in some cases for years. The importance of this network became evident in 1933, when he left Germany with his wife, Luise, in the spring of that year after the Nazis came to power. In his first country of refuge, England, he was far from unknown, for he had given lectures there in previous years and his work had been published in professional journals. He was received with open arms and immediately permitted to work, while other, lesser-known architects were placed in detainment. When he finally received British citizenship in 1938, he changed his first name to Eric; from that point on Luise also called herself Louise, though not entirely consistently. This change of name has been incorporated into the essays, for it strikingly illustrates the degree to which Mendelsohn distanced himself from Germany in view of the fate of his fellow Jews, circumstances that made it impossible for him to ever return there. In this respect he was not alone: Salmann Schocken, Mendelsohn's main client in Germany and his great supporter in Palestine, likewise changed his name to Salman in exile.

Eric Mendelsohn's greatest hopes and probably also his greatest disappointments were associated with Palestine: as a devoted Zionist, he sought to contribute to the development of the land, establishing an office in Jerusalem in 1935. Political and economic circumstances, however, forced him to leave Palestine with his wife in 1941, after he had already dissolved his London office in 1939.

He found asylum for a third time in the United States, yet he arrived there at a time when there was nothing to build and his colleagues, previously emigrated from Germany, had already divided up the professorships and commissions among themselves. Since Mendelsohn had the reputation of being self-confident to the point of arrogance, their support for him was limited. Yet we—as the next generation with access to the thousands of letters exchanged by Eric and Louise throughout their lives—can view Mendelsohn's personality, thought, and action in another, more differentiated light. To us he appears as a man of unusual integrity, a personality both visionary and analytical. Mendelsohn found it difficult to establish himself in America; he had been enthralled too long by Palestine and Europe. The Académie Européenne Méditerranée that he and others sought to found as a center for research and training marks him as a man ahead of his time—conceived as an international, European institution, it was to become realizable only many decades later in the context of a united Europe. In the United States, the focus of Mendelsohn's work shifted.

Indeed, in general one can say that his stays in different countries set different architectural accents in his work. This observation applies not only to building types, but to their structure as well, for Mendelsohn—every inch a pupil of Theodor Fischer—strove above all to integrate his buildings into their urban and landscape setting. His buildings are always dialogically developed, designed for their particular context. It might not even be an exaggeration to say that if his architecture had been embraced in the American academies of the 1950s, our cities would not have taken on such monotonous, inhospitable forms. Mendelsohn's architectural approach acquires enormous significance in light of the growing interest in existing urban structures in contemporary architecture—an effort summed up in the motto: "Bauen im Bestand" ("Enhance the Existing"). One of our goals has been to illuminate this significance.

A project such as this one cannot be realized without a broad base of support. First and foremost, I would like to thank the archives, building authorities, libraries, institutions, and private persons who supported us in our research, made materials available to us, and agreed to their publication. To name them all would exceed the scope of this preface, yet one institution deserves particular mention: the Kunstbibliothek of the Staatliche Museen zu Berlin–Preussischer Kulturbesitz. Its director, Bernd Evers, has generously supported and promoted our work for years, and without him many insights would not have been possible. With great patience and interest, Bernd Meier uncovered the treasures of the Erich Mendelsohn Archive and made them available to us. Thus we would like to express our deepest gratitude to the Kunstbibliothek in Berlin as well as to the photographers who reproduced the archival material, in particular Dietmar Katz, who contributed the most recent photographs.

Without the publisher, however, there would be no book, and the best ideas would have remained in manuscript. The publishing house Verlag Gerd Hatje supported the project from its inception. My sincere thanks go to business director Annette Kulenkampff for her energetic involvement and commitment, without which this book could not have been realized. I am also grateful to Ute Barba for her excellent, very precise editing, and Christine Müller for her tireless, highly competent work on the production. It was a great pleasure to work with this team, and I would like to express my heartfelt thanks to them in the name of my co-authors as well.

Esther Mendelsohn-Joseph, the daughter of the architect, was informed of the progress of the work at every stage. She supported, motivated, and informed us to the best of her ability. Her great interest was both an incentive and a reward. To her, as well, we owe a great debt of gratitude.

Finally, I would like to thank my husband, Peter, for his untiring support during the two and a half years from the original idea to the final publication. This book is dedicated to him.

Regina Stephan

Erich Mendelsohn was born on March 21, 1887, in Allenstein, East Prussia, the small capital town of an agricultural district. He was the fifth of six children of a milliner and a clothing salesman.[1] According to his wife, Mendelsohn "was a born architect. He told me . . . that even as a child he did nothing but build: with sand, with any kind of material."[2] Like all the Mendelsohn children, he was stimulated by his mother's enthusiasm for music.[3]

After completing studies at the secondary level, Mendelsohn worked as a business apprentice in Berlin, but quickly decided to study law and registered for the 1906–07 winter term at the University of Munich.[4] After two terms he changed his major from law to architecture; he enrolled in the School of Architecture at the Technische Hochschule in Berlin on April 16, 1908, and studied there until May 10, 1910.[5] At that time, he transferred to the Technical University in Munich. This move was surprising, since Berlin was then the center of the attempts to define a contemporary architectural style. Peter Behrens (1868–1940) did his influential work for the All-gemeine Elektrizitäts-Gesellschaft and Hermann Muthesius (1861–1927) lectured at the Commercial College there. Munich at that time seems to pale in comparison, showing innovative work only in the field of applied arts, e.g., in the work of Richard Riemerschmid (1868–1957) for the Vereinigte Werkstätten für Kunst und Handwerk. The move may have been influenced by artistic considerations. Mendelsohn may have hoped to receive a different type of education in Munich. Commenting later on his intentions, he stated, "As a student . . . I rebelled against the then prevalent teaching of historical styles."[6] Accordingly, Mendelsohn chose to study with the architect Theodor Fischer (1862–1938), who had been appointed to a professorship in Munich in 1907. Fischer was involved in the efforts to modernize architecture through his participation in the Deutscher Werkbund. The founding meeting of this body had been held in Munich on October 5–6, 1907. At this session Fischer was elected chairman of the Werkbund.[7] When Mendelsohn came to Munich, the city was a widely acclaimed artistic center. Through the activities of the Blauer Reiter group it was fast becoming one of the focal points of progressive art. At the very end of 1911 the *Blue Rider Almanac* was published, and during October and November 1912 the first exhibition of futurist paintings was held in Munich.[8] Mendelsohn's artistic inclination was illustrated by his extracurricular activities, as noted by his wife: "[He] earned enough money to support himself during his student years. He did store window displays, designing graphic layouts of programs for concerts, for the theatre, for dancing performances and by selling his paintings."[9]

Mendelsohn graduated in the summer of 1912.[10] He recalled that he "started working on my own the very day of my final examination."[11] He designed the stage set for the 1912 Press Ball in Munich. The theme was the theatrical spectacles of Max Reinhardt: *Oedipus, Oresteia,* Offenbach's *La Belle Helene,* and *Orpheus in the Underworld.* The artistic direction of the ball, which consisted of the decoration of the auditorium of the Deutsches Theater and the design of a festive procession of about four hundred people, had been entrusted to Mendelsohn and the sculptor Caspar Theodor Pilartz.[12] Mendelsohn's stage design consisted of a temple facade with polychrome columns, statues, and a frieze.[13] Mendelsohn received this same assignment each year for the next two years. For the 1913 Press Ball, the theme was "Richard Strauss Week." Mendelsohn's stage decoration was again a pastiche of details taken from classical architecture.[14] For the 1914 ball, the theme was Richard Wagner's *Ring of the Nibelung.* Mendelsohn transformed the stage into the throne room at Valhalla. The throne of Wotan was placed into a deep niche with giants supporting the ceiling in the fashion of caryatids.[15]

Mendelsohn also created costume designs for the 1914 ball.[16] Ten sketches still exist, which depict dresses in rather flat compositions mixing linear configurations with fully painted color patches.[17] Mendelsohn revealed himself to be a competent master of his medium.[18] These events induced Mendelsohn to consider seriously a career as a stage designer. During spring 1914 he was engaged in the controversy over the Munich Artists' Theater. A number of progressive artists and theater professionals planned to take over the direction of this establishment for the 1914 season.[19] Mendelsohn would have been in charge of stage design.[20]

All of these experiences predisposed Mendelsohn toward thinking of himself as an artist with clear ideas about art and its purpose. His thoughts on these matters can be pieced together from the correspondence he began with his fiancée, Luise Maas, in August 1910.[21] Mendelsohn considered the work of art to be "the discharge of a person's own rhythmic sense," which he described as the waves of the tensions of the soul.[22] This may well be an elaboration of Wassily Kandinsky's (1866–1944) ideas that paintings consist of forms that cause the human soul to vibrate, and that the goal of art is the expression of the artist's inner meaning.[23] Mendelsohn stated that "a work can be created only when its author is completely filled with one vision, when he is no longer himself but the mouthpiece and hand of the spirit that drives him."[24] The concept of vision may have been suggested to Mendelsohn by the artist Hermann Obrist (1863–1927), who had had a vision one evening and began to treat the capacity of the human mind to experience visions as a valid source for the creation of new forms.[25]

Mendelsohn listed loneliness among the most important character traits of the artist. He believed that the artist lived outside the social mainstream.[26] He was convinced that artists sense a conflict within, between the artistic will and the desire for life. These two conflicting forces produce melancholy. From this suffering the work of art is created.[27]

There was also a development in the visual arts that influenced Mendelsohn's thinking. In 1910, Wassily Kandinsky began his breakthrough into the abstract. He harbored doubts about the scientific view of the world and turned toward self-expression through color.[28] The idea of abstraction became important for Mendelsohn. Influenced by Adolf Hildebrand's (1847–1921) book *Das Problem der Form in der Bildenden Kunst,* he regarded space as the essential characteristic of the artistic perception of nature. In Hildebrand's opinion, human knowledge of the plastic nature of objects originally derived from "kinesthetic ideas."[29] Mendelsohn took from Hildebrand the thesis that the seed of artistic design lies in the capacity of the human senses to conceive space.[30]

Through actual work, he learned that he had to accommodate this rather artistic outlook to the pragmatic concerns that determine architecture. His first architectural commission was a cemetery in his hometown.[31] The chapel was made up of an atrium and a big hall, which was covered by a cupola. The walls were painted in a reddish purple and the floor was covered with a carpet in an ancient oriental pattern. The walls of the main hall were broken by occasional niches painted in the same pattern as the carpet.[32] Mendelsohn's design is traditional, as a domed space with an anteroom was a frequently used plan for such buildings. Although a Star of David is clearly visible on the floor of Mendelsohn's chapel, the decoration makes his design part of the oriental revival movement in synagogue architecture, which began in Germany during the latter half of the nineteenth century.[33]

In 1913, Mendelsohn began to deal with ideas pertaining to architecture. He stated: "The sublime magnitude of the passion of the soul gives birth to everything in sublime form, at once chaos and a miracle of harmony."[34] He began to equate order with structure, sections, and proportions. A dualism between reason and soul developed in Mendelsohn's mind, which reflected the dispute between two major philosophies of art. Mendelsohn's theory seems to be a mixture of Alois Riegl's assertion of the individual as it is revealed in the *Kunstwollen* and Gottfried Semper's materialistic explanation of art forms, i.e., that art forms arise out of function, material, and technology. Mendelsohn's affirmation of the artist's personality and soul appears to be influenced by Riegl, while the emphasis on rationality and order in architecture seems to come from Semper. Mendelsohn could have learned about both theories through Wilhelm Worringer's (1881–1965) book *Abstraktion und Einfühlung* (published in English as *Abstraction and Empathy,* which was published in 1907. It expressed what many a progressive artist felt in those years.[35]

Worringer was also influential in helping to refocus Mendelsohn's ideas about movement and dynamism in architecture. Mendelsohn had stated that "only in movement lies infinite charm."[36] Movement and dynamism were important for Mendelsohn on an expressive level as well. He interpreted certain architectural forms as indicating energy and strength. Worringer's contribution to this idea came through *Form Problems in Gothic,*[37] in which he emphasized that the architectural language of the Gothic style was abstract; its laws were not organic laws, but mechanical ones. The structural idea was seen as the major, guiding part of this expression. Mendelsohn combined these thoughts about dynamic forms with a particular structural system in architecture, as used by Max Berg's (1870–1947) Century Hall (Breslau, 1913), a monumental exhibition hall built in reinforced concrete.[38]

During spring 1914, Mendelsohn saw architecture as rising from "falseness in tectonics and ornamentation" to a simple and sublime greatness.[39] However, he believed himself incapable of reaching the depth of soul he considered necessary for artistic creation. He was still only a reproducing artist, not a producing one.[40] He had to overcome his doubts about his artistic abilities. The insecure drawing technique of his earliest designs follows from this uncertainty. Projects such as the Machine Exhibition Halls[41] show delicate and sensitive linear configurations.[42] The lines used to draw the buildings are "hesitant, often fading into series of dots which leave corner and perspective problems unsolved."[43] "The line serves to trace architectural forms, but, as yet, neither creates nor determines them."[44] Indeed, these sketches seem to depict existing buildings, not original designs.

Interior of Railway Station, 1914.

Equally hesitant is Mendelsohn's stylistic association. These projects show that he began his work as a follower of the Jugendstil.[45] He must have become fascinated by this style because it was an artistic form of architecture. Guided by forms found in nature, artists attempted to design ornaments that would express force, energy, and movement.[46] Mendelsohn emphasized such expressive qualities in his own forms: "But, if I may ask you to go along this contour with me—and contour means the linear element of space—then you will be able to infer from its uninterrupted flow the later, conscious, spatial coherence."[47]

Mendelsohn's sketch depicts a building put together from cubical volumes stacked on top of one another. This compositional system was influenced by buildings designed by Joseph Maria Olbrich (1867–1908), whose Secession Building (Vienna, 1897–98) is assembled in a similar manner. The emphasis Mendelsohn put on the unbroken contour of the exterior shape is a feature that could have been influenced by Josef Hoffmann's (1870–1956) Palais Stoclet (Brussels, 1905–10).

Mendelsohn tended to emphasize the continuous exterior surface. It is above all the particular perspective in which Mendelsohn's designs are drawn that is responsible for this impression. The buildings are situated so that a corner is closest to the viewer, thus allowing for two facades to be seen simultaneously.[48] Interestingly, Adolf Hildebrand advocates exactly this type of perspective as correct for the arrangement of objects in a painting: "For instance, if something near be placed in the middle of the picture, and on the sides to the right and left things which are more distant, the result will be that the retrogressive movement into depth begins with the central part as being close at hand and proceeds by stretching backwards to either side. Think now of the reversed arrangement. Our ideas of movement into depth, our retrogressive spatial judgments, begin here with the full extension of the canvas only to traverse narrower and narrower areas as they approach the further distance. From the very start such an arrangement opposed our true and normal relation to Nature. Our feeling for space is curtailed rather than incited to infinite stretches."[49]

Subsequently, Mendelsohn turned away from Jugendstil toward the forms and shapes used in industrial design to develop a new style better suited to the new world. He focused on using new building materials and exploiting their structural possibilities in his attempt to renew architecture. This direction may have been suggested to him by efforts among Munich avantgarde artists to find a new form of painting. Kandinsky proposed in *On the Spiritual in Art* that the new style should be based on the constituents of painting: line and color.[50] Mendelsohn transposed this goal into architecture, by conceiving of a structural solution different from the classical post-and-lintel system.

This new concept changed the appearance of his projects. The sketch for the interior of a Railway Station shows a huge hall whose glass exteriors are supported by rows of arches. The building lacks ornamentation and consists of straightforward, structural forms. From the beginning of critical review of Mendelsohn's sketches, industrial architecture has been mentioned as a source for his early sketches. Julius Posener identified Mendelsohn's "point of departure [as] a certain monumentality that governed industrial architecture immediately before . . . the war."[51] In a lecture given in 1919, Mendelsohn stated that the shift in spirit of the era before World War I meant new building tasks set by industry, transportation, and religion, and new structural possibilities through new materials.[52]

Two changes in Mendelsohn's designs demonstrate this influence. He began to introduce round shapes, similar to Gothic vault structures, and he began to design exteriors that were more immediately expressive of structural forces. This goal was achieved by the use of cantilevered building parts on one hand, and by the expression of a sense of energy on the other hand. An untitled sketch depicts a structure that rises from the ground and ends in high over-hangs on the other side. Following the contour of this building gives the viewer one of Hilde-brand's "kinesthetic ideas," thus imparting a feeling of movement.

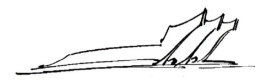

Untitled, 1915.

The sketch for the Factory in Steel and Concrete presents these new forms. The building volumes are arranged in a row of square arches. Light to the interior is provided through taper-ing windowpanes hung between these supports. Three pilasters, each made up of a steel skele-ton, buttress the end walls. The arched building volumes are intended for steel construction. They must be seen as an assemblage of cut steel planes welded or riveted together and to an underlying steel frame.

To exploit steel construction as a catalyst for a new architectural style was a common inter-est of architects at the turn of the twentieth century. Hermann Muthesius had studied the aes-thetics of steel forms, mentioning among other aspects the rows of rivets used in steel construc-tion as an architectural motif.[53] In his essay "Der stilbildende Wert industrieller Bauformen" in the 1914 Werkbund yearbook, Walter Gropius commented on a trend toward enclosed shapes in contemporary industrial buildings, especially in factories and bridges for the railway.[54]

The growing impact of industrial forms reveals itself mainly in the distribution of the build-ing volumes. In 1923 Mendelsohn stated in his lecture "Die internationale Übereinstimmung des neuen Baugedankens oder Dynamik und Funktion" that industrial machines, e.g., the turning lathe, "reflect an inescapable organization of technical exigencies. They give it the purity of its

Factory in Steel and Concrete, 1914.

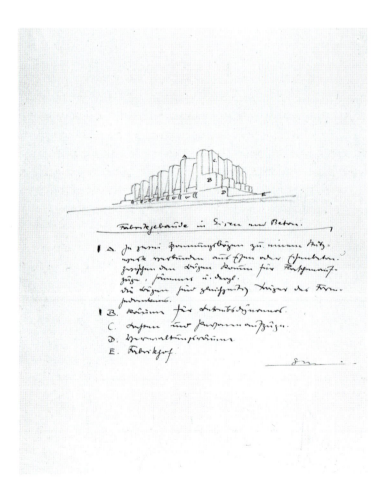

Esther, Luise, and Erich Mendelsohn
on a Sunday outing, ca. 1919.

organized form. The variation in size of the individual machine parts is scaled to their respective power stresses."[55]

In the Industrial Building, Mendelsohn emphasized that the contour reflects the curved form of steel[56] as well as "the technical form of the machine as we all know it from ignition magnets and from armatures in a dynamo."[57] The overall shape of the Industrial Building is compact and coherent. The exterior form is independent of interior function and becomes the main expressive feature of the design. The various purposes of this complex were incorporated in a unified spatial organism.[58] The uninterrupted contour line of this building added the expression of dynamic movement to the repertoire of industrial design features in Mendelsohn's earlier designs. The smooth exterior, the line of rivets along the edges, and the overall shape make this project look like an ocean liner. Thus, the building is treated as a working machine, although the exterior form is given an independent dynamic expression.

This clarification of design intentions went along with attempts to formulate a comprehensive theory of architectural design. On November 10, 1914, Mendelsohn wrote about Hermann Obrist, complimenting him for having "shaped his rich imagination . . . in an evolutionary manner, i.e., both structurally and organically."[59] Quite interestingly, Mendelsohn mentioned structure and organism as the two guiding principles of design. These were the two aspects which had preoccupied him since beginning his architectural designs.

On November 22, 1914, Erich Mendelsohn left Munich for Berlin. He seemed intent on further defining his theoretical intentions by letting himself be guided by intuition: "Projects which are . . . like the images of an overstrained imagination. . . . And yet all are intended for the needs of the most lucid calculation, and of technical demands. . . . Ideals, where figures are the masters!"[60]

This contradictory explanation of the designs as the outcome both of intuition and calculation suggests that he attempted to adhere to his earlier conception of artistic creation, while acknowledging that architectural structures have to satisfy certain material requirements, i.e., structural engineering. The acceptance of engineering as one of the unchangeable constituents of architectural design may also reflect the growing influence of the Werkbund on Mendelsohn. Leading members of this association had increasingly begun dealing with contemporary industrial and engineering structures. In his essay "Stilarchitektur und Baukunst" of 1901, Hermann Muthesius stated that a novel economic situation and new circumstances in transportation, combined with new building materials, had brought forth new developments in architecture during the nineteenth century. Muthesius went on to proclaim that a new architectural style would be generated either by these new building types or by such nonarchitectural objects as "bridges, steamers, or railway coaches," rather than from buildings imitating historic styles or natural forms.[61] The 1913 Werkbund yearbook was entitled *Die Kunst in Industrie und Handel* and con-

Automobile Factory, 1915.

Illustration p. 16:
Poster for the Ostdeutsche
Gewerbeausstellung (East German
Trade Exhibition) in Allenstein, 1910.

Illustration p. 17:
Costume design for the 1914
Press Ball in Munich.

GUNTHER

213

Observatory, 1917.

tained essays on industrial architecture by Muthesius and Gropius.[62] The 1914 Werkbund year-book was titled *Der Verkehr* and included an essay by Walter Gropius on engineering buildings[63] and articles on ship and car design.

How vision and calculation could combine to generate a design is shown in the project for an Automobile Factory. Mendelsohn admitted that he "tackled the project in an unrealistic manner for the sake of a new idea. The factory derives its dynamism fully from the forces in its steel construction. The row of gantries, indicated as lattice trusses, pulls the high tracts of the form shops together while at the same time the corner blocks lean forward."[64]

With this project Mendelsohn further advanced toward the establishment of symbolic architectural forms. This interpretation is suggested by one puzzling feature of this factory: the row of metal truss beams on top, connecting the four higher corner volumes of this building. These gantry cranes do not serve the purpose of moving car bodies along an assembly line but merely seem to hold the four corner buildings together. Apart from this structural function, the gantries seem to be a symbolic reference to the purpose of the whole building.

In 1915 Mendelsohn began sketching projects intended for construction in reinforced concrete. He became interested in shell construction, a system that relies on curved planes held in tension. Due to this influence, Mendelsohn began to use regular cylindrical shapes in his designs. These new forms are shown in a group of sketches for grain elevators. The central part of the building is formed by two parallel rows of high cylindrical shafts emerging from a lower, terraced base.

Mendelsohn joined the army shortly thereafter. On October 5, 1915, Erich and Luise were married.[65] His active duty interrupted his architectural endeavors. He resumed work in 1917 and began to formulate the coherent theoretical framework of his new architectural style. His concepts focused increasingly on genuine problems of architecture. This process was influenced by Martin Buber's book *Drei Reden über das Judentum,* which may have given Mendelsohn reason

House of Friendship, 1917.

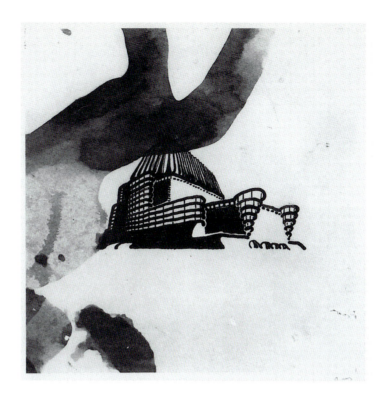

to put the artist on an equal level to the biblical creator, by suggesting that artistic creation—bringing form to chaos—is similar to the creation of the earth—creation out of nothing.[66] Already earlier, Mendelsohn had hinted at such a definition of the act of creation: "Conception means fertilization; it describes the moment when for the first time the idea takes shape, that is, when it takes on the form of the material in which it is conceived. The intensity of the moment often precipitates conception and birth together and renders tangible what has hitherto only been present in one's subconscious."[67]

Here artistic creation is compared to the creation of life—birth. Mendelsohn began to realize that artistic conception goes beyond mere scientific analysis of function, form, and material. He treated architecture as art and believed artistic creation to be an act of genius.

This outlook generated a number of designs for observatories. Intended for construction in reinforced concrete, these designs feature domes, which are appropriate for this type of construction. Obviously, the use of a dome in such a design is not exclusively the result of reinforced concrete construction, as an observatory is generally defined by a large domed hall on top that houses the telescope. A further source for this particular shape can be found in war materiel: the compressed building mass with the dome as the only notable protrusion shares features with contemporary artillery guns.

The increased practicality of these designs influenced Mendelsohn to explain artistic creation more specifically. In a letter of May 28, 1917, he wrote: "With me the everyday becomes something more than the everyday. I do not really know if it is because of my inclination towards the fantastic. . . . Problems of symmetry, and of the elasticity of the building components, and of the closed contour and of methods of construction concern me at every line and act as discipline, self-criticism, and a universal rule."[68]

Such statements indicate that Mendelsohn began to realize that a design that is too fantastic might not be an appropriate solution. He emphasized design principles governing the

Silo, 1915.

Airport for Dirigibles and Airplanes,
1914.

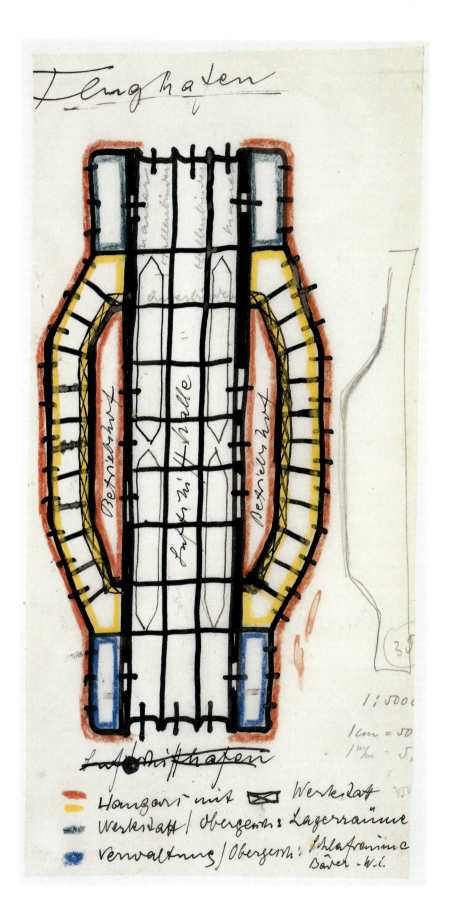

exterior of a building. Mendelsohn focused on the factual side of architecture, attempting above all to formulate a design theory that would govern both the structure and the exterior appearance of his buildings. The ultimate goal of this theory was to define dynamic masses. This definition was included in Mendelsohn's text "Gedanken zur neuen Architektur (Im Felde 1914–1917)." For the most part this manifesto contained his fundamental architectural theory. For him, architecture was the enclosure of space.[69] He intended his own buildings to consist mainly of walls and roofs, or planar envelopes in various forms. Furthermore, Mendelsohn stated that mass and light are the means by which architecture is made visible.[70]

In this attempt to establish an aesthetic theory for his designs, Mendelsohn was influenced by ideas promoted by other architects. The most probable source for the concept of architecture as enclosed space is found in the design philosophy of Hendrik Petrus Berlage (1856–1934). Berlage's three principles of architecture, "the primacy of space, the importance of walls as creators of form, and the need for systematic proportion," are strikingly similar to Mendelsohn's ideas. Berlage also stated: "The art of the master-builder lies in this: the creation of space. . . . A spatial envelope is established by means of walls, whereby a space . . . is manifested."[71]

What was left for Mendelsohn to do now was to produce the designs that would breathe life into his theory. In his quest for a novel architectural style, Mendelsohn began to reject the straightforward application of mechanics in building. What is shown in the drawings is the symbolic essence of the design, not necessarily its realistic form. Drawn in a freehand style, the designs are rendered with precise outlines. In his intuitive design mode, Mendelsohn was primarily interested in showing "dynamic masses," rather than providing expedient solutions for factory designs.

Mendelsohn found it difficult to capture his fleeting visions. In a letter of August 11, 1917, the translation of vision into design is once more mentioned: "The visions are once more behind every ring of light and every corpuscle in my closed eye. Masses standing in their ripeness flash past in a moment and slip away, so that it is almost impossible for the hand to note them down even approximately. I lament the fact that hand and vision are not linked together mechanically."[72]

Nevertheless, Mendelsohn now had the confidence that led to the breakthrough of his early period. In winter 1917/18 he was finally creating designs that combined his earlier intentions and ideas into the forms for which he was searching. These sketches depict projects that are worked out in detail. In the design for the House of Friendship, glass seemed to become the predominant building material. It must be concluded that the ridges on the exterior of the super-

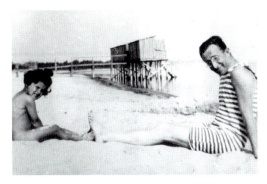

Erich Mendelsohn with his daughter, Esther, at the Baltic Sea, probably summer 1919.

structure of this project are meant to be posts between windowpanes. These vertical ridges also imitate those used on the exterior of combustion chambers of motors.[73] Indeed, this project displays a closer resemblance to machinery than to architecture. With the exception of the glass walls, the building consists of solid walls lined at the corners with openings that imitate ventilation holes in machines. The tapered overall shape seems to come from ship design. However, one can also see an organic quality in these designs. As the above sketch does not contain features that would indicate its scale, the horizontal ribbon windows can be mistaken for "a bent arm complete with five bent fingers."[74]

A design that seemed to preoccupy Mendelsohn at the time was Optical Factory. Reinforced concrete and glass—due to their fitness for molded forms—seem responsible for the resulting shapes. The series of designs discussed above must be looked upon as the quintessential outcome of Mendelsohn's search for architectural forms that would adequately express their time. These designs were intended for construction in new building materials. They employ reinforced concrete in daring structural configurations, adequate to its possibilities, mainly through exploiting the ability of this material to support cantilevered building parts. These projects were created intuitively, emerging from Mendelsohn's visions. The forms of these projects took features from industrial design, mainly the forms of ships, cars, airplanes, and machines.

However, after years of intellectual struggle, especially regarding the nature of architectural creation and the dualism of vision and reality, these designs must be more than simply imaginary transformations of achievements in industrial design. These projects must be looked upon as instinctual art works. They are similes without consideration of reality. Expressionist designs cannot be understood simply as projects to be built eventually. The greatest potential of these designs is their social and political commentary. Resulting from the pure act of drawing, they became an intensely human manifestation, not the representation of actual conditions and requirements. Most Expressionist designs are multidimensional. Not only form, elevation, plan, and section, but also the social and political meaning can be read from a single drawing.

Like the artists of the Blue Rider group in Munich, Mendelsohn created pure solutions for the future that were not influenced by reality. This true creation produced "object-less" works of art.[75] The value of Mendelsohn's sketches is primarily ethical, not practical. Mendelsohn's goal was to point out a new direction for architecture that would express its era. His main intention was to formulate an architectural style adequate to the industrial progress of the twentieth century. In this respect, Mendelsohn could be criticized for producing only an intellectual manual for the new architecture, not its definitive form.

On November 7, 1918, the day of the cease-fire, Mendelsohn returned home to Berlin and opened his own architectural office. He brought his early period to an end with an exhibition of the early sketches and a lecture at the renowned Paul Cassirer Gallery in Berlin, on December 1919, titled "Architektur in Eisen und Beton."[76]

With regard to the forms and purposes of his designs, Mendelsohn's work was part of the machine-aesthetic movement in modern architecture. Within this movement, Mendelsohn's contribution was unique. His designs display many formal similarities to the Futurist projects of Antonio Sant'Elia (1888–1916).[77] Whereas other representatives of machine-aesthetic architecture—Le Corbusier, Russian Constructivist architects, and a number of German architects—used formal details from machines for their functional value, Mendelsohn was mainly impressed by their power to evoke symbolic meaning.

Notes p. 262.

Three sketches for the Villa Becker in Chemnitz, 1915: bedroom, living room, and view from street.

"Organic!"
Einstein, Finlay-Freundlich, Mendelsohn,
and the Einstein Tower in Potsdam

Kathleen James

Few architects have the chance to begin their careers with buildings guaranteed to attract public attention, regardless of the details of their design. Mendelsohn's acquaintance with the astrophysicist Erwin Finlay-Freundlich and, through him, with Einstein's Theory of Relativity deeply influenced the young architect's understanding of the relationship between mass and energy in ways that reverberated throughout his career; for him modernity was never a static force. It also provided him with an extraordinary opportunity: the commission for a building which served simultaneously as monument to and a laboratory for research into the controversial new theory.[1] The result was a declaration of an approach that, even if it proved in the end to be untransferable to other buildings, remains one of the most imaginative moments in the history of modern architecture.

Mendelsohn met Freundlich through Luise Maas, the woman he was soon to marry, and who, like Freundlich, was a cellist. Through Freundlich, he became acquainted with the details of Einstein's emerging General Theory of Relativity almost as it was being formulated and long before it came to the attention of the public at large. Freundlich was well positioned to explain Einstein's startling new ideas about the relationship between light, space, and time. In 1911 Einstein suggested that his hypothesis that light could be bent by gravity could be proven by measuring the deflection of sunlight during an eclipse. Freundlich was the first astronomer to undertake such an effort, although the outbreak of World War I prevented him from completing the requisite observations.[2] The two men remained in close contact despite this setback. In 1916, working in close conjunction with Einstein, Freundlich published *The Foundations of Einstein's Theory of Gravitation,* the first book about relativity.[3]

Even before he received the commission for the Einstein Tower, Mendelsohn's acquaintance with relativity encouraged him to speculate about the implications for architecture of Einstein's famous equation of mass and energy. In a 1917 letter to his wife with which he enclosed several drawings of observatories, Mendelsohn described his interest in the depiction of motion in language that recalled relativity: "The balance of movement—in mass and light— mass needs light, light moves mass—is reciprocal, parallel, complementary. The mass is clearly constructed, if the light balances the mass. Returning in conclusion to the contour! The light is properly distributed, when it equalizes the moving mass. Returning in conclusion to the representation! This is the general law of the art of expression."[4] Throughout his career Mendelsohn would seek to represent the energy he saw as latent in architectural mass, substituting this implied movement for the impossibility of converting the material fact of the building into actual energy.

Meanwhile, Freundlich was busy trying to raise funds for a facility in which he could continue his relativity-related research. He hoped through a comparison of the spectra of artificial light and sunlight to find that sunlight was the redder of the two, evidence of a gravitationally caused shift in its mass. After being refused access to the Babelsberg Observatory, where he had worked earlier, he received an offer in 1918 from Gustav Müller, the director of the Astro-

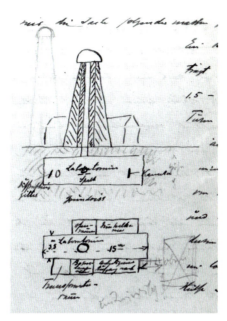

physical Observatory, also in Potsdam, of a site on its grounds.[5] Freundlich quickly sent Mendelsohn, who was by then stationed on the French front, a detailed description of the building's program complete with sketches of a possible elevation and two different ground plans.[6]

Freundlich's letter, written at the beginning of June, revealed the influence upon his thinking of a series of solar telescopes built at the Mount Wilson Solar Observatory near Pasadena, California, under the supervision of George Ellery Hale. For two decades Hale, a pioneering astrophysicist, had experimented with new scientific equipment and the structures necessary to house it adequately. Hale had been troubled by the way in which the mounting of extremely powerful telescopes precluded experimentation with rigidly mounted spectographic instruments. He attempted to rectify this situation at Mt. Wilson in three telescopes built between 1905 and 1912 in which a coelostat (a pair of rotating mirrors) reflected light directly through the fixed telescope into a horizontal spectographic chamber. In the second he raised the coelostat high above the spectographic chamber, which he now located underground. Freundlich's specifications were apparently based on a photograph of the Snow telescope's long shingled laboratory and this tower. In the third of the Mt. Wilson telescopes the cupola was for the first time completely enclosed so that the coelostat, too, could be kept at a constant temperature while light from it reached the laboratory through a separate freestanding lightwell.[7] Freundlich's major contribution was to place a horizontally oriented chamber under the tower. This combination would produce far more generous work and circulation spaces than existed at Mount Wilson.[8]

Mendelsohn began to design the observatory almost immediately. His earliest perspective sketches, sections, and plans share little of the dynamism of the final building, as he apparently conceived of the project at this date as an exclusively scientific one.[9] Germany's defeat made a mockery of Freundlich's original optimistic prediction that construction would begin in August 1918.[10] By the time Mendelsohn resumed serious work on the project in the spring of 1920, the aftermath of the November Revolution had politicized German science and radicalized the country's young architects. These changes dramatically transformed his approach to the commission.

On November 6, 1919, the Royal Society and the Royal Astronomical Society met in London to announce that the experiment Freundlich had hoped to perform August 1914 had been completed by two British groups, producing proof of Einstein's General Theory of Relativity. Back in Germany, the theory's popularization was accompanied by fierce controversy. Supporters of the newly founded Weimar Republic found in Einstein, a Jewish pacifist with a Swiss passport, a welcome demonstration of the continuing renown of Germany's intellectuals. Rightwing nationalists, on the other hand, labeled Einstein's seemingly objective theory irrational and thus "undeutsch" (not German). Both the advocates and opponents of relativity carried the debate outside the normal channels of scientific discussion. In August 1920 Einstein published on the front page of a Berlin newspaper a response to critics who had earlier held an anti-Relativity meeting in the city's Philharmonic Hall.[11]

It was in this climate that Freundlich raised much of the money for his observatory through a public appeal, rather than the usual government sources, and that Mendelsohn added to the program the task of commemorating the first of the many controversial modernities with which he would be associated during the Weimar Republic. Only a month after Einstein and his theory became world famous, Freundlich organized a foundation in Einstein's name to fund the construction of his observatory. Freundlich worked quickly. Appealing for half a million marks for the building and its equipment, he secured the support of eight of the country's leading scientists, including Max Planck. The call, couched in nationalistic terms, pleaded for the money for just one site where German research could be given a chance to hold its own against that being conducted in England, France, and America. Freundlich also lobbied the Prussian state government for the funds with which to purchase a spectrograph, the proposed observatory's most important and expensive instrument.[12]

By May 1920 Freundlich had raised enough money for Mendelsohn to preoccupy himself with the project, about whose technical details he now had new information from the engineers at Carl Zeiss, the Jena optical firm who manufactured and donated many of the instruments it housed.[13] More importantly, the utopian speculation that preoccupied many of the younger members of Berlin's architectural community in the wake of the November Revolution encouraged the young architect to believe that his wartime sketches were buildable and that their fusion of technical functions and monumentality was appropriate to the Einstein Tower. Nonetheless Mendelsohn remained somewhat apart from Bruno Taut and many of the architects who contributed to the Arbeitsrat für Kunst's exhibition of unknown architects. Unlike them, he preferred astronomy to astrology. Furthermore, his connections to scientists reinforced his faith in technology at a time when most of his contemporaries were concerned above all with the spiritual.[14]

In a lecture delivered in 1920 to the Arbeitsrat, Mendelsohn defined the principles which would shape his design of Freundlich's observatory.[15] Here he touted construction in new materials as the basis of a new architecture answerable to Einstein's theories: "Whereas in the classical principle of support and load a quietness of massing is declared as the highest goal, here [in his sketch for an optical instruments factory] the building's massing itself has overcome gravity and inertia and has compressed all energy together into the center of its own spatial being. . . . The cult of construction seems to be the only expression of determined honesty, its strictness merely introspection, its force expressing the will to create monuments."[16]

Earlier, Mendelsohn had planned to build the observatory in a mix of brick and concrete.[17] Now he aspired to construct it entirely out of the material whose capacities had so strongly influenced his wartime drawings.[18] Mendelsohn greatly admired the plasticity of such recent concrete buildings as Max Berg's Centennial Hall in Breslau, which he had visited in 1913, and Henry van de Velde's Werkbund Theater of the following year in Cologne.[19] Already a perspective drawing

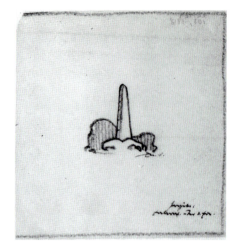

Einstein Tower, Potsdam, perspective sketch, 1918.

Einstein Tower, Potsdam, perspective
sketch, 1919.

of 1919 shows him experimenting with ways to impart the sense of mass shedding energy as the building appeared almost ready to leap out into the landscape. Despite a brief flirtation with a more stable scheme drawn only in elevation, side views of the building drawn in the spring of 1920 continue to show it lunging forward into space.

By the end of June, Mendelsohn had largely settled on the building's exterior appearance.[20] A less expressively rendered plan and section dated July 7, just under a week before the receipt of a building permit, show that the interior details of the building's organization were, however, quite different from what was eventually built.[21] For the relatively inexperienced young architect, the task of translating his visionary scheme into construction documents was an enormous challenge, one which was exacerbated by difficulties with building authorities and by economic conditions that, along with the technical difficulties of the design, impinged upon his hope of constructing it entirely out of concrete. Throughout the summer and fall, even after construction had begun in mid-July, Freundlich diplomatically steered the unusual design through the approval process, ensuring that it did not run aground on the objections of a variety of government officials.[22] Along the way, Mendelsohn completed three more sets of plans, the final one illustrating the mix of concrete and stuccoed brick out of which the tower was in fact erected (see the illustration on page 37, in which the concrete is denoted by gray, brick by orange, and the torfoleum insulation of the underground laboratory by green).[23]

In a description of the building, Mendelsohn stated: "The architectural form meets the inner needs and adheres to the formal conditions of reinforced concrete."[24] His failure to so coordinate form and material greatly diminished the satisfaction he took in the finished building. Why, in the end, was he unable to construct the building entirely out of concrete? Certainly, if anyone in Germany could have executed the design in this material, it would have been Dyker-hoff-Widmann, who along with A. F. Bolle were the contractors.[25] Among Germany's leading experts in reinforced concrete construction, they had already built the Centennial Hall in collaboration with the local firm of Lolateisenbeton.[26]

Years later Mendelsohn denied the story that he had had problems with the formwork and blamed the substitution entirely on a shortage of concrete.[27] In fact, the need to economize, cited in a report to the Prussian Ministry of Culture of October 28, was primary.[28] This explanation is supported by contemporary accounts of the impact of inflation on the cost of building materials.[29]

Having struggled to "give birth" to the building's design, Mendelsohn failed to redesign the tower shaft midway through construction to reflect the materials of which it was actually being built.[30] The revisions he did make instead involved the organization of the interior. Although the basic disposition of an entrance porch leading to a vestibule and tower—with the underground laboratory and, above it, a workroom extending to the rear—remained constant, many details were refined during the summer, probably in consultation with engineers familiar with the technical requirements of the building's scientific equipment.[31] Most importantly for its exterior appearance, Mendelsohn changed the lidded windows that peek out of the ground to illuminate the underground workrooms.

The structure of the Einstein Tower was erected in a mere twelve months.[32] It took more than three years, however, to complete the furnishings of the interior, installation of the technical apparatus, and landscaping of the surrounding site.[33] This last was executed by Richard Neutra, who was at the time an employee in Mendelsohn's office. The building was finally dedicated on December 6, 1924, once the collapse of hyperinflation enabled Freundlich and his donors to properly equip the building.[34]

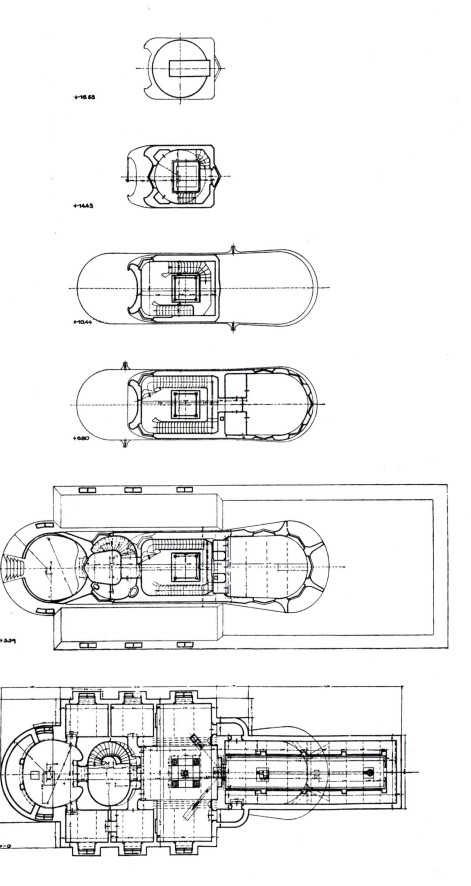

At its core, the Einstein Tower consists, as Freundlich from the first intended, of a vertical shaft and, perpendicular to it, a horizontally placed underground laboratory. Plunging from the observatory cupola to the basement, the shaft, around which also wrap stairs leading to the observatory, encircles and shelters an inner tower. Comprised of two independent wooden lattices, this structure supports the coelestat, whose mirrors can be adjusted to capture sun-, moon-, or starlight and deflect it into the underground laboratory. Here, broken by the prism of the spectrograph, the color of that light can be measured and photographed. The interior tower, set in concrete, must be impervious to motion; for the laboratory Freundlich demanded a constant temperature.[35] About these aspects of the building's basic organization Mendelsohn had little choice.

The disposition of the ancillary spaces provided him with greater opportunities. Anchoring the building in the landscape, the spaces located below ground were devoted to the housing and maintenance of additional instruments. Atop the laboratory and behind the tower shaft, which they appeared to stabilize, Mendelsohn placed the building's two most habitable interiors, a workroom and, above it, a smaller chamber to accommodate scientists who often worked through the night. These were the only interiors to be artistically decorated. Designed only after the completion of the exterior shell, the furnishings, of wood with angled vertical surfaces and legs that taper to sharp points, are the only aspect of the building that hint at the contemporary fashion for faceted, crystalline forms.[36]

The extraordinary appearance that the Einstein Tower presents to visitors approaching it from the crest of a hill crowned by a previous generation of telescopes would seem at first to have little relationship to these mundane details of the building's program. Except for the cupola, whose function as an observatory is easily discernable, nothing about the willfully sculpted monolith apparently emerging organically from a turf-covered platform hints at its scientific purpose. In fact, Mendelsohn designed the shell encasing Freundlich's program to represent the theory the scientists inside were striving to prove. While Freundlich and his assistants sought to demonstrate Einstein's postulate that gravity shifted the color of light, Mendelsohn attempted to express architecturally Einstein's fundamental claim that mass and energy are interchangeable. The building appears almost able to stride across the landscape, its solid mass swept back by the unseen forces that are converting its substance into animate energy. The embracing curve of the entrance porch, its concave echo in the skirt of the tower, and the downturned lids of the tiered windows all contribute powerfully to this effect. In a lecture delivered in 1923, Mendelsohn described the relationship between technology and organic form that inspired this aspect of his design: "Ever since science has come to realize that the two concepts matter and energy, formerly kept rigidly apart, are merely different states of the same primary element, that in the order of the world nothing takes place without relativity to the cosmos, without relationship to the whole, the engineer has abandoned the mechanical theory of dead matter and has reaffirmed his allegiance to nature. . . . The machine, till now the pliable tool of lifeless exploitation, has become the constructive element of a new, living organism."[37] Mendelsohn's determination to monumentalize what could have been simply a scientific facility can be attributed to two interlocking sets of circumstances. First, in the last years before the war, inspired in part by the activities of the German Werkbund, prominent German architects had embraced the artistic design of factories as a means for controlling the cultural dislocations wrought by industrialization. From Peter Behrens's heroic recasting of the Greek temple front for the AEG Turbine Factory in Berlin, it was but a short jump to the equally self-conscious design of an observatory. Secondly, relativity was, far more than industry, in need of defenders; at stake

Illustration p. 32:
Einstein Tower, Potsdam, elevation sketch, 1920.

Illustration p. 33, above:
Einstein Tower, Potsdam, perspective sketches, 1920.

Illustration p. 33, below:
Einstein Tower, Potsdam, perspective sketch, 1920.

was not only a scientific theory, but the cultural direction of the new republic. In these circumstances the Einstein Tower served as the first of Mendelsohn's many celebrations of Weimar-era modernity.

In the first years of the new republic, monumentality continued to be a crucial issue for German architects, as it had been during the last years of the Wilhelmine era. Then nationalist as well as more politically progressive architects had vied to create ever-larger markers of a political stability the country in fact lacked. Intended to foster loyalty to the status quo, these buildings were erected in a variety of quasi-historicist primitivizing styles, although Berg's Jahrhunderthalle, built by advocates of change, was rigorously abstract in its elementalism. Architects who supported the November Revolution initially attempted to create futuristic antidotes to such examples of Wilhelmine bombast as Bruno Schmitz's Völkerschlachtdenkmal in Leipzig, dedicated in the presence of the Kaiser in 1913.[38] With Bruno Taut's schemes for city crowns and Hans Poelzig's Grosse Schauspielhaus, the Einstein Tower was among the most prominent of these experiments.

Mendelsohn's political sympathies were diametrically opposed to those of Schmitz's patrons, yet critics correctly noted a relationship between the two buildings.[39] Mendelsohn went far further than his predecessor in creating dynamic new forms unconnected to any but the most recent past. He shared with Schmitz, however, a belief in the efficacy of bold gestures—the Einstein Tower appears in photographs to be far taller than its twenty meters. Furthermore, it was from Schmitz, rather than any of the Art Nouveau architects he wholeheartedly admired—Joseph Maria Olbrich, Hermann Obrist, or Henry van de Velde—that Mendelsohn learned how to create a vital connection between the building and its site, out of which the structure appears to grow as if it were a living plant or, at the least, a geological formation.

Almost no one recognized the specific ways in which Mendelsohn intended to memorialize Einstein's theory.[40] Nonetheless, as much because of its relation to Europe's most famous scientist as its unusual appearence, the Tower quickly became one of the best-known German buildings of its day. In September 1921, within weeks of the completion of the exterior, it was promi-

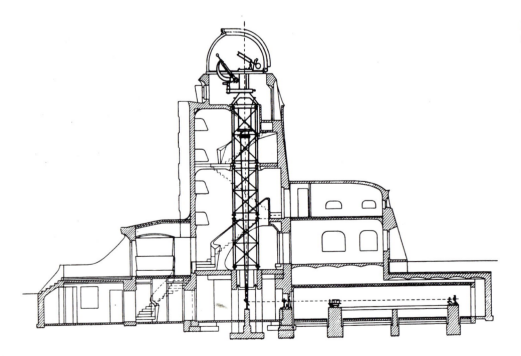

Einstein Tower, Potsdam, longitudinal section, 1920.

Einstein Tower, Potsdam, workroom, 1921/22. The chairs, tables, cabinets, and light fixtures were designed by Mendelsohn.

nently published in Berlin's popular press.[41] Meanwhile, the design was already familiar to many fellow architects throughout Europe through its inclusion eleven months earlier in an issue of the Dutch architectural journal *Wendingen* devoted to Mendelsohn's work.[42] Featured in a number of prominent surveys of modern architecture, the Einstein Tower was also included in books on reinforced concrete construction.[43]

Fame did not always equal praise. The often critical reception of the building served as a bellwether of the shift from individual expression back toward functional form. From the beginning, even those who admired the building tended to associate it with the occult-like views popular among the Crystal Chain rather than with the spirit of scientific inquiry in which experiments were actually conducted within it. Hermann Scheffauer, for example, wrote in the first publication of the Tower in English: "The building, mysterious even in its outward aspects, attains to something of an esoteric scientific uncanniness within. We are in the brilliant crypt of the modern alchemists and sorcerers, in an arcanum of subtle discovery, one of the radiant poles where the ultimate mysteries of the cosmos, of time, of space, and of the eternal forces are being weighed, analyzed, and interpreted."[44]

And for exactly these reasons, it was an appealing target for proponents of a more sober, functional architecture. The first and most bitter of these attacks was written by Paul Westheim, one of Germany's leading art critics and an opponent of Expressionism. Writing in 1923, he condemned the Tower's outdated monumentality and dismissed Mendelsohn's attempts at symbolism as pure advertising.[45] Five years later, the Swiss critic Peter Meyer struck the same tone in his book *Moderne Architektur und Tradition.*[46]

Although its was through its role as a monument that the Einstein Tower initially transcended its purely technical purpose to become the building that most fully embodied the cultural aspirations associated with the fledgling Weimar Republic, the same willful grandeur also brand-

ed it in the end as the product of a brief moment of Expressionist experimentation. In 1930 Paul Schmidt labeled the Tower "a final tribute to the emotional and chaotic time of the revolution, a direct transfer of the dynamic principle to crystalline structure."[47] Mendelsohn's own stylistic debts were above all to the Jugendstil, and the Blue Rider paintings it had helped inspire, rather than to other Expressionist architects, but he shared the optimism of Taut and his circle that in the wake of the November Revolution a better world was possible and that architecture would be integral to its creation.[48] The impracticality of the paper architecture that flourished in the Revo- lution's immediate aftermath and the extreme willfulness of what little was actually built, including the Tower itself, by 1923 triggered a sobering reengagement with the realities of mass production and easily buildable rectilinear forms. Mendelsohn, who during the early 1920s was perhaps the busiest German architect of his generation, blazed this trail himself in his Steinberg, Hermann hat factory in Luckenwalde of 1921 to 1923 and the many Frank Lloyd Wright–influenced projects his office produced while Richard Neutra was working for him. For its architect the process of creating the Einstein Tower demonstrated that the wartime sketches on which it is so clearly based did not in fact provide a template for a new architecture. Although it proved inimitable, the building nonetheless clearly established the direction Mendelsohn's career would take, espe- cially as long as he remained in Germany. Always he sought to represent his enthusiasm for the dynamism and the excitement of modern life, often through the use of dramatically curved forms. But the Tower's legacy transcended issues of style or form.

    Mendelsohn achieved fame through his association with tradition-defying ideas of Einstein, a fellow supporter of the Weimar Republic and of Zionism. For the rest of his life, as in the design of the Einstein Tower, he unwaveringly championed the new against the old, espoused demo- cracy over nationalism, and remained fiercely loyal to his embattled German-Jewish community.

Notes p. 263.

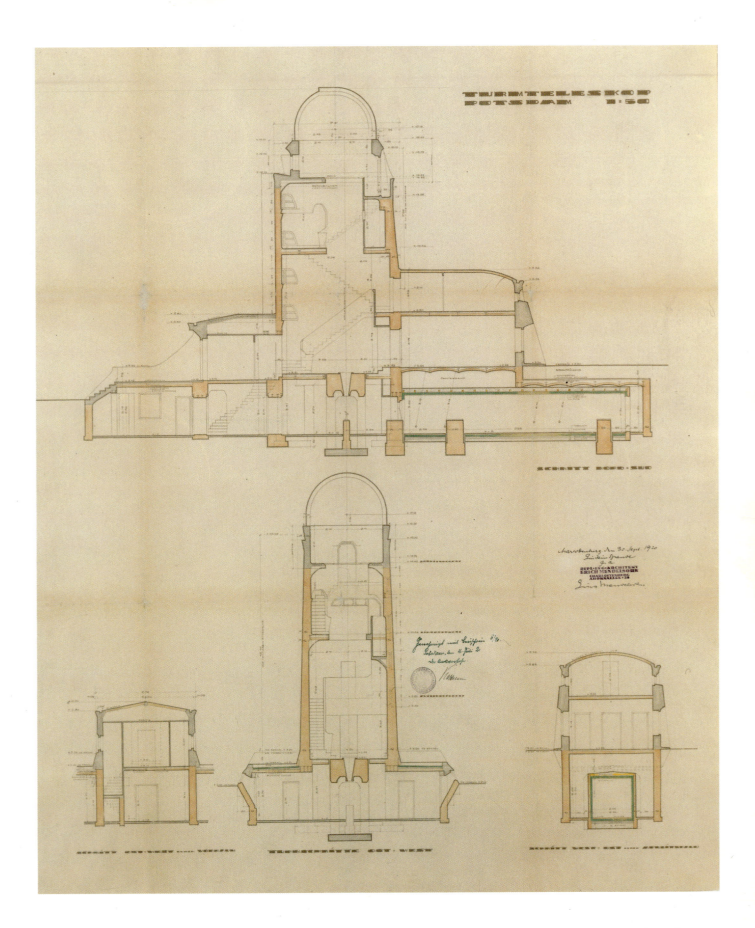

Regina Stephan

"Thinking from day to day, where history takes great turns, leaving hundreds of thousands unsatisfied"

Early Expressionist Buildings in Luckenwalde, Berlin, and Gleiwitz

"In January and February of 1919, I intend to give a series of eight to ten lectures to a select audience on the subject of architecture. The lectures are intended to correct subjective and false attitudes toward art in general, to do away with distortions of judgment produced by historical and temporal bias, and to prepare the ground for the demands of a new epoch. In this context, the rules of architecture are foundational and comprehensive. Knowledge of them seems to me to be a pressing need. Photographs and sketches will illustrate the lectures, discussions will clarify and stimulate."[1]

The lectures announced in this invitation were to be decisive for Mendelsohn's career. He had opened his architectural office in Berlin immediately following his return from the war on November 7, 1918, and was urgently seeking commissions. Thus it was fortunate that Molly Philippson, a friend of his wife, Luise, from her youth, was interested in architecture and made her excellent social connections available to Mendelsohn, a stranger in Berlin.[2] The lectures took place in her salon, and it was there that Mendelsohn met a number of his later clients: Gustav Herrmann, for whom he built a residential development and a hat factory in Luckenwalde as early as 1919; Dr. Hans Heymann, who shortly thereafter commissioned him to remodel a house on Dorotheenstrasse; Hans Lachmann-Mosse, for whom he renovated the publishing house on Jerusalemer Strasse; and Dr. Walter Sternefeld, who commissioned Mendelsohn to build a villa on Heerstrasse.

In his didactically well-organized lectures—"Entwicklungsgesetze der Baukunst" ("Developmental Laws of Architecture"), "Gesetze der Baukunst" ("The Laws of Architecture"), "Der Monumentalbau" ("The Monumental Building"), "Die Stadt" ("The City"), "Das Haus und der Garten" ("The House and the Garden"), "Der Innenraum" ("Interior Space"), "Kritik der jüngsten Produktion" ("Critique of Recent Productions"), and "Die neue Zeit" ("The New Age")—Mendelsohn explained why the time for a new architecture had come and what its conditions were. He illustrated his explanation by comparing monumental buildings from four past epochs: the Egyptian pyramids, the Greek temple, the Gothic cathedral, and buildings of "recent production." While for him the first three represented genuine developmental stages in architecture, closely associated with building technique, society, and religion, he had no sympathy for the architecture of the Wilhelmine age. He compared its design to a dress "hung by a clever tailor around some construction or another, so that it can be seen in public. A play of variations on the uncreative."[3] Instead, he demanded that the new methods of construction now be translated into design as well. He criticized the Eiffel Tower in Paris, as well, stating that steel skeleton buildings of this kind revealed only the construction, "but . . . not yet the flesh, which makes it a body in the first place," and for this reason represented "not yet art, but naked construction."[4] To Mendelsohn, the solution to this problem was clear: "Only one step further and the scaffolding of bones becomes a complete wall, entirely of steel; the supports fall and a completely free space is created. . . . Only one step further and the filling material is found. Steel is joined by concrete, reinforced concrete." In the discussion that followed, he advocated the use of this

Lecture manuscript of 1919 showing Mendelsohn's central thesis, according to which building technique and design are innovatively combined in the outstanding works of architecture from all epochs.

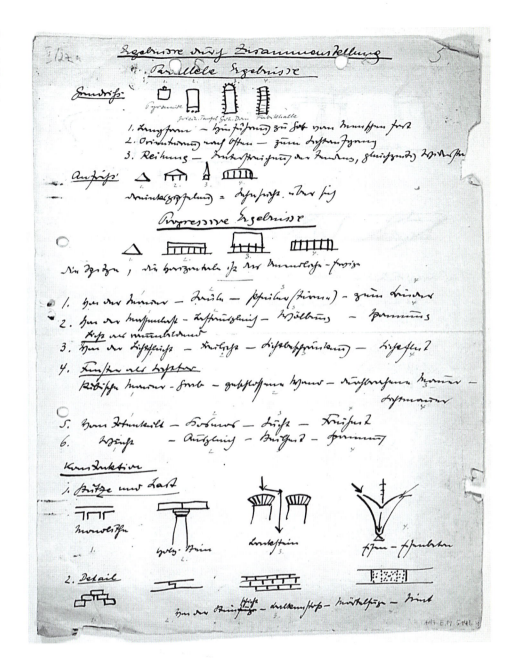

new building material, on the one hand justifying it with arguments from design and construction, and on the other developing theses on the social structures of each epoch made visible in its buildings. For the new age, marked by the dominance of capital and industry, he demanded a new architecture adapted to this changed society. His lectures conclude with the thesis, "As numerous examples in my lectures have shown, we may now assume that the new form will develop from industry. This is the beginning, not the goal of the development." The lectures led to vehement controversy among his listeners as well as to his first private commission from Gustav Herrmann, owner of the Gustav Herrmann & Co. hat factory in Luckenwalde, which had been manufacturing hats since 1883.[5]

Mendelsohn was already working on the first plans for Herrmann when, in the fall of 1919, an exhibition of his sketches entitled "Erich Mendelsohn. Architekturen in Eisen und Beton"

("Erich Mendelsohn: Architecture in Steel and Concrete") was mounted in the gallery of Paul Cassirer. The show later traveled to Hannover, Hamburg, Breslau, Chemnitz, Stuttgart, and Cologne. For this exhibition, Mendelsohn's sketches from the Russian front, many of them very small, were enlarged with the help of a *laterna magica* and published in a catalog. The fine reproductions in the latter won Mendelsohn notoriety beyond German borders. Among those who saw the exhibition were Salmann Schocken, later one of Mendelsohn's most important clients, as well as the art historian Oskar Beyer. The latter wrote in retrospect: "In the fall of 1919, Paul Cassirer had sent out an invitation that read: 'Erich Mendelsohn. Architekturen in Eisen und Beton.' At the time I was reporting on events in the art world, but I waited a few days to go—not very expectantly, for the title sounded a little dry and joyless. And of course no one had ever heard of this architect. Only a handful of people shuffled through the spaces; hung at eye level were sketches, rather small sketches on large white areas, with detailed designs above, greatly enlarged like posters. Strangely, from the first glance I felt myself drawn into a stream, seized by a rhythm that I could not resist. The effect was so strong that on the very same day I called the Dipl. Ing. Erich Mendelsohn . . . in order to arrange a meeting soon. . . . Understanding between us essentially occurred without a word; what connected us was the experience of the music of J. S. Bach, whose name appeared on many of the sketches."[6] In the following year, Beyer's enthusiasm for Mendelsohn and his architectural ideas led to a long article with numerous illustrations in the Dutch architectural magazine *Wendingen,*[7] thus bringing Mendelsohn to the attention of the architects of the Dutch avant-garde. In fall 1920, Mendelsohn was invited to lecture in Holland, and the interaction with colleagues such as Theodor Wijdeveld and J. J. P. Oud began. In England, Mendelsohn aroused the interest of the Russian engineer Pinchas Ruthenberg, who in 1923 invited him to travel to Palestine to discuss the architecture of future power plants.[8] A direct commission, however, did not result from the exhibition.

Garden pavilion for Gustav Herrmann, Luckenwalde, sketch.

Works for Gustav Herrmann in Luckenwalde

In 1919 Mendelsohn built a small garden pavilion for Herrmann, for which he prepared a series of fantastical sketches. The octagonal, wood-boarded pavilion that was ultimately built, however, was essentially simpler and more conventional than the complex, zoomorphic forms visible in the sketches, forms that could only have been produced in cast reinforced concrete.[9] The pavilion no longer exists.

In the same year he received a commission to build a small residential development in Luckenwalde, which was executed in rational construction methods and largely conventional forms.[10] Mendelsohn entrusted the direction of the project to his assistant Arthur Korn.[11] The work progressed so quickly that by May 1920 the design of the exterior was under discussion. Mendelsohn wanted to use colorful paint on the exterior and wrote in early May 1920: "[The colors] must be lighthearted yet serious. The choice remains with blue and yellow. After all, I can't allow this love to remain unenjoyed."[12] Shortly thereafter, he reported that he had also made a "color chart for the interior rooms."[13] The first houses were finished on July 1; Mendelsohn, however, was not entirely satisfied with the result: "I think it will be cheerful, although something has been lost through Korn's interference."[14] He may have decided not to publish this residential development—the only one executed after his design—because the revolutionary color scheme would have gone unnoticed in black-and-white reproductions, while the ground plans and elevations were still largely conventional.

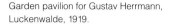

Garden pavilion for Gustav Herrmann, Luckenwalde, 1919.

The Steinberg, Herrmann & Co. Hat Factory in Luckenwalde

In fall 1919, Mendelsohn began working on plans for a new hat factory for Gustav Herrmann. As the company grounds lay in the middle of the residential district of Luckenwalde, the emissions from industrial textile production represented a danger to the population. The city, therefore, sought to move Herrmann & Co. along with its local competitor, Friedrich Steinberg, to a newly developed industrial district outside of town. Herrmann, however, wanted to remain in his traditional location and expand the factory onto an adjacent piece of property, an expansion he commissioned Mendelsohn to plan.

One element in the conception was a steel framework building—erected in 1920 as the first structure—that was to form the front wall of the newly planned factory yard and would have set an important accent in the overall image.[15] Unlike other works by Mendelsohn, with its rectangular form defined by the steel skeleton, large windows with iron frames, and whitewashed filling walls, it resembled Gropius and Meyer's Fagus Works of 1911. Yet the hall differed from its famous predecessor in important respects: it was one-story, the center windows were subdivided into vertical rectangles, and the low windows continuing around the corner were slightly inclined toward the exterior, serving to subtly break open the boxlike space. In 1925 the hall was destroyed by fire.

The general plan for the factory grounds presented by Mendelsohn in spring 1920 called for unified facades connecting the existing factory buildings with the new structures.[16] For this purpose, he chose lucid forms free of any of the decoration common up to that point in industrial architecture. As he himself wrote on May 14, 1920: "The Herrmann & Co. factory will be very—'brutal.'"[17] The plans show facades articulated by large horizontal windows, interrupted only by projecting stairwells whose narrow vertical rows of low, broad windows draw attention to their function as circulation spaces. In their sculptural character the window frames still strongly recall earlier sketches of industrial buildings.

While negotiations with the city were still underway, a decisive change occurred that rendered all planning obsolete: in 1921, Herrmann & Co. merged with Friedrich Steinberg, a longtime competitor who had manufactured hats in Luckenwalde since 1870. The result was removal of the factory complexes of Steinberg, Herrmann & Co. to the industrial district.[18] Naturally this completely undeveloped site offered Mendelsohn considerably more latitude for design than had been the case with the first project.

In a number of sketches from 1921, Mendelsohn sought an adequate solution for the intended function and the site. The sketches are marked by the horizontal positioning of industrial manufacturing halls, a form justified by the weight of the production machines. An early, dramatically intensified perspective sketch, still strongly related to sketches from the war years, shows a large power station before a seemingly endless series of manufacturing halls. When their number had to be reduced, the power station too was executed in a quite smaller form.

For the dyeworks, Mendelsohn developed a completely new approach to function and design, an innovation that at the same time greatly improved working conditions: a considerable increase in height enhanced air circulation in the building, thus protecting the workers from harmful chemical pollution. A sketch published by Mendelsohn, now lost,[19] impressively demonstrates the dynamic building design with its riblike ventilation slits.

In accord with the sequence of production, Mendelsohn planned a symmetrical complex with a dominant central axis along which the primary buildings were arranged: the main entrance with the porter's buildings, the dyeworks, the four manufacturing halls, and the boiler and machine building.[20]

The plans for the first phase of construction with the dyeworks and the manufacturing halls were submitted to the municipal building office of Luckenwalde in late November 1921. Employed there at the time was Richard Neutra, a man five years Mendelsohn's junior who was gaining his first professional experience after studies in Vienna. Neutra recalled: "One day my colleagues in the building office . . . showed me a few bold color sketches for a hat factory. These drawings had been submitted by a man named Erich Mendelsohn. I thought they looked like Expressionist art, and in any case it was unusual to dare to show them to a municipal building inspector in Luckenwalde."[21] Neutra traveled to Berlin to see Mendelsohn, introduced himself, and was hired.

The manufacturing halls and dyeworks were built in the first half of 1922. The bearing system of both buildings consisted of reinforced concrete supports and trusses, elegantly tapered on the lower and upper bearing surfaces. All sense of heaviness was thus avoided and an elegance attained that was unusual for an industrial building. In the manufacturing halls, transmission shafts and pulleys for the production process ran through openings in the supports at the forking of the roof girders. The halls, with a floor area of 56 by 150 meters, were open on the interior and well supplied with daylight through pitched glazed roofs and windows.

Steinberg, Herrmann & Co. hat factory, Luckenwalde, elevations, 1921.

A

B

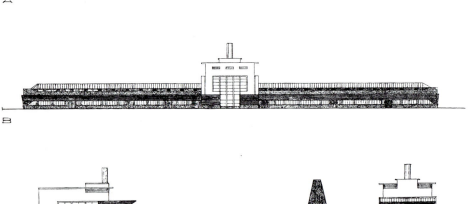

C

Steinberg, Herrmann & Co. hat factory, Luckenwalde. All photographs of the hat factory were taken from a lateral perspective, emphasizing their resemblance to the design sketches.

The dyeworks, which Mendelsohn placed in front of the row of manufacturing halls, later became the trademark of the company. In its design he succeeded in translating technical necessities into striking architectural form. The roof of the dyeworks was considerably taller than that of the manufacturing halls and concealed a complex ventilation system that, with the help of natural draft as well as fans, could completely replace the air in the building within half an hour, ridding it of the formic and sulphuric acid produced by the dying process.[22] This significant step in protecting the health of the workers found a lively echo in the architectural press and won Mendelsohn the commission for a large textile factory in Leningrad in 1925.[23] The construction method was once again based on a skeleton of reinforced concrete, whose bent trusses traced the form of a pointed arch.[24]

In late August 1922, the building application for the boiler house was submitted, and by June 1923 the building was in operation. Its inclusion had become necessary since in the early 1920s the uncertain supply of electricity made it impossible to run the machines around the clock. At the same time, it constituted an important symbol of modernity for the company. Standing at the end of the symmetrical axis, it towered over the manufacturing halls by double the height. On the narrow north side, the coal platform extended to the industrial tracks, ensuring a quick supply of coal.

Steinberg, Herrmann & Co. hat factory, Luckenwalde, interior of manufacturing hall. The large glass areas provide generous daylight, while the supports, elegantly tapered like the trusses, have openings at the top for the transmission shafts.

The final step in the building process was the construction of the two gatehouses on the street side. A detailed sketch by Mendelsohn, unusually finely articulated, reveals their function: with their strongly projecting roofs and ribbon windows continuing around the corners, they served both as weather protection and as guardhouses for the entrance. At the same time, the shape of the opening provided an introductory motif for the factory complex, anticipating the roof form of the dyeworks.

A consistent facade design throughout all the parts of the factory joined the functional buildings into a unified complex whose double function—both the manufacture of hats and the creation of corporate identity—was emphasized in the architectural press of the time. In contrast to the Einstein Tower of the same period, the architect rejected curved wall surfaces and chose sharp, angular forms, emphasized even more through the use of different materials.

Atop a reinforced concrete base, all the factory buildings show homogeneous bands of brick on the wall surfaces between the eaves and the edges of windows and base. The lowered brick areas at the corners of the buildings and the corresponding slanted edges of the windows, along with the brick wainscoting on the gables of the manufacturing halls, give the otherwise

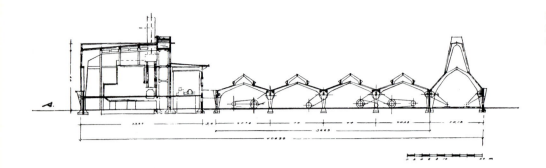

Steinberg, Herrmann & Co. hat factory,
Luckenwalde, section of dyeworks and
manufacturing halls, 1921.

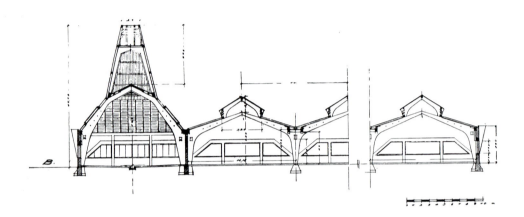

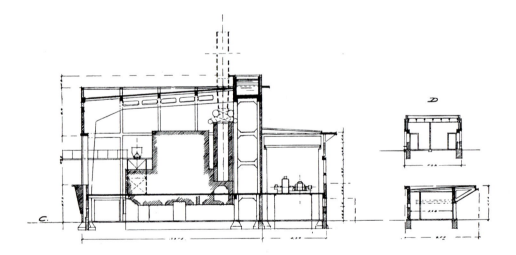

Steinberg, Herrmann & Co. hat factory, Luckenwalde, sketch of entrance, 1922.

Steinberg, Herrmann & Co. hat factory, Luckenwalde, boiler and turbine building after completion.

purely functional buildings a strongly accentuated, rhythmic character. At the same time, the viewer's gaze is led around the corners of the building, transforming the static symmetry of the ground plan into dynamic movement in the elevation. In addition to the high roof of the dyeworks, the lively contour produced by the glass roofs of the manufacturing halls is of central significance for the overall effect, as is the boiler house towering above the rest with its centrally positioned smokestack.

In its remarkable functionality and tremendous strength of expression, the factory is a key building for understanding Mendelsohn's successes of the 1920s. The step taken here toward his architecture of functional dynamism, with buildings composed of varying heights, is made clear by a comparison of the ground plan—defined entirely by axial symmetry—with photographs of the factory published by Mendelsohn. The photographs are consistently taken from a lateral perspective, thus considerably intensifying the drama of the complex and producing a close relationship to the sketches. Quite obviously Mendelsohn at least suggested, if not prescribed, the particular angle to the photographers, as becomes clear from a comparison of images by different photographers. In his Berlin period, he preferred to work with Arthur Köster, but also made use of the services of local photographers in remote areas; yet all the photographs show a similar view of Mendelsohn's architecture, revealing the same intention.

In a lecture given to the Arbeitsrat für Kunst, Mendelsohn himself identified the models for the unusual entrance to the Luckenwalde hat factory: the entrance to the 1901 Mathildenhöhe exhibition in Darmstadt and the Wedding Tower of six years before, both by Joseph Maria Olbrich, whom Mendelsohn viewed as an immediate precursor whose inventions were now to be continued in modern building techniques.[25] The Wedding Tower and the ticket booth in Darmstadt were of central significance for the hat factory of Steinberg, Herrmann & Co., in comparison to which other factory buildings, such as Peter Behrens's AEG Turbine Factory, played only a subordinate role.

The hat factory changed hands a number of times, serving among other things as an armament and roller bearing factory. Subjected over the years to thoroughgoing changes, it awaits reconstruction to this day.[26]

Steinberg, Herrmann & Co. hat factory,
Luckenwalde, sketch, 1920.

Steinberg, Herrmann & Co. hat factory,
Luckenwalde, sketch of boiler and
turbine building, June 1922.

The Administrative Building of the Hausleben-Versicherung Insurance Company in Berlin
In 1920, Dr. Hans Heymann, owner of the Hausleben-Versicherung insurance company, commissioned Mendelsohn to renovate his administrative building on Dorotheenstrasse in the Mitte district of Berlin. A new facade was applied to the old building and a number of its interior spaces redesigned. The brilliant colors used in both measures caused quite a stir.[27] We know of the coloration of the building only from polychrome sketches, while a single photograph of the facade shows that here, too, Mendelsohn met with only limited success in realizing the motion-filled forms conceived in reinforced concrete. At times there are huge gaps between idea and realization. Perhaps for this reason, too, the building—like the garden pavilion and residential development in Luckenwalde before it—is not included in Mendelsohn's own survey of his work, *Das Gesamtschaffen des Architekten.*

Administrative building of the Hausleben-Versicherung insurance company, Berlin, sketch, 1920.

The Rudolf Mosse Publishing House in Berlin
In fall 1921, Mendelsohn's architectural office began work on the renovation and expansion of the Rudolf Mosse publishing house in downtown Berlin, in the newspaper district around Kochstrasse. For the first time, Mendelsohn was able to realize his architectural ideas in an urban context, although the project was a renovation rather than a new building. It initiated the series of significant renovations and expansions with which Mendelsohn was commissioned in the 1920s and which won him considerable success. Mendelsohn's Mosse building resembled the Luckenwalde hat factory only in the bearing frame of reinforced concrete; in all other respects, it differed fundamentally.

The Rudolf Mosse publishing house was one of the most respected journalistic ventures in the empire. In 1867, Rudolf Mosse founded an advertising agency that was soon so successful that, through advertising, newspapers became affordable to the masses for the first time. In 1871, Mosse founded the newspaper *Berliner Tageblatt,* a publication that later numbered among the opinion-makers of the Weimar Republic and represented the left-liberal spectrum. The publishing company moved into a large, monumental building with historicist sandstone facades, erected 1901–03 after plans by Cremer & Wolffenstein. At that point, it also included a book publisher and produced various magazines.

Administrative building of the Hausleben-Versicherung insurance company, Berlin. The color scheme was striking: "The blue-gray windows against the red, the red display windows in the blue-gray base begin to enliven the building and provide a transition from the abstract to the life of the street. It will always be strange. How did I think of that?" Mendelsohn wondered in 1920.

In 1920, after the death of Rudolf Mosse—who had become one of the wealthiest and most respected businessmen in Germany as well as a leading representative of the assimilated Jewish upper class—the management of the publishing company and book publisher was assumed by his son-in-law, Hans Lachmann-Mosse. The direction of the *Berliner Tageblatt,* however, was taken over by Theodor Wolff, permitting Lachmann-Mosse to devote himself to other interests. These included above all real estate, and in the course of the 1920s he repeatedly employed Mendelsohn for renovations and new buildings. Lachmann-Mosse was only two years older than Mendelsohn and was so impressed by the Einstein Tower in Potsdam that in 1921 he commissioned him with the remodeling and expansion of the publishing house itself.[28] In the Spartakus rebellion of January 1919, the corner of the building had been heavily damaged during skirmishes between the rebels and government troops. Commissions for the main hall of the Mosse-Haus (unrealized) and for a newspaper stand at the automobile exhibition followed in 1924, and in 1927 for the boiler house of the publishing building, the Rudolf Mosse pavilion at the "Pressa" in Cologne, and finally for the WOGA buildings on Kurfürstendamm.[29] Lachmann-Mosse became one of Mendelsohn's best clients, with whom he also cultivated a close social relationship. For the renovation of the damaged corner of the publishing building and the addition of auxiliary stories—a project of prime significance both urbanistically and in terms of the

"Erste Skizze R. Mosse" ("First Sketch R. Mosse"), 1921.

Rudolf Mosse publishing house, Berlin, corner design on a text page of the *St. Matthew Passion* by Johann Sebastian Bach, 1921.

Erſter Teil.

Doppel-Chor mit Choral.

Kommt ihr Töchter, helft mir klagen,
Sehet — „wen?" — den Bräutigam,
Seht ihn — „wie?" — als wie ein Lamm.
Sehet — „was?" — ſeht die Geduld,
Seht — „wohin?" — auf unſre Schuld.
Sehet ihn aus Lieb und Huld
Holz zum Kreuze ſelber tragen.

Mosse self-representation—Lachmann-Mosse had previously requested designs from a number of architects.[30] As these merely adopted the historicist forms of the old building, however, he found them unsatisfactory, and instead sought a completely new design that could also be used for advertising purposes.

For this project Mendelsohn collaborated with Richard Neutra and the sculptor Paul Rudolf Henning, likewise a member of the Novembergruppe, giving them free reign with entire portions of the building. The collaboration process, however, was not always easy, as we learn from the intense correspondence of 1922 between Erich and his wife, Luise, who was spending time in the Black Forest. For Mendelsohn it was unusual to collaborate on a project, and he vacillated between optimism, culminating in the desire to make Neutra a partner, and the skepticism that finally won out regarding the delegation of aspects of the design to equal associates. It was with Henning's approach above all that he had difficulties. In June 1922 he wrote, "The ceramics are causing problems due to the nonchalance with which Henning—as if in passing—took care of these things. He is still in Switzerland, despite supposedly urgent business in Berlin, and cannot be found. This morning I corrected the models as best I could. Since my solutions can only be of a functional nature, it is ridiculous to involve a sculptor, especially someone so unreliable in his feeling of 'free creativity.'"[31] To some extent, Neutra assumed the role of mediator between these radically different artistic personalities.

Mendelsohn's first design for the facade, shown in a drawing entitled "Erste Skizze R. Mosse" ("First Sketch R. Mosse"), was exactly what the client didn't want: a continuation of the old building. Shortly thereafter, however, he found a fitting solution during a performance of Bach's *St. Matthew Passion,* a design involving strict separation between the vertically articulated old building and the horizontally articulated new one, a strongly cantilevered baldachin rounding the corner, ribbon windows, and the addition of dynamically inclined stories. Bach's music played a significant role in the subsequent planning of the Mosse building as well. A letter to his wife written in August discusses the problem of the projecting baldachin, which met with vehement resistance from the building authorities: "Yesterday the entire day, today all morning with the sculptor on account of the Mosse model. . . . The side view and attachment of the baldachin . . . were not yet resolved, especially after the baldachin bands were replaced by moldings. Neutra, Henning—three men at the same time are too many to find a solution. Today, alone, I threw out the details from yesterday and in a happy moment came upon the connecting element, and thus also the detail. I hope that with the model I can make it clear to the bigwigs

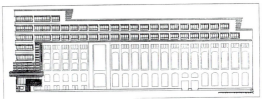

Rudolf Mosse publishing house, Berlin, elevation of Schützenstrasse facade, 1922.

why the baldachin rings project out from the facade so brutally. . . . The baldachin has to be pushed through, otherwise the bass is missing from the fugue. . . . The next thing is the entrance from the inside, which absolutely must be changed, i.e., remodeled, deconstructed, reconstructed. How, is already clear."[32] In numerous meetings—despite the resistance of the municipal building authorities—the eight-story structure, towering up over the existing building by three additional stories, was successfully approved and completed by fall 1923.

The work was overshadowed by a serious accident occasioned by inexperience with the new material of reinforced concrete. The construction manager had caused "considerable quantities" of gravel to be put on the ceilings while they were still in formwork, and shortly thereafter ordered the removal of the formwork. Four days later, the ceiling collapsed and the masses of stone and gravel came crashing down into the old building, where the publisher's work had continued in the meantime. A safe was carried away in the avalanche and broke through to the floors below. The end result was horrifying: twenty-four of the publisher's employees were plunged to the depths, thirteen of them to their death, while the other eleven suffered severe injuries. Court proceedings following the accident revealed that no regulation had been violated, but that inexperience with the building material was at fault.[33]

The center of the composition is the rounded corner structure with the projecting baldachin over the entrance and five high, very broad bands of windows, suggesting a different number of stories than on the interior. The window bands are subdivided into many small, vertical, rectangular panes with dimensions taken from the attic story windows of the old building, thus establishing a subtle connection between the two structures. The new building projects into the old like a wedge, at the same time providing it with two additional stories on the wings and three in the center. While these added stories are marked by large, simple forms, the entrance area and baldachin are remarkable for the complex, fine-grained articulation of detail. Vertical bands of windows establish a transition between these contrasting portions of the new structure and serve to both mark and soften the boundary to the old building.

The Mosse building clearly manifests Mendelsohn's conception of modern facade design: only those portions visible to pedestrians at short range should be articulated in detail, while parts of the building seen only from a distance or even from a moving automobile should react to this altered mode of vision with simple horizontality, articulated in large forms.[34] This contrast is seen here in the lower and upper portions of the facade. Mendelsohn developed the details of the facade together with his colleagues: Henning designed the ceramic facing, Neutra the window frames of the additional stories.[35]

Rudolf Mosse publishing house, Berlin, office of Lachmann-Mosse on the top floor of the building corner.

While Mendelsohn played the decisive role in both the detail and overall design of the exterior, the office of publishing director Lachmann-Mosse was designed by Neutra in all its details.[36] Here Neutra was strongly influenced by the architecture and interior design of Frank Lloyd Wright, whose work had been known and respected in Germany since the major publication on Wright by the publisher Wasmuth-Verlag in Berlin in 1910. Along with Henry van de Velde and Joseph Maria Olbrich, Wright became one of Mendelsohn's most venerated models. Neutra's debt to Wright is particularly evident in the executive office, which reflects numerous motifs from interior designs by the latter. The contrast in style between Neutra and Mendelsohn is made clear by a comparison with Mendelsohn's more or less contemporaneous designs for the interior of the Einstein Tower or the double villa at Karolinger Platz.

The finished Mosse building caused a sensation: it was widely discussed in both the daily and the architectural press and was included in architectural guides to Berlin. Even more than the Einstein Tower or the hat factory, it represented Mendelsohn's ticket to success, for here for

the first time a renovation was also extraordinarily successful in enhancing the advertising presence of a client. This approach spoke to the needs of other potential clients as well, their desire for effective advertising and an increase in sales with comparatively low investment.[37]

Numerous puns made the rounds. The Mosse building was described as the "S. M. Rudolf Mosse steaming along Jerusalemer Strasse," while in Mendelsohn's office "the arrival of the Mauretania in the west harbor of Berlin" was noted.[38] Mendelsohn himself described the Mosse building as follows: "Just as the overall expression visibly echoes the rapid tempo of the street, the movement intensifying to an extreme toward the corner, at the same time, through the balance of its powers, it tames the nervousness of the street and the passersby. . . . By dividing and channeling traffic, the building stands, despite its tendency toward movement, as an immovable pole in the agitation of the street."[39]

All of these descriptions evoke the steamship or aerodynamic motifs popular in the second half of the 1920s. Yet in the Mosse building, such allusions remain bound to the overall form and are not visible in the design of the details.

After suffering considerable damage in the war, the publishing house was rebuilt in a simplified form and now stands in a completely altered urbanistic environment in Berlin-Mitte.

The Weichmann Silk Store in Gleiwitz

The broad stylistic range of Mendelsohn's early work is likewise apparent in the Weichmann silk store in Gleiwitz. It was his first commission for a store, if only a small one in the province of Upper Silesia. In this building, too, Mendelsohn collaborated closely with Neutra, to whom he delegated the construction supervision and probably part of the design.[40] Remarkably, no hand sketch by Mendelsohn exists for the silk store—a great exception in his work. For other, albeit more significant, commissions he produced up to thirty sketches.

The commission dates to spring 1922. The client was the Jewish silk dealer Erwin Weichmann, who had come to Gleiwitz after World War I. He had acquired a small, extremely inconveniently shaped plot on the corner of Wilhelmstrasse, the main business street of Gleiwitz, and Promenadenstrasse. Here he decided to erect a building with sales and storage rooms as well as an apartment. Toward Wilhelmstrasse the plot was less than eight meters wide, while along Promenadenstrasse it extended to thirty-one meters. These extreme proportions prompted Mendelsohn to design his first asymmetrical building. In so doing, he used the tension between bearing and projecting elements, between open and closed, horizontal and vertical, planar and three-dimensional, light and shadow to produce a contrapuntal design that, despite its objectively small scale, gave the building the impression of size and spaciousness.

The elements of design used here differ radically from those of the contemporaneous factory in Luckenwalde and the Mosse building, although the bearing frame was once again constructed of reinforced concrete. The shallow depth of the building made it possible to engage the supports in the facades and freely span the interior spaces. The grid of supports thus articulate the facades, while the spaces between them on the ground level and the first upper floor are completely occupied by windows. These windows, behind which lie the sales rooms, are framed above and below with broad, deep cornices, giving the facades a strong sculptural effect. In contrast, the second upper story, with the apartment, was smoothly plastered up to the flat roof, its windows flush with the wall.

Toward Wilhelmstrasse, the upper stories were designed to project 1.25 meters beyond the building line, a feature that led to vehement conflicts with the building authorities. Only the dispensation for the baldachin of the Mosse building enabled Mendelsohn to obtain the permit.[41] At the other end of the long facade toward Promenadenstrasse, a counterweight was provided by a four-story stairwell, before a one-story office annex for Weichmann struck the final chord of

Weichmann silk store, Gleiwitz, corner view of facade toward Promenadenstrasse/Wilhelmstrasse.

the contrapuntal composition. The annex is connected to the sales room on the ground floor by a cornice band, a motif Mendelsohn had already used in Luckenwalde.

The interior spaces were furnished in a simple, functional manner. Since a portion of the neighboring building intruded into the plot, the sales room narrowed from a maximum of 5.7 meters to a minimum of 3.3 meters. The zigzag of the sales tables responded to this form, as did the ceiling tracks for advertising signs and lamps. The lighting of the interior spaces, however, was achieved primarily through the windows inserted directly below the lintel, thus fulfilling an important prerequisite for the sale of fabric: natural daylight. For the first time in commercial architecture, decorative elements were completely absent from the interior design of the silk store. This was exactly what the client wanted, as his head clerk noted in retrospect: "Mendelsohn departed in a particularly striking way from current building methods and created a new style whose modernity can be described in the terms functionality, uniformity, and simplicity. His building program corresponded to the wishes of the client, and thus the architect found a solution to symbolize the stylistic sensibility uniquely characteristic of our age."[42] For Mendelsohn, the most important achievement was that "space, the fundamental element of architecture, is recognized again, three-dimensionality dominates."[43]

The original architectural substance of the Weichmann silk store still exists in Gleiwitz today.

In his early work, Mendelsohn developed numerous design elements that he continued to use in his subsequent projects, elements including the energetic placement of building volumes, the playing out of design opposites in the creation of dynamic facades, and finished surfaces in glass, shiny metal, and tile. With the hat factory, the Mosse building, and the silk store he attracted the attention of a clientele whose businesses were rapidly expanding in the 1920s. When inflation ceased in 1923, he was nearly inundated with commissions. Mendelsohn's architectural office was to become the largest and most successful in the German empire. Nonetheless, by mutual agreement he separated from his colleagues Henning and Neutra. In his office, he wanted to be the sole designer.

Notes p. 264.

Weichmann silk store, Gleiwitz, sales room on the first level.

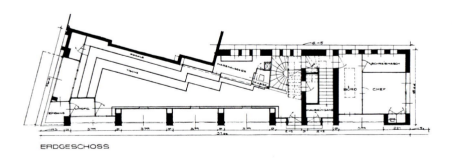

ERDGESCHOSS

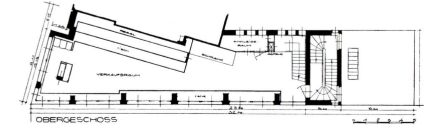

OBERGESCHOSS

Weichmann silk store, Gleiwitz, plan of ground level and first level, 1922.

Administrative building of the
Hausleben-Versicherung insurance
company, Berlin, interior, sketch, 1920.

"Around noon land in sight"

Ita Heinze-Greenberg

Travels to Holland, Palestine, the United States, and Russia

For Mendelsohn, there were different kinds of journeys: short trips from which he planned to return, longer ones that raised the possibility of a permanent move, and a few "one-way tickets." Many trips were associated with lectures devoted to his own work, the fundamentals of modern architecture, or philosophical and political questions of the time. Such lecture tours included trips to Holland in 1921 and 1923, to Spain in 1929, and to London in 1930. Many trips were connected with projects: Mendelsohn always refused to draw up designs without firsthand knowledge of the site and its surroundings. This principle took him to Palestine in 1923 and 1934, to the Soviet Union in 1925 and 1926, and to Norway in 1932.

Erich Mendelsohn at the Ammersee, mid-1920s.

Although the purpose and goal of his travels varied, they were always an integral part of the creative work to which his life was devoted. His major journeys abroad at the beginning of the 1920s doubtless played an especially important role as formative influences in his professional and personal development.

There were three countries in particular to which he traveled at the start of his career: Palestine, the land of his fathers; Holland, Germany's European neighbor; and America, the land of unlimited opportunity. Palestine, the old/new Jewish homeland, assumed an extraordinary position *a priori,* one that was emotionally, politically, and, in a broad sense, religiously charged. He traveled to Palestine for the first time in 1923, at a time when most German Jews knew little of Zionism. This trip confronted him with his roots, with questions of his own personal and national identity. It opened up a new sociopolitical dimension in his architecture, and from that point on he always viewed his architecture in its social and geographical context.

At first, Mendelsohn's interest in Holland and America appears to have been of a purely professional nature. In an essay on Mendelsohn for the Dutch journal *Wendingen* in 1920, his advocate Oskar Beyer wrote: "As far as I can tell, there are at present only two countries of essential significance with regard to new architectural creations: America and Holland. With its pronounced industrial culture, America has created great things in the realm of new types of work buildings; the resulting 'American style' is of high quality, not only technically but also artistically. In Holland, a century-old architectural culture is now manifesting itself in amazingly innovative solutions and projects, which transcend all bourgeois narrowness and torpor and seem to open up a cosmopolitan horizon. What the new artists in both countries share is a cultivation of the technical and a breadth of imaginative achievement, and it is this that allows the German steel architect [Mendelsohn] to take his place at their side."[1]

Mendelsohn established contact with both America and Holland relatively early. He made his first trip to Holland two years after the end of World War I in early 1921, the second in 1923. In 1924, he was among the first German architects to visit America. In addition to a purely professional interest, however, it was doubtless the human contact, the dialogue with colleagues, that Mendelsohn sought in these lands. He found it above all with other Jewish architects. He established personal relationships with Hendricus Theodorus Wijdeveld and Michel de Klerk in

Holland, Ely Jacques Kahn in the United States, and later El Lissitzky in the Soviet Union with comparatively greater ease than with the German colleagues of his own generation.[2]

Mendelsohn's travels to these countries, however, were always undertaken with a view to exploring his own professional chances there as well. Palestine and America in particular represented potential destinations for emigration from a crisis-weakened Germany whose politics were progressively shifting toward the right. Palestine promised him the national affirmation of his Jewish identity, America the assimilation into the "melting pot." Politically, he vacillated between the two possibilities. For him, the "Promised Land" was wherever an attractive field of endeavor opened up for his creative work.

In the end, he remained in Germany—until the political situation became intolerable. The temporary economic recovery after the currency reform very quickly brought him to the top of his field for the few glorious years of the Weimar Republic. His extensive travels in the early 1920s had helped turn the young Expressionist architect into an experienced builder whose self-confidence was rooted not least of all in a thorough acquaintance with the architectural happenings in other countries as well as the successes he himself had enjoyed abroad.

Travels to Holland, 1921 and 1923

It was from abroad, in fact, that Mendelsohn received the first positive responses to the sketched visions exhibited by Cassirer in 1919 at the beginning of his career. The swelling, towering volumes drawn by the young, still unknown architect at first found few admirers in Germany, with the exception of Oskar Beyer. The reaction from Holland, however, was quite different. The architect Hendricus Theodorus Wijdeveld of Amsterdam initiated contact with Mendelsohn after visiting the exhibition. Wijdeveld was one of the editors of the mouthpiece of the Amsterdam architects' association Architectura et Amicitia, *Wendingen,* a publication that had existed since 1918. In addition, the magazine was associated with the so-called Amsterdam School, a circle of architects around Michel de Klerk with which such figures as Mathieu Lauweriks, Jan Frederik Staal, Pieter Lodewijk Kramer, Johann Melchior van der Meij, and Willem Marinus Dudok were loosely associated. *Wendingen* appeared monthly until 1931 and published articles in Dutch, German, French, and English dealing with all areas of the visual arts. Without doubt, the main accent lay on illustration, and Wijdeveld's typographic ornaments gave the journal its special, almost orientalizing flair.[3] The exquisite graphic quality of Mendelsohn's sketched architectural visions may also have stimulated Wijdeveld's interest in publishing them in *Wendingen.*

The entire October 1920 issue was devoted not only to Mendelsohn's architecture, but above all to his drawings, accompanied by two lengthy essays by Staal and Beyer.[4] As a result, Mendelsohn attained a notoriety in modern Holland that hardly any other architect enjoyed and that long remained denied to him in Germany. During a subsequent lecture tour in 1921 at the invitation of Architectura et Amicitia, he spoke on "Das Problem einer neuen Baukunst" ("The Problem of a New Architecture"), a speech he had presented shortly before to the Arbeitsrat für Kunst. Its theme was a problem whose solution he had striven for in the Einstein Tower: the development of a new form of architecture derived from the material of reinforced concrete.[5]

For Mendelsohn, this first trip to Holland was a complete success, both professionally and personally. He became acquainted with and came to appreciate works by the Amsterdam School, but also those of de Stijl in Rotterdam. As divergent as they were, both directions were to influence his own work. There he saw, as it were, the two defining poles of his own architecture in their pure form, and from this experience he developed his concept of the synthesis of dynamics and function. His "Holland letter" of August 1923, written to his wife following Oud's lecture at the

Bauhaus in Weimar, has become well known in this context: "Oud is . . . functional. Amsterdam is dynamic. A union of both concepts is conceivable, but cannot be discerned in Holland. The first puts reason foremost—perception through analysis. The second, unreason—perception through vision. Analytic Rotterdam rejects vision. Visionary Amsterdam does not understand analytic objectivity. . . . If Amsterdam goes a step further towards ratio, and Rotterdam does not freeze up, they may still unite. Otherwise both will be destroyed; Rotterdam by the deadly chill in its veins, Amsterdam by the fire of its own dynamism. Functional dynamics are the postulate. Holland is a brilliant example of its analysis."[6]

Hendricus Theodorus Wijdeveld, design for a bridge in Amsterdam (detail), 1920.

Mendelsohn's second trip to Holland in November 1923 was likewise conceived as a lecture tour. In Amsterdam, The Hague, and Rotterdam he spoke on "Die internationale Überein- stimmung des neuen Baugedankens oder Dynamik und Funktion" ("The International Agreement in the New Idea of Architecture, or Dynamics and Function").[7] This lecture, too, is striking for its historical and social analyses, which always maintain a grasp on the whole without forgetting the details. Ideas that resulted from his above-mentioned "Holland letter" can be identified between the lines. Once again, the insistent search for new formal principles stands in the foreground; here, however, these principles are derived not only from the new building material, but also from political, socioeconomic, and scientific revolutions that demand adequate expression. In Mendelsohn's view, this development can be observed worldwide, as already indicated in the title of the lecture. Yet this international character by no means signals the propagation of a universal formal sameness, but rather is intended to stimulate an international dialogue—a prac- tice Mendelsohn himself pursued with an increasing number of friends and colleagues abroad.

Mendelsohn cultivated personal relationships above all with Oud, de Klerk, and espe- cially with Wijdeveld. The contact to Jacobus Johannes Pieter Oud resulted in an extensive correspondence beginning in the early 1920s and continuing into the 1950s,[8] as well as in occasional visits.

At Berlage's recommendation, Oud had been an assistant in Theodor Fischer's office in Munich for three months in 1911. It is not inconceivable that as a student Mendelsohn had already made his acquaintance at that time, though probably only briefly. Certainly the shared experiences and the person of Theodor Fischer provided a welcome point of contact between Mendelsohn and Oud. Their letters, however, contain no references to Fischer. In addition to con- gratulations on various occasions and a few letters of recommendation, the correspondence contains an interesting exchange on the concepts of dynamics and function continuing through a number of letters, an exchange initiated in response to Oud's lecture during the exhibition week at the Bauhaus in Weimar in the summer of 1923.[9] Oud and Mendelsohn's correspondence likewise includes another lengthy exchange continuing for almost two years on the subject of the

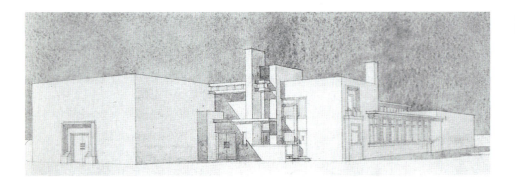

J. J. P. Oud, design for a factory in Pumerend, 1919.

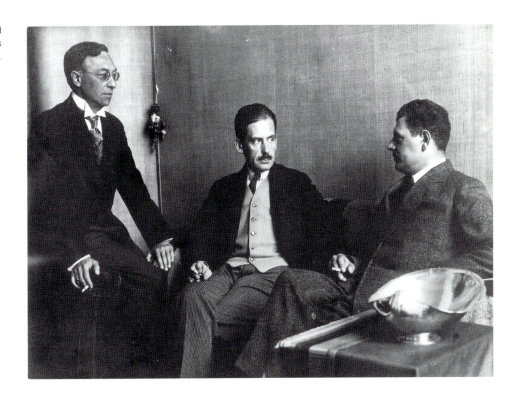

architecture critic Werner Hegemann, whom Mendelsohn attacks with some vehemence, though he concludes by relenting, "He is certainly an amusing and clever fellow, but he lashes out too often and in all directions."[10]

Oud was certainly one of Mendelsohn's most important contacts in Holland, one that he cultivated until his death. His friendships with de Klerk and above all with Wijdeveld, however, seem to have been much more personal, due not least of all to the fact that both were Jewish, giving rise to something like an *a priori,* nonverbal agreement. De Klerk was the shining star of the Amsterdam School. Unlike most of the German Expressionists, he had actual buildings to show. His residential developments in Amsterdam, above all Spaarndammerbuurt, were impressive examples of the brick Expressionism that Mendelsohn had already admired during his first trip to Holland.

De Klerk was three years older than Mendelsohn. He had grown up in the lively Jewish quarter of Amsterdam and was left to make his own way at age fourteen after the death of his parents.[11] For many years he worked in the office of Eduard Cuypers, where he became acquainted with Piet Kramer and Wijdeveld. Mendelsohn met him during his first trip to Holland and intensified the contact during his second stay in November 1923. He felt a spiritual kinship with de Klerk, which he found expressed in his buildings and projects as well. He attempted to win him to Zionism, and the two planned a trip together to Palestine. The plan remained unrealized, however, when de Klerk died only a few days after Mendelsohn's return to Berlin. In a letter to his former fellow student Richard Kauffmann in Palestine, he expressed his great esteem for de Klerk: "My dear Kauffmann, terrible news! De Klerk, with whom I was only just together, has died suddenly. Since you knew him, the man and his work, you know what a great loss we must all lament. We had only just agreed to travel to Israel together. Through that trip I hoped to awaken his interest for the Jewish roots that were in him and to which the generosity and pathos of his work bore witness far more than he himself was aware. Young architecture mourns, and

Israel has reason to mourn as well. . . . You can imagine what his death means for our circle of friends in Amsterdam. You will have received the card we sent you, of which he spoke with pleasure even on the last day. You have not yet seen his most recent works, which manifest a significant leap forward from decoration to clear spatial form and in which the agreement with my ideas came to clear expression, in his own awareness as well. Remember him, as many of the best will always remember him."[12]

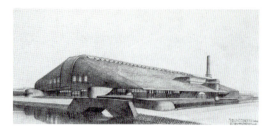

Michel de Klerk, design for an auction hall for the flower market in Aalsmeer, 1923.

The third of Mendelsohn's Dutch friends was Wijdeveld, at whose initiative Mendelsohn had come to Holland in the first place. In time, Hendricus Theodorus Wijdeveld acquired the nickname "Dutchy," and the two families became close friends. Whenever the Mendelsohns spent time in Holland, they were welcome guests at the Wijdeveld home.[13] Ellen Wijdeveld née Kohn came from Germany and like Luise Mendelsohn was a musician. Wijdeveld himself was an amusing dreamer and a well-traveled cosmopolitan who had spent part of his childhood in South Africa, later attended evening classes at the Lambeth School of Art in London for three years, and subsequently spent a number of months in France and Germany. As an architect, he did not attain the level of recognition he enjoyed for his stage designs and journalistic activities. He achieved international recognition for his work as editor of *Wendingen*.[14] Wijdeveld was known as an enthusiastic and busy man involved in many extraordinary and interesting projects, including the planning of the Académie Européenne Méditerranée together with Mendelsohn.[15]

Journey to Palestine, Spring 1923
In early 1923, Wijdeveld decided on the spur of the moment to accept an invitation from Mendelsohn to accompany him to Palestine. He sent a telegram confirming his participation with the words "Freunde ich reise mit euch brief folgt" ("Friends I will travel with you letter to follow").[16]

Erich Mendelsohn on a Mediterranean beach.

A few days earlier, Mendelsohn had written a long letter to him explaining the circumstances of the journey: "The engineer Ruthenberg, who has received permission and money from the English government to exploit the hydraulic energy of the Jordan river, has . . . become acquainted with my work. Ruthenberg immediately communicated to me that he was extraordinarily interested in my work and that he would soon visit me in Berlin. —Last Tuesday . . . Ruthenberg appeared in my office and asked me to work over the whole object with him after we have discussed the project in more detail and I have shown him my works now under construction.— I then suggested to Ruthenberg that he travel to Palestine with me, since it was impossible for me to draw up designs for a strange country without knowledge of the land and climate.— Ruthenberg eagerly agreed to travel with me. . . . The project calls for the construction of a large power plant along with a dam and settlement on the Jordan and power stations in Haifa, Jaffa, and Jerusalem, as well as everything else that could result from it.—It is an extensive project, on which the entire problem of the incipient Jewish state naturally depends. Ruthenberg has turned to me as an architect and a Zionist. He made such an outstanding impression as a man honestly wrestling with the issue that I accepted with great joy."[17]

Mendelsohn's reference, if only in passing, to the significance of this project, on which "the entire problem of the incipient Jewish state" depended, was justified. Up to this point, the land of Palestine had no supply of electricity.[18] In 1919, Ruthenberg had emigrated from Russia to Palestine. A mechanical engineer by trade, he adopted an already existing plan for the electrification of the country and after skillful diplomatic negotiations in 1921 was able to obtain an official concession from the British mandate government permitting him to exploit the hydraulic powers of the Jordan and Yarmuk rivers for the production of electricity. This produced a vehement counter-

Jaffa ca. 1920. In the foreground, building activities for the city of Tel Aviv, founded in 1909.

reaction in the land, whose spokesman was Charles Robert Ashbee, a British proponent of the Arts and Crafts movement and at that time architectural adviser to the governor of Jerusalem. He resisted the industrialization of Palestine advocated by Zionist Jews, a plan that hinged on the availability of electricity. Ashbee and most of the British sought to preserve the oriental-biblical character of Palestine that had remained unchanged for centuries, largely protected from the Industrial Revolution. In his *Palestine Notebook*—a kind of philosophical diary—Ashbee's thoughts on the matter are recorded in the chapter "Allah and the Machines," which concludes with the remark "The future of the West may lie in the machines, but not the future of Palestine."[19]

Ruthenberg emerged victorious from this controversy and in so doing made a decisive contribution to the increasing industrialization of Eretz Israel (the land of Israel, as Zionists referred to Palestine).

For Mendelsohn—whose early sketches from the period around World War I include three for the AEG company—Ruthenberg was something of a reincarnation of Emil Rathenau, who would have represented Mendelsohn's ideal client. Indeed, it now looked quite as if Mendelsohn was about to become the Peter Behrens of the Palestinian AEG.

The small entourage that arrived in Palestine in late February consisted of Mendelsohn, his wife, Luise, and Wijdeveld. For all three, this trip was to be an unforgettable experience. Mendel-

Mendelsohn and Wijdeveld's postcard to Oskar Beyer from Jerusalem with a sketch of the "approach to the Wailing Wall," dated March 9, 1923.

sohn used the time to prepare initial sketches for a power station in Haifa.[20] In Jerusalem he was reunited with Richard Kauffmann, a former fellow student from Munich and pupil of Theodor Fischer who had been involved in settlement planning in Palestine since 1921. In addition, he made new contacts with significant leaders in the Zionist Organization such as Chaim Weizmann, who in turn put him in contact with important Jewish circles in Berlin.[21]

The journey proved to be an overwhelming emotional experience for Mendelsohn. From Jerusalem he wrote to Oskar Beyer: "My dear Beyer, don't wait for something to be written. What I have experienced is great beyond all expectation and I must have time to digest it. Once I have, it can only strengthen what was always strong: blood and space, race and three-dimensionality!" In a less melodramatic vein, Wijdeveld added: "Send two Arab peasants to a European architecture school for a year and we would know what architecture is."[22]

Several months later, Mendelsohn analyzed his impressions again in his lecture "Palästina als künstlerisches Erlebnis" ("Palestine as Artistic Experience"): "As the offspring of the oriental Jewish people, a more or less essential part of our blood existence is connected with the soil of Palestine, whose sometimes shocking oppositions have produced the unequivocally monumental structure of the Bible and its moral law—regardless of the extent that the individual has inherited this blood connection in a pure or mixed form in his psyche. . . . Nowhere do we so power-

Business center in Haifa, 1923. Aerial perspective from an aircraft approaching Haifa from the Mediterranean.

Haifa power station, 1923.

Site plan for the garden city on Mount Carmel, project sketch, 1923.

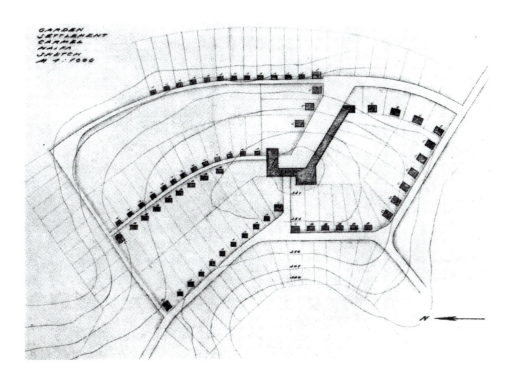

fully experience the fate of belonging to two spheres of sensibility—the atavistic oriental and the contemporary Western one—as in Palestine itself."[23]

Despite the initial euphoria with which Mendelsohn rushed into the Ruthenberg project, it ended in disappointment for him. His designs for the power station in Haifa were not executed and the collaboration was discontinued. The reasons for this swift end to an initially promising effort are unclear. Years later, Mendelsohn himself construed an amusing anecdote as the answer to this question: "The Haifa power station with its projecting cornices as sun protection for the windows beneath, which in turn were reduced to a minimum, responded to the climatic conditions of the East. Its clear spatial impression shocked the then High Commissioner, who described it as 'too European.' At the same time I was building the first modern villa in Berlin. A German general was shocked and described it as 'too oriental'!"[24]

The journey to Palestine gained Mendelsohn two other extensive commissions, to which he devoted himself during the months that followed in his office in Berlin. The first resulted from an exchange of ideas with Richard Kauffmann, an exchange probably begun verbally and later continued in writing.[25] It involved the planning of a settlement on the craggy ridge of Mount Carmel in Haifa. In 1923, the Berlin contractor and Gropius patron Adolf Sommerfeld acquired a large piece of land for development on the south side of Carmel. Richard Kauffmann assumed the on-site direction of the planning as the settlement architect. Presumably, Mendelsohn first became acquainted with the project during his trip to Palestine. Back in Berlin, he continued to correspond with Kauffmann, but also contacted Adolf Sommerfeld himself. In June 1923, he sent Kauffmann six sketches with an attached commentary. These drawings are one of the few occasions on which Mendelsohn devoted his attention to the design of a small dwelling. He presented two types, a three- and a four-room house, describing them as "developed from the cube and brought to a certain spatial intensification even in their relatively small dimensions by stairways, projecting halls, cut-out windows, and flower-box ledges.—I hope they will help in the development of the type necessary for the old/new homeland."[26]

Additional correspondence with Kauffmann suggests that while at first Mendelsohn was involved in the planning for a short time, he was soon forced to abandon his efforts. In January 1924, he resigned from the project, not before uttering vehement criticism of Sommerfeld.[27]

In early March, while Mendelsohn was still in Palestine, an international competition for a business center in Haifa was announced in the Jewish newspaper *Jüdische Rundschau*.[28] The Business Centre Company Haifa, a Jewish firm, had purchased a large downtown plot between the lively Jaffa Street and the railroad tracks along the coast. According to the competition announcement, a solution was sought that would combine the bazaars, cafés, businesses, residential blocks, a cinema, banks, office spaces, and a hotel within a single organism. Presumably, Mendelsohn heard of this project already during his stay in Palestine and was able to view the building site. Back in Berlin, he drew up designs for the competition project in partnership with Richard Neutra, at that time his most trusted assistant in the office. He himself described the project as follows: "The project combines the various businesses into a unified architectural organism, beginning on the beach with the low bazaar structures and spiraling upward to the high tract of the office building. The transverse placement of the latter serves to separate the noisy bazaars from the official buildings grouped around the Centre Place. The aerial approach shows the spiraling upward movement, while the view from the shore promenade reveals the steep ascent from the low bazaars to the high office building. The program calls for the Centre Place development to include an old Arab hall building, gradually incorporating it into the rhythm of the new structures."[29]

Garden city on Mount Carmel, design for two house types, 1923. (The version seen here, published in 1930 in *Das Gesamtschaffen des Architekten*, mistakenly shows the perspective view of the upper house with the plan of the lower, and vice versa.)

Alexander Baerwald, competition entry for the business center in Haifa, 1923.

Mendelsohn and Neutra won first place in the competition, with a prize of one hundred Egyptian pounds—a significant source of income in view of the escalating inflation in Germany. The commission for the execution of the lucrative project, however, was awarded to the essentially more modest and conservative second-place design of Fritz Kornberg, a Berlin architect who had lived in Jerusalem since 1920.[30] This turn of events once again represented a great disappointment for Mendelsohn. He had already considered emigrating to Palestine, but only on the condition that the country offer him enough work and influence.[31] Still, Mendelsohn and Neutra received the prize money, and with it Neutra was able to realize a longtime dream: "It was a monumental project, and we received payment in Egyptian pounds. My share was large enough to allow me to make the jump to the United States."[32]

Journey to America, 1924

Neutra left Mendelsohn's office and emigrated to America. In the months that followed he worked alternately for the large architectural firm Holabird and Roche in Chicago and the office of Frank Lloyd Wright at Taliesin in Spring Green, Wisconsin. Shortly after beginning to work with Wright, Neutra was able to arrange a meeting between the great master and his own former boss from Berlin. In the new environment, the relationship between Mendelsohn and Neutra was reversed: here it was Neutra who called the shots, who had a better command of the language, and who found himself in a more advantageous position with respect to Mendelsohn. This was to remain unchanged until Mendelsohn's death.

Neutra was by no means the only European of his generation to view America as the "Promised Land"—pointing the way to the future, a bastion of individual freedom and social prosperity. The prosperous America with its (for German standards) extravagant metropolitan centers lived up to its reputation as a pulsating modern world—with skyscrapers and big cities, unlimited expansion both horizontally and vertically, jazz, Charlie Chaplin, and Hollywood, rationalization and optimal work performance, Ford and the "car for everyman." Americanism was the new, powerful slogan of the age. Many architects of the Neues Bauen found their way to America; Adolf Loos was one of the first. In the 1920s, it was already clear that the "Grand Tour" of the twentieth century led to America. Mendelsohn shared the European fascination for the "land of unlimited opportunity." His early lectures already contained many images that had become icons of modern architecture: Wright's Larkin building, Buffalo's giant grain silos, the Ford factory in Detroit, and an aerial view of Manhattan.[33]

Mendelsohn had played with the idea of visiting America since 1920,[34] yet the unstable German currency of the early 1920s presented insurmountable financial obstacles. In July 1924, however, Mendelsohn excitedly wrote to his wife that the Mosse publishing firm had agreed to pay for the trip: "October 2 on the 'Deutschland.' First Class. C Deck 67."[35] From the same letter we learn that the journey was initially planned as a group excursion: in addition to his wife, Mendelsohn had also invited the Wijdevelds and Ouds. When the other couple canceled, however, he decided to travel alone, leaving even his wife behind, in order to have the freedom "that I need to make all the decisions that may be required of me in America. There are very real thoughts of gaining commissions and perhaps even emigrating or moving there."[36]

On October 3, Mendelsohn embarked from Hamburg on the *Deutschland*. Eight days later, on October 11, he reached New York. Probably the most interesting fellow passenger on board, and the one with whom Mendelsohn spent the most time, was the filmmaker Fritz Lang. Mendelsohn wrote humorous remarks about Lang to his wife: "The most elegant of all is Lang's

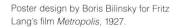

monocle, which I hope will fall overboard at the next opportunity." Or: "Apart from the monocle and similar Viennese affectations, Fritz Lang . . . is a thoughtful, active, and bold person."[37] And then, Mendelsohn's first impression of New York, still from the deck of the *Deutschland:* "Around noon land in sight. . . . Suddenly appearing for a moment in the evening fog—the Woolworth Building. Like a phantom, towering up in the sky. No one ever thought that high. . . . Lights just above the bay, ascending, stretching up to the sky—red light—the top of Woolworth. The ship turns—Babylon. Ghostly in the moonlit darkness. Towering up with verticals of light. Rapid entry, turns, curves—a battle of space in the darkness, in the light of the embedded streets. A thrust to the heart, lost in such dimensions—the tragedy of madness, insane power, the power of space, the unending intoxication of victory."[38] Mendelsohn's dramatic description seems to anticipate Lang's *Metropolis.*

Lang's own impressions of the arrival at the New York harbor, which he later published in the journal *Film-Kurier,* so resemble the tone of Mendelsohn's that we may imagine the two men standing together at the railing, exchanging their ambivalent impressions of this Mephistophelian seduction. Lang's text, too, contains the highly symbolic word "Babylon," which he later developed into a key scene in the film that he himself said was born that very hour.[39]

For both artists, this first glimpse of New York, reinforced by additional travel impressions, was to be formative for their later work. For Lang, these experiences came to expression in his cinematic masterpiece *Metropolis,* for Mendelsohn in direct form in his book *Amerika. Bilderbuch eines Architekten* and indirectly in a new kind of big-city architecture. Both manifestations, however, bear witness to an extremely critical response to America and European Americanism.

Mendelsohn began his tour in New York, followed by brief visits to Buffalo, Pittsburgh, Ann Arbor, and Detroit. The rest of his two-month stay was devoted exclusively to Chicago, from which point he undertook his two-day excursion to see Frank Lloyd Wright.

Mendelsohn was not entirely unknown in the United States; several articles by Herman George Scheffauer—the first published as early as 1921—had preceded him.[40] Against this

background, it was easy for Mendelsohn to arrange lectures on his work at architecture schools in Pittsburgh, Ann Arbor, and elsewhere, engagements that on the one hand helped finance his trip and on the other provided an ideal introduction to important circles in various cities. In addition, he also carried with him a long list of Jewish contact addresses, including a number of architects such as Ely Jacques Kahn. The visit to Kahn was a noteworthy experience for Mendelsohn, confronting him with the scale of the successful American architectural office: "Mr. Kahn . . . has an office of 300 architects, engineers, and mechanics. He only draws and supervises, in a well-furnished Renaissance room on the seventeenth floor of the Marguet building. A splendid, refreshing man, a Jew, about fifty years old. Loves Messel and in his heart of hearts—his architectural heart—is quite averse to me, but otherwise certainly sympathizes with me. Here, such a thing is possible, out of Fairness, out of Friendship."[41] For the sake of comparison, one should remember that at the height of his career in the late 1920s, Mendelsohn maintained a staff of forty, placing his architectural office among the largest in Europe.

Mendelsohn's appointment calendar filled, and the invitations became so numerous that he was finally forced to decline them—"because I am full and because I am accustomed certainly to strain the boundaries of elasticity, but also to respect them."[42] An exception was doubtless the meeting with Frank Lloyd Wright, who invited him to spend two days at Taliesin. For this meeting, Mendelsohn took as much time as the master allowed him, and it proved in every respect to be an incomparable experience. In a long letter to Luise, Mendelsohn writes: "I had two days at Taliesin with Frank Lloyd Wright; two days in the marvelous current, expectant and giving, tensed and relaxed. . . . He is sixty-five; so I am twenty years younger. But we were friends at once, bewitched by space, holding out our hands to one another in space; the same road, the same goal, the same life, I believe. We understood one another at once, like brothers. A verbal hint is all the explanation we needed. We drew close to one another at once, quite naturally. We conversed easily and found plenty to say. We could soon communicate fluently because we understood one another. I brought him the greetings of the whole of the young movement in Europe—to him, the father, the champion. He spoke at once about my work.

Ford Factory, October 1924.

New York, Entrance to Broadway, close-up shot, 1924. From *Amerika. Bilderbuch eines Architekten* (Berlin, 1926).

'Original, powerful—the future.' He knew it through Neutra, who has been working with him for the past four weeks. His opinion—and I think Neutra's as well—that I am perhaps more of a sculptor than an architect, more of a modeler than a builder, could at once be easily refuted, and later again in sketches I had with me. The reasons for such a view, which certainly exist, I dismiss as part of the process of development." Following this valuable self-assessment and qualification of his early projects as first attempts to forge ahead into the future of architecture, Mendelsohn indulges in a euphoric description of Taliesin and the rural, patriarchal life on Wright's farm. Amidst all the guests invited to Sunday breakfast—the architects with their wives, the fathers, mothers-in-law, babies, chauffeurs, and service personnel—Wright, the great master himself, shone as the centerpiece. He was the star, all others were extras in this play for the patriarch's favor—but Mendelsohn says nothing of this; rather, he describes the scene following breakfast, in which he himself had a role to play: "Then I had to change into clothes like his; a fantastic garment with something Indian about it—more or less without buttons (which he detests). Bark shoes, a long staff, gloves, and a tomahawk; and so we went up a marvelous road, to the surrounding hills, land that a hundred years ago was still no-man's-land. Now it is abandoned by the redskins and growing wild where it is not taken over by falling trees and landslides. In a curve about us was the Wisconsin River; the two of us were ahead. He turned and said to Neutra:

'Mr. Mendelsohn is very strong, powerful.' He meant my stature and my way of walking, heel first, but springily." No word of praise by the master was forgotten and every stroke of his hand was a creation: "We had a competition in the sand. Wright drew with angular lines a massive garage which he is working on at the moment, with a fantastic superstructure. I did a sketch with a rounded contour. He drew ornaments spontaneously, circular and angular in contrast; interpreted them like a sage, like an actor!" And then the farewell in grand style, to which Mendelsohn was always very receptive: "He said I was the first European to come and seek him out and truly to find him. I said that people will ask, everyone will—and I shall say, 'I have seen him, I was with him.' He said the same thing to me, out of courtesy and the wisdom of age—but I felt more; dream and purpose, happiness and hope."[43]

For all the almost embarrassing pathos of the two days in Taliesin—whether derived from Mendelsohn's own interpretation of the events or a part of Wright's staging—Mendelsohn's euphoria was rooted not least of all in the fact that in Wright he had finally found the modern America he was seeking. With few exceptions, Wright's buildings were the only ones Mendelsohn saw during his entire trip for which he had real enthusiasm. They alone fulfilled the demand for organic unity with nature and regional culture, representing a truly American architecture, rather than eclectic copies imported from Europe. Chicago and Oak Park, the entire span of Wright's architecture became the high point of his tour. Barry Byrne, his trained guide through Chicago and a former assistant of Wright, also introduced him to the now classical developmental line of the Chicago School of Architecture from Richardson to Sullivan to Wright.[44]

In other respects, however, Mendelsohn radically revised his original image of America. The fascination that America had always held for him cooled noticeably in the face of reality: "This land is only an intensified version of European civilization. By no comparison is it a new world like that of the Orient or archaic cultures. This land demands nothing of our love, but wants to be firmly gripped on a mutual basis."[45] Again and again, he criticized the chaos resulting from the irresponsible, inhumane politics of laissez-faire capitalism, making highly critical remarks concerning American consumerism and its methods of production. He became acquainted with the latter at Ford in Detroit, where he recognized the same mechanisms and driving forces at work as in American architectural practice: "Detroit revolves. It asserts that it is 'dynamic.' It is growing rapidly and is amazed at itself. The architects keep pace by maintaining offices of two- to three-hundred architects which are organized entirely like Ford's own factories. The cheap columnar recipe with pillars deceives the clients on the imponderables of creative architecture and satisfies the architects with an always dignified and hallowed appearance."[46] His ruthless, telegram-style remarks on the condition of the United States ring like slashes: "Land too young and uncertain, instinctual, exploitative, record delirium, unconsolidated, traditionless."[47]

Back in Berlin, Mendelsohn published several articles based on the travel experiences he had recorded in diary form in the letters to his wife. Among them was an article on New York for the *Berliner Tageblatt* and two on Frank Lloyd Wright.[48] His most important publication, however, was *Amerika. Bilderbuch eines Architekten,* printed in late 1925 by the Mosse publishing house. The remarkable success of this large photo album, already printed in multiple editions the first year after its initial publication, as well as the history of its reception and influence on figures from Brecht to Rodchenko have been studied and analyzed in detail elsewhere.[49] The book played a considerable role in Mendelsohn's growing fame and served to revise the general image of America, in terms of both form and content. In texts and photographs, Mendelsohn succeeded in representing both poles of the magnet America, its attractive and repulsive side, the ambivalence of the heights and depths of its metropolitan centers. Formally, he achieved this in the texts through an expressive, choppy language, direct and aggressive, and in the illustrations through unusual perspectives that did not aim at the "objective" representation of individual buildings, but at a very personal, individual perception of architecture within its urban situation.[50]

Mendelsohn sent one of the first copies of his book to Lewis Mumford, whom he had met in America and with whom he enjoyed a friendly relationship for the rest of his life. Fearing that his critical approach might offend Mumford personally, he enclosed a letter stating: "Dear Mr. Mumford . . . I am sure that in looking at, and reading, my book you will perceive the positive side and not merely the sharp criticism of your country's historical vertigo."[51]

From the opposite corner of the world, El Lissitzky, to whom Mendelsohn likewise sent a copy of his America book, wrote a glowing review, in which he advised the viewer of the photographs to rotate them over his head in order to understand them correctly.[52]

Wologda Gouvernement, door of the church of St. Vladimir. From Erich Mendelsohn, *Russland—Europa—Amerika. Ein architektonischer Querschnitt* (Berlin, 1929).

Travels to the Soviet Union, 1925 and 1926

Only a little later, El Lissitzky was delighted to welcome Mendelsohn to the Soviet Union: "With the Leningrad commission, you have caused an uproar among our architectural people and raised the question of 'involving technical powers from abroad in our reconstruction.' . . . If you would like to make a statement on this issue, please write to me, I will be glad to publish it. The relationship to you personally is the very best, the concern is for organized collaboration with our Western colleagues. When are you coming again?"[53]

Between 1925 and 1926, Mendelsohn made a total of three trips to the Soviet Union. The opportunity presented itself in connection with a commission for a textile factory in Leningrad,[54] and Mendelsohn was the first Western architect to visit the land at the invitation of the new regime. During his trips to the building site in Leningrad, he planned excursions to Moscow as well as sightseeing tours to the most important new projects in the country. Thus he was able to gain a relatively clear picture of the new Russia, with which Germany had resumed diplomatic relations since the Treaty of Rapallo in 1922 and which in the early 1920s as well as long afterward represented the "big brother in the East" for the German left, a model and source of political and cultural impulses. Next to the United States, the Soviet Union was the state that offered the most raw material for future-oriented visions and concepts. The artistic avant-garde from the East was received with enthusiasm; the Constructivists celebrated great successes in German galleries, and no film enjoyed more popularity in the cinemas of the Weimar Republic than Eisenstein's *Potemkin*. The cultural and artistic exchange between the two countries looked back on a long tradition and doubtless reached new heights in the first quarter of the twentieth century. In the area of visual arts as well as in the fields of literature, music, theater, and film, the Berlin-Moscow axis was strengthened by parallel developments in both lands, as manifested, to name only one example, in the substantively similar concepts of architectural education at the Bauhaus and Wchutemas.[55]

Mendelsohn made his first trip to the Soviet Union together with his wife in November 1925. In her memoirs, Louise Mendelsohn draws a colorful, detailed picture of the new Russia in the first year after Lenin's death, "when the spirit of the Revolution still lived in Russia." She describes the rather formal reception by the Leningrad association of architects and engineers, the empty stores on Nevsky Prospekt, the women's envious gazes at her wardrobe, the shabby, decaying hotel with vodka and caviar at every meal, the luxurious suppers at dachas outside of Leningrad with heartrending gypsy music in the background, and then the excursion from Leningrad to Moscow. Alexei Victorovich Shtshussev, the architect of the Lenin Mausoleum, had asked Mendelsohn to give a lecture at the school of architecture at the University of Moscow. For

El Lissitzky, project for a high-rise on cantilevers, Moscow, 1925.

Mendelsohn, Moscow unequivocally represented the new center of Russia, and Louise Mendelsohn's memoirs become noticeably livelier in their description of the sights and experiences there: Red Square; the Kremlin, where they were received by President Kalinin, Trotsky's sister, and Cultural Secretary Kameneva; the performances of the Russian Ballet and the many theater visits, among which the Meyerhold Theater made a particular impression; as well as the tours, sightseeing, and endless conversations that filled their days in Moscow. Mendelsohn was repeatedly implored to stay in the country and play an active role in its reconstruction.[56] For Mendelsohn, however, the idea of emigrating to the Soviet Union never represented a serious possibility.

Of the contacts made by Mendelsohn during this trip and the two following ones the year after, that with El Lissitzky was certainly the closest. Mendelsohn and Lissitzky had already met during the famous Bauhaus Week in Weimar in 1923, and their paths crossed repeatedly thereafter. Yet despite the memorable impressions, Russia remained an isolated, self-contained episode for Mendelsohn, one whose end coincided with the completion of the textile factory in Leningrad. Russia remained foreign to him: "Russia then and now a riddle."[57] Mendelsohn once again put together a collection of superb photographs from Russia, at first intended for a book along the lines of his America album. Finally, however, he decided in favor of a comparative contrast, thus revealing the relative importance that the experience of Russia had for him. In 1929, the Berlin publisher Rudolf Mosse published Mendelsohn's *Russland, Europa, Amerika. Ein architektonischer Querschnitt,* whose text contains the following words: "America's forms of existence are supported by the cultural stem of Europe—Russia draws its primary nourishment from the Orient and the Far East, or at least is fed by Asia, the Mediterranean, and the West together. America, therefore, signifies only the continuation of our accustomed horizons and patterns of thought; Russia, however, means a rethinking in terms of Asia, a cultural sphere that is opposed to Europe in climate, land, race, and religion. . . . Between America and Russia, these two poles of the will, Europe will mediate, if it comes to itself again and unites in solidarity, if it preserves moderation, establishing a balance between idea and brain, spirit and reason."[58]

Notes p. 265.

"The merchandise is primary—all architectural means serve its praise"
Department Stores in Berlin, Breslau, Chemnitz, Duisburg, Nuremberg, Oslo, and Stuttgart, 1924–1932

Regina Stephan

Although it was above all Mendelsohn's department stores that made him one of the most successful German architects of the 1920s, he always maintained a certain inner distance from them.[1] For him, the department store was a building type subject to such diverse requirements as urbanistic integration, economic functionality, technical modernity, and a high level of advertising effectiveness through the use of the newest lighting techniques. Through precise analysis—demanded above all by clients from the business world such as Salmann Schocken—he became increasingly successful at concentrating on the essentials of the department store. In retrospect, his lecture of 1929 on the "modern commercial building" reads like a summary of his experiences with this building type, one that had been radically altered by the political and social changes following World War I.[2] Mendelsohn's first design for a store, the small Weichmann silk store in Gleiwitz, was created together with Richard Neutra. There, despite the extremely inconvenient proportions of the site, the building turned out to be so economical, advertising-effective, and formally innovative that it served as an important point of departure for later commissions. In addition, his renovation and expansion of the Rudolf Mosse publishing house towered over the surrounding buildings in downtown Berlin like the beacon of a new age. Both projects established Mendelsohn's reputation as a builder of commercial and industrial structures that were advertising-effective as well as innovative in design and technology. For this reason, Mendelsohn remained largely independent of the public commissions for large residential developments upon which most of his colleagues relied. Private clients approached Mendelsohn personally with attractive commissions for new buildings, renovations, and expansions. In addition, he also participated in competitions, from which further commissions resulted. From 1924 on, Mendelsohn's office pursued a number of major projects simultaneously.

Another factor in his extraordinary success were his incisive reports on architecture in America, which appeared in 1924 in the widely read newspaper *Berliner Tageblatt* and were published the next year in his book *Amerika. Bilderbuch eines Architekten* along with expressive photos and comments. There he criticized the use of lighted advertising signs applied without any relation to the architecture, denouncing them as the site "grandiose boorishness of a cosmopolitan fair," which, "unbridled and wild," only shouts itself down.[3]

C. A. Herpich & Sons in Berlin

The currency reform of November 28, 1923, put an end to inflation and drew large numbers of foreign, above all American, investors to Germany. In the ensuing period of economic recovery, Mendelsohn's first commission was marked by vehement conflicts with the building authorities.

In 1835, Carl August Herpich founded a coat business located on Leipziger Strasse from 1875 on. This street, leading from Potsdamer Platz to Spittelmarkt via Leipziger Platz, developed into Berlin's most elegant shopping district. Along its length of about a kilometer and a half, a number of important department stores and other shops grew up that were to influence department store architecture throughout Germany. Of particular significance were Bernhard Sehring's

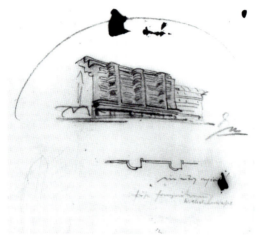

C. A. Herpich & Sons store, sketch, Berlin, 1923–24.

To the left, the C. A. Herpich & Sons store before the renovation and expansion by Mendelsohn; to the right, the architect's clay model of the project, published in 1925.

Tietz department store (1899–1900), whose glass facade represented the first curtain wall in Berlin, in Germany, and perhaps even in the world, and Alfred Messel's Wertheim department store. The latter was realized in a number of building phases and defined the appearance of German department stores until Mendelsohn's innovations of the 1920s. With its Gothicizing natural stone facades and splendid interiors, its elegant atriums and stairways, restaurants and thematically designed sales rooms, the Wertheim store constituted an early example of experience-oriented shopping, an approach that was replaced after World War I by functionally designed buildings.

The circumstances of the commission from the furrier C. A. Herpich & Sons are unknown. Julius Herpich had lodged his business in two former residences and had also purchased a third, neighboring one. Neither the interior structure of the buildings nor their facades, however, corresponded to modern tastes; furthermore, the valuable property was built over with only four stories. Mendelsohn was called in to help, and probably received the commission in late 1923.

In all of his sketches, the three plots are connected by a single facade whose horizontal bands of windows find their vertical counterweight in oriels in the center and on the sides. The developed plans were presented to the expert committee of the city of Berlin in April 1924 and approved with a large majority.[4] At that point, however, Gustav Böss, then mayor of Berlin, intervened. Probably under the influence of Ludwig Hoffmann, who as retired city building commissioner still represented his unfilled post, Böss spoke out against the design and in May 1924 refused to grant a permit as director of the building inspectors. The project was blocked.

Objections were raised first of all to the planned addition of two stories, which would have caused the Herpich store to tower over the rest of the neighborhood. A special exemption was required for this feature. Secondly, Mendelsohn broke with the German department store tradition by replacing the verticality and plasticity of Messel's building with horizontal ribbon windows alternating with smooth wall surfaces faced in limestone. In addition, he proposed a flat roof instead of a pitched roof and enclosed the ground floor entirely in glass, while two oriels projecting out into the street space were to attract the interest of passersby even at an oblique angle. This, too, represented a radical break with Messel's department store architecture, whose closely spaced pillars produced the impression of a solid wall when viewed at an angle.

The resistance of the municipal authorities to this design aroused more than just the interest of the architectural press. It led to the first architects' union of the Neues Bauen, the Zehnerring (Ring of Ten), which was later enlarged to become Der Ring.[5] Mendelsohn found continuing support with his colleagues from the German architects' association (BDA), particularly the older and more experienced Peter Behrens and Hans Poelzig, who approached the

Ministry for Public Welfare on his behalf in the name of the BDA. The ministry intervened and
engaged in difficult negotiations for a solution to the problem.

Preparation for construction began in January 1925. In order to keep from interfering with
sales activities, the construction was divided into two phases. In the first phase, the two existing
houses were remodeled and given a new facade; in the second, the newly acquired building was
torn down and replaced by a new structure, connected to the old ones by a unified facade design.

An innovative feature was the use of a construction fence that was both functional and
decorative, extending the height of the old buildings. Its sharply tapering supports constituted a
last echo of Mendelsohn's expressionistic furniture design. By providing a covering at ground
level, it served to protect passersby from the construction work overhead and at the same time
draw their attention to the store. The director of retail trade described this invention as "the obvious solution" and recommended its emulation.[6]

The struggle to acquire a building permit dragged on into the second half of 1925 and
was accompanied by complaints, polemics, negotiations, and expert opinions. In a letter to
his wife from August 1925, Mendelsohn himself alluded to the open resistance to his project:
"In the meantime the newly submitted—and oh, so old and harmless—Herpich facade has
been rejected by the mayor on the grounds that Mendelsohn buildings have no business on
Leipziger Strasse."[7]

C. A. Herpich & Sons store, Berlin,
night view, 1927.

C. A. Herpich & Sons store, Berlin,
facade section and detail of lighted
cornice, 1925.

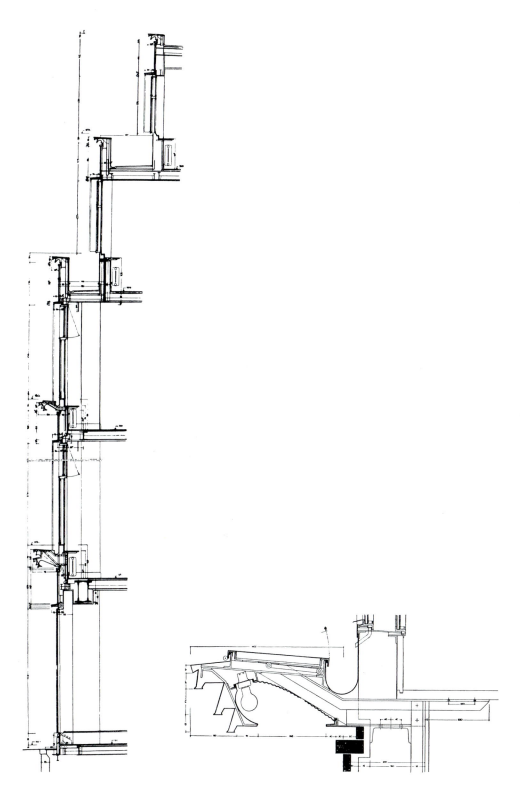

As with the Rudolf Mosse publishing house, the national art curator Edwin Redslob was asked to step in on Mendelsohn's behalf. Erwin Finlay-Freundlich, who had procured for Mendelsohn the commission for the Einstein Tower in Potsdam, invited Redslob, Adolf Behne and Werner Hegemann—two of the most powerful architectural critics of the day—as well as others to the Einstein Tower to win their support for the Herpich project. A petition was circulated among architects and building experts and signed by twenty-two of the twenty-three persons approached.[8] In the journal *Wasmuths Monatshefte für Baukunst und Städtebau*, Hegemann later published a diagram by Mendelsohn showing the "bureaucratic labyrinth of a building application in Berlin," demonstrating why a normal building application required at least a quarter of a year. With the Herpich building, the process took considerably longer because of the necessary exemptions. The first building phase was not completed until May 1927, and work on the second phase dragged on into spring 1929. No other building by Mendelsohn took so long to plan and construct.

For the facade, Mendelsohn adopted elements from Sehring's Tietz department store with its glass curtain wall. From the perspective of sales, however, this feature was useful only to a limited extent, since no sales racks could be placed in front of the exterior walls and the display windows in the upper stories were not visible to passersby. Mendelsohn corrected these deficiencies by introducing alternating bands of wall and window. This ensured the penetration of natural daylight deep into the sales areas, since the ceiling-high windows allowed indirect, reflected light to fall onto the merchandise as well. The wall areas in the Herpich building accommodated the heating elements; in his subsequent department stores in Nuremberg and Stuttgart, Mendelsohn took this solution to its logical conclusion by installing merchandise shelves in their place. Since the facade of the Herpich building was completely nonbearing, the ground floor could be glazed in its entirety, while the windows ran continuously through the upper stories, uninterrupted by supports. In accord with the building code in Berlin, the two added stories were recessed so as not to shade the street space.

Only the finest materials were used: large panes of glass, limestone panels, and letters, window frames, and cornices of bronze. The latter, above all, served to relieve the flatness of the facade and incorporate subtle tension in the alternation of projecting bronze cornices in the center and bronze roofs on the oriels. The cornices also concealed electric lights that accentuated the alternation of window and wall even at night by illuminating the areas of natural stone. In this way, Mendelsohn put his criticism of American lighted signs into practice by providing his own modern solution to the problem: the image of the store by night was to be defined not by applied ornament, but by the illumination of individual architectural elements.

The facade of the Herpich building was a great success and found numerous imitators. In 1928, Ernst May, city building commissioner of Frankfurt am Main, wrote: "In recent times, increasing use has been made of the lighted cornice. . . . Lighted cornices are mounted story by story . . . illuminating the letters below them on the wall areas by means of reflectors."[9]

The interior of the Herpich store was designed in a simple yet elegant manner, with spherical lamps of white frosted glass, smoothly veneered cubical cabinets with large mirrors along the walls, elegant armchairs upholstered in leather, glass display cases, and—as the only ornament—patterned floor coverings.

Like almost all of Leipziger Strasse, the Herpich store was heavily damaged in 1944–45. In the 1970s, high-rise apartment buildings were built on the site of the finely articulated late-nineteenth-century structures.

C. A. Herpich & Sons store, court entrance.

Illustration right:
C. A. Herpich & Sons store, Berlin, after its completion, 1929.

C. A. Herpich & Sons store, salesroom in the annex.

Works for the Schocken Company

While the controversies in Berlin were still underway, Mendelsohn received a commission from the Jewish department store owner Salmann Schocken, who was to become one of his most important clients. Together with his brother Simon, Salmann directed the Schocken department store company, founded in 1906 in Zwickau in Saxony. In 1919 the Schockens had founded two new stores, raising the total number to eleven;[10] the years of inflation, however, at first permitted no further expansion. Finally, in spring and summer 1924 trade recovered noticeably, and for the first time in ten years the Schocken company could once again organize a "summer fair," a kind of end-of-the-season sale.[11] By the late 1920s, it had become the fifth largest chain in Germany.

While up to this point the Schocken stores had been housed in existing old buildings in small and medium-sized towns in Saxony, in 1924 the Schocken brothers decided to expand beyond the borders of the province and erect new, innovative department store buildings. Salmann was the leading figure in this process. His attention had been captured already in 1919 by the Mendelsohn sketches exhibited at the gallery of Paul Cassirer;[12] only now, however, did the economic situation permit the Schockens to commission Mendelsohn with the design of new department stores. The Schocken department stores in Nuremberg (1925–26), Stuttgart (1926–28), and Chemnitz (1927–30) were to number among Mendelsohn's most famous buildings in Germany. His work on these projects, moreover, consisted of more than just the design, planning, and construction supervision, but embraced the design of posters, brochures, and typefaces as well. For the Schocken company, the architect created a "corporate design"—one of the first in Germany—used in all the Schocken stores in the second half of the 1920s.

The Nuremberg Schocken Store

In November 1925, the company acquired a plot in the Nuremberg workers' district of Steinbühl. In the interest of economy, Schocken wished to remodel the existing factory building into a department store by renovating the street facades and erecting a new building on the corner of the site. The building materials were to be simple and inexpensive. In Schocken's view, costly building materials were as little suited to modern times as luxury articles and elaborately decorated sales rooms. He conceived it as his company's mission to make industrially manufactured, aesthetically satisfying, inexpensive mass products available to the broad base of consumers thanks to wholesale purchase in large quantities. Like the photographs of merchandise commissioned from Albert Renger-Patzsch, the leading photographer of the Neue Sachlichkeit, the architecture of Schocken's stores was to lend expression to this business philosophy.

In December 1925, Mendelsohn submitted the preliminary project, which called for the construction of the department store in two building phases. The design was marked by cubic volumes that attained great spatiality through their varying height and depth. According to the building application of January 1926, the first building phase was to involve the renovation and remodeling of the factory structure, the second a new building on the street Ziegelgasse.[13]

In Nuremberg as well, however, Mendelsohn's plans met with stubborn resistance. The Nuremberg city council recommended a change in the facade plans, since "through its oppressive building mass the new building . . . will severely damage the image of the plaza and probably destroy it."[14] The architectural commission also rejected the project for its "unquiet distribution of masses and the design of the details."[15] In the controversies that followed, Mendelsohn announced that he wanted his design to be evaluated by a "committee of the most significant German architects."[16] The project was supported by the local trade unions, who

C. A. Herpich & Sons branch store, on Leipziger Strasse, 1927.

Advertising photo of stacked aluminum pans, photographed by Albert Renger-Patzsch for the Schocken company, ca. 1927–28.

Schocken department store,
Nuremberg, sketch, 1925.

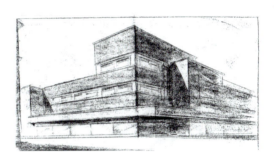

Schocken department store,
Nuremberg, perspective drawing from
the preliminary building files,
December 1925.

emphasized the new jobs that would result. But still construction was stalled. Although the demolition of the villa located on the site had begun already in January 1926, the work proceeded so slowly that in June, Schocken felt compelled to give the city an ultimatum. By this point, work on the shell of the old building had already been completed and the interior construction begun. In late June, the building authorities relented and issued a building permit. Since the first building phase had to be finished in time for the opening on October 11, the delays were followed by a tremendous exertion of effort. Mendelsohn once again closed the gap to the new building with a specially designed wooden construction fence.

The Nuremberg Schocken store was a steel skeleton building with brick masonry infill, whose ground floor was dominated by large display windows. The supports were incorporated into the facade and formed a light counterweight to the dominant horizontals, which were further underlined by the ribbon windows in the upper stories and the straight upper edge of the masonry. The structure was identifiable as a warehouse on both the exterior and the interior. Mendelsohn's interior design was perceived as a significant achievement for department store architecture: below the ceiling-high windows, which permitted both direct and indirect sunlight to penetrate

Schocken department store, Nuremberg,
ground plan of the preliminary project
(showing the first building phase to the
right and the second building phase to
the left), December 1925.

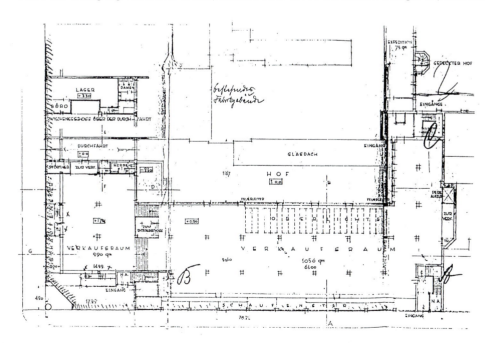

far into the sales areas, merchandise shelves were installed, serving at the same time to insulate the walls. Stairwells at the ends of the building, emphasized on the exterior by vertical bands of windows, provided for circulation throughout the building. The simple, cubic furniture was likewise designed by Mendelsohn's office and became the standard furnishings of Schocken department stores.

The grand opening of the Nuremberg Schocken store on October 11, 1926, drew huge crowds and was shown in the news features in the cinema. Both client and architect gave speeches at the festivities. In his speech, Salmann Schocken quoted the painter Max Liebermann's remark that "the art of drawing consists in omission" and continued: "The art of the master shows itself in the ability to select and reduce, in the ability to dispense with the nonessential, to limit the material, to recognize the principal pillars and design what is necessary with a few main lines."[17] Mendelsohn emphasized the relation of period and style. In his speech, he used short, concise theses to formulate his answer to the question: "Why this architecture?":

Think back only a hundred years:
Riding frock and wig
Tallow candles and spinning wheel, litters and mail coaches
Grocers' shops and craftsmen's guilds
Then think of us:
Knee-length pants and short hair
Radio and film
Automobile and airplane
Banana specialty stores and department store chains.
Don't think that these are just externals. The internals lie behind them.
Both a hundred years ago, and today. . . .
And so—to want to disavow our way of life is self-deception, is pitiful and cowardly.
To want even to retard its development is self-sacrifice, is foolish and futile.
So be courageous and shrewd! Seize life by the scruff of the neck, right where its liveliest heart beats, in the midst of life, in the midst of technology, traffic, and business. . . .
Everything demands functionality, clarity, simplicity. Everything must be functional, because all labor is too valuable to be senselessly squandered.
Clarity, because it should be understood not merely by a select few, but by everyone.
Simplicity, because the best solution is always also the simplest.
Never has a powerful age expected more from another age than from itself.
So should we architects be the only ones to limp along behind and wear wigs, we engineers and builders who construct your houses, your cities, the entire visible world? . . .
You say there are no building patrons. Don't fall for such weakness. Here they are!
But palace facades, decorators' catwalks, and dollhouse windows lie far behind.
The masses pile up into the space conjured into the air from the ground plan.
Here lie the stairs, here the entrance, here the bands of windows above the shelves.
Stairs, entrance, windows pass into the rhythm of speeding cars in the booming traffic. . . .
Don't be fooled, you are the master. Be a creator, shape your time.
That is your obligation; render your responsibility, be a leader!—
Thus, this architecture.[18]

Illustration right:
Schocken department store, Nuremberg, sales area on an upper floor, 1926.

Schocken department store, Nuremberg, stairwell B, 1926. "Shading in yellow" and brownish-black handrails defined the space.

The critics' responses to the Nuremberg Schocken store were unanimously positive. It was praised even by writers who up to that point had not identified themselves as adherents of the Neues Bauen. Justus Bier, for example, spoke of the "magnificent overcoming of the old . . . laws of support and load," of the "simplicity and sureness of the overall impression," and testified that with this building, the site had attained "architectural significance . . . in a single stroke."[19]

The great success of the Nuremberg Schocken store is all the more surprising in view of the fact that the second building phase was not yet realized, a deficiency that noticeably disturbed the overall impression. Nearly all contemporary publications on the building used retouched photos that did not correspond to the actual appearance. Yet even this could not diminish Mendelsohn's achievement for department store architecture. For the first time, a department store had been built solely on the basis of functional considerations: uninterrupted sales areas, continuous ribbon windows, no atriums, the transfer of the stairwells to the ends of the building, and the complete rejection of applied ornament on both exterior and interior. A new type of store had been created, one that was to be widely imitated in Europe in the 1920s and early 1930s. Only in the 1950s was it replaced by windowless machines for selling, structures that did not, however, attain the architectural quality of Mendelsohn's buildings.

The Nuremberg Schocken store was heavily damaged in World War II and reconstructed in altered form. Nothing of Mendelsohn's design has survived.

Mendelsohn designed more than just department stores for the Schocken company. His sketches were strategically used in the company's publicity.

The Stuttgart Schocken Store

The success of the Nuremberg store, which was reflected in excellent sales figures as well, confirmed Salmann Schocken's decision to commission Mendelsohn with the design of another department store in Stuttgart. The company's decision to build a new store in the capital city of Württemberg was based first of all on the extraordinary economic advantages of the location, "for it was hard to imagine a population in Germany with more buying power than that of Stuttgart . . . in the 1920s."[20] Furthermore, in June 1925 the first statement was published on the Werkbund exhibition *Die Wohnung für den modernen Großstadtmenschen,* scheduled to take place in Stuttgart in 1927. Ludwig Mies van der Rohe's Weissenhof development of 1927 and the exhibitions accompanying it would attract a public interested in art and architecture to Stuttgart, an influx from which a new department store would profit as well. Perhaps for the same reason, the building was to be constructed in a manner used relatively seldom up to that point for multistory buildings in Germany: steel skeleton construction.

The plans for the building site—located amid the old city of Stuttgart and bounded by four streets of varying width—began in January 1926 with discussions between Schocken and Mendelsohn.[21] In a series of sketches, Mendelsohn first developed the distribution of building volumes and the facade design. The restrictive building regulations stipulated that construction had to be conform to the width of the street and leave space for an inner courtyard; the height of the structure had to correspond to the widely differing heights of the buildings in the vicinity. In addition, from Eberhardstrasse, a street lined with late nineteenth-century commercial buildings, to the rear side of the plot on the narrow Geißstrasse with its low half-timber houses, the terrain sloped as much as an entire story.

Finally, in June 1926, the purchase contract for the plot was signed by the Schocken company.[22] In the meantime, Mendelsohn worked intensively on the design for the department store. The decisive idea came to him on June 26, during a Bach recital organized by the art historian

Schocken department store, Stuttgart, site plan, July 25, 1926.

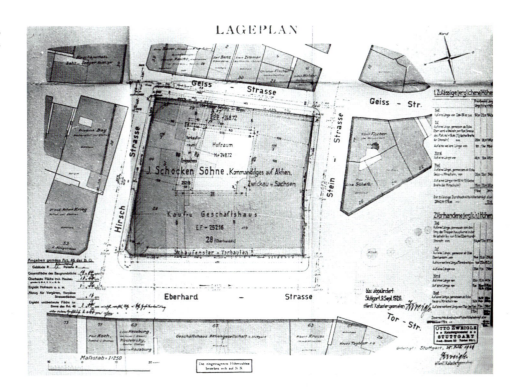

Oskar Beyer, at which Luise Mendelsohn performed on the cello. Mendelsohn's sketches on the recital program are the first to show the building in the form in which it was realized.[23] Interestingly, although the building was designed for a clearly defined urbanistic context, the sketches give no indication whatsoever of the surroundings. As usual, Mendelsohn chose perspective and bird's-eye views for the representation of the design, which, however, is easily recognizable due to the form of the terrain. Finally, in July 1926, Mendelsohn submitted the first building application.

The department store was to consist of four wings of varying height grouped around an inner courtyard. Access to the wings was provided by clearly emphasized stairwells. In an essay of 1925, Mendelsohn had discussed "harmonic and contrapuntal structure in architecture," thus establishing a direct connection between musical and architectural composition.[24] The contrapuntal compositional principle is represented above all by the fugues of Johann Sebastian Bach, music that Mendelsohn prized and loved to listen to while sketching. In the Stuttgart Schocken store, the stairwells form the vertical counterpoint to the horizontal bands of windows.

Only after he had found a solution for the exterior did Mendelsohn turn his attention to the interior design, for the interior of the department store had relatively simple demands to fulfill: it was to provide lucid, comprehensible, well-accessed sales areas, illuminated by daylight and interrupted by as few supports as possible. Once the customers were in the building, the center of attention was to be the merchandise, not the architecture; to draw them into the building, on the other hand, was the task of the architecture.

Mendelsohn succeeded in fulfilling this demand through the skillful design of the facades, whose arrangement of vertical and horizontal elements led the customer around the corners to the entrances. The main entrance on the corner of Hirschstrasse and Eberhardstrasse was situated where the projecting stair tower met the recessed display windows of the main facade. Through this device, passersby were to be subtly and ineluctably led into the store. Mendelsohn

Illustration right:
Schocken department store, Stuttgart, page of sketches drawn during a Bach recital on June 26, 1926.

Schocken department store, Stuttgart, ground floor plan published by Mendelsohn, 1927–28.

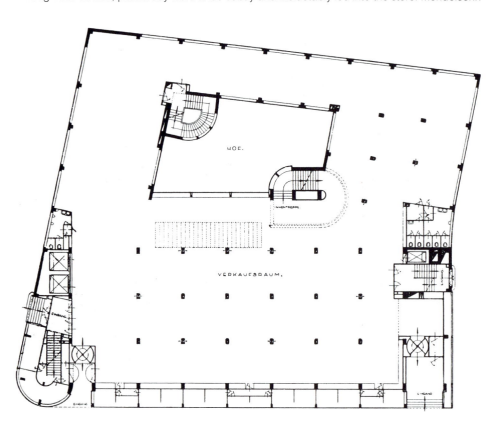

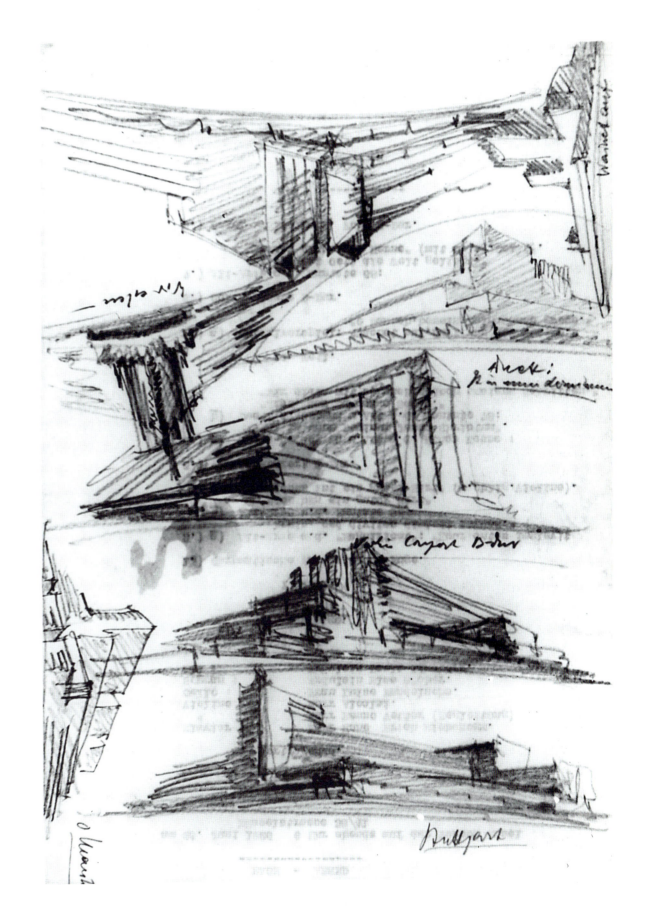

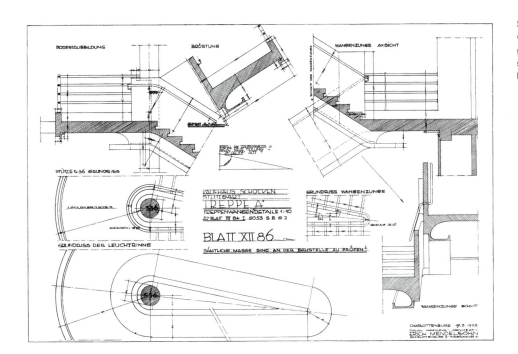

Schocken department store, Stuttgart, working diagram of stairway in the glass tower at the corner of Eberhard-strasse and Hirschstrasse, May 19, 1928.

Schocken department store, Stuttgart, stairway in the glass tower.

Schocken department store, Stuttgart, main facade with the glazed stair tower at the corner of Eberhardstrasse and Hirschstrasse, 1928.

himself was persuaded of the high quality of his design. He wrote: "We have finished the preliminary project for Stuttgart; the enclosed sheet shows the clarity of the spatial organism. To change it—to take away from or add anything to it, would require renewed efforts and a new design."[25]

In July 1926, Mendelsohn traveled to Stuttgart for meetings with the building authorities. On this occasion, he also met with Paul Bonatz, who like Mendelsohn had studied with Theodor Fischer in Munich. Ten years older than Mendelsohn, Bonatz was professor of architecture at the Technical University of Stuttgart and a central figure in the Stuttgart architectural scene.

Mendelsohn wrote to his wife: "Stuttgart. Stuffy and filled with indescribable art gossip. The meetings with the building commissioners went very well and my report card—required to pacify Schocken—is better than in school. . . . It appears that our project will be approved with no difficulty; with the colored model we have finally found the most practical and thus the quickest way to communicate."[26]

Schocken department store, Stuttgart, sales area on the ground floor, 1928.

The role of the model in the design process should not be underestimated. It was used to work out the details of the building, almost completely ignored by Mendelsohn in his sketches;[27] in addition, the models were more visually suggestive than building plans and provided an important basis for negotiations with the client and building authorities. Mendelsohn always worked with models; initially they were fashioned of clay, later of wood, and finally, in the United States, of plastic.

The joy over the prospect of quick approval for the project was short-lived. While a temporary building permit was issued in late August 1926, the neighbors now raised vehement objections, causing considerable delays in the beginning of construction. Once again, Schocken had to threaten to break off the project in order to get negotiations started again. After numerous meetings between the architect, client, city, and Ministry of the Interior, after changes and additions to the project and the issuing of exemptions, the building permit was finally approved in July 1927, one year after the first application had been submitted. From then on, construction proceeded rapidly. The steel skeleton was completed by mid-December, the shell work by April, and in September 1928 the building was handed over to the client. On October 2, 1928, the grand opening took place.

After its completion, the Stuttgart Schocken store was discussed in all the current architectural magazines. It was *the* department store of the 1920s and served as a model for count-

Schocken department store, Stuttgart, gallery at the interior angle of the Eberhardstrasse and Steinstrasse wings, 1928.

Schocken department store, Stuttgart, cafeteria on the third floor.

less imitations in Germany and abroad. The technical innovation of the steel skeleton was particularly admired and was photographed and published in all stages of its construction. Such publicity emphasized the advantages of steel skeleton construction over traditional building methods: rapid construction, precision in planning, low material and labor costs, easy expandability, and tremendous stability.[28]

The steel skeleton of the Stuttgart Schocken store stood on strip foundations and consisted of riveted U-girders, which also accommodated utility conduits for heating, roof drainage, and the like. On the facades, the pumice block infill was covered with dark, hard-burned clinkers. On the main facade toward Eberhardstrasse, this facing was embellished with small strips of travertine, a lustrous, gold-brown natural stone quarried in the Stuttgart suburb of Bad Cannstatt. The Cannstatt travertine combined with the bronze window frames to create a harmonious color scheme into which the illuminated letters SCHOCKEN, mounted over the large, recessed display windows, were integrated as well. The letters consisted of bronze side pieces 2.3 meters high and "travertine-colored opalescent flashed glass" on the front. It proved difficult to gain a building permit for the letters, for fear of their falling down during a storm. Finally, Mendelsohn had them fashioned of cardboard and mounted on a trial basis, emphasizing their significance in an accompanying statement: "I would like to point out that the letters have been a part of the design from the very beginning and thus represent a part of the architecture as a whole. For this reason, they do not simply float at an arbitrary place on the front wall, but are organically connected to the form and material of the projecting structure over the display windows as an integral part of the building. The proportions of the letters are oriented to the height of the window jambs as well as that of the entire building. . . ."[29]

The design of the Stuttgart Schocken store was precisely tailored to the specific urbanistic situation. Consequently, the building would be much less effective on a different site, for in

Eisenlohr and Pfennig, E. Breuninger A.G. department store, Stuttgart, completed 1931.

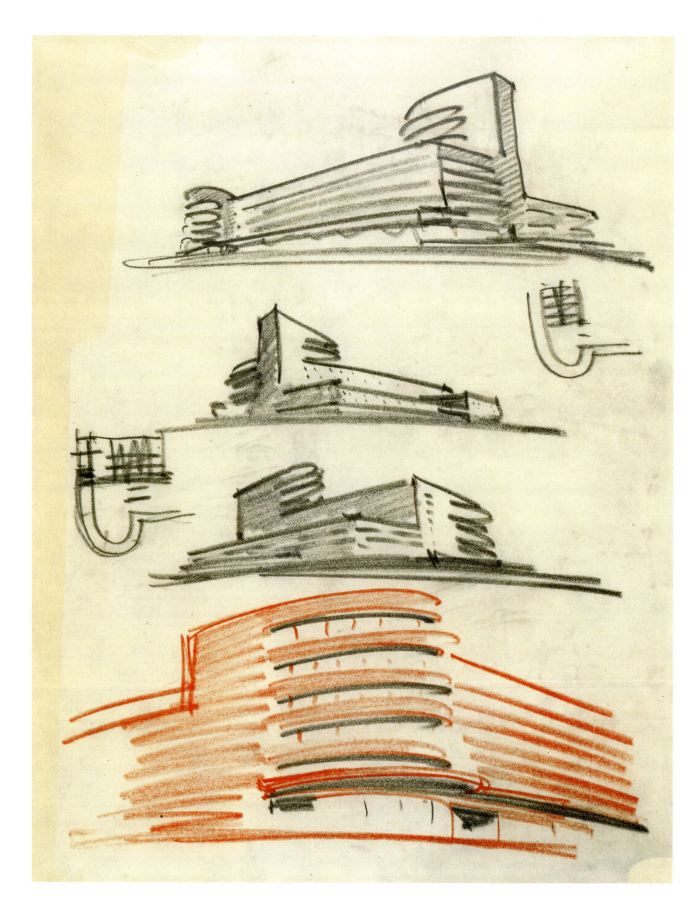

FÜHRER
DURCH DAS KAUFHAUS SCHOCKEN STUTTGART

Kaufhaus Schocken Stuttgart

Ideen-Skizze von Erich Mendelsohn, Berlin

Left: Schocken department store, Stuttgart, page of sketches with four perspective views and two ground plans of the stair tower on the corner of Eberhardstrasse and Hirschstrasse, 1927–28.

Above: "Guide to the Schocken department store in Stuttgart" with two-color sketch by Mendelsohn on the title page and plans of sales floors.

preparing his design Mendelsohn carefully studied such elements as visual axes, exposure, and wind directions.[30] In this respect his work differed fundamentally from that of other contemporary architects, whose buildings were designed without reference to the specific site.

The stairwells played a dominant role already in the sketches; in the finished building, they constituted significant vertical accents. The glass stair tower at the corner of Hirschstrasse and Eberhardstrasse consisted of a two-layer steel skeleton construction with an outer bearing skeleton and an inner steel stairway and center support. At night, the bottom side of the stair stringers and steps were illuminated with "light gutters," transforming the outer bearing skeleton into a glass skin for the building. The stairwell on Steinstrasse, on the other hand, was almost completely enclosed by masonry, punctuated only by a narrow, vertical strip of windows; in addition, it stood at a 90-degree angle to the glass stair tower. Thus the two main stairwells of the Stuttgart Schocken store were both contrasted and unified at the same time. A shared modular system defined the proportions of the windows in both stair towers as well as those in the rest of the building. Mendelsohn departed from this scheme only on Eberhardstrasse, where he adopted an old motif from the Chicago School. There he divided the horizontal windows vertically into three parts, with a fixed center pane and two side casements. This feature may well reflect the influence of one of the most famous department stores in America, Louis Sullivan's Carson Pirie Scott & Co. store in Chicago, which Mendelsohn had seen and admired during his trip to America in 1924.[31]

On the interior, the purist, utilitarian design of the Nuremberg Schocken store was further refined, with shelves built into the exterior walls. Slogans mounted on the walls above the shelves served to inform customers and motivate employees, while large horizontal windows just below the ceiling on all floors supplied the sales areas with ample daylight. In order to economize on electricity, the simple spherical lamps could be switched on and off individually.

View of boiler house erected by Mendelsohn in 1927 in the rear yard of the Rudolf Mosse publishing house, a building he had remodeled in 1921–1923. The steel frame construction with brick infill is strongly reminiscent of later buildings by Ludwig Mies van der Rohe in Chicago.

The Rudolf Mosse pavilion at the "Pressa" trade fair in Cologne, 1928. This temporary structure was based on the idea of international news broadcasting; accordingly, Mendelsohn chose the radio antenna as the point of departure for his design. The pavilion was intended to display the international orientation of the Mosse publishing company. On the interior, the latest news broadcasting equipment was presented, as well as an exhibition on the publishing company and its products. Otto Bartning's steel church appears in the background of the photograph. Right: plan of ground floor and upper story.

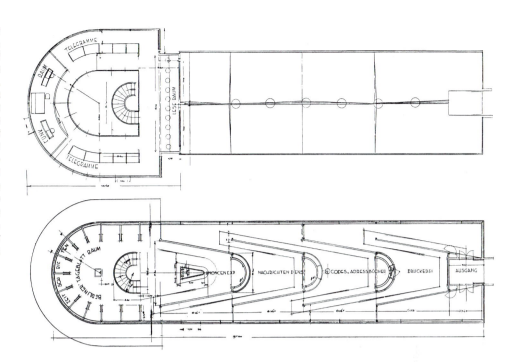

The furnishings of the Stuttgart store were even simpler than those of Nuremberg and consisted of smoothly veneered furniture with only a few moldings. Mendelsohn's choice of wooden furniture represented a departure from the contemporary avant-garde, which propagated steel pipe furniture at the Weissenhof development in 1927. Yet steel piping was not stable enough for sales furniture, and a unified appearance with respect to the other Schocken stores had to be considered as well. Even the conference room on the top floor of the Steinstrasse stair tower was no exception: the room was adorned only by a spectacular view of the Stuttgart city center and the surrounding hills.[32]

The Stuttgart Schocken store was designed by Mendelsohn down to the smallest details. His goal was to create an urbanistically integrated, advertising-effective, and striking modern department store whose design was capable of attracting customers. Its interior was to present them with a carefully devised spatial design appropriate to the claims advanced by the exterior and reflective of Schocken's business philosophy.[33] The success of the building, which manifested itself in an increase in sales as well, was enormous. In response, the local competition sought to secure their share of the market by erecting their own new structures.[34]

Like all of downtown Stuttgart, the Schocken department store was heavily damaged in the air raids of 1944–45, although its steel skeleton enabled it to withstand the fire much better than the half-timber structures around it. Sales resumed as early as 1945. A controversy over whether the Schocken store would be allowed to expand onto an adjoining, ruined plot dragged on for years; finally in 1960, despite international protest, the store was torn down in order to widen Eberhardstrasse, plans that have long since been discarded.

The Cohen & Epstein Department Store in Duisburg

One of Mendelsohn's smaller commissions was a renovation and expansion project for the firm Cohen & Epstein, which had operated a department store in downtown Duisburg for four generations. In the period after World War I, Hermann Muthesius had been approached in connection with the modernization of the original building, erected from 1895 to 1905, as well as its expansion with an annex on an adjacent plot. Due to the rapid inflation of 1922–23, however, these talks failed to result in a concrete commission, and when the economic situation improved, the owners of the store—the Jewish families of Cohen and Epstein—found themselves wishing for a more modern solution to the task.

In January 1925, Dr. Harry Epstein approached Mendelsohn on behalf of the company; Mendelsohn wrote to his wife, Luise: "The preliminary project has been agreed upon with Epstein. Sketches 5000 marks. . . . A man of modern stamp, clear, taken with Mosse, expects my work to give his business a boost. He claims there is a 9/10 chance of a commission against Muthesius and a local architect."[35]

In a number of sketches, Mendelsohn developed his design for the renovation of the department store, which was to incorporate a display window pavilion at a distance of approximately thirty-five meters. The project was to consist first of the construction of a new building on the neighboring plot, followed by the demolition and reconstruction of the facades.[36] The first building application was submitted already in June 1926. Unfortunately, the plans submitted with the building application have not survived; thanks to the sketches and the building description, however, the project can be reconstructed. The overall configuration was an interesting one: as a major opening motif the department store was to be connected to the display window pavilion by means of a kind of bridge. Pavilion and store were to be fused into a single formal unit by the continuation of the wall band of the bridge above the display windows. On the main facade,

Mendelsohn envisioned the windows as fully glazed display cases cut deep into the front of the building, while on the other sides of the building the windows were to be flush with the facade. The corner of the building at Beekstrasse and Münzstrasse acquired central significance. Only two stories high, it was to be used as an open-air terrace for the refreshment room. This urbanistic accent was to be intensified and balanced by another, higher building corner at Beekstrasse and Kühlingsgasse.

Shortly after the project was submitted, the client began to experience financial difficulties. In vain, Mendelsohn attempted to save the project through reductions and his personal presence on a number of occasions. In August 1925, he was forced to withdraw the building application, and negotiations came to a complete standstill.

Only in late 1926, a year and a half later, was the project resumed, though in a considerably reduced form. The building application now proposed only the construction of a new department store on the site of the adjacent building, the enclosure of the atrium, and the renovation of the display windows on the ground floor. The building permit was not issued until May 1927. Furthermore, construction was hindered by disagreements between the architect, the steel construction firm, and the building authorities regarding the static calculations of

Cohen & Epstein department store, Duisburg, sketch of the first major renovation project, 1925.

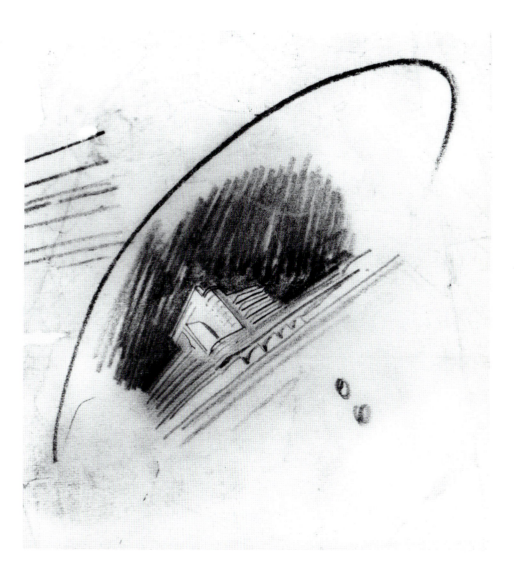

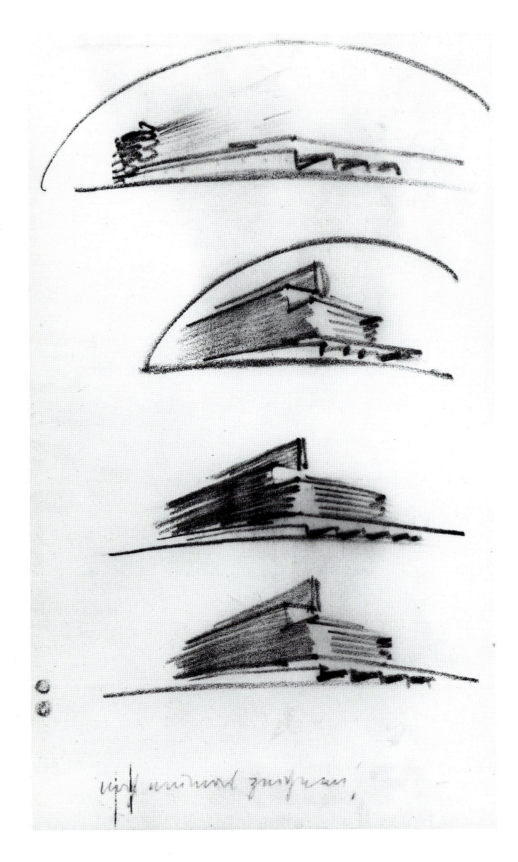

Cohen & Epstein department store, Duisburg, sketches showing the second, reduced renovation project, December 1926.

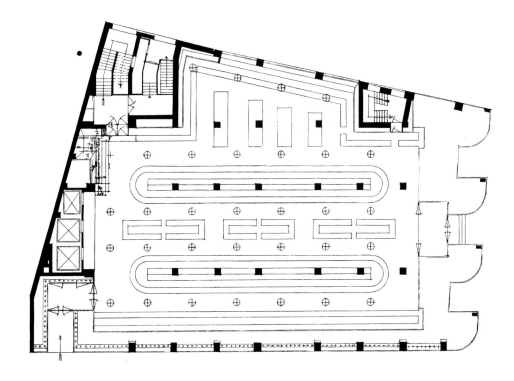

Cohen & Epstein department store,
Duisburg, ground floor plan, 1926.

Cohen & Epstein department store,
Duisburg, display windows toward
Beekstrasse, 1927.

the supports, so that the building was not handed over to the client until November 1927. At the grand opening on November 28, 1927, Harry Epstein gave a speech outlining his basic theses regarding the task of the modern merchant: "A commitment to what is truly necessary in the selection of merchandise, along with correct guidance of the customers in their needs, the exclusion of all superfluous, and therefore unjustified, profit for the middleman . . . But also a commitment to what is truly necessary in the design of the sales room as a warehouse, a 'house full of wares.'"[37]

Probably because the project was realized only in an extremely reduced form, it attracted little attention in contemporary architectural criticism. On the interior, moreover, Mendelsohn had few opportunities for design, since only the atrium was enclosed, while the old stairwell remained.

In the facades, the main concern was to unite the extension with the old building without imitating its late-nineteenth-century style. As Mendelsohn had written to Luise, Epstein was "taken with Mosse," that is, with the way in which the architect had combined old and new structures with radically differing architectural languages. In Duisburg, as in Nuremberg and Stuttgart, the ceiling-high bands of windows served to illuminate the sales areas in the extension building. As in the side facades of the contemporaneous Stuttgart Schocken store, the height of the windows decreased toward the top; in Duisburg, however, the strips of masonry separating the window areas was only as wide as the floors themselves. A round oriel marked the transition to the existing building and at the same time provided the point of departure for a lighted cornice extending around the old building all the way to the rear. It created a transition to the main facade, whose ground floor featured deep, fully glazed display windows rounded on one side.

A carefully devised system of lighting lent the Cohen & Epstein store a striking appearance by night, illuminating the new parts of the building while leaving the old shrouded in darkness. The display windows formed a brightly illuminated base topped by the lighted cornice, which

connected the illuminated oriel with the main facade and with the lighted pillars modeled after it in the middle of the ground floor.

This building, too, was used as an advertising device for the store. An advertising campaign in the local press initiated by Epstein before the grand opening on November 28, 1927, used sketches by Mendelsohn as well as texts by Epstein.

The Cohen & Epstein department store was destroyed in World War II and never rebuilt.

The Rudolf Petersdorff Department Store in Breslau

The Rudolf Petersdorff store was likewise renovated during the extremely productive period of 1927–28 and expanded with a sensational new building.[38] The company, a high-quality coat merchant, had long resided in the Silesian capital; the sales rooms themselves, however, no longer met modern demands, nor was the exterior of the building particularly appealing. The department store was housed in a former residence as well as a new building from the first years of the twentieth century, structures that were incoherently juxtaposed. The site, on the other hand, was ideal: located in the immediate vicinity of the old city ring with the famous Gothic town hall, the department store occupied the corner of the "narrow, medieval Ohlauer Strasse"[39]—one of the main streets leading to the city center—and the cross street Schuhbrücke. This location, a site visible from the ring, was now to be exploited to the commercial advantage of the firm.

Mendelsohn was commissioned to erect a new building in place of the former residence and to unify it with the existing department store building. In addition, he was expected to compensate for the company's loss of almost 370 square meters of floor area, a change that had occurred through an alteration in the municipal development plan. The city had used the opportunity to push back the building line on the Schuhbrücke more than seven meters to facilitate a widening of the street. The latter, however, was never carried out, and to this day the firewall of the neighboring building on the Schuhbrücke terminates the Petersdorff building to the right.

As always, Mendelsohn used sketches to arrive at the solution of the problem. All of them show one or several oriels, a device aimed at compensating for the loss of floor space. In addition, two additional stories set back behind the building line were to increase the usable floor area. The old building with its bearing skeleton of iron supports was altered only on the facade toward Ohlauer Strasse, where it received a smooth covering of travertine panels and a dense series of vertical rectangular windows. In a reversal of conventional window design, the frames and panes of the windows were raised in slight relief from the surface of the facade.

For the new structure on the Schuhbrücke, Mendelsohn added two rows to the old building's grid of supports. The outer row carried the five-story oriel on the street corner, whose window bands ran continuously over the entire length thanks to the nonbearing facade construction. The oriel, which projected outward a distance of four and a half meters, was built using a construction method borrowed from railway platform halls. Together with the giant display windows in the ground floor—subdivided only by slim bronze frames—the facade toward the Schuhbrücke thus received an extraordinary visual lightness.

Petersdorff department store, Breslau, preliminary sketch, 1928.

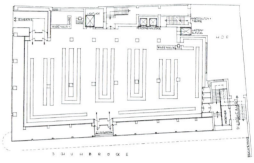

Petersdorff department store, Breslau, ground floor plan. The heavier, square supports are left over from the existing building of 1924, while the more delicate, rectangular ones were added by Mendelsohn in 1927.

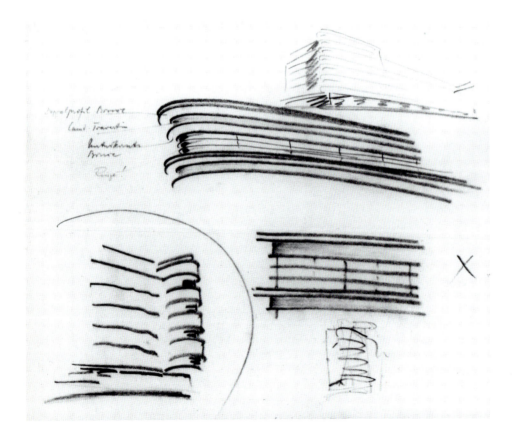

Petersdorff department store, Breslau, sketches of oriel on the Schuhbrücke side indicating the materials to be used, 1927.

Illustration right:
Petersdorff department store, Breslau, night view, 1928.

The building—visible as far away as the city ring thanks to the oriel—made a striking impression both day and night. By day, the alternation of matte and glossy surfaces, the contrast of rest and motion, was intensified still more by advertising banners mounted on the roof edge of the Ohlauer Strasse facade. By night, however, a lighting scheme transformed the building itself into an advertisement. Here, too, the display windows on the ground floor formed a brightly lighted base for the building, illuminated by lighted bands parallel to the edges of the panes on the interior. The upper stories of the oriel were illuminated over their entire length by lighted strips beneath the windows, whose effect was intensified still more by the sheer white drapes behind the windows. Mendelsohn himself gave the reason for this as follows: ". . . we illuminate the curtains—draw an outstanding architectural element out of the night."[40]

Writing on the building was reduced to a minimum: the letters PETERSDORFF in bronze were affixed to the display windows, while toward the neighboring building on Ohlauer Strasse a narrow lighted sign extended the entire height of the building.

The interior was furnished not by Erich Mendelsohn, but by the Breslau architect Heinrich Tischler.[41] The surfaces of the simple sales furniture varied from polished white paint in the children's department to oak veneer in the tailoring division to ebony in the fur department.

The Petersdorff building earned the highest praise in the retail trade press; "this newest creation by Mendelsohn" was characterized as "an absolutely exemplary achievement for which the Petersdorff company can only be congratulated, since the propagandistic value of such a building can hardly be overestimated."[42] Also praised was the extremely short construction period, extending from August 15 to September 26, 1927, for the steel construction including the roof, with the finishing work completed by March 31, 1928.[43]

The Petersdorff department store survived the war with negligible damage. Today, it stands in the middle of Wroclaw (Breslau) in nearly its original architectural fabric and is still used as a department store.[44]

Petersdorff department store, Breslau, interior of the oriel, over fifty meters tall and four and a half meters deep with seating for customers, 1928.

Petersdorff department store, Breslau, view from the "Ring," 1988.

Petersdorff department store, Breslau, corner view, 1928.

Petersdorff department store, Breslau,
sketch.

The Schocken Department Store in Chemnitz

Beginning in December 1927, while construction on the Stuttgart Schocken store was still under-way, Mendelsohn entered into negotiations for a third Schocken department store, in Chemnitz. More than any other department store created by Mendelsohn, its materials and interior design give it the character of a sales warehouse for industrially manufactured mass products.

The negotiations between Salmann Schocken and Mendelsohn for the Chemnitz store proved extremely difficult. Schocken wanted to pay the architect a set fee; Mendelsohn consid-ered this too risky in view of the delays and losses incurred with the two previous Schocken build-ings through conflicts with the building authorities. Furthermore, Schocken wanted to hand over the construction supervision to his own building office, which Mendelsohn perceived as a painful intrusion into his own competence. As a conciliatory correspondence from December 1927 makes clear, however, both parties were interested in maintaining a good business relationship.[45]

The surviving sketches for the Chemnitz Schocken store reflect the special urbanistic situ-ation of the building.[46] The quarter-circle-shaped plot lay on Brückenstrasse, an important down-town street not far from the main railway station. The significance Mendelsohn attributed to the form and location of the site is reflected in the fact that he sketched the ground plan at all; usu-ally, he confined himself to elevations and views, often only of the main facade, while the ground plans were adapted to the exterior form of the building. In the design of the Chemnitz Schocken facade, Mendelsohn explored two questions in particular: the graduated stacking of the building elements, and the mounting of the company name. At an advanced stage in the planning, he developed a very reserved and thus very appealing solution for the project.

Nevertheless, the planning progressed slowly. In September 1928, Mendelsohn supplied a sketch of the Chemnitz store for the brochure for the grand opening of the Stuttgart Schocken store, a design that already closely approximates the realized version. Yet only in spring 1929 were concrete steps taken toward construction: in March and April, the plans for the building application were developed, and in the summer of the same year construction began. Up to that point, Mendelsohn had provided all the drawings for the building and the interior furnishings; now, however, Schocken entrusted the construction supervision and minor changes in the plans to the company building office, which had already gained experience with Mendelsohn's approach during work on the Nuremberg and Stuttgart stores. In any case, the interior furnishings were standardized on the basis of these buildings and had already been used in other Schocken stores without the involvement of Mendelsohn's office, for example in 1928 in Crimmitschau in Saxony. On May 15, 1930, two and a half years after the start of negotiations, the building was opened.

As the photos of the Luckenwalde hat factory show, the beginning of Mendelsohn's career was marked by contrapuntally designed buildings that, though in reality symmetrical, were visually represented from extreme vantage points. The Schocken building in Chemnitz, on the other hand, marks a departure from this principle. Mendelsohn now returned to quiet, symmetrical designs and gave this quality particular emphasis in his publications. Goaded by contemporary criticism of his architecture, which stood outside the Neue Sachlichkeit, he reduced his architectural lan-guage to only functionally necessary elements. For department stores, however, the "functional-ly necessary" included not only generous sales areas on the interior, but also the exterior effect of the building, aimed at luring customers into the store.Two ideal ground plans published by Mendelsohn show a perfect circle segment with regular, widely spaced supports and symmetri-cal entrances, stairwells, elevators, and escalators: an ideal sales space. Due to objections from the neighboring property owners, however, neither of the two plans could be realized. But this remains unnoticeable to the public.

Wertheim department store, Breslau, competition entry, 1927.

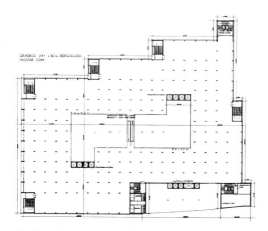

Wertheim department store, Breslau, proposed ground floor plan, 1927. Mendelsohn's proposal called for steel skeleton construction.

Schocken department store,
Chemnitz, sketch, 1927–28.

Schocken department store,
Chemnitz, front elevation.

Schocken department store, Chemnitz,
ideal ground plan and site plan, 1928.

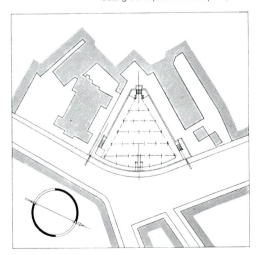

The complex was built in reinforced concrete skeleton construction, a technique Mendelsohn had used in the early 1920s in the Rudolf Mosse publishing house, the Weichmann silk store in Gleiwitz, and the hat factory in Luckenwalde. In these earlier buildings, however, the structure of supports and girders had remained hidden to the observer, covered over with masonry and plaster. In the Chemnitz Schocken store, after a hiatus of a number of years, Mendelsohn returned to this technique and even took special care to emphasize it.

One reason for Mendelsohn's reversion to this building method may be that in the intervening years, the reinforced concrete skeleton had become the dominant construction method for factories. During his trip to America, Mendelsohn himself had seen numerous American factories in Chicago and Buffalo with warehouses articulated by regularly spaced pillars of reinforced concrete.[47] According to Schocken's philosophy of business, the department store was a sales warehouse where attention was to be focused exclusively on the industrially manufactured merchandise. Furthermore, in recent years Mendelsohn's preeminence in German department store and commercial architecture had been increasingly challenged by the designs and buildings of architects from the Ring group. Since his successful direction of the Weissenhof development in Stuttgart in 1927, Ludwig Mies van der Rohe, in particular, had laid claim to leadership among the ranks of German architects. Mies was increasingly successful in obtaining interesting commissions, among them the German Pavilion for the World Exposition in 1929 in Barcelona, which earned him international fame. His curtain wall had already caused a sensation during the first competition for a high-rise building at the Friedrichstrasse railway station in 1922, while his unbuilt design for an office building from the same year showed reinforced steel supports developed in a manner similar to Mendelsohn's Schocken store in Chemnitz.[48] The latter, therefore, might in fact represent Mendelsohn's response to increasing competition from other German architects and an attempt to translate his own individual modes of expression into the language of functionalism.

The elevation of the Chemnitz Schocken store is striking first of all for its subtle orchestration of size relationships between individual window types and for its stepwise receding facade. Here, too, the ground floor consists of giant panes of glass interrupted only by the frames, followed by the close succession of wall and window bands in the upper stories. Yet the elevation alone cannot convey the true quality of the building, which manifests itself only in natura. Only by experiencing the building in person does the viewer see the gentle convexity of the first to fifth upper stories, which project outward by a meter over the entire facade length of fifty-six meters. The continuous ribbon windows and the supports and girders of the reinforced steel skeleton, visible on both the exterior and the interior, clearly identify the facade as a nonbearing curtain wall. The same purpose is also served by another detail: the insertion of a low, continuous ribbon window between the large display windows and the projecting upper stories. The weight of the latter could never be borne by these window strips. In size and proportion, the small windows exactly match those of the stairwells at either end of the facade, connecting them with each other and framing the central block of projecting upper stories on three sides.

The clear window panes with their wooden frames lie flush with the limestone-paneled facade. The facade is tremendously advertising-effective, both by day and by night;[49] the dominance of light-dark contrasts give the two views the character of a photographic negative-positive reversal. The three-and-a-half-meter-high supports behind the facade are clearly visible at all times. While the sketches still showed the company name in giant letters on the roof of the building, in the finished structure it appears only on four low bands above the entrances. Clearly, increasing trust in the advertising-effectiveness of the architecture itself had developed over the course of the planning.

The interior was furnished in the style introduced in Nuremberg and continued in Stuttgart. The sales rooms are articulated by supports in an axial grid of 6-meter intervals. Beneath the window bands stand 1.45-meter-high shelves, while low tables and cabinets furnish the sales areas. The building has a ventilation system with outlets over the doors to the stairwells.

In the Chemnitz Schocken store, Mendelsohn achieved optimal balance between expense and effect. The building represents his response to the ever more insistent demands of functionalism, interpreted in light of his own postulate of functional dynamics. Like Mendelsohn's other department stores and commercial buildings, the Chemnitz store was designed especially for the site and took advantage of its urbanistic context for advertising purposes. Mendelsohn placed the emphasis exclusively on the rounded curtain facade toward Brückenstrasse; the side facades were not meant to be viewed and were not in fact visible until after the destruction of the surrounding buildings in 1944–45. Originally, the side facades served only to accommodate large windows to provide the interior with as much light as possible and were otherwise simply plastered.

The Chemnitz Schocken store suffered relatively little damage during the war. After a short hiatus, sales could once again resume. The department store changed hands a number of times; today, much of the original building fabric can be seen in a completely altered urbanistic situation.

Schocken department store, Chemnitz, the carpet department, 1930.

The Dobloug Garden Department Store in Oslo
Interestingly, the basic concept of the Chemnitz Schocken store was modified by Mendelsohn himself in spring 1932 and sold to a company in Oslo. In early March 1932, he had traveled there to give his lecture "Der schöpferische Sinn der Krise" ("The Creative Spirit and the World of Crisis"). On this occasion, he became acquainted with the head clerk of the Dobloug Garden company, which was planning to erect a new building in downtown Oslo. While a local architect, Rudolf E. Jacobsen, had already been hired, he had apparently failed to present a convincing design. Up to that point Jacobsen, only eight years older than Mendelsohn, had not produced any significant modern commercial buildings, and his works retained a historicist character until the end of the 1920s.[50] Mendelsohn's slide lecture served among other things to make the owners of Dobloug Garden aware of the deficiencies of their architect.

Mendelsohn's new project, its nine stories towering far above the rest of the neighborhood, required special exemptions in Oslo as well; these, however, were quickly issued by the municipal committee in April 1932. Mendelsohn traveled to Oslo to present the plans and on April 19, 1932, wrote to his wife: ". . . and so the plans received 100% applause at Dobloug. In the meantime, the Norwegian under contract has devised another project, one that is bungling and idiotic. But he seems to be going with his contract and grafting his ridiculous clothes onto my spirit. I have just come from a meeting, and—now that I have turned in the plans and know how good they are—feel sad. I feel like someone who has let himself be robbed, and had fun doing it. For I don't want to say that I *had* to let myself be robbed—in order to come up with money."[51] At that point Mendelsohn's participation in the project was therewith concluded, and the construction supervision was transferred to Jacobsen.

Like the Chemnitz Schocken store, the Dobloug Garden department store was erected on a street corner. It resembled the Schocken building to an amazing extent in design and construction technique, although it lacked the dynamics achieved in the Chemnitz store by the projecting upper stories framed on both sides by stairwells. The Dobloug Garden building had only a single, lateral stairwell on the street side.

The circumstances under which the Oslo department store originated are unique in Mendelsohn's oeuvre and can be explained only by the uncertain commission situation of 1932

Schocken department store, Chemnitz, entrance to stairway B, 1930. The openings over the doors are a part of the ventilation system.

Schocken department store, Chemnitz. The reinforced concrete supports are clearly visible through the clear glass panes. Photo taken in 1930.

Schocken department store, Chemnitz. The view at night shows a complementary effect: now the windows are brightly illuminated, while the strips of wall between the window bands are black. Photo taken in 1930.

and the debts he had incurred through the construction of his house Am Rupenhorn and the transfer of his office to the Columbushaus. Today, the building stands unchanged in the city center of Oslo, but no longer serves as a department store.

It would be no exaggeration to number Erich Mendelsohn's department stores of the 1920s and early 1930s among the most important German contributions to twentieth-century architecture. In terms of style, they set the standard for countless imitators. In his designs, Mendelsohn replaced the Wilhelmine merchandise palace with a department store adapted to changing ways of life and economic structures. In addition, he introduced numerous technical innovations that considerably shortened construction time and lent the buildings an innovative character.

In 1929, at the height of his success, Mendelsohn gave the lecture mentioned earlier on the modern commercial building at the meeting of the German retail trade association. In it, he formulated his point of departure for commercial design:

"The meaning of every store is the merchandise, i.e., its sale in as rapid and useful a manner as possible. The merchandise, therefore, is primary, i.e., all commercial and architectural measures serve the necessity of its highest praise. The building, in particular—aside from the self-evident accommodation of technical needs—must be defined by this basic requirement of business in every phase of its planning and execution.

"Light and circulation are the testing points of its quality. Light: i.e., sufficient natural illumination of the sales spaces and the merchandise through windows and courtyards, as well as effective artificial lighting conducive to sales. Circulation: i.e., coherent sales spaces, the lucid arrangement of the storerooms. The proper location for stairs and elevators. Unhindered entrances and exits. In sum: easy orientation for the customer."[52]

In his own department store architecture, Mendelsohn consistently fulfilled these demands. By the late 1920s, moreover, he had succeeded in freeing himself from applied sculptural

Dobloug Garden department store, Oslo, 1932, executed by Rudolf Emil Jacobsen, after Mendelsohn's plans.

Philipp Schaefer, Karstadt department store, Berlin-Neukölln, 1928–29. One of the rare contemporary examples of department stores not in Mendelsohn's manner.

elements and in finding increasingly constructive, functional design solutions. Nonetheless, the adaptability and range of variation of such designs shows his continued adherence to his own conception of functional dynamics. For Mendelsohn, it was especially important that his facade designs be recognizable as consistent expressions of the interior structure and not be misunderstood as mere fashionable decoration. In his lecture, he uses the example of the Nuremberg Schocken store to explain: "Thus . . . the structure of this building and the articulation of its facade clearly correspond to the logic of the internal workings. It is the warehouse, presenting its merchandise for sale above the display windows in layers, floor by floor—in the Nuremberg Schocken building, this recognition creates a new kind of store."[53] At the same time, he defended himself against the accusation that the dominance of the horizontal in his department stores represented mere fashion, for "vertical or horizontal architecture—that is not the mark of a new age. Fashion is always external—and thus quickly changes its face. It has nothing to do with a fundamentally altered way of very differently stratified periods of time. Horizontal or vertical— only someone with no judgment believes in such outer signs; only the fellow traveler hides his lack of persuasion behind others."[54]

In addition to the pure design of the building, Mendelsohn was especially interested in its urbanistic setting and its advertising function as the embodiment of corporate identity, aspects that are integrally related to each other and of fundamental significance for department stores. He believed that the buildings should be tailored to the site and blend with the surroundings yet still arouse the interest of passersby. Mendelsohn achieved this end by emphasizing individual building parts—usually the stairwells so important for a department store—as well as through the use of select materials and refined lighting. In this way, his department stores became so expressive that the buildings themselves became synonyms for the companies, their names mounted in ever smaller letters on the facades. The buildings spoke for themselves.

Notes p. 266.

"No stucco pastries for Potemkin and Scapa Flow"

**Metropolitan Architecture in Berlin: The WOGA Complex
and the Universum Cinema**

Kathleen James

For the most part, accounts of urban planning in Europe during the 1920s focus on radical unrealized schemes, such as Le Corbusier's City for Three Million, and on suburban housing like the *Siedlungen* Ernst May's office built on the outskirts of Frankfurt. Overlooked are the ways in which central cities were transformed during these years as new uses and densities were accommodated within traditional street networks. In Germany, poor economic conditions limited the bulk of such building to the years 1924 to 1929 and to renovations and expansions rather than entirely new projects. Mendelsohn was fortunate enough to realize the most important exception erected in Berlin during the years of the Weimar Republic, the Wohnhausgrundstücksverwertungs AG (WOGA) development, designed and built between 1925 and 1931. Here he integrated a dynamic celebration of the new mass culture into the existing streetscape of Berlin's busiest boulevard, demonstrating in this mixed-use development that modern architecture could co-exist with, indeed even enhance, nineteenth-century urban patterns.

Mendelsohn's approach to urban planning is, besides the plasticity of almost all of his architecture, the principal legacy of his days in Munich as a student of Theodor Fischer. Fischer was the principle German disciple of the Austrian planner Camillo Sitte, who advocated the

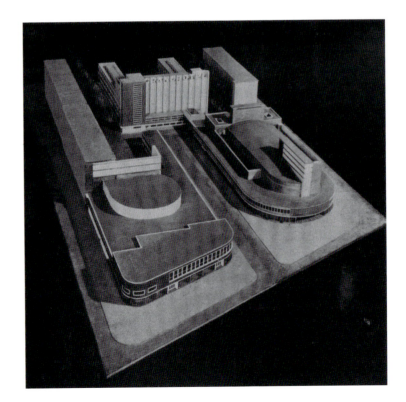

WOGA complex, Berlin, model, 1928.

WOGA complex, Berlin, site plans, 1925/26.

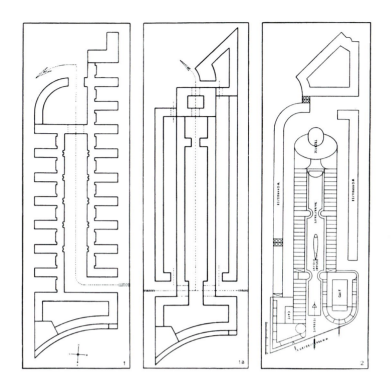

abandonment of neoclassical rationalism in favor of a more picturesque approach to the formation of urban spaces.[1] Fischer and Sitte favored small, tightly defined and irregularly shaped urban plazas in place of the vast open expanses of Vienna's Ringstrasse or, for that matter, Le Corbusier's tower-in-the-park schemes. Although Mendelsohn adamantly rejected his former teacher's nostalgia for the vernacular, he never wavered from Fischer's lessons about the siting of urban buildings.

The WOGA complex consisted of a cinema and cabaret facing the Kurfürstendamm, with an interior street of small shops between them leading to a hotel, and, on the side streets, two long blocks of generously scaled apartments. In the wake of the crash of the American stock market in 1929, the investors were forced to substitute a third block of more compact apartments for the hotel.[2] This combination of entertainment, shopping, and housing had characterized the boulevard from the time it was laid out in the 1880s.[3] Entirely new, however, was the organization of the block itself and the style in which it was built. While existing buildings were organized around private courtyards, with shops fronting the street and apartments above, Mendelsohn broke open the middle of the block to achieve maximum light and air for the apartments and more rentable commercial space for the developers. In the absence of the hotel, the shopping street failed to attract sufficient pedestrian traffic. The Kabarett der Komiker, Café Astor, and Universum Cinema, however, became prominent fixtures of Berlin nightlife.[4]

Built for the bourgeoisie rather than the working class, the WOGA complex was not a utopian imposition of the latest architectural theories upon tenants who had little choice about the conditions in which they lived. Despite the fact that he was building for tenants wealthy enough to afford spacious units, in some cases even with maid's rooms, Mendelsohn used much the same idiom, however, for his own apartment block, which lined Cicerostrasse, as Bruno Taut and Martin Wagner were employing during the same years for their much more efficiently laid out blocks in the suburban Britz Siedlung.[5]

Nonetheless, Mendelsohn's design reflected his accountability, which Taut and Wagner did not share, to the market and to investors, most importantly Hans Lachmann-Mosse, who had earlier commissioned him to renovate the Mosse publishing house and whose wife, Felicia, had inheirited the land from her father, Rudolf Mosse.[6] Lachmann-Mosse, thinking that Mendelsohn would either not be interested in or appropriate for such a speculative commission initially turned to Jürgen Bachmann, another architect, but Mendelsohn eventually secured all of the commission save the apartments on Albrecht-Achilles Strasse, which Bachmann retained.[7] The commercial character of the WOGA development did not deter either Lachmann-Mosse in the end or, for that matter, his architects, from espousing an entirely unornamented architecture. It did, however, prompt Mendelsohn to once again animate stark surfaces through a deft manipulation of tactile materials and, above all, curvilinear forms. The latter also served to enhance the definition of urban edges.

Mendelsohn organized the apartments along Cicerostrasse, for instance, along the same principles as Taut and Wagner's more modest units: floor-through flats with balconies. This emphasis on cross-ventilation means that they are grouped around staircases rather than disposed along corridors. Cicerostrasse was a quiet sidestreet, and he placed no stores along it. The undulating rhythm, however, of the red brick balconies set against the cream-colored, stucco-covered walls of the rest of the block established a firm and interesting boundary, its horizontals corresponding, as usual, to the flow of traffic.

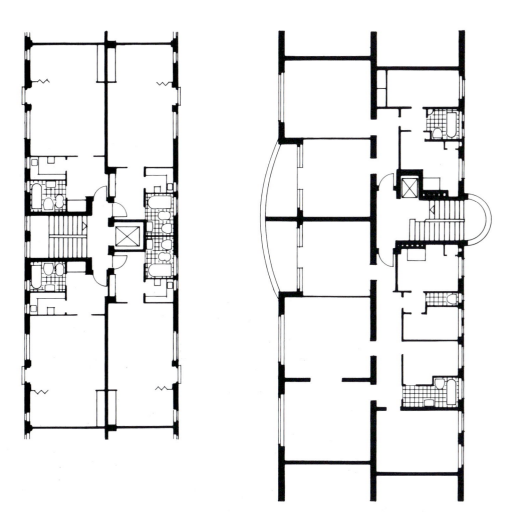

On the Kurfürstendamm itself, a far bolder gesture was necessary in order to compete against the rival nightspots located further east toward the heart of the city. On one side of the pedestrian street stood the Kabarett der Komiker, Café Astor, and six shops. Mendelsohn laid out a detailed plan for this block, but was not responsible for the decoration of any of its interiors. Opposite, Mendelsohn placed the Universum Cinema, whose tall ventilation stack, located perpendicular to the boulevard, served as a bold marker for the complex's leading tenant. Adolph Donath likened the result in a review written in 1928 to "an island in the old 'water' of the Kurfürstendamm."[8]

From the opening in 1919 of Hans Poelzig's Grosses Schauspielhaus until the completion of Rudolf Fränkel's Lichtberg Cinema in 1930, Berlin witnessed the transformation of the architecture of theater and cinemas to attract a new mass public. Beginning with Poelzig, architects inspired to create new democratic forms exciting enough to attract substantial audiences substituted dazzling new lighting effects for historicist ornament.[9] Immaterial technology replaced vicarious re-creations of aristocratic palaces as the architectural lure as cinema architecture in particular began to represent as well as serve this affordable new type of mass-produced entertainment. Floodlights, signage, and even the very shape of the Universum attracted attention at night, while inside a panoply of colors and lighting effects sustained the magic of the movies themselves. Mendelsohn himself wrote of the result:

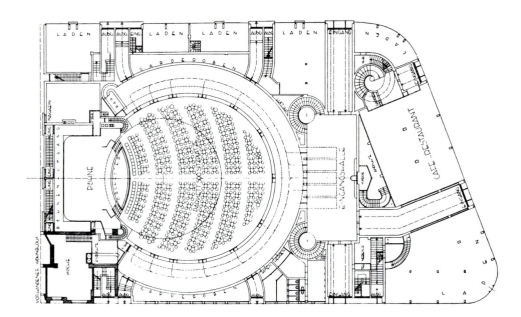

Kabarett der Komiker, Berlin, ground floor plan, 1926–28.

Thus no rococo palace for Buster Keaton.

No stucco pastries for Potemkin and Scapa Flow.

But, also no fear!

No sober reality, no claustrophobia of life-weary brain acrobatics.—Fantasy!

Fantasy—but no lunatic asylum—dominated by space, color, and light.[10]

Having the design of almost an entire city block at his disposal also enabled Mendelsohn to rethink two key aspects of cinema design: plan and elevation. The Universum's position within the WOGA complex eased the problems of integrating a sufficiently dramatic front, profitable rental space, and the requisite number of escape routes by leaving both side facades accessible.[11] Shifting the shopfronts to the side meant that they did not detract from the compositional emphasis on the cinema entrance. Meanwhile, Mendelsohn's elimination of the horizontal mullions in the second-story windows left a vertically divided band that Theodor Böll aptly compared to a strip of film.[12] And although the curve of the Universum's ground plan was slightly skewed to accommodate the two-story shops, most of which faced the pedestrian street, Mendelsohn established here an unprecedented correlation between exterior form and interior plan.[13]

The Universum was built to showcase the new sound films of Ufa, Germany's leading film production company. Mendelsohn balanced efficient circulation and an understated luxuriousness in the entry sequence of what quickly became one of Europe's most prominent cinemas.[14] A broad covered alcove led into a spacious lobby flanked by staircases to the second-floor balcony and opened onto wide corridors that in turn encircled the orchestra seating. Patrons could thus proceed quickly into the theater and at the conclusion of the show leave with equal ease through paired doorways opening onto Cicerostrasse. The lobby, a galleried two-story atrium, marked a calm, but carefully lit, moment in the procession from the boulevard into the auditorium. Here moviegoers paused to buy tickets and shed coats. The cashier's window, a pavilion of opaque glass and bronze mounted on a stone-faced base, divided the flow of traffic swirling toward the auditorium. Its bow echoed the curve of the balcony and of the horseshoe of glass set into the ceiling above. Bands of light troughs tucked behind matte-finished glass radiated from this central motif outwards over the lobby balcony.[15]

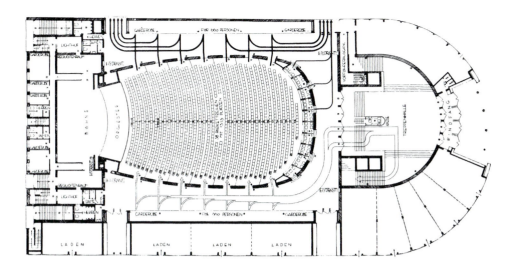

Universum Cinema, Berlin, ground floor plan, 1926–28.

Universum Cinema, Berlin, lobby, 1928. The interior color scheme consisted of yellow stone floors, ivory walls, and a deep blue ceiling.

Beyond was the auditorium, a tight curve whose every detail focused one's attention toward the screen. The shape of the space, which seated 1,800, echoed in Mendelsohn's own mind his fascination with the "moving" quality of movies and responded to the specific sightlines required by film.[16] Older cinemas, following the precedent established by conventional theaters, were often too wide for the new concentration on a single flat surface. The architect compared the effect—enhanced by the striped housing of the organ pipes at either end of the balcony, the great curve of the balcony itself, and the linear panels of ceiling lights—to that of a camera.[17] Because the theater was designed primarily for the new "talkies," the sunken orchestra pit was small and even the organ of secondary importance. An English visitor commented: "The sensation is of a hall which leaps out from the proscenium and is caught as it were on the rebound and immobilized. The interior shimmers and moves; yet it is static in the sense that the vault is static. One feels that in these forms there is latent a fine adjustment of mechanical forces. It is not inert architecture, in the sense of load and ample support. It is cantilevered, stressed, tense, yet strong in the same way that the wings and stays of an airplane are strong. One might almost say that this is aeroplane architecture."[18]

Foreign reviews of the Universum Cinema nonetheless demonstrated how unusual Germany's technologically infused architecture still seemed in countries where traditional formulations of luxury had not been challenged by defeat and revolution. British critics, for instance, remained largely immune to the fantastical qualities of the Universum. Instead they saw it as an

Universum Cinema, Berlin, auditorium, 1928, with mahogany paneling and seats in matching red-brown velvet. The rear walls of the balcony were painted in parallel bands of yellow, blue-gray, and soft red.

Illustration right:
Universum Cinema, Berlin, night view, 1928. At night the Universum literally glowed, attracting audiences from up and down the Kurfürstendamm.

example of the characteristic austerity of contemporary German architecture, which they understood to be the product of economic hardship.[19] J. R. Leathart, for instance, writing in 1930, noted the building's "functional severity" and described it as an example of "extreme Teutonic efficiency and directness of purpose."[20] With the onset of the Depression, however, cinema architects across Europe and the United States were faced with smaller budgets. In these conditions, the Universum became a popular model, particularly in England, where it inspired a series of cinemas designed by Harry Weedon for the Odeon chain.[21]

The WOGA complex amply demonstrated Mendelsohn's ability to rethink typological conventions in ways that enhanced the dynamism of the cityscape without exacerbating its chaotic appearance. Moreover, it was Mendelsohn's celebration here of precisely the programmatic aspects of these commissions that accounted for this success. For Mendelsohn, advertising and the mass culture of which it was a part were forces to be exploited as well as tamed, just as the modern city was to be enjoyed as well as reformed. The spectacles he mounted on his city-scaled stage led to an image of luxury far more democratic than its Wilhelmine predecessor and provided a model for the United States and much of the rest of Europe.

Notes p. 267.

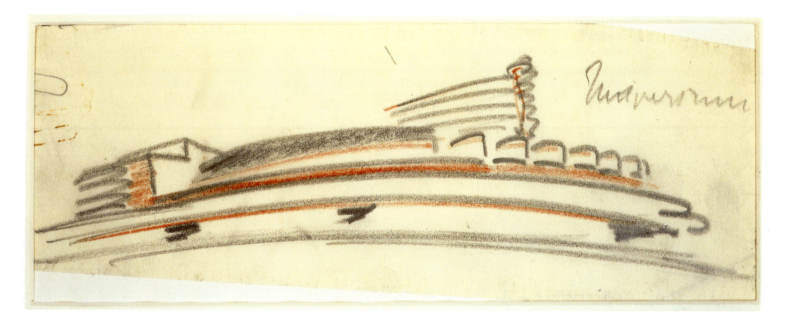

Universum Cinema, Berlin, perspective
sketch, 1927.

"We believe in Berlin!"

The Metal Workers' Union Building, the Columbushaus, and Other
Office Buildings in Berlin

Regina Stephan

From November 1918 to March 1933, Mendelsohn's office was located in Berlin, first in the Westend district and later in the Columbushaus on Potsdamer Platz. During this time he participated in architectural events in the capital city in a variety of ways and produced a number of interesting designs for commercial buildings in Berlin. Not all of them were built, either because they were competition entries or because their realization was hindered by the changing economic situation. Those commercial structures that were realized, however—including the building for the Deutscher Metallarbeiterverband (German Metal Workers' Union) in the Kreuzberg district and the Columbushaus on Potsdamer Platz—aroused widespread public interest even outside architectural circles. They were notable for their modern, metropolitan design and construction methods as well as their short building periods; in addition, they numbered among the few high-rise buildings realized in the capital city.

In the early 1920s, interest in high-rise construction—initiated in 1910 by the "Wettbewerb Gross-Berlin" ("Competition for Greater Berlin") and interrupted only by World War I—had flared up again. The dramatic increase in population and traffic had given rise to a high volume of investment, above all in downtown districts. The construction of high-rise buildings was intended to channel this development and at the same time create urbanistic accents in the burgeoning commercial metropolis.[1]

The High-Rise on Kemperplatz in Berlin
Mendelsohn developed his first high-rise project for the "Wiederaufbau-Aktiengesellschaft für die Errichtung von Hochbauten" ("Reconstruction Corporation for the Erection of High-Rise Buildings"—Widag for short). In 1921, under its director and main shareholder, the Berlin contractor Heinrich Mendelssohn, the company had announced a general competition for a commercial high-rise on Kemperplatz. By the deadline on September 30, 1921, seventy-six designs had been submitted, yet none was satisfactory. Thus in a second phase, Peter Behrens, Erich Mendelsohn, Max and Bruno Taut, Hans and Wassili Luckhardt, and Arthur Voigdt were invited to submit projects. With the exception of the latter three, their designs were published in the magazine *Frühlicht*.[2]

Mendelsohn designed a flat-roofed building with sections of differing heights. Its defining characteristic was the powerful contrast between strongly projecting, deeply shadowed cornices and horizontal window bands. The ground floor was to be recessed beneath a bridge-like construction whose supports tapered to a point at the ground. The height of the building was to increase stepwise to eight stories at the street corner, dropping to four stories where it adjoined the neighboring plots in accord with the typical Berlin building height. The different levels were set off from each other not at right angles, but at a 75-degree incline, while the bands of windows continuing around the corners created a strong, dynamic effect. The most important element in this design was its emphatic horizontality, here proposed for the first time by Mendelsohn for a large commercial building. The innovative character of this feature becomes clear from a com-

Competition entry by Mendelsohn for high-rise building on Kemperplatz, Berlin, 1921.

Competition entry by Max and Bruno Taut for high-rise building on Kemperplatz, Berlin, 1921.

Peter Behrens's design for the high-rise on Kemperplatz shows the influence of projects for the "Competition for Greater Berlin" of 1908–9.

parison with the designs by Peter Behrens and the Taut brothers. While Behrens's nine-story tower, rounded and faced in natural stone, evoked high-rise designs from before World War I, the Tauts planned vertically articulated towers with pilaster strips, vertical rectangular windows, and pitched or pyramidal roofs, designs that manifest a clear affinity to the Gläserne Kette.

None of these projects was realized; instead, a revised design by Heinrich Kaiser and Eduard Jobst Siedler from the first competition was built, of which Adolf Behne said: "They are building a pathetic school-book exercise that inspires pity, but is bound to get good press."[3] Mendelsohn's Kemperplatz project, however, was to exert considerable influence on commercial architecture in Berlin into the early 1930s, as is manifested by examples such as Bruno Paul's Kathrein high-rise or the Shell-Haus (now the Bewag administrative building) by Emil Fahrenkamp, both from 1930.[4]

By the late 1920s, the economic and political situation in Germany was rapidly deteriorating. Even more than before, Mendelsohn felt compelled to secure the continued existence of his large office by participation in competitions. In late 1928, he expressed his foreboding in a letter to his wife that is remarkable and moving for its perceptive analysis of the times: "We are young, young enough, not to be blind. War is coming and will seize even us."[5]

In 1929, the Mendelsohn office participated in three major competitions, from which only one commission resulted, although his designs made a successful showing in all of them. The three projects were the headquarters of the German Metal Workers' Union, the administrative building of the Deutsches Stickstoff-Syndikat (German Nitrogen Syndicate), and the high-rise building at the Friedrichstrasse railway station.

The German Metal Workers' Union Building in Berlin

In 1928, the German Metal Workers' Union resolved to move its headquarters from Stuttgart to the capital city of Berlin. Initially, the union considered renovating one of its own buildings in Berlin to provide inexpensive accommodation for its directorship, but finally decided to erect a new structure. The plot acquired for this purpose took the form of an equilateral triangle and was located on Alte Jakobstrasse across from the national patent office, in the immediate vicinity of the Belle-Alliance-Platz and the newspaper district around Kochstrasse. The union had intentionally chosen a site in the center of the capital city and wished for an architecture appropriate to its significance for economic life in Germany.

Paul Bonatz of Stuttgart, Erich Mendelsohn, Rudolf W. Reichel, Max Taut and Franz Hoffmann of Berlin were invited to submit designs for the new union headquarters. The latter two architects already had experience with union buildings: in 1922–23, Max Taut had designed the office building of the Allgemeiner Deutscher Gewerkschaftsbund in Berlin-Mitte and in 1925 the headquarters of the German book printers in Kreuzberg. At the time of the competition, Taut and Hoffmann were preparing plans for the miners' union building in Wilmersdorf. In 1927, Mendelsohn, too, had developed a preliminary project for a union building in Zwickau, which was likewise to contain administrative spaces, assembly rooms, and a printing press.[6] Simon Schocken, the brother of Salmann and co-owner of the Zwickau-based Schocken company, had arranged the commission for Mendelsohn;[7] the project, however, never went beyond the initial stages.

In 1930, the union official Karl Schott reported on the results of the competition for the metal workers' building: "Not all of the designs submitted were satisfactory. Two were essentially the same in their basic features: those of the architects Erich Mendelsohn and Rudolf W. Reichel. We have entrusted the realization of the building to them. . . . The details were worked out in the office of Mendelsohn, where there was a large staff of experienced architects."[8]

The projects by Mendelsohn and Reichel do in fact agree in their overall conception: both show two side wings converging into a taller central building. In the design of the details, however, the two projects differ considerably. In its realized form, the building bore exclusively Mendelsohn's signature, raising the question as to why he was not awarded the sole commission, especially since Reichel erected no other significant buildings in Berlin either previously or subsequently.[9] The surviving documents provide no explanation for this circumstance, which may simply have resulted from personal connections between Reichel and the leadership of the union.[10]

In 1928, Mendelsohn had already developed an extensive project for the union building as well as an adjacent plot. His point of departure was the revised plan of the municipal administration of Berlin for the urbanistic redevelopment of the area. The new plan was intended to relieve Friedrichstrasse, which, as the main connecting street between Leipziger Strasse and Unter den Linden, bore the brunt of the increase in automobile traffic. The newly planned Lindenstrasse was to direct traffic toward the Spittelmarkt and Alexanderplatz.

The plans of 1928, which called for an elaborate, large-scale complex, are among Mendelsohn's few urbanistic projects. A new building for the printing and editorial offices of the Social Democratic newspaper *Vorwärts* was planned across from the union building.[11] This attenuated structure was to follow the course of the new street and was connected to the union building by a four-story bridge. Mendelsohn was working on its design as early as July 1928.[12] At this stage of the planning, the union building occupied almost the entire triangular plot. Later, Mendelsohn deeply regretted the fact that the ensemble remained unrealized: "The horizontality of my initial sketches and of my first buildings spread everywhere. It reached its high point in the city plan of 1929, which placed the press of the Weimar Republic to the left and the main administrative building of the metal workers' union to the right—architecturally close, but not politically! By the

Rudolf W. Reichel, competition entry for Metal Workers' Union building, Berlin, 1929.

Model of the complex designed for the site on Alte Jakobstrasse in Berlin-Kreuzberg, planned in 1928 but unrealized.

Metal Workers' Union building, Berlin,
page of sketches, January 1929.

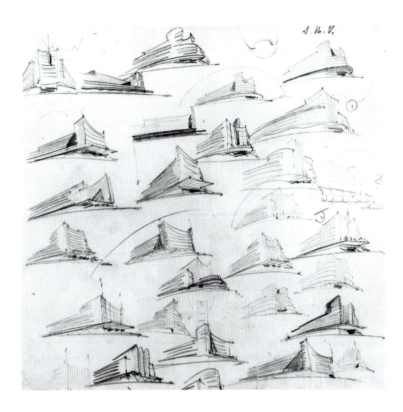

time the union building was finished, all hopes of association had been dashed, thus shattering the entire scheme."[13]

A letter from Mendelsohn to his wife on January 14, 1929, serves to precisely date the beginning of work on the union building: "I am sitting in the atelier, have begun the metal workers. . . ."[14] A single sheet of sketches with a total of thirty-three designs shows him wrestling with the right solution for the building. The task of the architect was to provide representative spaces for the union leadership, administrative offices, and spaces for the union's own printing press as well as ground-floor shops to be rented out to help finance the project.

The triangular form of the plot and its urbanistic orientation placed the main accent on the tip of the triangle pointing toward the Landwehrkanal. Accordingly, Mendelsohn located the spaces of the directorate within a central structure, into which two wings with administrative spaces converged. The printing office was to be located on the ground floor along with shops.

On April 26, 1929, Mendelsohn submitted the first building application for the structure, designed with a bearing frame of reinforced concrete. Discrepancies in the facades led to revisions, and a second set of plans was submitted in mid-May 1929.[15] The building permit was issued unusually quickly, so that the work of construction, under the direction of Ernst Sagebiel, would have progressed rapidly if it had not been interrupted by a four-week strike.[16] The strike resulted from the fact that the metal workers' union had not turned over the execution of the building to the Bauhütte (construction workers' union), but had awarded the contracts to the lowest bidder. After seeing the building shell, Mendelsohn decided to alter the main facade. For "purely architectural reasons," the "main cornice was to be raised by 65 cm" without changing the height of the uppermost story.[17] The change was approved and the building completed by August 1930; on the fourteenth of that month, it was inaugurated with a grand union celebration.

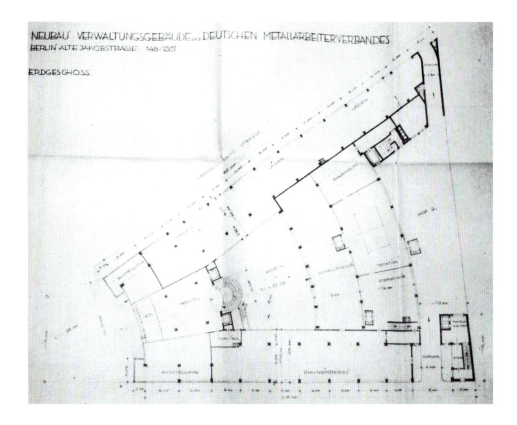

In many respects, the Metal Workers' Union building represents a synthesis of Mendelsohn's earlier department stores and commercial buildings. Once again, he devised a fitting
response to the urbanistic situation and the specific building type. Unlike the earliest designs for
the project, the building as it was realized left the tip of the plot completely unoccupied, thus
creating space for a plaza. The concave line of the main facade terminated the building in a
harmonious manner, while at the same time directing traffic into the two adjacent streets.

The center of the axially symmetrical building was emphasized in a number of ways. The
central structure, which housed the monumental spaces of the union directorate, was faced with
vertical panels of shell limestone, mounted not in a staggered masonry bond but with continuous
horizontal and vertical joints. In this way, Mendelsohn made it clear that the natural stone served
no structural purpose. Horizontal window bands with tall bronze-framed windows provided
abundant daylight for the interior spaces behind the main facade; in an earlier stage of the
planning, Mendelsohn had considered glazing the entire main front.

The top story of the central structure is considerably taller than the other stories and
houses the most important space in the building: the conference room, which is also emphasized on the facade. Its windows are double the height of those below, while a narrow, rounded
oriel emphasizes its center. The sole sculptural element in the facade, the oriel projects outward
like a command tower, gaining urbanistic weight through a flagpole mounted atop it, towering
high above the building. The whole thus evokes the image of a flag-bearer marching at the head
of a demonstration, proclaiming the cause of the workers. The flanks of the central building have
no windows and are adorned only with the union logo mounted on the facades.

On the interior of the main structure, the centralized composition is repeated: the entrance
is sheltered by a strongly projecting canopy, whose underside takes the form of a luminous ceil-

Metal Workers' Union building, Berlin, main facade, 1930.

Metal Workers' Union building, Berlin, view from the ground floor into the elegantly curving ensemble of stairway and light fixture, 1930.

ing fixed with bronze moldings radiating outward from the imaginary center of a circle. Like the display windows on the sides of the building, the entrance hall is completely glazed. In a manner reminiscent of his design for Chemnitz, Mendelsohn placed a strip of glass between the large windows and the ceiling, thus calling attention to the skeleton of reinforced concrete and the nonbearing curtain wall in front of it. The bright entrance hall leads to a light-flooded stairwell, the building's most important adornment. In an elegant curve, the seemingly self-supporting stairway spirals around an open core, half surrounded by a glass cylinder subdivided only by the necessary supports. In the center of the spiral, a light fixture hangs down from the ceiling on top of the building. At the floor levels, it is composed of hemispheres and round horizontal panes of glass punctuated with light bulbs; between the floors are vertical fluorescent tubes. For the design of the entrance hall, the union announced a competition in which Rudolf Belling, Ludwig Gies, and Oskar Schlemmer also participated.[18] Probably due to the precarious economic situation, none of the designs was executed.

The design of the conference room on the top floor, as well, was compositionally oriented to the center, with floor beams and parquet converging toward the tip of the site like the radii of a circle. The side walls were faced with wooden panels on which vertical fluorescent tubes were mounted. The rear wall of the room was adorned by a mural showing industrial metal workers at their labor. According to a newspaper article by Adolph Donath, the furniture in the conference room was manufactured after designs by Mendelsohn.[19]

The situation in the administrative quarters of the union, housed in the side wings of the building, was quite different. For these spaces, used furniture was brought in from Stuttgart. This part of the building is much simpler than the central structure. The absence of natural stone facing and the use of wooden window frames is clearly apparent on the exterior. Above the display windows on the ground floor, the windows were cut into the smoothly plastered walls in narrow, even rows and connected with continuous sills, thus disguising the supports in the facade. The girders resting on the facade piers completely span the offices, their abutment resting on supports on the interior side of the office corridors. The advantages of this solution are obvious: the office spaces can be subdivided at will, while the hallways on the courtyard side are well supplied with daylight from the continuous window bands. In addition, extremely attractive views of the rear courtyard result, creating an interior echo of the restrained dynamics of the street facade.

While on the street sides a clear distinction is made between central structure and wings and respectively between management and administration, at the rear all sense of hierarchy is avoided. The exterior facades are smoothly plastered and painted white, windows flush with the wall. The center of the composition is marked by the glass-enclosed cylinder of the stairwell framed on either side by two narrow vertical bands of windows, providing light for the elevators. It is here that the vertical circulation within the building takes place. Quite different are the corridors of the administrative wing, whose continuous ribbon windows evoke horizontal circulation with equal clarity. At the end of each wing, vertical bands of glass clearly mark the location of side stairwells and elevators. If ever an example of *architecture parlante* was created in the 1920s, it is Mendelsohn's Metal Workers' Union building, a structure that avails itself of an entire syntax. Here Mendelsohn made use of his experiences with department stores to captivate the viewer. However, the goal was a different one: in both its interior and exterior appearance, the building was intended to render visible the social and political claims of the German Metal Workers' Union.

After the Nazi takeover of the unions in 1934, the Deutsche Arbeitsfront occupied the building, removing the union logo from the side facades of the central structure. After suffering heavy damage in the war, the building was returned to the metal workers' union IG Metall and repaired. Since its most recent restoration, it bears witness as one of Mendelsohn's few large-scale buildings to the high architectural and urbanistic quality of his work as well as to his *architecture parlante*.

Metal Worker's Union building, Berlin. Corridor in the side wing showing the advantage of the chosen construction: a continous band of windows.

Metal Workers' Union building, Berlin, view from the rear, 1930.

Illustration right:
Metal Workers' Union building, Berlin. The main stairwell, flooded with light through large windows during the day, was illuminated at night by a light fixture with a variety of glass elements.

The Administrative Building of the German Nitrogen Syndicate in Berlin

In 1929, the Mendelsohn office also participated in a competition for the administrative building of the Deutsches Stickstoff-Syndikat (German Nitrogen Syndicate) in Berlin. With a usable area of 18,000 square meters, the complex was to provide offices and assembly rooms for 1,200 officials and accommodate an on-site experimental station for nitrogenous fertilizer. Fritz Höger and Siegfried Budeus also took part in the competition,[20] submitting designs that differed markedly from Mendelsohn's. Mendelsohn's project called for three north-south wings connected by an east-west tract. The sunny exposures accommodated office spaces, while the north sides were reserved for corridors and stairwells, reducing energy use to a minimum. The supports of the steel skeleton were located within the facade, making it possible to "divide the tract at will into rooms measuring 4 or 6 or 8 meters, without any structural modification."[21] An additional wing one story shorter than the others with an entrance hall and reserve rooms was to adjoin the west part of the building. From here, a pergola would provide access to the greenhouses.

Here for the first time, Mendelsohn dispensed with all dynamic elements of design and arranged rooms and wings according to purely functional considerations. The smooth facades of the stairwells were punctuated by vertical window bands, those of the offices by horizontal ones. The design is compelling for its orientation to the points of the compass, its interior spaces expertly attuned to exposure. In addition, the grounds are optimized with the experimental station for nitrogenous fertilizer located at the center of the complex. None of the designs was realized.

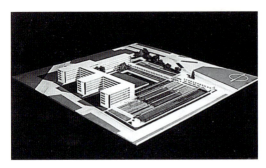

Model of competition design by Mendelsohn for the administrative building of the German Nitrogen Syndicate, Berlin, 1929.

The High-Rise at the Friedrichstrasse Railway Station

The last and most significant unrealized competition entry by Mendelsohn from 1929 was designed for a site between the south bank of the Spree near the Reichstag, Friedrichstrasse, and the Friedrichstrasse railway station. A competition for this site had already been announced in 1921–22, sponsored by the corporation Turmhaus-Aktiengesellschaft. This first competition had aroused great interest among architects, many of whom were unemployed at the time. For numerous reasons the project was never realized.[22] In May 1929, the corporation Berliner Verkehrs-Aktiengesellschaft (BVG) purchased the plot and in late September announced a second competition. In addition to the BVG company architect Alfred Grenader, the architects Heinrich Straumer, Paul Mebes and Paul Emmerich, Ludwig Mies van der Rohe, and Erich

Sketch for a high-rise at the Friedrich-strasse railway station, Berlin, 1929.

View of model looking toward the Friedrichstrasse railway station, 1929. In addition to restaurants, offices, and shops, Mendelsohn planned a swimming pool with artificial waves; a sliding glass roof would have enabled it to be used as an open-air pool as well.

Mendelsohn were invited to participate.[23] The deadline for submission was November 30, 1929. The jury included City Councilman Ernst Reuter, City Building Commissioner Martin Wagner, and Otto Bartning. Two first prizes were awarded, going to Mebes/Emmerich and Mendelsohn.

Mendelsohn's design was based on a precise analysis of the urbanistic situation, which he illustrated in eight models,[24] deriving his examples from the first competition. In his search for an adequate urbanistic solution for the new building, he sought to establish its relation to the railway station, the Spree, and the five-story buildings on Friedrichstrasse; at the same time, he wanted to permit as much daylight as possible to enter Friedrichstrasse. There were to be as few north rooms as possible; instead the site was to be optimally exploited with office floors that could be subdivided at will.

The surviving sketches are difficult to match with the more developed plans and model. The latter shows a multipurpose building, successful both urbanistically and in terms of design, whose architectural elements also suggest an *architecture parlante*. The three wings of differing height made use of insights gained from the study of light conditions. The eighteen-story high-rise parallel to the banks of the Spree would have housed offices in the upper stories with uniform square windows cut into the smooth wall like a pattern of holes. The first and second upper stories, on the other hand, were to accommodate a café with panorama windows extending over the entire six-story wing to Friedrichstrasse. The remaining corner of the plot, oriented to the south toward the railway station, would have been occupied by a swimming pool with artificial waves and a sliding glass roof that allowed year-round use. Once again, Mendelsohn created a design perfectly tailored to the urbanistic situation, a solution hardly conceivable in any other location.

A very different approach was taken by Mies van der Rohe, whose designs are marked by interchangeability of location. He had suggested this idea already in 1921 in his famous design for a glass high-rise building for the same site and now adopted this concept again.

In retrospect, it is clear that Mies van der Rohe's typical designs, which emphasized qualities other than that of urbanism, triumphed over the individualized solutions proposed by Mendelsohn and others—a development that in the end was to lead to the monotonous, uniform appearance of metropolises throughout the world.

The Galéries Lafayette and the Columbushaus in Berlin

Mendelsohn's last great building in Germany, the Columbushaus in Berlin, likewise began as a major urbanistic project. In the end, however, the rapidly deteriorating economic situation prevented the realization of all but a single building.

The point of departure for Mendelsohn's urbanistic scheme was a 1928 project for the redesign of Leipziger Platz and Potsdamer Platz by Martin Wagner. Since 1926, Wagner had been the progressive-minded successor of Ludwig Hoffmann as city building commissioner of Berlin. He had engaged in a detailed study of modern housing and urbanism, producing numerous lectures, essays, and books on their conditions and demands.[25]

In his project of 1928, Wagner suggested the reorganization of Potsdamer Platz and the octagonal Leipziger Platz. Streetcar stops as well as subway and elevated railway stations were to be accommodated in a large, round, glass-enclosed traffic island in the middle of the former Potsdamer Platz. Automobile traffic was to flow around the island and directed in a straight line into Leipziger Strasse. Wagner wanted to redesign the edges of the plaza with buildings of uniform height and emphasize the central axis of Leipziger Strasse with a high-rise tower. The buildings were intended to be completely written off as a tax deduction within twenty-five years, so that nothing would stand in the way of alterations and adaptations perhaps necessary by that time.

A number of architects used Wagner's ideas as the point of departure for their own projects, among them Mendelsohn and Hans and Wassili Luckhardt with Alfons Anker. Individual buildings around the edge of the plaza were planned in detail, but could not be realized due to the client's financial difficulties. The Luckhardt brothers had almost completed the plans for the "Haus Berlin"—a high-rise in the central axis of the plaza that was to serve as a *point de vue* for Leipziger Strasse—when the decision was made to abandon the project. In 1930–31, the architects once again proposed a building for this central site, known as the "Josty" plot, as well as a "twin" or mirror-image of the Columbushaus, at that time under construction.

Mendelsohn developed three urbanistic projects for the double plaza. In all of them, he rejected the idea of a high-rise tower and proposed buildings of uniform height all around the edge of the plaza. The commercial building planned for the central plot between Potsdamer Strasse and Bellevuestrasse was conceived as a jetty or pier dividing the flow of traffic from Leipziger Strasse and conducting it into different directions. In his first project, he suggested tearing down the "corner obstacles," i.e., the buildings at the interface between the two plazas.[26]

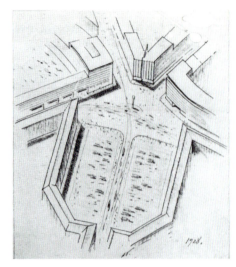

Project for redesign of Potsdamer Platz and Leipziger Platz, Berlin, 1928.

Hans and Wassily Luckhardt with Alfons Anker, project for the redesign of Potsdamer Platz, 1931, showing their own design for the "Haus Berlin" as well as Mendelsohn's Columbushaus.

Page of sketches for the
Columbushaus, 1930.

Extremely high real estate prices, however, made it impossible for the city of Berlin to acquire the
property necessary for a complete urbanistic reorganization, and soon only a smaller-scale
solution was under discussion, one that preserved the two-part plaza structure.

Since early summer 1928, Mendelsohn had been engaged in negotiations for the construction of a large department store on the site between Bellevuestrasse and Friedrich-Ebert-
Strasse, which led to the Brandenburg Gate. A consortium equipped with German and French
capital had acquired the plot—one of the most attractive building sites in all of Germany—and
agreed to the construction and operation of a department store of the French chain Galéries
Lafayette.[27] Eighty percent of the capital lay in German hands, a factor considered particularly
important by the city. By late 1928, plans for the department store had progressed so far that in
December, the Hotel Bellevue on the site was demolished, since architect and clients were
confident of speedy receipt of the building permit.

In January 1929, Mendelsohn engaged the architect Ernst Sagebiel specially for the
Galéries Lafayette. Concerning Sagebiel, Mendelsohn wrote to his wife: "Dr. Sagebiel is here,
somewhat uneasy about the tempo and a lot of things—he is certainly no sensationalist, no
salesman—but he is devoted to the thing with seriousness and constancy. We have to give him
time."[28] Mendelsohn was not at all pleased with the progress of work on the Galéries. In the same
month he wrote: "I have had to give the Lafayette duck a hard push to get it through the bureau-

cracy. . . ."[29] At this point, the plans called for a twelve-story department store with a two-story restaurant at the top and an entrance hall on Potsdamer Platz with direct access to the subway and elevated railway stations. The building was to be erected in steel skeleton construction with a "large display facade of glass and metal."[30] Above the pitched roof, giant illuminated letters spelled out GALÉRIES LAFAYETTE. The building had already been planned in detail and logistical preparations made when the work was discontinued. Mendelsohn closed the gaping hole in the edge of the plaza with a 20-meter-high wooden construction fence that essentially followed the old building line, incorporating temporary shops and later the construction office. As with the Metal Workers' Union building, the city used the change in plans as an opportunity to alter the original development scheme and enlarge the area of the plaza. A total of 550 square meters of buildable area was added to the public space at the street corner.[31]

The reasons for the halt to construction were various. In February 1929, Wagner and the municipal traffic authorities rejected the construction of a twelve-story high-rise for fear of further increasing automobile traffic. With the ratification of this decision in June, the Galéries Lafayette decided to erect their store elsewhere in the western part of the city. For this purpose they engaged the architect Philipp Schaefer, who had just built the large Karstadt store on Hermann-platz in Berlin, one of the few department store buildings of the 1920s in Germany that eluded the dominant influence of Mendelsohn. Thus the beginning of construction, originally scheduled for September/October 1929, had to be postponed. Meanwhile, the stock market crash in New York on October 25, 1929, posed tremendous difficulties for the German economy, in whose recovery American investments had played an essential role since 1924. A political climate of growing nationalism, moreover, made it difficult for a French company to invest in Berlin.[32]

Columbushaus, Berlin, view during construction, showing the cantilever beams and the slender steel supports in the upper stories, 1931.

By 1930, the successor project Columbushaus was already underway.[33] The client, the real estate company Bellevue-Immobilien-AG, wanted to erect a multipurpose building with restaurants, shops, offices, and medical practices with the option for later use as a department store, a factor that particularly affected the statics of the building.

Mendelsohn prepared sketches for this project, as well, which largely preserved the facades developed for the Galéries Lafayette as well as the constructive bearing frame of steel with only a few modifications. The main differences consisted in the subtraction of three stories and of the large illuminated letters. Instead, an innovative lettering system was developed for the facades. The plaza edge was to be defined by a unified main cornice at a height of thirty-four meters; the only exception was the building on the "Josty" site, for which Luckhardt/Anker had already developed plans in 1928.

In spring 1931, construction could finally begin. While the planning had progressed slowly up to this point, the perfect logistical preparation of the site enabled the Mendelsohn office to finish the Columbushaus—one of the largest office buildings in Germany, with an enclosed space of 54,000 cubic meters—in a record time of only eleven months.

In late April, the three Berlin steel construction firms Breest & Co., Krupp-Druckenmüller GmbH, and Thyssen Eisen- and Stahlbau-AG received the commission for the erection of the steel skeleton; the mounting work was scheduled to begin on July 29. The work had to be completed in only sixty-eight working days, for which reason the project was divided up into three precisely coordinated phases of construction. The prominent location of the site on one of the busiest plazas in Europe posed particular problems; thus even the removal of the excavated material and the delivery of building supplies had to be carefully planned in advance.

By mid-October 1931, the steel skeleton had been completed on schedule. Construction continued at the same tempo: "The installation of the reinforced concrete floors followed immediately everywhere the state of the steel skeleton permitted. Working from gunite scaffolds, the construction of the masonry followed in a quick tempo, as well as the mounting of the freestone facing, so that the shell was officially completed only a month after the steel skeleton, i.e., in mid-November."[34] By March 1932, the interior had been finished.

The Columbushaus received considerable publicity in the architectural press both at home and abroad. It was a highly innovative building in terms of both design and technology and marked the beginning of a new phase in Mendelsohn's work. The rise to power of the Nazi party in January 1933 and Mendelsohn's emigration in March of the same year, however, prevented the continuation of this new artistic direction either in Germany or in his host countries. Only in the 1950s did younger architects once again begin to draw inspiration from the Columbushaus.[35]

The point of departure for the design was the corner plot, with street fronts measuring approximately 35 meters on Bellevuestrasse and 63.5 meters on Friedrich-Ebert-Strasse. Mendelsohn himself described the central goal of his conception as follows: "In accord with the actual function of the building as a framing element for the plaza, all conspicuous emphasizing of the corners is avoided. Only the roof form and the bands of windows point toward Potsdamer Platz in a pronounced manner. . . . A slight curvature of the facade was necessary along Friedrich-Ebert-Strasse in order to preserve a right angle at the corner of Bellevuestrasse. The curve rather than the oblique line is the most vital way of architecturally mediating between two intersecting building lines. . . . The floor plans of all the stories are reduced to the simplest possible formula. The primary aim was to accommodate every conceivable use from the beginning, without requiring essential remodeling should changes become necessary later. This demand is largely taken into account in both the construction and the technical facilities."[36]

In this innovative construction, the steel skeleton was incorporated into the facades, creating large spaces 6.7 meters deep and over 90 meters long, uninterrupted by any supports. Since the facade nonetheless had to look elegant, Mendelsohn reduced the width of the facade supports (including casing) to only 16 centimeters "to enhance the effect of the window areas."[37] The necessary stability was ensured by supports with a center-to-center distance of 1.3 meters. The same grid also set the parameters for the interior subdivision of the floors, determining the placement of partition walls and the size and position of heating elements as well as the arrangement of openings for the air conditioning system.

The design of the first two stories, intended for shops and restaurants and thus dominated by large display and panorama windows, proved to be problematic. For this purpose, the load of the second to ninth upper stories had to be diverted from the facade to supports on the interior of the building. This was accomplished by means of large summer-beams in the facade "which . . . at a length of 6.5 meters bore four individual loads of 34 tons each."[38] The summer-beams, in turn, were supported by cantilever beams, which Mendelsohn wished to keep as narrow as possible. At 30 centimeters, they were in fact relatively delicate, considering the enormous weight they had to bear. Nonetheless, 48 percent of the total quantity of steel was used in the first two stories.[39]

Mendelsohn's desire to arrange "all the roof trusses on Friedrich-Ebert-Strasse parallel to the Bellevuestrasse facade . . . out of consideration for the architectural design of the roof area" led to further structural problems. The terrace of the restaurant on the ninth upper story was to be protected by a monopitch roof six and a half meters in depth, extending without supports over a length of ninety meters. The trusses, which would normally have been oriented to the imaginary center of the circle described by the rounded facade of the building, instead diverged from it at various angles, and for this reason were cut to size on site.

The facades were covered with limestone panels, whose finely pored surface could weather the heavy air pollution on Potsdamer Platz better than the Cannstatt travertine so prized

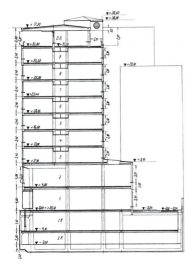

Columbushaus, Berlin, section through wing on Friedrich-Ebert-Strasse, 1932.

Columbushaus, Berlin, unfurnished office floor.

Columbushaus, Berlin, after completion, spring 1932.

Columbushaus, Berlin. On the rear side of the building, the ground floor and first upper story projected into the courtyard, thus enlarging the valuable shop and restaurant space, 1932.

by Mendelsohn. The panels separating the continuous window bands on each story also covered the structural steel framework, opposing the strong verticals of the latter with a horizontal accent. Above and below the natural stone facings, tracks were mounted for interchangeable illuminated letters. The rear side—described by Mendelsohn as a "mirror image of the street side"—repeated the facade design of the plaza front. Also at the rear were openings through which the air conditioning system could draw in fresh air, which then—filtered, mixed with purified air from the interior, and heated or cooled according to the season—was conducted into the interior spaces.

The Columbushaus was the first office high-rise in Germany with air conditioning, and the other technical installations were innovative as well. Unlike the gravity heating systems customary up to that point, the building was centrally heated with a warm-water pump system. Heating coils in the glass skylights of the monopitch roof enabled the terrace to be used even in winter. Water was drawn from the building's own thirty-two-meter-deep well, passed through a number of filters, and fed into the pipes. Numerous stairs and elevators—self-bearing elements of the steel skeleton—provided for circulation throughout the building.

The interior of the building was conceived to allow as many different uses as possible. The lower stories above the reinforced concrete foundation trough with reinforced concrete beams above—a measure made necessary by the high ground water level—extended over the entire

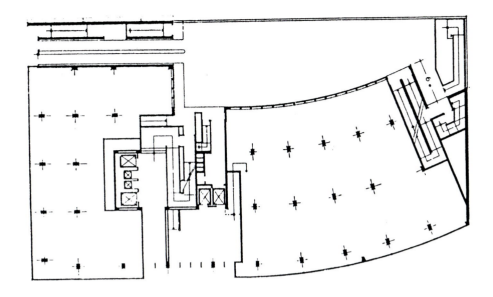

Columbushaus, Berlin, ground floor plan, 1931.

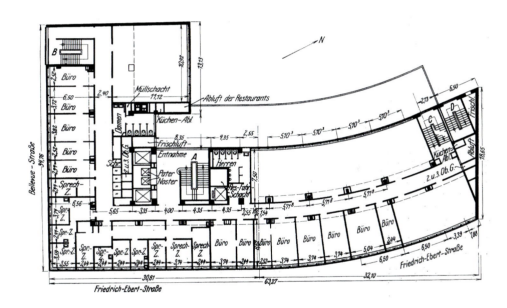

Columbushaus, Berlin, plan of second to sixth upper stories with typical interior arrangement, 1932. The steel supports were incorporated into the facades, permitting the free arrangement of office spaces.

site area of 2,150 square meters. The lower basement level housed the central heating and ventilation systems, while the upper basement level accommodated the restaurant kitchen as well as a wine and beer taproom. On the ground floor were the entrances with large shop areas between them, projecting out beyond the building line on the rear side. The steel supports positioned behind the facades permitted the installation of large display windows. An additional restaurant occupied the first upper story, its large panorama windows overlooking the roaring traffic on Potsdamer Platz.

The plans and sections show a change from the first upper story to the second to sixth upper stories. In addition to the steel supports, three blocks with elevators, stairs, and restrooms are the defining constants of the plan. In the first upper story, however, the supports along the street fronts clearly stand behind the facades, while above they are flush. The interior spaces are interrupted only by a hallway formed by a double row of supports in the center. On the roof story,

the outer row of supports defines the wall of the roof terrace, while the sides toward the neighboring buildings are recessed to establish a transition to those structures.

The Columbushaus marks the final climax of Mendelsohn's oeuvre in Germany.[40] Not surprisingly, it was built at the same time as his private house Am Rupenhorn, and on October 1, 1932, he moved his office into the Columbushaus. Yet he was to be permitted only a short time in either of these high-tech buildings, having left Germany in March 1933.

Under the Nazis, the Columbushaus became the headquarters of the state tourist agency and the Berlin offices of significant industrial enterprises as well as the revenue office for Berlin-Mitte.[41] During the war, the Columbushaus was long spared damage, but in the air raid of February 3, 1945, it was hit and went up in flames. After the war, it was located in the Soviet-occupied sector of Berlin. In 1950, at the request of the magistrate of Greater Berlin, a million marks from the "Sonderprogramm für das Columbushaus" ("Special Program for the Columbushaus") were to finance its reconstruction as a department store of the state HO chain and seat of the chief finance committee. In November 1950, however, the Politburo suddenly halted the work.[42] An unfinished ruin, the building housed an HO shop and a Volkspolizei station until June 1953, when it was set on fire during a revolt and later demolished.

In his projects for downtown sites as in his department stores, Mendelsohn established the relation to the urban context with painstaking precision, paying attention to exposures and the direction of the winds as well as visual axes and other buildings in the immediate vicinity. Interestingly, however, this concern for context does not come to expression in the sketches; the latter show the buildings isolated, without any relation to their surroundings. By the late 1920s, Mendelsohn was able to completely dispence with ornamental accessories and expressive gestures, yet without neglecting his postulate of functional dynamics. The goal remained the same—only the language changed.

Notes p. 267.

The exhibition halls at the Zoological
Garden were designed by
Mendelsohn in 1927 but never realized. They were to accommadate
shops and offices as well as a projecting corner restaurant. The small round
tower at the corner was to facilitate the
mounting of illuminated letters on the
advertising surface.

Red Flag factory, perspective sketch
for powerhouse.

Soviet Buildings and Projects

In 1930 the socialist Alexander Schwab, writing under the pseudonym Albert Sigrist, commented: "The New Building has a Janus face. It is indeed both bourgeois and proletarian, high capital-istic and socialistic. One can even say autocratic and democratic."[1] He was specifically thinking of Mendelsohn, whom, he noted, had worked for the both the Mosse publishing company and the Soviet government. Trade union officials and Soviet functionaries, like the heads of publishing, manufacturing, and department store businesses, came to Mendelsohn for efficient and innovative architecture, and the architect, although his experiences in the Soviet Union led him to criticize its government, did not turn them away.

In 1925 a Soviet delegation visited Mendelsohn's office in Berlin. They requested that he expand a knitwear and hosiery factory for Leningrad's Textile Trust.[2] Mendelsohn was the first foreign architect to receive such an offer. It came, not because he was a Communist—he was not—but because the complex included two dyeworks and a bleaching facility for which the Soviets wanted to duplicate the innovative ventilation he had developed in the Steinberg, Herrmann & Co. hat factory in Luckenwalde. Although Mendelsohn eventually became so contemptuous of Soviet standards of construction and of the liberties taken with his design that he disavowed any connection with the Red Flag (Krasnoje Snamja) factory, he frequently published photographs of the model.[3]

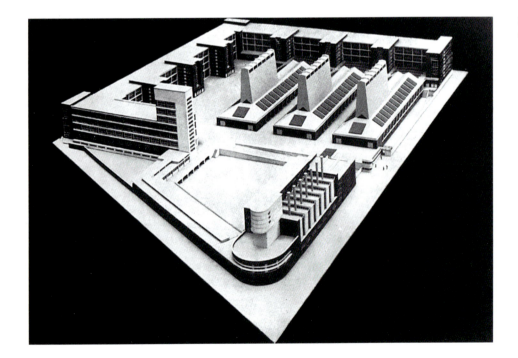

Red Flag factory, Leningrad, 1926, model.

Red Flag factory, Leningrad, 1925,
ground plan.

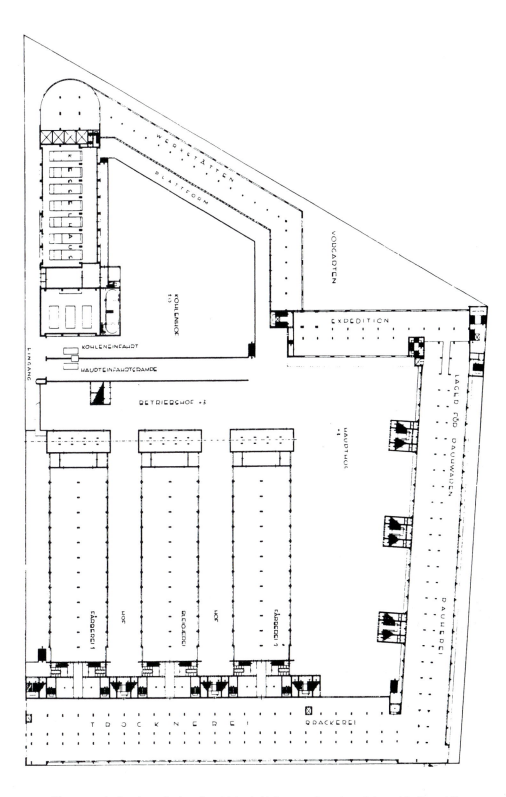

The commission for a factory in which eight thousand workers labored in two shifts was enormous; in collaboration with two consultants, Erich Laaser and an engineer named Salomonsen, the Mendelsohn office prepared hundreds of sheets of technical drawings.[4] Mendelsohn placed the main weaving facilities along the two interior edges of the site. Four stories tall, their regular facades were to be accented by extruded stair towers. Turning a corner, this factory block was transformed into offices. Within the arms of this sat two dyeworks and, between them, a bleaching facility, each featuring the ventilation stack Mendelsohn had developed for the hat factory in Luckenwalde. At the corner, the project was anchored by the powerhouse. All were to be built in reinforced concrete faced in brick.

Characteristically, Mendelsohn focused on the most urbanistically important aspects of the project without depicting any of this context in his sketches. In particular he set the two most prominent elements, the powerhouse and the tower of the shipping department, against each other to achieve his usual sense of dynamism. But it was the powerhouse that offered the most exciting opportunities. Located on a prominent corner, it is an early example of the architect's return to the curvilinear forms so prominently featured in his wartime sketches and in the Einstein Tower. In particular the play of rounded corner against a strong vertical accent anticipates the design of the Universum Cinema.

The Red Flag commission took Mendelsohn to the Soviet Union once in 1925 and twice the following year.[5] There Mendelsohn resumed his friendship with El Lissitzky and met the Vesnin brothers, Konstantin Melnikov, and Alexei Shtshussev.[6] In 1926 he started planning what became his second book, *Russland—Amerika—Europa. Ein Architektonischer Querschnitt*.[7] Here and in his private letters to his wife, he voiced his criticisms of a country from whose architects he was nonetheless to learn a great deal. Mendelsohn's experiences in Moscow and Leningrad made him distrust the government. More than an abstract political critique, his abhorrence of the Soviet system was based on its inability to better the lives of its citizens. "Russia, the former colossus with clay feet, lives today from its heart after chopping off its feet for, rather than continuing to vegetate, it preferred to cripple itself." The country was too busy, he continued, keeping alive the flame of revolution through dictatorship and too little concerned with freedom for the people.[8] Furthermore, he found that despite the ultra-modern schemes proposed by the country's leading architects, Soviet construction was labor-intensive and largely unmechanized, a situation that he believed instead called for pragmatic designs which responded to these realities, as he himself would do when working in the British Mandate of Palestine in the 1930s.[9]

Competition entry for Palace of Soviets, Moscow, 1931, model.

Although the building itself was a disappointment, the Red Flag factory signaled Mendelsohn's international stature, while his firsthand knowledge of Soviet architecture established his authority in evaluating all of the strains of modernism familiar to his German audience. Furthermore, despite his willingness to work for revolutionaries, Mendelsohn continued to cherish above all the individual expression found in his design of the textile factory's powerhouse, a point that escaped those critics of modern architecture who attacked the style as Bolshevist.

The competition to design the Palace of Soviets definitively exposed the gap between the propaganda needs of the Soviet government and the aesthetic goals of Europe's most prominent modern architects. In 1931, the Soviet government invited nine foreign architects, including Walter Gropius and Le Corbusier as well as Mendelsohn to submit designs for what was intended to become Moscow's most prominent building, a hall housing two enormous auditoriums seating audiences of 15,000 and 5,900, as well as two smaller theaters.[10] Charged as well with capturing "the character of the epoch and the worker's desire to construct socialism" and creating "a monument of architectural art in the capital of the Soviet Union," Mendelsohn offered none of the overt symbolism of the winning entry by Boris Iofan, a skyscraper capped with a colossal statue of Lenin. Indeed, nothing about the surviving model, section drawing, or plan demonstrate the talent Mendelsohn had so frequently exhibited in his German buildings for advertising his patron's businesses. Instead, the somewhat bulbous form of the two halls, separated by a taller and rectilinear flytower, are curiously static examples of his characteristically curvilinear forms. Emphasizing function over image, Mendelsohn solved the technical aspects of the brief in a design that featured efficient circulation but did little to represent the cultural and political ambitions of the revolutionary state.

Notes p. 268.

"Even if the Berlin buildings had been well underway, I would have kept on fighting"
Small Buildings for the Jewish Communities in Tilsit, Königsberg, and Essen

Kathleen James

During the 1920s, German architects, most notably Otto Bartning and Dominikus Böhm, trans-formed the architecture of German churches by emphasizing the creation of community through the rituals of Christian worship over individual mystical experience.[1] Germany's Jews also embraced modern architectural forms and construction materials in buildings whose functions were not necessarily limited to the provision of sacred space.[2] Although the three buildings Mendelsohn erected during the Weimar Republic for specifically Jewish purposes were not widely published in the architectural press, they establish an important link between his first executed commission, a cemetery chapel in his hometown of Allenstein, and the synagogues that represent his most important contribution to the history of American architecture. The Lodge of the Three Patriarchs (Loge zu den Drei Erzvätern) in Tilsit (then on the East Prussian border with Lithuania and now the Russian city of Sovetsk) of 1925–26, the Jewish cemetery in his wife's hometown of Königsberg (now Kalingrad, Russia) of 1927–29, and the Jewish youth center in Essen of 1930–33, are also significant examples of the way in which Mendelsohn, who during these years specialized in commercial architecture, could adapt his talent for dynamic massing to suit commissions that called for greater restraint.[3]

The plan and program of the lodge in Tilsit indicate that, although there was a small syna-gogue on the second floor, this was above all a social hall. A ballroom with balconies for both audience and musicians dominated the first floor, which also included a lounge, cloakroom, toilets, and kitchen. On the mezzanine Mendelsohn placed a gaming room and a caretaker's apartment. Above were, in addition to the temple, a library and other community rooms, includ-

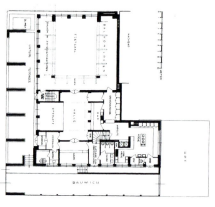

Lodge of the Three Patriarchs, Tilsit, ground floor plan, 1925–26.

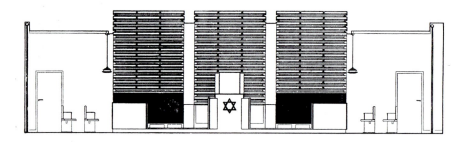

Lodge of the Three Patriarchs, Tilsit, interior elevations and plan of synagogue (second floor of Lodge).

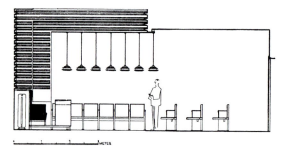
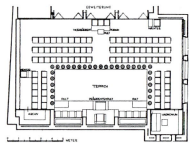

Lodge of the Three Patriarchs, Tilsit, corner view with alternating horizontal and vertical motifs.

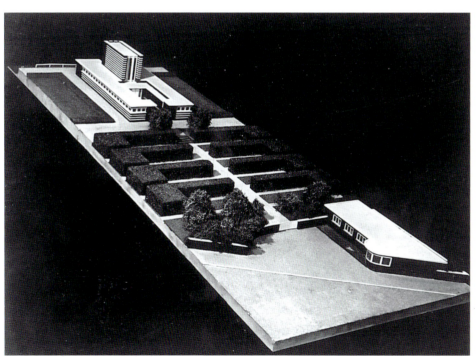

Jewish cemetery, Königsberg, view of model, 1927–29.

ing a separate one for women.[4] Mendelsohn arranged these functions almost domestically, creating an informal rather than ceremonial path through the building. One entered, as in Frank
Lloyd Wright's Unity Temple, along a path tucked parallel to the street, approaching the primary
interior space from the side rather than on axis.

Inside and out Mendelsohn eschewed symbolism; the only overt reference to the Jewish
faith was the Star of David he placed upon the lectern in the temple. This understatement,
true of all of his buildings for Germany's Jewish community, has several possible sources
in addition to the architect's resolutely modernist aesthetic. The second commandment's
restriction against graven images continued to constrain Jewish interest in representational
religious art. More importantly, although during the Weimar Republic Germany's Jews were
more active in the country's political, economic, and cultural life than ever before, they also
faced mounting anti-Semitism as Nazis and other right-wing nationalists made them scape-
goats for the country's defeat during the First World War and for the political and economic

crises that ensued. In this climate, few of the religious buildings German Jews erected during the 1920s demonstrate the self-confidence of such late Wilhelmine synagogues as the one Edmund Körner built in Essen between 1908 and 1914, Germany's largest, or its counterparts in cities like Cologne and Frankfurt.[5]

Until reaching America, Mendelsohn largely avoided in his religious commissions the bold curves that once again became a prominent feature in his work during the second half of the 1920s. The Lodge of the Three Patriarchs was no exception. In sharp contrast to the direct relationship Mendelsohn was creating during these same years between pedestrians and shop windows, here terraces and loggias buffered the building from the two streets it faced. And yet the corner is one of his most complex compositions, as the play of vertical brick bands against horizontal windows, and of the projecting corner of the Stiftstrasse facade in opposition to the recessed upper story on Fabrikstrasse, replaced history and ornament in establishing a commanding presence.[6]

Mendelsohn's design of a Jewish cemetery in Königsberg is unusual, above all as the only known example of his work as a landscape architect, and for the strong axial planning, which—if not unprecedented—remained unusual in his mature work. The city's Jewish community was small—only 3,500 in 1933—but diverse enough to support five synagogues.[7] Königsberg's second Jewish burial ground was located on Steffeckstrasse, on the city's western edge.[8]

Jewish cemetery, Königsberg, consecration hall. The focus of this space was a tall stained-glass window designed by Carl Grossberg in an abstract pattern of deep brown, blue, and gold.

A low-key entrance pavilion contained a flowershop, a gardener's apartment, and administrative space.[9] An allée, flanked on both sides by spaces for graves, led from here directly to the main building. In Mendelsohn's perspective drawings, drawn from the side, this building appears to float above the landscape, an effect that was accentuated in the finished building by the same projecting bands of bricks he had used in Tilsit, but the symmetrical entrance elevation was appropriately sober.

Built like its Tilsit counterpart of stone and steel, with stucco and brick facing and wooden window frames, this small pavilion provided rooms for the ritual washing of the dead. The simplicity of the three-aisled consecration hall impressed the critic Curt Horn, who included it in an essay on contemporary church buildings: "A chancel, flanked by two great illuminated columns, and a lively colored window in abstract forms are the only appointments furnishing this room, that in other respects only through its happily proportioned compelling masses."[10] The window, designed by Carl Grossberg, was also published in *Die Form*.[11] In one of the few continuities between his German and American work, Mendelsohn at the end of his life reused the motif of a projecting rectangular roof with a clerestory window positioned in the resulting pediment-like space over the entrance in his Mount Zion synagogue in St. Paul, Minnesota.

Both of Königsberg's Jewish cemeteries and four of its synagogues were destroyed in 1938 on Kristallnacht, the same day on which, on the opposite end of the country, Mendelsohn's final German building, a Jewish youth center in Essen, was torched by the Nazis.[12] Rabbi Hugo Hahn had got the idea for this center from Christian counterparts who had made ministering to young people an important aspect of German religious life in the 1920s. Pastors, priests, and rabbis alike sought to counter the influence of cafés and cinemas among adolescents who increasingly spent their time together independent of their families.[13] Located almost within sight of Bartning's Round or Resurrection Church and only a few blocks from Böhm's St. Engelbert Church, the youth center comprised one of a trio of buildings that made the city's Rüttenscheid neighborhood a showpiece of modern religious architecture.

Jewish youth center, Essen,
exterior, ca. 1933.

In Essen, as in Tilsit, secular uses predominated, with a dining hall, kitchen, library, music room, meeting rooms, and gymnasium—the last doubling as an auditorium—overwhelming the small chapel in importance. This range of activities, along with the example of Bartning's circular church, may have been what encouraged Mendelsohn to abandon the strict rectilinearity of his earlier religious buildings. The presense of a semicircular, single-story wing fronting Ruhrallee backed by a characteristically contrapuntal play of vertical stair tower against horizontal bands of windows nonetheless failed to dramatize the building's steel frame with the boldness displayed, for instance, in Columbushaus, his commercial commission of the same date.

Few in number and small in size, Mendelsohn's buildings for Jewish communities in Germany were but a minor aspect of his wide-ranging architectural practice during his Berlin years. The focus in two out of three cases on the social rather than ritual dimension of Judaism was appropriate for a Zionist well aware of the limits of assimilation but whose independence from a wide range of confining traditions encompassed religious orthodoxy as well as architectural eclecticism. No architectural forms, whether understated or dynamic, sacred or secular, could in the end shield the way of life these buildings were intended to nurture. The earliest of Mendelsohn's works to be demolished, their destruction pales in the face of the extinction of the communities they served.

Notes p. 268.

"One of the most lovable people and at the same time one of the most unpleasant"
Mendelsohn and His Assistants in the 1920s and Early 1930s

Regina Stephan

Erich Mendelsohn believed in the principle of the division of labor and worked unusually closely with highly qualified assistants, to whom he entrusted nearly the entire task of transforming his design sketches into building plans. His assistants thus played a central role in the success of the office; at the same time, however, Mendelsohn himself remained the sole responsible designer and undisputed chief of staff. Initial attempts to cooperate with partners failed.

Louise Mendelsohn described her husband's working method as follows: "Although Eric never worked in an office he always told his students that they needed that type of experience. There were many practical things that he never learned, such as detailing of windows and so on, and in these matters he had to rely on his own assistants. . . . He was always doing something that had never been done before—not that he necessarily wanted it that way, but because it just had to be that way. He would then have great difficulty executing his ideas, and that was where his more mechanically minded assistants came in. Often the engineers and draftsmen had a hard time accepting Eric's ideas. When that happened Eric would say, 'It must be done and it can be done'—even when he himself did not understand how it would be done. . . . Eric always hired people who were willing to experiment and to help execute designs the way he wanted them. Frank Lloyd Wright worked in much the same way, and by hiring talented and flexible engineers they could invent by collaboration things which did not exist before."[1]

Mendelsohn's creative process, from the receipt of the commission to the execution of the building, attracted attention already in the 1920s. First of all he studied the site; in Louise's memorable description, "He would go to the site and study it for hours on end—he would notice which way the wind blew, where the sun was the hottest, what kind of views there were, what the surrounding buildings looked like, and so on."[2] Later, at home in his study, he prepared the design sketches.[3] "He liked peace and quiet and therefore liked to work at night. . . . He really was annoyed by most noises except music, which acted like a curtain between him and the outside world. He always did his creative work at home, not at the office. He would retire to his little cubicle, put on some Bach and begin to work. . . . Actually he did not put music on especially to sketch by, but it seemed that when music was playing he became more inspired to sketch."[4] The sketches themselves often make direct reference to the music of Bach, with the names of specific pieces noted on them.[5] Mendelsohn also frequently sketched on programs during a concert. Louise recalls: "Many of them were drawn during concerts we attended, which sometimes embarrassed me because his pencil made a little noise and people would turn to look at him." The same was true of the chamber music recitals the Mendelsohns gave in their home, at which Luise performed with Lili Kraus and Albert Einstein. She writes: "When we had chamber music in our home Eric would listen for a while, then all of a sudden he was no longer listening, but sketching."[6]

Almost all of his sketches are drawn as perspective views with low vanishing points. More infrequent are designs shown from a bird's-eye view. The buildings are usually rendered on a small scale, presumably due to the architect's poor eyesight. After the removal of a cancerous eye in late 1921, Mendelsohn had only one, likewise weak eye.

Suggestions of the urbanistic context of a building or atmospheric details such as trees, clouds, or people are virtually nonexistent in Mendelsohn's sketches from the years before 1933. Equally seldom are representations of architectural details. In his sketches, Mendelsohn clearly sought to explore the architectural whole and the articulation of its parts as a dynamic spatial unity. The details were developed only much later. Usually, the sketches show a number of variations for a particular project, framed and separated from each other by large curving strokes. Ground plan sketches are very infrequent. Once the desired form had been achieved, Mendelsohn strictly adhered to it.

The transposition of sketches into building plans was the job of Mendelsohn's assistants. Julius Posener, who worked for the architect in Berlin and Jerusalem, gives a vivid description of this process: "Arriving in the morning, the assistants responsible for the various parts of a project would find a sketch on their drawing board, which they were to transpose into a construction drawing. Around the middle of the morning, Mendelsohn would appear and discuss the project with the assistants."[7] At that point, Mendelsohn would decide upon the subsequent course of work. Posener described this too: "I . . . learned that he was really the man of the rapid sketch, but that he watched over the transformation of this sketch into detailed building plans with almost painful meticulousness."[8] Mendelsohn's extreme perfectionism was described by the architectural draftsman Hans Bernhard Reichow: "I have seen him take a design that had already been worked out to a scale of 1:50 and consign it to the wastebasket, because something better had occurred to him over the weekend."[9] Understandably, such conditions were not always easy. Architects who had their own ideas about design and wanted to work with him on an equal footing remained for only a limited time. Mendelsohn could brook no partners in his office.

In early November 1918, Mendelsohn opened his office in Berlin and began to consistently and adroitly disseminate his architectural ideas through exhibitions, lectures, and publications.[10] Already in 1919, he engaged Arthur Korn to supervise the construction of his first commission, the residential development in Luckenwalde. He had met Korn, only two years younger than himself, in the Novembergruppe. Mendelsohn, however, was not satisfied with Korn's work and even perceived it as interfering with his design.[11] After only six months, the collaboration was terminated by mutual agreement. Nonetheless, Korn viewed this short time as very important: "I owe my entire later development to Mendelsohn."[12] In 1922, Korn opened his own architectural practice with Siegfried Weitzmann. Together, they realized a series of interesting commissions in Berlin, including the Haus der deutschen Turnerschaft (German Athletic Club, 1922–24), the Goldstein house (1922–24), the Wasservogel house (1924), and the store renovation for Kopp and Firle (1924), as well as the Fromm rubber factory in Köpenick (1930–34). In 1924, Korn received unusually unequivocal praise from Paul Westheim: "The name of one young architect will be remembered: *Arthur Korn*. . . . Korn differs from most of the others who are working toward a new architecture in Germany . . . in that he does not take on problems, but knows how to formulate them in the first place. . . . Korn once said that today he has the ability to hold a large slab with a single lateral point of support, i.e., he no longer needs four pillars to bear a 'load.' To cling to a statically unnecessary system of supports would be insipidity or empty talk."[13] In June 1919, Mendelsohn hired the draftsman and construction supervisor Petzold, who remained until the office was dissolved in 1933 and was to become one of Mendelsohn's mainstays.[14]

In 1921, when the commission for the Einstein Tower entered the decisive phase, Mendelsohn added a number of assistants to his staff. One of them was another architect from the Novembergruppe: Heinrich Kosina, who had come to Berlin from the Kunstgewerbeschule in Vienna. He assisted Mendelsohn in the details of the Einstein Tower, but was unable to satisfy

The sculptor Paul Rudolf Henning. His artistic temperament and unreliability were the cause of numerous conflicts with Mendelsohn.

him. After a visit to the tower, Mendelsohn stated: "What I did not do on my own is immediately apparent. That should not be the case at all; the lines of the stairway, in particular, are unclear— not in the arrangement, but only in the formal execution. Kosina's fault!"[15] Only a year later, Kosina set up his own office after winning the competition "Lufthafen Berlin" ("Airport Berlin").[16] He described the procedure in Mendelsohn's office: "His perspective sketches were so precise . . . that the draftsman Pilzing . . . could enlarge them with a 'laterna magica' and trace them in charcoal."[17] Later, Kosina produced buildings including a commercial structure for Adler-Auto-mobilwerke as well as private houses and residential developments in the early 1930s.[18]

In October 1921, inspired by the plans for the Luckenwalde hat factory, Richard Neutra answered an advertisement and applied for a position in Mendelsohn's office. At that time Mendelsohn was in desperate need of help, since his serious eye operation had necessitated a number of weeks of recovery. Like Kosina, Neutra came from Vienna, where he had previously worked with Otto Wagner and Adolf Loos. Mendelsohn valued him highly and entrusted him with the design of the details on the additional stories of the Rudolf Mosse publishing house and the office of Hans Lachmann-Mosse as well as the surroundings of the Einstein Tower.[19] The collaboration was very fruitful. In August 1922, they discussed a possible partnership, which Neutra desired as a prerequisite for marriage. Mendelsohn was skeptical for two reasons: first of all, he wanted to gain his school friend Charles Du Vinage for the office, but at the same time—and probably more important—he wished to maintain final control over the design process. The latter is made clear in a letter to Luise: "For the future . . . the association with Ch[arles] would be a good safeguard—Ch. would naturally agree to things to which I could no longer obligate N[eutra] in the long run, even in a close partnership. He is much too much of the Jewish intelligentsia for that, and racially not capable enough of sacrifice. In terms of my feelings, I am naturally far more disposed to Ch. . . . Reason speaks for N., because at the moment he is indispensible. . . ."[20] Shortly thereafter, Mendelsohn decided against Neutra: "It is quite certain that he is not the ideal and at this point I do not want *any* partnership. My nature would not be able to endure it in the long run."[21] The collaboration ended with a contract obliging Neutra to refrain from setting up his own office in Berlin for three years.[22] A letter to his fiancée, Dione, in July 1922 contains Neutra's clear-headed analysis of the situation: "Mendelsohn has made a tremendous career all by himself, has made a name for himself and has connections. He needs much technical help and he can always find it when he pays a fee. He is and can be choosy. He is financially independent and has a well organized office above all probability. . . . His proposals show a higher regard for me than whatever flattering words he could tell me. That he makes such ridiculously difficult conditions to prevent me becoming his competitor . . . is of course also flattering for me. So I have all reasons to be in good spirits."[23] Subsequently, Neutra left Germany and went to work with Frank Lloyd Wright in Chicago. In 1926, he set up his own office in Los Angeles and became one of the most important representatives of the International Style. Richard Döcker, Hans Scharoun, and Hugo Häring all sought to take his place in Mendelsohn's office; Mendelsohn, however, could not bring himself to hire any of them on a permanent basis.[24]

In late 1921, E. A. Karweik applied as construction supervisor with Erich Mendelsohn. He became one of the architect's most invaluable assistants, supervising the execution of numerous projects ranging from the silk store in Gleiwitz to the Columbushaus. He describes the way in which the details of the projects were worked out: "Mendelsohn's design procedure was essentially such that he began by sketching. Then, a plasticine model was produced. On this basis, corrections and new sketches were made and the facades designed. Later came the plaster model, etc." When Karweik arrived, Richard Neutra was serving as architect in chief; Karweik

Heinrich Kosina was a member of the Novembergruppe and worked on the Einstein Tower as Mendelsohn's assistant.

Mendelsohn's best friend was Charles Du Vinage, nicknamed "das grosse Heimattier" ("the old home fellow"). Here he appears at center, to the right of Mendelsohn.

In the summer Mendelsohn traveled regularly to southern Germany, including the Ammersee, Lake Constance, and Herrlingen near Ulm.

later described Mendelsohn as a seeker "for new forms, new materials. . . . What he sought was not the generally acceptable form, but the unique form, his form. There were many discussions about this in the office."[25] Only in 1932, when radical reductions in staff became necessary due to the precarious economic situation, did Karweik leave Mendelsohn's office and set up his own practice with Charles Du Vinage.

Charles Du Vinage was a school friend of Mendelsohn's from Allenstein who worked for him beginning on September 1, 1922. He had been a major in World War I and was now in search of a new beginning. Without great artistic ambitions of his own, he became Mendelsohn's right-hand man. He was entrusted with the organization and probably also the business management of the office. With the arrival of Charles Du Vinage, the core team of the office was complete. Petzold, Karweik, and Du Vinage—whom Mendelsohn himself referred to as "the old faithfuls"[26]—worked for him until the dissolution of his office in 1933. In early 1925, Mendelsohn considered making Du Vinage a partner; in the end, however, he decided against it, as the following passage from a letter makes clear: "Charles himself has retreated from the status of aspiring partner to 'mere assistant.' I cannot change my nature for love—even a childhood love."[27]

In 1923, the office found itself in a difficult situation with commissions declining due to unchecked inflation. Mendelsohn was forced to consider "whether circumstances do not compel us to further reduce the office staff. If there is nothing to build, the overhead costs cannot remain the same."[28] Only after the currency reform and a steady increase in commissions after 1924 could he think of expanding his office. The building projects, scattered over the entire country, required Mendelsohn to hire construction supervisors to represent him on site. While Mendelsohn generally conducted the negotiations with local authorities and clients in person, he entrusted the supervision of the construction work to assistants. Rudolf Overberg and the construction supervisor Heibeck, of whom nothing further is known, worked in this capacity in Nuremberg, Duisburg, and Stuttgart. Overberg also served as business manager in Mendelsohn's absence, as is documented for late 1927 and early 1928. Hans Bernhard Reichow and Joseph Neufeld worked on the Stuttgart Schocken store, H. Arnade worked on the Petersdorff department store in Breslau, and Ernst Sagebiel worked on the Metal Workers' Union building and the Columbushaus in Berlin. In addition, the staff of the Berlin office also included a number of draftsmen to transpose the sketches into building plans, such as Johannes Schreiner and Gunter Ascher, who later worked for Mendelsohn in London and Jerusalem as well. A document of December 1933 contains Mendelsohn's evaluation of Schreiner's work in the context of efforts to obtain a work permit for him from the Ministry of Labour in London. In his application he wrote: "Mr. Schreiner has been my assistant for eight years, and has taken part in the preparation of all drawings in connection with the biggest projects of my practice, because his particular knowledge of modern steel and reinforced concrete constructions and his great practical experience and ability have specially recommended him for this position. For that reason Mr. Schreiner is almost essential to my work."[29]

Today, the exact number of assistants and the organization of the staff can no longer be determined, as the office records from Mendelsohn's Berlin years have been lost. In general, we may assume that at the height of his success around 1928, his office numbered among the largest architectural practices in Europe with a staff of around forty.[30] Mendelsohn's assistants were rewarded for his success with higher-than-average salaries. Occasionally, Luise Mendelsohn worked in the office as well, mailing photographs of projects to publications all over the world.[31]

Ernst Sagebiel worked for Mendelsohn from 1929 to 1932 and served as chief construction supervisor for the last two major projects in Berlin, the Metal Workers' Union building and the

Columbushaus. Later in the 1930s, Sagebiel was to place the technical achievements of the Neues Bauen at the service of the Third Reich. His most famous buildings are the Reichsluftfahrtministerium on Leipziger Strasse (1935–36), the Berlin-Tempelhof airport (1936–41), and the Stuttgart airport (1936–38).

Julius Posener described the climate in Mendelsohn's office from the perspective of a young assistant: "I worked for E. M. in the summer of 1931 in Berlin, on the Columbus-Haus. First in the office, at that time still in Westend, then at the construction site. Then in thirty-three, I worked for him in Jerusalem, in the office. On both occasions I found him authoritarian. One could have a very nice conversations with E. M.—outside of office hours. He also had something like a hierarchy in the office, which manifested itself especially in Berlin. There was the inner circle, at the very center Duvinage, whom he had known already in Allenstein. In the office they called him 'das grosse Heimattier' ('the old home fellow'). Then came a group of assistants such as Sagebiel, who later became a famous Nazi architect. Karweik, the top construction supervisor, and others. . . . In Berlin the atmosphere was even more Prussian than in Jerusalem. I have to say . . . if I may describe it from the perspective of an assistant, that his person aroused antipathy in us, even a certain contempt on account of the marked pencils and the whole fuss of achievement with which he flattered himself. At the same time we admired him. In the end, we felt grateful to him . . . which had to do with the culture of the man. He was one of the most lovable people I have ever met—and at the same time one of the most unpleasant."[32] Sagebiel as an established architect, however, perceived the situation differently: "E. M. was generally much appreciated among the assistants for his unpretentious behavior and tactful respect for the personality of each helper. He possessed great pedagogical gifts."[33]

Concerning the office, Louise wrote: "Eric's most productive building period was between 1920 until we left Berlin in 1933—thirteen years of uninterrupted hard work. His architectural office was the largest in Germany. He had excellent and highly paid assistants, over whom he

Esther, Luise, and Erich Mendelsohn in St. Moritz, probably 1929.

The construction office for the Stuttgart Schocken store, ca. 1927. To the left is construction supervisor Rudolf Overberg, and in the middle Joseph Neufeld, who later emigrated to Palestine.

This undated card made fun of the rapid pace in Mendelsohn's office: "Donnerwetter, Donnerwetter: Bureau Mendelsohn – 10 Entwürfe innerhalb 10 Minuten" ("By Jove! Mendelsohn office—10 designs within 10 minutes").

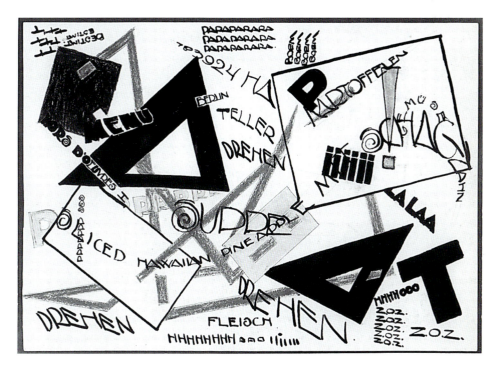

exerted strict control. He went so far that he kept account of the pencils and did not permit the slightest waste, though this was no sign of lack of generosity. He was a most generous man. It was an excellently organized office and I cannot remember any discord of importance. Architects were not unionized and, if they wanted, they could stay as long as they liked in the evenings. Eric was very spoiled in this respect. For the Leningrad job, everybody stayed and worked until midnight on a voluntary basis."[34]

The office moved repeatedly from 1918 to 1933.[35] For Mendelsohn, his architectural practice was more than an office, as Louise reported: "One can almost say that Eric Mendelsohn lived in his office. He even slept there frequently."[36] Finally, on October 1, 1932, he was able to move his office into the Columbushaus, a building he himself had designed—only to give it up again already in March 1933.

Tragically, Mendelsohn's closest assistant and childhood friend Du Vinage was the final catalyst for the Mendelsohns' emigration on March 31, 1933. Louise writes: "Another experience also stirred us deeply. Eric's birthday on March 21st approached and, with it, the traditional Bach celebration. All our musician friends assembled. The friend who used to be the first one to appear usually, and who was a great Bach lover, just as we were, did not arrive until very late. We had been waiting for him nervously. When he did arrive, we found his whole personality drastically changed, he seemed very excited. Eric asked him what happened. . . . He apologized for being so late but he had been in Potsdam to take part in the rebirth of the Prussian army in the presence of Hindenburg and, as he emphatically said, 'I have seen the Fuehrer.' Of course this was Hitler. His eyes were glowing, he seemed deeply excited."[37]

From a technical point of view, the buildings planned and executed by Mendelsohn's office from 1918 to 1933 were highly innovative and received extensive coverage in the architectural press. Particular attention was paid to the extremely short construction periods, which helped reduce the client's building costs. Even today, it is amazing to consider that the renovation of the Schocken store in Nuremberg, from the initial demolition work to the grand opening, was completed within nine months, the Petersdorff department store within seven months, the two new buildings for the Schocken company in Stuttgart and Chemnitz as well as the Metal Workers' Union building within ten months each, and the ten-story Columbushaus within a year.

This rapid pace was made possible by a six-day work week for all staff as well as extensive travels by Mendelsohn himself and the use of the most modern building techniques. These new construction methods were highly prized by the clients, as well, for two reasons: first because they minimized losses during the construction period, and second because the innovative buildings served as synonyms for innovative business practices, as the expression of modern commercial management.

An additional means of limiting the client's losses during the building period were Mendelsohn's attractive construction fences, which closed gaps, protected passersby from dirt and danger, and provided advertising space for the client, architect, and contractors. The largest and most advertising-effective construction fence was that of the Columbushaus, which even accommodated rented shop spaces and the construction supervisor's office.

As we have seen, the success of Mendelsohn's office was based on a variety of factors. Nonetheless, it was decisive that the architect's own abilities—acquiring commissions, designing, structuring, negotiating, persuading—were perfectly complemented by his assistants' skill in constructing, detailing, and executing.

Notes p. 269.

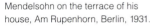

Julius Posener worked in the Mendelsohn office in Berlin as well as in Palestine in the 1930s. Photo taken in 1940 in Jerusalem.

Mendelsohn on the terrace of his house, Am Rupenhorn, Berlin, 1931.

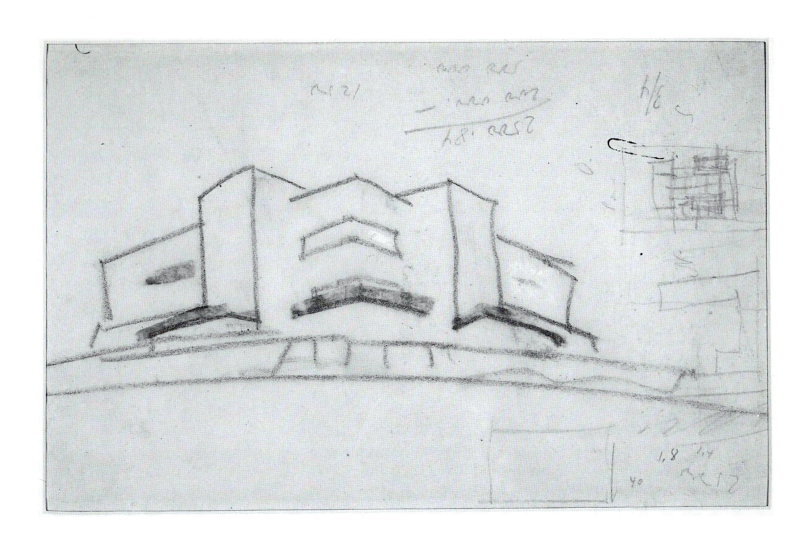

Double Villa at Karolingerplatz, Berlin,
sketch, 1921.

"The same means, the same end"
Private Houses in Berlin and the Influence of Frank Lloyd Wright

Regina Stephan

The private houses built by Mendelsohn in Berlin in the 1920s represent a peripheral theme in his work, both because of their small number—a total of only five—and their relatively small building volume. Without exception, the commissions came from the circle of Jewish academics with whom the Mendelsohns had associated since the lectures at Molly Philippson's salon. All but one of the houses were built in Westend, a villa district of Charlottenburg in southwest Berlin. With convenient access to the city center via the elevated railway and Heerstrasse, Westend offered fine suburban living with all the amenities of the big city.[1] Together with other villa districts such as Lichterfelde, Friedenau, Grunewald, and Zehlendorf, it formed part of a green belt surrounding the metropolitan area of Berlin with its population of millions. Before receiving his first commission for a villa in 1921, however, Mendelsohn had briefly devoted himself to a project for a residential development.[2]

Waldsiedlung
In spring 1920, the architect Erwin Gutkind approached Mendelsohn with a project for a *Waldsiedlung* (wooded residential development). The only references to the project are found in Mendelsohn's letters. "I have just come from Gutkind. He had invited me to discuss a residential project he has thought up for himself and us and a small circle. At this point it is only a wish, arising more from fear of an insufficient budget than from inner resolution. . . . First he has to find cheap and attractive sites, and then he will come again."[3] Shortly thereafter Mendelsohn reported: "Meanwhile Gutkind and I are planning a residential development for next spring—in Dahlem or near the Grunewald railway station. Beuster has promised us cheap land and subsidies. The conditions are that the situation has halfway stabilized and that we keep within our budget."[4] Once again plans changed, as Mendelsohn wrote to his wife: "A new plan: a development in Dreilinden near the Wannsee. Woods, hills, and waterfront property for a very low price. I am very much in favor of it, if enough residents can be drummed up. I think the location completely outside the city will be very nice for our life in every respect, and it can be managed with the office as well. We will inspect the site for the first time a week from tomorrow. By then, Gutkind will have inquired concerning the price and the availability of subsidies. I am letting him take care of those things, since they are inessential to the design, and even that is only interesting to me for the sake of our own future life."[5]

In 1920—probably because of the deteriorating economic situation, but also because of the site's considerable distance from the city center—the project was discontinued.[6] With it, Mendelsohn's interest in participating in the design of a residential development in Germany ended as well.[7] Only in 1935 in England did he once again devote himself to such a project: the likewise unrealized "White City" planned near London.

The Double Villa at Karolingerplatz
Mendelsohn's first villa dates to 1921, and it is interesting that here, as well, he considered using part of the Double Villa for himself and his family. Obviously during this period he was seeking an alternative to the Westend boarding house of Fräulein von Rebay, where the Mendelsohns had

Double Villa at Karolingerplatz, Berlin,
corner view, 1922.

rented three rooms, at first only for a limited time. Yet he was also reluctant to take on the responsibility of his own household. The first building application of September 1921 for the Double Villa at Karolingerplatz, only a few steps away from the office on Ahornallee 25, names the clients: Dr. Kurt Heymann and Erich Mendelsohn. Already in late 1925, however, Mendelsohn sold his share of the unfinished structure to Dr. Theo Meyer.[8]

This building, too, met with resistance from the authorities. As Mendelsohn wrote to his wife in summer 1921: "The Charlottenburg building office has raised objections to the house at Karolingerplatz, 'how such a thing could be hindered in the future'! As if one could turn back the clock. I referred the building commissioner to his 'big brother' in Berlin and advised him to abandon all hope of deterring me. Beer brains like to flaunt their power, since they are faint in spirit."[9] By this point, the building was near completion, making it a strange time indeed for the municipal authorities to articulate their objections. In another letter dated only slightly later, Mendelsohn described his primary concern with this building: "The Karolinger corner is becoming ever more amusing, the fence is standing, it's beginning to dawn on people."[10]

In fact, the corner situation at Karolingerplatz is of central significance for the Double Villa. The site itself was the point of departure for the design, as the surviving sketches clearly show. The plot is bounded by two streets meeting at nearly a right angle, its cut-off point oriented toward Karolingerplatz. The architect's concern was to tailor the design to this location while ensuring privacy for both families, even under a single roof.

Mendelsohn responded to this problem with an interesting solution. As always, his primary concern was the design of the street facade; only later did he puzzle out the arrangement of the living spaces within the angular exterior form. The latter consists of two wings running parallel to the streets, meeting at Karolingerplatz in nearly a right angle. The wings recede stepwise at the center, creating an open space behind the garden fence. The fence, which continues around the corner at a 45-degree angle, plays an important role in the overall effect of the building. Together

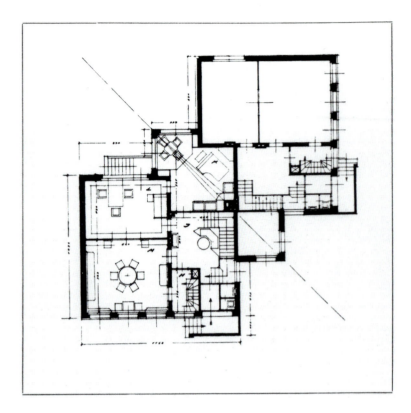

Double Villa at Karolingerplatz, Berlin, ground floor plan, 1921. The diagonal line marks the central axis of the "symmetrical complex," as Mendelsohn conceived the building.

with the unconventional use of materials on the facades, it helps lead the eye past the breaks in the exterior form that were necessary for the function, but not ideal for the design.

In a reversal of traditional facade design, the street side on the ground floor is covered with rough, light-colored plaster up to the window sills of the first upper story. The upper stories, in contrast, are faced with conspicuous red-brick masonry. This device enabled Mendelsohn to enliven the exterior skin of the building and intensify the effects of light and shadow. An additional roof story with attic spaces and access to a roof garden creates further height at the center of the Double Villa, which springs back and then forward again.

As the ground plan reveals, the Double Villa consists of two overlapping squares[11] with additional quadratic spaces inserted between them, one for each of the two dwellings. The two halves of the building differ in area by fifteen square meters per story, an imbalance clearly visible in the plan of the fire wall running through the house at a right angle. Thus on the interior, the symmetry of the complex is abandoned in favor of increased functionality.

While the exterior is highly innovative in its spatial design and surface texture, the dwelling spaces are arranged and used in an entirely conventional manner. The basement level accommodates the kitchen as well as storage and maids' rooms, the ground floor the living, music, and dining rooms, the first upper story the sleeping area, and the second upper story the attic spaces. Nowhere in the building do flowing, continuous spaces occur.

For the half of the house belonging to Kurt Heymann, Erich Mendelsohn also designed the furniture of the vestibule, bedrooms, and dressing rooms as well as a buffet. A design sketch of the latter has survived. With its conical legs and projecting sides, the furniture shows numerous similarities to that of the Einstein Tower. While the furniture in the Rudolf Mosse publishing house was the work of Richard Neutra, that of the Double Villa was unquestionably designed by Mendelsohn.[12]

A variety of influences is visible in the design of the building. Muthesius's angular villas in Berlin, which Mendelsohn certainly knew, are early examples of such complexes; they, in turn, were based on buildings of the English Arts and Crafts movement, with which Muthesius had become acquainted and on which he had published a three-volume work.[13] The design of the facades shows the influence of the Amsterdam School, whose representatives Mendelsohn had known at the latest since his first visit to Holland in early 1921 and who had long worked with material combinations of plaster and brick. Particularly important in this connection are Willem Marinus Dudok and Michel de Klerk, with whom Mendelsohn cultivated an intensive exchange of ideas.[14] Today, the Double Villa still stands at Karolingerplatz, largely unaltered on the exterior; as the villa has changed hands many times, however, the furniture designed by Mendelsohn has been lost.

The Sternefeld Villa

In summer 1923, Mendelsohn began planning a villa for the medical doctors Ruth and Walter Sternefeld on Heerstrasse in the Westend district of Berlin. In one respect, at least, the design of the Sternefeld villa advanced far beyond the Double Villa that had preceded it: it was the first residence in Berlin to be constructed of reinforced concrete. Up to this point the new building material—which Mendelsohn had propagated for years—had been used only in factory and commercial buildings. Now Mendelsohn had found two clients who were prepared to allow experimentation with this method in the construction of a private house as well.[15] The villa, moreover, was to have a flat roof, likewise unusual for Germany. Thus in January 1923, Mendelsohn wrote to J. J. P. Oud, requesting him to send a section of the "roofing skin (waterproof) . . . as you use it in your buildings."[16] The proposed use of reinforced concrete delayed the issuance of the building permit until April 1924, and then only after modifications had been made in those elements planned in reinforced concrete.[17] Finally, in November of that year, the building was handed over to the client for use.

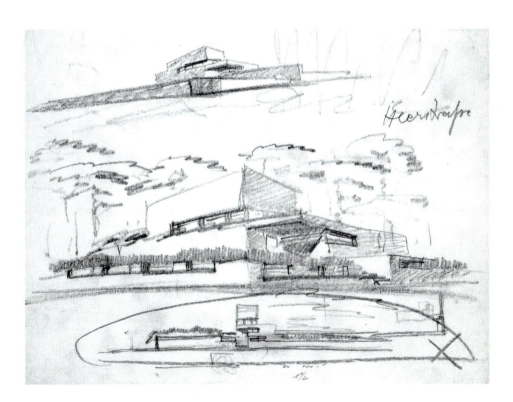

Sternefeld villa, Berlin, sketch, 1923.

Mendelsohn's ideas for this building are illustrated in four sheets of sketches. As in his other projects of 1923, the design is dominated by cubic forms combined with low, cantilevered slabs into a dynamic composition of complementary elements. Allusions to the painting of de Stijl are unmistakable. The building corners acquire particular significance, mediating between two views and at the same time establishing the boundaries between them. And—once again—the fence plays an important role as a base and therewith as an indispensable element of the architectural complex.

The ideal conditions of the level, rectangular site, planted with pine trees, were marred only by the municipal development plan of 1909, which called for the front corner of the plot to be cut off at an angle. This measure, however, was abandoned in early 1924 as a result of the project developed by Mendelsohn,[18] thus establishing the basis for the realization of a house that differed strikingly from the Double Villa. The latter had been dominated—at least on the exterior—by symmetry; now, however, Mendelsohn replaced the symmetry with a pronounced asymmetry in a move paralleling the development from the Rudolf Mosse publishing house and the Luckenwalde hat factory to the silk store in Gleiwitz. He justified this asymmetry, moreover, with reference to function: the villa was to accommodate not only the dwelling of the Sternefelds, but their medical practice as well, necessitating the division of the complex into public and private areas. This contrast is visible in the articulation of the garden into an open flower garden visible from the side street and a private garden with vegetables and flowers, enclosed by a high wall, as well as the use of the bearing wall of reinforced concrete to divide the ground floor into separate office and dwelling spaces. The two upper stories, on the other hand, were reserved for private use, culminating in an open roof courtyard enclosed by high walls for use as a sunbathing space, safe from the eyes of strangers.

The Sternefeld villa was the first single-family house in Berlin built of reinforced concrete.

Sternefeld villa, Berlin, plan of ground floor and first floor: on the ground floor, the office spaces for the doctor couple were located on the east side, while the dwelling areas with the terrace lay to the west.

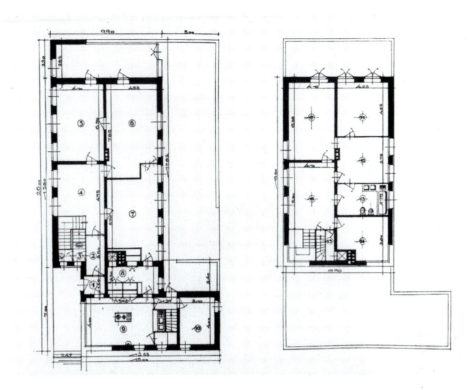

Toward Heerstrasse, the Sternefeld villa appeares closed and withdrawn.

On the exterior, the building was covered with rough plaster in combination with dark, hard-burned clinkers on the top edges of the walls, cornices, and stairs. The effect of the villa differs widely from varying points of view: from the street it appears closed and withdrawn, from the private garden open and inviting. Naturally, exposure plays a decisive role as well: the street front is oriented to the north, while the terrace in front of the living, dining, and music rooms faces west.

The conception of the villa was criticized early on, above all for the tenuous connection between exterior form and inner disposition. The placement of the windows is determined solely by exterior effect and reveals nothing of the arrangement of the interior; today, the building

Sternefeld villa, Berlin, entrance, 1924.

accommodates four dwellings rather than just one, while the exterior has remained almost the same. Even Mendelsohn himself is said to have noted the "preponderance of the formal" and suggested the remodeling of the roof story.[19] In 1932, the courtyard for sunbathing had to give way to a rented apartment, while the exterior west wall was opened up with a tight series of vertical rectangular windows. Thus only a few years after its completion, the character of a closed, cubic block was abandoned in favor of functional considerations.

The Sternefeld villa is considered the building by Mendelsohn most strongly influenced by the architecture of Frank Lloyd Wright.[20] Comparison with the structure often named as its inspiration, Wright's Robie house of 1909 in Chicago, reveals numerous similarities as well as fundamental differences. Common to both is the horizontal staggering of cubic building volumes, their illumination with horizontal bands of windows, and the close relation of interior and exterior spaces through terraces and balconies. For Wright as well, the garden wall constitutes an integral element of the building complex, inseparably connected to the house in its proportions and building materials. Fundamental differences, however, consist in Wright's use of slightly inclined, projecting roofs and, even more significantly, in the inner subdivision of the house. In the Robie house, the main dwelling spaces are located in the first upper story and flow into one another, both connected and separated by the fireplace in the middle. Mendelsohn, on the other hand, divided the interior of the Sternefeld villa into conventional rooms clearly distinguished from one another, in a manner far removed from Wright's principle of the open plan. Whether this arrangement primarily reflected the wishes of the clients remains uncertain. In any case, we may assume that Mendelsohn had long been aware of the significance of Wright's ground plans from various publications. During his visit to Chicago in November 1924, he analyzed Wright's development following visits to a number of his houses.

Back in Germany, he produced a number of articles and lectures responding to attacks on Wright,[21] works in which he vigorously defended the American architect: "His work stands in the midst of our time, and his negation of the traditional is thus entirely positive. His development from this idea occurs logically according to organic laws, even if, in the nature of the case, it is still without any inner compulsion to completely transform the new constructive material in a monumental sense. The organization of his buildings is exemplary; it is objective, free, open, moved. The richness of his formal ideas is inexhaustible, the harmony of his colors enchanting."[22] If we view these remarks in light of statements on the new architecture propagated by Mendelsohn in numerous lectures and essays, it becomes clear that he saw himself as seeking to continue the renewal of architecture initiated by Wright. For Mendelsohn, the appropriate use of the new material of reinforced concrete was an essential precondition of this development, and from this point of view the Sternefeld villa may indeed be seen as progressive, though in its inner arrangement it failed to incorporate Wright's innovations.

The Sternefeld villa was completely restored in the 1970s and on this occasion divided into four dwellings.

Villa Aron

Only recently has it been discovered that Mendelsohn planned and executed the renovation of a villa for the engineer and industrialist Manfred Aron. The house, located on Kastanienallee in Westend in Berlin, had originally been built in 1872 and later expanded in 1905.[23]

Like other works with which he was not satisfied, however, Mendelsohn never published the Aron villa, for which reason it has never appeared in the literature on the architect. To be sure, the project was an extremely thankless, unsatisfying one, since Mendelsohn was able only to free the facades of historicist ornamentation and make small modifications to satisfy contemporary aesthetic sensibilities. The interior, on the other hand, remained nearly unchanged. The villa, remodeled between February 1925 and February 1926, could never have satisfied Mendelsohn.[24]

Country House for Dr. Bejach

Mendelsohn, however, was obviously persuaded of the quality of his next single-family house, for he published it with numerous plans and photographs. The country house designed for Dr. Curt Bejach and his family was erected between August 1926 and December 1927 in Steinstücken, an exclave of Zehlendorf. Once again, the site was a very large, slightly inclined plot, bounded on its short sides by a residential street and a railway line.

The country house, though located far away from the street, was connected to it by a pergola at the right edge of the plot. The pergola led the visitor from the garden entrance to the house, positioned crosswise "for the sake of an east-west location."[25] Once again, he clearly distinguished between the public side of the house, oriented toward a lawn along the street, and the private rear side toward a "quiet garden." The entrance door was located on the side in the angle between the house and the projecting stairwell, which serves both to separate and to connect the two sides.

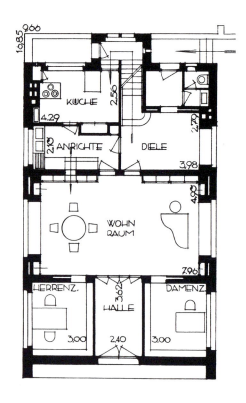 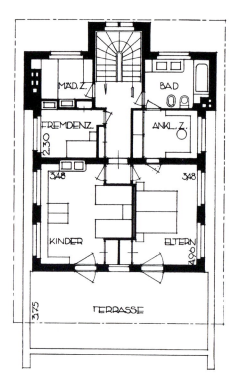 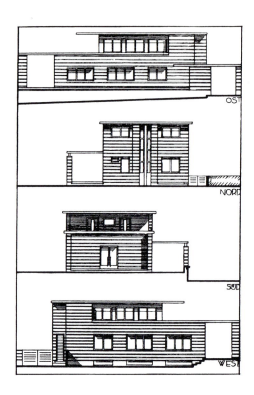

The two-story house has a markedly low-lying, horizontal character, which Mendelsohn reinforced with a number of motifs. Most important among them is the articulation of the facade in alternating strips of brick and light-colored plaster, a solution that harmoniously combines with the horizontal windows, terraces, and projecting roof slab to define the appearance of the building. The pergolas attached to the short sides of the house intensify this effect and make the building seem to occupy the entire width of the plot. In fact, however, the interior area is only 220 square meters, one of the smallest single-family houses—if not the smallest—that Mendelsohn ever built. His declared intention was to "expand the small house with pergolas." The original design as submitted with the first building application in August 1926 called for the living area on the ground floor to flow into a veranda. At the client's wish, however, the veranda was replaced by two smaller spaces, the ladies' and the gentlemen's rooms. This change is all the more regrettable since the veranda, with its southward orientation, would have been especially conducive to a lifestyle oriented entirely to nature. The interior arrangement, too, would have more closely approached the ideal of the open plan, at least on the ground floor. As it is, however, the disposition of the interior remains conventional.

As with all his previous single-family houses, Mendelsohn placed great emphasis on the unified design of house and garden wall. The latter, connected with the house, was conceived as part of the overall concept; in the end, the architect succeeded in ensuring its realization by threatening to put up a simple wire fence, "which would by no means provide a closure suitable to the value of the building, but would rather disfigure the street."[26]

All of these single-family houses, however, were only stages on the way to the planning of Mendelsohn's own house, about which he had been thinking for a long time and toward which he took concrete steps beginning in 1928. Am Rupenhorn, as the house was called, was to become the

Country house for Dr. Bejach, Steinstücken, ground floor, first floor, and the four elevations published by Erich Mendelsohn.

Country house of Dr. Bejach, Steinstücken. The unusual facade design shows alternating bands of plaster and brick on both house and pergola.

ideal dwelling, intimately connected with nature. There, the living spaces on the ground floor flowed into one another and, in the summer, into the terrace as well, fusing the whole into a single space for nature and dwelling with large windows that could be lowered completely.[27] Wright's Coonley house (1907–8), which Mendelsohn had seen in 1924, provided the inspiration ever afterwards for his own house: "Terraces with expansive views from every room into bushes still in bloom, the view toward the neighbors protected with projecting peninsulas of shrubbery. . . . Masterful, enchanting! That's the way our house should be!"[28]

Notes p. 269.

Success has many faces. In this chapter we are concerned not with the inner triumphs Mendelsohn enjoyed in his exploration of artistic form, but with the material, outwardly visible success that came to expression in numbers, property, and status. Success is the positive result of an effort, the attainment of a desired goal. With respect to his architecture, Mendelsohn took this kind of success for granted, and as far as his clients were concerned, no doubts were permitted to arise in the first place.

Each and every client received a complete "Mendelsohn," and the architect knew how to assess his own value. He asked for and received good money for his buildings—extremely good money, in fact, by the end of the 1920s. This income permitted him to build his "little palace," Am Rupenhorn, and enjoy the luxury of a staff of service personnel. In the garage stood a Mercedes he himself had designed, driven by a chauffeur.[1]

By the late 1920s, his office had become one of the largest architectural firms in Germany, with major commissions at home and abroad. In addition to his buildings in Germany, his oeuvre also included projects in Russia, Palestine, Spain, Norway, and Czechoslovakia, works that brought him international recognition.[2]

Mendelsohn was invited to lecture in Holland, America, England, France, and Denmark. In addition, his work was honored in exhibitions at well-known museums and galleries, with milestones such as the solo exhibition in the renowned Galerie Neumann-Nierendorf in Berlin in 1928 and his participation in the "Contempora" show of art and industry at the Art Center in New York in 1929. His buildings were presented to a larger audience in numerous publications, both his own and those of famous art and architecture critics such as Hermann Georg Scheffauer, Paul Westheim, and the Englishman Aldous Huxley. The prestigious journal *Wasmuths Monatshefte für Baukunst* devoted an entire issue to him in 1924, while the Dutch journal *Wendingen* had already discussed his sketches and first projects in Germany years before. Mendelsohn's *Gesamtschaffen* was published in 1930 in a special edition of the French magazine *L'Architecture vivante*, while the French critic Jean Badovici characterized him as one of the prophets of modern architecture.

In the late 1920s, Mendelsohn was awarded honorary membership in two renowned international associations: the International Association of Modern Architecture in Tokyo in 1927 and the Arts Club in London in 1930. One year later, in 1931, culture minister Adolf Grimme made him a member of the Prussian Academy of the Arts along with twelve other artists including Emil Nolde, Karl Schmidt-Rottluff, Otto Dix, Ernst Ludwig Kirchner, Ludwig Mies van der Rohe, Bruno Taut, and Martin Wagner. These are a few of the highlights of Mendelsohn's brilliant success during his Berlin period from 1919 to 1933.

Yet Mendelsohn was acquainted with the other side of success as well. As the president of the Prussian Academy of the Arts, Max Liebermann, once ironically stated: "I had too many enemies. Indeed, I was vulnerable on three fronts: first, I was a Jew; second, I was rich; and third, I had talent. Any one of these would have been enough."[3]

"Rupenhorn Club" soiree at the Hotel Esplanade, winter 1929–30. From left to right: Dr. Heymann, Renee Sommerfeld, Adolf Sommerfeld, Luise Mendelsohn, Fräulein von Kardoff-Oheimb, Herr Tuteur, Gräfin Tegtmayer, Graf Platen.

Illustration p. 171:
This sketch shows three views of the Mendelsohn villa Am Rupenhorn (1929–30). At top is the street side, with two views of the garden side below.

To be a Jew was one thing, but success had always been held against the Jews, and Mendelsohn was no exception. His triumphs and rich legacy have been successfully suppressed from certain quarters—during his lifetime, but even afterwards, to this very day.

Despite his renown and extensive architectural activity, Mendelsohn was repeatedly excluded from decisive events that today are considered milestones in the curriculum vitae of modern architecture. To name a few particularly striking examples, no works by Mendelsohn were shown at the 1927 Werkbund exhibition at Weissenhof in Stuttgart.[4] Nor did he number among the elite of Hélène de Mandrot. In 1928, the Congrés Internationaux d'Architecture Moderne (CIAM) was founded at de Mandrot's chateau at La Sarraz, Switzerland, without Mendelsohn, and he was not invited to participate in any of the group's further meetings. In 1932, Philip Johnson and Henry-Russell Hitchcock hindered Mendelsohn's participation in their "International Style" exhibition in the Museum of Modern Art in New York, while in 1941 Sigfried Giedion—one of the main protagonists in the founding of CIAM—actually managed to write his epoch-making book *Space, Time, and Architecture* without a single reference to Mendelsohn.

To this day, scholarly research has tended to neglect Mendelsohn's architecture. Apart from Bruno Zevi's foundational study of 1970 as well as books by Arnold Whittick and Wolf von Eckhardt, a handful of dissertations and masters' theses, and a few articles and chapters in architectural history books, the reception of Mendelsohn has by no means been appropriate to his stature.

The unbalanced and insufficient attention Mendelsohn has received is a symptom among other things of the obvious difficulty of placing and categorizing him. No "logical" line of stylistic development can be traced in Mendelsohn's architecture. His work has a relativistic character, reacting to its environment with the sensitivity of a seismograph. Mendelsohn registered and processed each new situation—whether of an urban, cultural, political, or psychological nature—for himself and his architecture. Dialogue, flexibility, and adaptation to new situations were integral elements of Erich Mendelsohn's system and may even be considered his characteristic trademarks.

For Mendelsohn, everything was caught up in movement. Architecture represented a petrified instant in the midst of this motion, a momentary, unique solution within an eternal flux. Even the smallest change in a single aspect influenced the whole and altered the result. Mendelsohn sometimes used the expression "elastic principle" for his early concrete constructions. This term doubtless also serves as a metaphor for his conceptual approach: "Genius must be thoroughly elastic, must always renew itself in order to fulfill itself."[5] Thus everything that hindered his freedom of motion and limited his flexibility was unnecessary ballast that must be thrown overboard: "Everything depends on being light and mobile. Whoever blocks his own movement—ossifies."[6] To be able to take new positions at a moment's notice, to change locations and adopt new perspectives—this was his sure foundation in life.

For Mendelsohn, the onset of material success was a double-edged sword. The most immediate expression of material success is money. Money was important to Mendelsohn—and he never made a secret of it—since it enabled him to enjoy essential independence and thus existential mobility. Money is a liquid, elastic principle, a means of achieving freedom of movement. Without money, he felt humiliatingly dependent.

Success, however, also gave rise to static structures, which the architect viewed as constraining in a fundamentally disturbing and dangerous way. These structures were the various forms of establishment that came to expression in property and prestige. The rigid character of establishment contradicted his maxim of free mobility. At a sociopsychological level, this dualism

Am Rupenhorn, garden facade, 1932.

of motion and rest, of flexibility and rigidity, evokes the image of the Wandering Jew on the one hand and values such as home, roots, and being settled on the other. It is precisely against this background that Mendelsohn's success revealed its ambivalent character.

The temptation to rest on the laurels of success was denied Mendelsohn—or rather, he denied it to himself, presumably in order to actively forestall suffering. Undoubtedly the most cherished fruit of his success was the construction of his own villa, the "little palace" Am Rupenhorn. Yet he could not freely abandon himself to the enjoyment of his luxurious dwelling. It was, as it were, too good to be true. A premonition that this would only be a temporary home for him in Germany seemed to cast a shadow on his achievement from the very beginning. Even immediately after moving into the new house, it became a burden to him, "its firm existence" perceived as something "confining and oppressive."[7]

The idea of a house of his own, on his own property, took on the significance of a kind of meta-idea. It represented the projection of all the hopes and longings that, in a certain sense, were "forbidden" for Mendelsohn the Jew, awakening as they did the "envy of the gods."[8] Here a variety of aspects came into play, one of them doubtless the architect's dream of the ideal project in which he himself was his own client. Yet there was also the outsider's desire for a ticket to the high society of the capital city, the businessman's calculation of an effective calling card and billboard, and the longing of the Jew for a home and roots. Not least of all, however, was the lover's desire to build a golden cage for the woman he idolized. To judge from Mendelsohn's correspondence with his wife, it was above all the latter aspect that represented the decisive motivating force in the creation of his house, although he undoubtedly projected all his other motives onto this one, using the desire to create an appropriate setting for his wife to legitimate his own suppressed aspirations. By transferring to his wife the static values associated with the idea of home, he absolved himself of what he perceived as an insoluble dichotomy between freedom and rootedness.

Luise Mendelsohn, née Maas, was an extraordinary woman whose mere appearance inspired the wish to lay the most precious gifts at her feet. The conquest of her heart was probably Mendelsohn's greatest personal success. Theirs was a marriage that survived all crises, characterized by mutual love and respect. From the first to the last moment of their life together, Mendelsohn adored his wife and treated her with great tenderness. Luise Mendelsohn subordinated her own career as a cellist to the professional goals of her husband, accepting his exceptional talent and the unbroken power of his will as her own calling. In this way she naturally fulfilled traditional expectations; yet her place in Mendelsohn's work goes far beyond the usual passive role of a wife. She played an active part in the creative planning process of the individual projects. Although apart from isolated exceptions she was not directly connected with the work in the office, she was a valuable partner for Mendelsohn, one whose judgment he highly respected: "Your letter from Rauschen just came with your opinion of the most recent sketches of the tower. It agrees entirely with my own feeling. I often send you variations actually only in order for your opinion to confirm the decision I have already made. What for me is the result of complex cognition, you recognize intuitively. That we have this is the finest sign of our communion, the final agreement, because the opinion proceeds from the opposite pole."[9]

Erich and Luise Mendelsohn, ca. 1935.

The intense dialogue between Mendelsohn and his wife is preserved for us in their letters.[10] Here the architectural historian finds precise records of the developmental stages of Mendelsohn's current projects—"Karolingerplatz is not getting off the ground, it is tiresome and is gradually becoming nauseating"[11]—or the labyrinthine complexities of building politics: "Meanwhile the newly submitted—and oh, so old and harmless—Herpich facade has been flatly rejected by the Major on the grounds that Mendelsohn buildings have no business in the Leipziger Strasse."[12] Nor does Mendelsohn decline to comment on his clients, for example his potential client from the Spanish house of Alba: "The Duchess is very young, elegant and charming—either very fastidious or very discontented."[13]

Amusing gossip about colleagues affords a glance behind the scenes: "Lissitzky is likable and serious except for a van Doesburgian black collar. . . ."[14] But Mendelsohn also shares with his wife more serious remarks on contemporary art: "Olbrich's Ernst-Ludwig-Haus a great decorative gesture. The Wedding Tower is wholly built. A strong impression and encouragement. You must certainly see it."[15] Or, on a critical note: "A 'little' letter from Taut. His misleading ideas must be stopped. Our time can no longer be shaped with art and mysticism."[16] The letters also contain analytical commentary on current political events, for example in connection with the murder of Walter Rathenau: "The citizens are an insipid people, as soon as they can fill their bellies, not realizing that with their fat they feed the slave-driver that will soon yoke them again."[17] And here and there, a glimpse into a private world: "Esther is sweet and maternal, and is giving me tango lessons—ten minutes every afternoon. It will be a surprise for you."[18]

For Mendelsohn, the letters he wrote to his wife were reflective interludes after the busyness of the day. They served the contemplative function of a diary, yet went far beyond it in their character of dialogue with an active counterpart. This intense "I-Thou" relationship gave rise to an exchange of ideas that represented an important foundation for Mendelsohn's creative work. Through this dialogue, Mendelsohn discovered his solutions in a process of dialectical synthesis—ever new solutions that flowed directly into his architectural work. This was exactly what the Jewish philosopher Martin Buber called the "dialogic principle," seeking its revelation in human interaction.[19]

Luise Mendelsohn was an exceptionally striking woman, a classic Apollonian beauty with finely carved features and heavy dark hair, which she usually wore in a knot at the nape of her neck. Wherever she appeared, her grace occupied the center of attention. Her portrait was created by numerous artists.[20] The villa Am Rupenhorn is Mendelsohn's architectural portrait of his

These fanciful sketches for Mendelsohn's house were gifts for Luise's birthday from 1915 and 1917.

wife. Her nobility and elegance set the standard for the creation dedicated to her. Both attracted attention; Mendelsohn proudly reported to his wife that at social receptions "everyone knew of you and our house, i.e., of the beauty of both."[21] He designed and built the house solely for his Luise, and without her it was unthinkable: "The house is empty without you, and it is good to feel this."[22]

The project began with fantastical sketches created every year for her birthday.[23] The first sketches were inspired by music—towering masses equipped with halls for dancing and music, but at the same time reminiscent of giant industrial forms. They are designs with a utopian character, going far beyond the exigencies of dwelling, and at the same time manifestos of a philosophical concept of harmony, a synthesis of various correlates: man and woman, architecture and music, form and content. "The ultimate plan must come from both of us. . . . It must be for us both, in the determined will to a happy life and in shared devotion to child and future. The latter revolves around our work. Around your music, which I see and await in all earnestness as the correlate to my work and the level of our future house."[24]

Yet for many years, the idea of his own house remained a utopia for Mendelsohn. Reality reflected another need: the need for self-imposed independence and flexibility. For eleven years, from 1919 to 1930, the Mendelsohns—along with their daughter, Esther, born in 1916—occupied first one, then two, and later three rooms in the attractive Pension Westend, a building by August Endell. When Mendelsohn rented the first room, he saw this solution as the most pragmatic option under the unstable circumstances. Moreover, "the life of the mind that I long for, that I carry with me, seems possible only by limiting the externals of life. . . . Only this kind of life can ensure a creative future for the artist, since it requires only little energy, freeing all intellectual powers for work."[25] Here a Romantic, nineteenth-century image of the ascetic artist appears to merge with a conception of nomadic Jewish life and freedom of spirit.

In mid-1926, the dream of a house had begun to assume more concrete form. Mendelsohn's first great works had been completed, and he used the profit to acquire real estate, purchasing a large plot in Babelsberg as well as a house in Westend from the 1870s. Initially, he considered using either one or the other as a point of departure for his own residence, but eventually rejected them as unsuitable for this purpose.[26]

Although the desire for stability comes to expression again and again in Mendelsohn's letters—"I have a burning desire for your house, our house, with you in it—for a whole life"[27]—the question of location remained unresolved throughout the next year and a half, with various sites and possibilities considered at various times. Whether explicitly or implicitly, Frank Lloyd Wright's Taliesin—a family refuge and artistic center in one—was the ideal that inspired many of the dream villas Mendelsohn created in his mind.[28]

The precise date of the final decision in favor of the site Am Rupenhorn, a plot with a breathtaking view of the river Havel and the surrounding lakes, cannot be determined from Mendelsohn's correspondence with his wife. In any case, in July 1928 he wrote to Luise from Berlin: "Am bringing everything along, raincoat and 'little Rupenhorn,'"[29] and by the end of the month the building plans had been submitted.[30] After a construction period of over a year and a half, the completed house passed its final inspection in early March 1930.[31]

The construction of Mendelsohn's dream villa did not proceed entirely without crisis. The precisely calculated financing plan for the elaborate project was thrown off course by the New York stock market crash in late 1929 and the beginning of the international economic crisis. In the process, the Mendelsohns lost a considerable sum of money they had invested in stocks.[32]

But Mendelsohn was also plagued by "qualms of conscience." A letter to his wife bears witness to the deep impression Trotsky's *Anklageschrift* had made on him. He questioned his own social responsibility: "And we? Each of us, both of us? Build a house modest enough not to be guilty ourselves? We throw away the best thing we have, quiet contemplation, productive simplicity—for whom? We burden ourselves with things that are not our own. We pay tribute for human rights to assert our own right; while against the capitalistic order in spirit, we fatten ourselves on capital. For whom? Out of habit, laziness, to swim with the flow, out of greed for property, for pleasure and to be able to afford everything! We like to embellish these vanities with the desire for beauty and faddish ideals—but reality pumps us dry and diminishes our spirit. Very well, we are young and ready to give it all up at any time—that's easy to say when the sun is shining. But where is our courage on cold days?"[33] Yet in the end, both financial difficulties and fits of Marxism gave way to the will for artistic expression and the desire for public recognition—"when Rupenhorn is not a phantom, but is alive and everyone can see instead of believing blindly."[34]

In summer 1930, the Mendelsohns moved into their own home, a project whose realization had taken fifteen years. As early as June 1915, Mendelsohn had written to Luise: "The villa is defined and is now being given form. I will send you sketches as soon as they are legible. I only fear it will be too good. . . ."[35]

"I only fear it will be too good"—the "envy of the gods" always hovered in the background. This ambivalent attitude is reminiscent of a traditional Jewish custom in which during a wedding—the act of supreme individual happiness—the blackest moment in collective Jewish his-

Erich Mendelsohn with his daughter, Esther, born 1916, in the apartment in the Pension Westend, Berlin, ca. 1923.

Am Rupenhorn, southwest corner, 1932.

tory is remembered as well, as the crushing of a glass recalls the destruction of the temple. Fulfillment and its potential destruction stand in close proximity.

Am Rupenhorn was the fulfillment of a dream for the Mendelsohns: a high-tech *Gesamtkunstwerk,* a perfect synthesis—as always for Mendelsohn—of art and technology, with nature incorporated as well. The large, parklike grounds of the Mendelsohn estate were located in the western part of Berlin between Charlottenburg and Grunewald, in a fine villa district preferred by the Jewish upper class. The area was connected to the city center by Heerstrasse, one of the most important old streets in Berlin, from which the quiet side street Am Rupenhorn branched off. The cul-de-sac, lined on both sides by villas, was adjoined to the north and west by the Jewish cemetery.

The long, narrow parcel was approximately 30 to 42 meters wide and 104 meters long. The terrain sloped downward toward the lake, with the house itself set at the highest point of the plot to take advantage of the spectacular view of the river and lake landscape of the Havel. All the main rooms of the house as well as the large terrace were oriented to the magnificent view of the lake plateau. House and site opened themselves to nature in a dialogue of natural and artistic aesthetics, the architect engaging in a tête-à-tête with the creator. Toward the outside—toward the street and neighboring plots—Mendelsohn's refuge appeared closed and inaccessible. A high wall rebuffed noise from the street. Entrance to the *hortus conclusus* was permitted only in a controlled, selective manner.

The entire building radiated a tranquillity that stood in utter contrast to the metropolitan dynamism of Mendelsohn's commercial buildings. The rather static character of the house's architectural form underlined its function as a private retreat. For Mendelsohn as for Frank Lloyd Wright, family and contemplative union with nature represented stable values, poles of rest in the hectic pace of business life. Yet while Wright was able to play out these values openly, Mendelsohn felt compelled to protect them, to architecturally concentrate and delimit them.

The invited guest passed a gate of iron bars and progressed toward the door of the house either along the driveway to the garage or on foot over a long straight path through the front

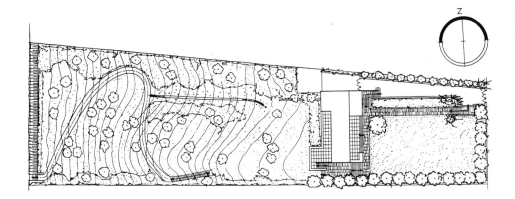

Am Rupenhorn, site plan.
The Mendelsohn estate comprised
almost 4,000 square meters and
bordered the river Havel to the west.

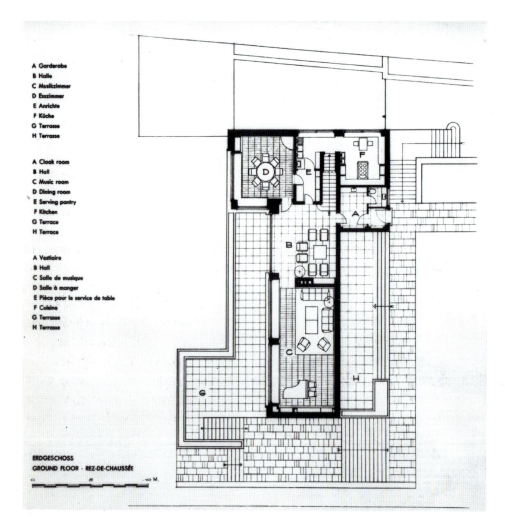

Am Rupenhorn, ground floor plan,
1932.

A Garderobe
B Halle
C Musikzimmer
D Esszimmer
E Anrichte
F Küche
G Terrasse
H Terrasse

A Cloak room
B Hall
C Music room
D Dining room
E Serving pantry
F Kitchen
G Terrace
H Terrace

A Vestiaire
B Hall
C Salle de musique
D Salle à manger
E Pièce pour le service de table
F Cuisine
G Terrasse
H Terrasse

ERDGESCHOSS
GROUND FLOOR · REZ-DE-CHAUSSÉE

Am Rupenhorn, footpath to the front
door, 1932.

garden. The entrance to the house, though visible from afar, was framed as simply and unpre-
tentiously as possible. The T-shaped plan of the house was striking for its clear and relatively
simple conception, fully tailored to the needs of its inhabitants. In addition to the entrance hall
and kitchen area, the ground floor accommodated the public spaces: the reception hall and,
adjacent to it along the same axis, the large living and music room. In the hall, a glass wall
capable of being lowered completely into the ground made it possible to open the room entirely

Am Rupenhorn, hall with view through completely lowered window onto the projecting terrace with the lake landscape of the Havel in the background.

Am Rupenhorn, window mechanism with lowered window, driven by a one-horsepower engine and counterweights, 1932.

toward the garden terrace. Diagonally to the northwest lay the dining room, a light-flooded space designed for the natural theater of unforgettable sunsets over the Havel lakes.

The upper story accommodated the private spaces: the bedroom and study of the man of the house, the lady's chambers, a room for the daughter, and a guest room: "The upper floor is a small hotel. Smallest measurements. Everybody independent, every room with bath, telephone and individual arrangements. . . ."[36] In addition to functional spaces, the basement housed a boiler room that looked like a small power plant and storage areas as well as an exercise room beneath the terrace. With the exception of the tiled boiler room, the walls in the entire house were smoothly plastered and painted in cream-colored enamel.

The house boasted a wealth of technical installations. In addition to the spectacular guillotine windows, Mendelsohn himself called special attention to the progressive oil furnace, which, with the help of a thermostat, could be automatically set for a particular temperature. Although Mendelsohn planned his house with a maximum of convenience, the machines that created the comfort were never shown, but were placed invisibly into the walls as internal organs. "In this house there are many motors and machines. But must they all be on show?" asks Amédée Ozenfant in his preface to Mendelsohn's publication *Neues Haus—Neue Welt*. And Ozenfant himself then provides the answer: "Mendelsohn was clever enough to cover the inner organs of this house with a beautiful skin. It is the fashion to admit the existence of every organ. A house is no council of revision, no confessional, no tribunal, no anatomical model, nor museum of mechanics."[37] Ozenfant, erstwhile fellow traveler with Le Corbusier on the paths of purism, swore off the machine aesthetic in his panegyric to the "little palace" Am Rupenhorn: "With all our experience no machine is equal to a masterpiece of architecture: the machine has no Acropolis,"[38] he writes in a clear reference to Le Corbusier's provocative contrast of the Parthenon and automobile in *Vers une architecture*.

Ozenfant created three large works for Am Rupenhorn. For the reception hall he painted a puristic mural—*Musik and die plastischen Künste*—which evokes Mediterranean, almost biblical, associations with motifs such as harp, lyre, and earthen vessels.[39] Behind the grand piano in the large living and music room hung his work *Orgelpfeifen:* "An Ozenfant in niche: organ pipes and gramophone records, radio volves and a horn. Cool in shades of blue by day. At night, indirectly illuminated, gleaming yellow gold and red."[40] Finally, in Luise's room upstairs was a smaller, more intimate picture entitled *Mutter und Kind*. All the works were originally commissioned in fresco technique; Ozenfant, however, persuaded Mendelsohn to let him execute them on canvas instead.[41]

Other works of art integrated into the program of the house were a version of Lyonel Feininger's *Gelmeroda* in the cloakroom and a relief image in copper by Ewald Mataré in the living room across from the music niche. For this large transverse wall, Oskar Schlemmer had already prepared a monumental mural design over three meters wide and more than a meter high, with rhythmically articulated statuary groups alternating with architectural elements. It is not known why Schlemmer's design was replaced by that of Mataré.[42]

Although much admired, Am Rupenhorn was also subjected to vehement criticism immediately following its completion and the publication of *Neues Haus—Neue Welt* in 1932. Mendelsohn was vulnerable to attack from both the right and the left; it was his elaborate publication, above all, that provoked the "envy of the gods." For this showpiece—a lesson in technical as well as aesthetic perfection—he opened gates and doors, cupboards and drawers to the photographer Arthur Köster, sparing neither Luise's manicure set nor the wine rack with its exclusive names and years. Accompanying each photograph was a short description by Mendelsohn himself, written in his characteristic, expressive telegram style. The sumptuous picture book was

Am Rupenhorn, music room with grand piano and wall cabinet for Luise's cello.

Am Rupenhorn, music room with grand piano and wall cabinet for Luise's cello.

prefaced with panegyrics by the national art curator Edwin Redslob[43] and Amédée Ozenfant. The book was doubtless misunderstood as immoderate pretension and reviewed accordingly. Among the causes of offense was Ozenfant's concluding assessment: "This is a house for a modern Goethe."[44] During the Goethe anniversary year 1932, Werner Hegemann took the bait and wrote a sarcastic critique for the journal *Wasmuths Monatshefte für Baukunst.* Aside from isolated positive remarks and a few truly justified points of criticism, Hegemann indulged in a polemic culminating in a social-political, pseudo-moralistic indictment: "Until we have succeeded in saving our fatherland from the threat of economic collapse and once again created healthy economic conditions for the broad masses of people and their intellectual champions, such luxurious, capitalistic private houses as the Mendelsohn house will continue to represent a purified and very dashing, yet very dangerous Wilhelminism."[45]

At a time when most architects were concerned with creating subsistence-level housing, Mendelsohn's employment of the full creative powers of every artist involved and his insistence on the best possible execution with the most expensive materials in the creation of a sumptuous villa was an untimely, "politically incorrect" undertaking.[46]

Mendelsohn himself did not feel bound to his house in the long term. Already in 1932, i.e., at the time of the Hegemann article, he seriously considered leaving Berlin to found a Mediterranean academy in the south of France together with Ozenfant and Wijdeveld.[47] And when in early spring 1933 he finally decided to turn his back on his house for good, it seems that it was not especially difficult for him. In mulling over this decision, he recalled the "proverb of the ancient Jews, that 'even this is for the good' [what at first appears to be suffering]. More than ever in the danger zone of our life here, I sense the sweet burden of the fate that caused us to be born Jews. . . . This new order for which I worked, lived—and against which we offended when we, like all the others, allowed ourselves to be blinded by the boom, the prosperity, of living outside ourselves. The beauty we created cannot be considered a sacrifice,

Am Rupenhorn, seating group in music room with copper relief by Ewald Mataré.

Am Rupenhorn, study of
Erich Mendelsohn in the
upper floor.

The lake Stössensee with Am Rupenhorn visible on the ridge of the slope.
Here Albert Einstein arrived in his
sailboat to share evenings of chamber
music with Luise Mendelsohn.

the sorrows cannot be considered penance. For before grace comes recognition, before liberation the will to repent, before sanctification, i.e., before purification, repentance itself. This is no accusation, no complaint. It only shows the wrong turn that was necessary in order to find our way back. . . ."[48]

For three years, the "luxurious, capitalistic private house" served as a meeting place for an international cultural elite. Regular guests in the Mendelsohn home included the French ambassador, the writer André Gide, the editor in chief of the *Berliner Tageblatt*, Theodor Wolff, and Oskar von Wertheimer, Prince Karl Anton Rohan, Victoria Ocampo, Chaim Weizmann and Kurt Blumenfeld, Salmann Schocken, Albert Einstein, and many more.

"Music filled the house on many occasions," recalled Louise Mendelsohn. "The climax of the regular chamber music evenings came on Eric's birthday which fell on the same date as Bach's birthday, March 21. All our musician friends would assemble as early as possible in the afternoon with their instruments, and we played until the early morning hours with only the interruption of a simple supper and drinks. The Brandenburg Concerti, Solo Violin Partitas, cello-gamba sonatas were played—Bach was honored and with him Eric. . . . Later we played trio a few times with Professor Albert Einstein. He was an excellent musician, technically an amateur, of course; sometimes he would play very well and sometimes his thoughts were probably deviated into other regions. . . . Einstein would take his sailing boat from his house, which was situated at one of the other lakes which the river Havel formed around Berlin, to our house, then climb up the hill with his fiddle under his arm. On one of these occasions, Eric said to him, 'Professor Einstein, did you sail this distance all alone? This is dangerous.' Whereupon Einstein answered, 'Mendelsohn, you need not be worried as the friends who gave this boat to me had it built in such a way that it cannot overturn.'"[49]

Notes p. 270.

Ita Heinze-Greenberg

"We'll leave it to the Schultzes from Naumburg to ignore the Mediterranean as the father of the international art of composition"
The Mediterranean Academy Project and Mendelsohn's Emigration

In January 1936, Mendelsohn dreamed a strange dream—three years after Hitler had been appointed chancellor, two years and nine months after Mendelsohn and his wife, Luise, had left Germany, and two years and four months after his name had been expunged from the books of the Bund Deutscher Architekten (Association of German Architects) since "Aryan" origin had become a requirement for membership. He dreamed: "I was in Germany. A man . . . was trying to talk me into assuming leadership of the School of Arts and Crafts, which was in a state of complete chaos. All was to be forgiven and forgotten. It rankled me that art and business were being brought together as before and that I had been asked mainly on account of my organizational skills. I received some papers and a form letter with an *apology—preprinted*. I replied that I would consider it, since I would still be in Germany for a good five days. That was a lie. On the very same evening I traveled to London without answering."[1]

Not until years later did Mendelsohn give his answer to Germany, a land in which he never again set foot after April 1933. In a letter of 1947 to his former colleague from the Ring group, the architect Richard Döcker, he wrote: "I would like to say only one thing: whether good or bad, Nazi or liberal—each German has to answer for Germany, for its monstrous crimes against 'humanity.' . . . Germany's desire that the world quickly forget is a utopia. This utopian view makes Germany presumptuous. . . . If you were a Jew, you would know firsthand what that means. The 'good' Jew counts for nothing, the 'bad' one is the token of all Jewry. It is Germany's fate to experience this pernicious stigma, after it hoped to gain the particular esteem of the world by murdering its Jews. The hope of the German for respect can be fulfilled only when he is quiet, does not blame himself, gives up trying to be the center of the world, works, helps himself through work, and for a long time accepts his own guilty fate."[2]

In 1951, when former Jewish colleagues were invited to participate in the Darmstadt exhibition "Mensch und Raum" ("Man and Space"), Mendelsohn once again thwarted the exhibition organizers' hopes for easy reparations and answered in a sharply accusing tone: ". . . as long as Germany lacks the courage or the insight to publicly extirpate the anticultural things that have occurred in its name and with its silent acquiescence, I as a Jew cannot contribute to the cultural significance of your country."[3] These unequivocal responses were written from America, the last station in Mendelsohn's migration. Here in the multicultural melting pot, like so many Jews before and after him, he had found if not a home, at least a livelihood.

Mendelsohn's 1936 dream about Germany occurred on board the *Patria* amid the waves of the Mediterranean Sea. For him, the name of the ship may have awakened memories of the lost fatherland. The steamer set its course toward the east coast of the Mediterranean, a place that at that time still inspired Mendelsohn with the vision of an "old-new" home in the "Promised Land": "Is not our place here—is not Palestine for eighteen millions the only island, the point of departure and the historical point of conclusion?" he asked in a letter to his wife.[4]

Yet even in Palestine, Mendelsohn—the "Oriental from East Prussia,"[5] as he often jokingly called himself—was not to find a home. Forced to leave the land of his birth and the soil of his

Erich Mendelsohn in the mid-1930s in Jerusalem.

childhood memories, he remained a man without a country for the rest of his life. As numerous letters to friends, (potential) clients, and influential personages in England, Palestine, and America in the 1930s and 1940s show, his suitcases were always packed; he was ready at a moment's notice to uproot and resettle elsewhere. Like a seismograph, he registered every political impetus and change, fleeing again and again from the threat of anti-Semitism and approaching war. The experience of World War I had disabused him of the youthful illusion that military conflict could be productive. Furthermore, even enlistment in the German army had failed to give him and his many Jewish comrades the national identity and integration they had hoped for. Within only fourteen years, their sacrificial service for the German fatherland was "rewarded" with the brutal deprivation of their rights as German citizens. For the Jews of the German Reich, the idea of home and fatherland became a sinister farce. Among those who sought to preserve their home under the new tormenters by adopting nationalistic attitudes or who simply could not conceive of things going so terribly awry in "their" Germany, the land of Goethe and Schiller, was Mendelsohn's old father, David Mendelsohn. He flew the swastika over his modest little house in Allenstein, and on Sundays a heavy and expensive weight adorned his double-breasted jacket: medals of the Prussian state, among them a number of Crosses of Honor First Class.[6] Mendelsohn's father died in 1937 in his own country, before the executioner could shatter his illusions; his son, however, never harbored hopes of a place for Jews in the new Aryan-Germanic order. Already during the Weimar Republic, he had viewed Germany as unstable for its Jewish citizens. He attempted to safeguard himself—intellectually and spiritually through his support of the Zionist movement, economically through professional contacts abroad—and considered emigrating to Palestine or the United States already in the early 1920s. The idea of emigration was Mendelsohn's constant companion. As he later remarked in retrospect from America: "*Ubi bene, ibi patria* is no opportunistic proverb. Wanderings from land to land are too difficult and energy-consuming for that. But it is the only solution for a man who loves freedom when confronted with the pestilence of tyranny."[7]

David Mendelsohn (1854–1937), Erich's father.

In the final analysis, the image of the dreaming Mendelsohn aboard the *Patria* in the Mediterranean is perhaps the most fitting, felicitous picture of his relation to the idea of a homeland. In the Mediterranean, he felt at home and secure: "The sea of eternal wandering, the Mediterranean bears me."[8] The sea was his element and his kingdom; the eternal flux of the waves was his beloved theme, a symbol of his dynamic approach to architecture as well as the restlessness of his life. The ambivalent dynamic of the sea as a moved and moving energy was his constant point of reference, an origin to which he returned again and again. His first love letter to Luise is an essay on the sea, for which he finds ever new fantastical, poetic descriptions. He writes of the "surging greatness of the sea," of "primeval creative forces as secretly moving powers," of the "dancing play of the waves far away on the horizon," of "foam kings" and "the mournful cries of exploded greatness down to their feet like the passing away of restless wishes."[9] His hymns to the azure of the eternally moving sea run through his life like a blue thread. In his last will and testament, he asked that his ashes be scattered on the waves of the sea, a wish fulfilled by his wife.[10]

It was above all the Mediterranean that enchanted and preoccupied him: "Its fullness, its tranquillity, its creations. Escorial and Toledo—Carcasonne and Côte d'Azur—Florence and Rome—Delphi and the Acropolis—Constantinople and the Greek islands—Galilee and Jerusalem—the pyramids and Karnak. Cruelty and austerity—voluptuousness and the art of life—wisdom and humanity—enchantment and volatility—faith and redemption—beginning and eternity. The Mediterranean contemplates and creates, the North rouses itself and works. The Mediterranean lives, the North defends itself."[11]

For Mendelsohn, the Mediterranean was "the father of the international art of composition," the "cradle of civilization."[12] It was here that he sought to establish one of his most interesting projects, one that, if it had been realized, would have overshadowed even the Bauhaus: the Mediterranean Academy, on which he began work in 1931. It was undoubtedly one of the most ambitious academy projects of the twentieth century, born of the spirit of the *Gesamtkunstwerk* and the synaesthetic interaction of a diverse range of arts.

The father of the idea was Mendelsohn's Dutch friend Hendricus Theodorus Wijdeveld, an architect who had been developing concrete ideas for an international art school since 1930 at the latest.[13] The French painter Amédée Ozenfant was persuaded to join them as the third member of the alliance. Within this triumvirate, Mendelsohn played the role of mediator between two strongly diverging artistic personalities, between the visionary Wijdeveld on the one hand and the purist Ozenfant on the other. Beginning in early 1931, Mendelsohn himself made numerous trips on behalf of the academy, travels that took him to Paris, Marseille, and the Côte d'Azur as well as Corsica. Already in January 1931—only a few months after the Mendelsohns had moved into their new home, Am Rupenhorn—he wrote euphorically to his wife, "in secret, I am already envisioning the Côte d'Azur with ateliers in Paris and London; for both, one would just have to set about it in the right way."[14] In summer 1932, Mendelsohn and "Dutchy," as Wijdeveld was known

Luise Mendelsohn in the mid-1930s in Jerusalem.

to his friends, traveled along the French Mediterranean coast in search of a suitable building site: "We are taking every roundabout way to find every beautiful place—we travel down the coast . . . marking our assessments on the maps. . . ."[15] Finally, they chose a beautiful site near Cavalière, for which Mendelsohn could find only superlatives in his letters to Luise: ". . . one kilometer from the beach, rising over about 300 meters to provide a distant view, a sea view, a dream view." He speaks of "the enchanted life of this smiling azure," "a plateau, whose view encompasses Grenoble, Montblanc, the Côte d'Azur far out to the sea," and a "Greek-sized beach between Corsica-like granite precipices, with a silver beach and pines up to the smoothly polished, transparent azure surface." In sum: "Up here, the academy we are planning would be an attraction and a mystical workplace."[16]

After leaving Germany, Mendelsohn at first devoted his full energies to the academy project. He single-mindedly pursued his plans for the site in Cavalière, developing the financial and administrative basis for the academy and the content of its academic curriculum as well as initial attempts at an architectural layout: "Always with thoughts of our future, which now means 'academy.'"[17] In the spring and summer months of 1933, Mendelsohn was doubtless the driving force behind the entire project, providing it with firm basis in reality.

On June 27, 1933, the enterprise was established to the point that a limited liability company—the Académie Européenne Méditerranée—could be founded in Paris with a second seat in London. Statutes with fifty articles were ratified and published and preliminary application forms distributed to potential students in an effort to make an initial determination of class sizes for each subject. An extensive brochure was published providing information on the ambitious goals of the new academy, whose advisory committee included renowned artists and scientists with Albert Einstein at its head.[18] In addition to an international regiment of famed architects such as Hendrik Petrus Berlage, Auguste Perret, Charles Herbert Reilly, Raymond Unwin, Henry van de Velde, and Frank Lloyd Wright, the committee also included the English stage designer Edward Gordon Craig and the German theater director Max Reinhardt, the musicians Leopold Stokowski and Igor Stravinsky, the poet Paul Valéry, and other famous artists and patrons. For each of the academy's courses of study—probably the most extensive selection of its day—the following were named as artistic directors:

Department of Architecture: Erich Mendelsohn, architect, Berlin

Department of Theater: Hendricus Theodorus Wijdeveld, architect, Amsterdam

Department of Painting: Amédée Ozenfant, painter, Paris

Department of Ceramics: Paul Bonifas, ceramist, Geneva

Department of Interior Design: Serge Chermayeff, architect, London

Department of Sculpture: Pablo Gargallo, sculptor, Barcelona

Department of Typography: Eric Gill, engraver, London

Department of Music: Paul Hindemith, composer, Berlin.[19]

At the time the brochure was published, directors for the departments of dance, textiles, photography, and film had not yet been selected. Wijdeveld was to occupy the post of general director and serve on the board of directors together with Ozenfant and Mendelsohn. All in all, the international character of the teaching staff listed in the brochure already suggested the high standards and potential attractiveness of the projected academy, an impression confirmed in the descriptions of the methods and goals of the individual courses of study. A few key sentences from Mendelsohn's text on architecture suffice to demonstrate the high level of the professional and educational approach:

Tuition begins with the study of materials, their formation and manufacture, in the workshops and actual construction on our own building site, where practice of all details of building technique is acquired. What is learned through practical work alternates with drawings and calculation in the studios. . . . Designing by means of perspective, photography, and film: building blocks as the component parts, and models as a check upon proportions. Designing section. Study of architectural expression. Line and outline, surface and volume, the principles of proportion, arrangement and sequence studied in three dimensions. Study of essential harmony between interior and exterior, purpose and plan, plan and form. . . . Construction section. Theory is translated into practice; work on practical structural problems: standard construction, economics of building, calculation, specification and quantities.

The course aims at unifying tradition and the desire for the expression of our own time, and directs them towards the formation of the future. It makes the young architect into a complete builder.[20]

This brief course outline, written in Mendelsohn's typical telegram style, leaves many questions unanswered. Nonetheless, even these few sentences manifest the basic synthesizing tendency that came to expression not only in the programmatic union of tradition and innovation in the content of the courses, but also in the didactic forms themselves. Rather than radically breaking

THE EUROPEAN MEDITERRANEAN ACADEMY

CAVALIERE, Cap Nègre, Le Lavandou, (Var) FRANCE

Société Anonyme: Académie Européenne 'Méditerranée'
Registered office: 10 rue des Marronniers, Paris, XVI

SECRETARY FOR ENGLAND
A. E. M. 173 Oxford Street, London W 1

¶ THE A.E.M. was formed on the 27th June 1933 in Paris as a limited liability company (société anonyme) whose purpose is the creation of an Academy of Arts on the Mediterranean coast. The Academy will concern itself with Architecture, Painting, Sculpture, Ceramics, Textiles, Typography, the Theatre, Music and Dancing, Photography and Films.

with conventional teaching methods, the program of study built on traditional ideas, above all in the field of engineering, but also in the basic principles of aesthetics such as the theory of proportion. New pedagogical and artistic approaches did not replace the old ones, but were added to them, as in the creative use of the new media of photography and film in architectural design. The brochure likewise alludes to the central role of "three-dimensional sketching" in the design process through the use of models and compositions of building blocks, recalling Gropius's "large-scale building set." Another concept likewise proposed by the Bauhaus (but never realized there) was the emphasis on practical experience through work on the academy's own construction site.

If it had been realized according to the program described in the brochure, the Mediterranean academy would doubtless have developed into the center of the collected *experiences* of the modern movement—in contrast to the Bauhaus, which became the focus of the collected *experiments* of modernism. Through direct contact between the masters and the next generation, the academy would have closed a gap in the continuity of modernism.

Mendelsohn spent the summer months of 1933 in Cavalière, busying himself with preparations for the architectural design of the academy campus. After the stressful years in his Berlin office and the political tensions of the last months in Germany, he enjoyed the peacefulness of nature, using the opportunity as well to bring closure to his past and establish a new inner foundation. As a symbol of this closure, he altered his handwriting. As he wrote to Luise: "You will notice—I only write in Latin characters anymore, already Mediterranean lands. . . . I see nothing good coming from Germany."[21] In Latin script, Mendelsohn wrote one panegyric after another on the charms of the Mediterranean to his wife, who in the meantime was staying with friends in Switzerland together with their daughter, Esther. Unmistakably mingled with his declarations of love toward the Mediterranean are Zionistic longings: "The Mediterranean is a first step towards a return to that country, to that final stage where we both belong. One is glad to know that."[22]

At this point it will be helpful to briefly sketch the background of these emotionally charged wanderings of spirit toward the east coast of the Mediterranean: namely, Mendelsohn's attitude toward Zionism and his relation to Palestine and the national Jewish project in "Eretz Israel" (the land of Israel), as the land was called by its Jewish inhabitants.

While Luise Mendelsohn always kept a certain distance from the Zionist movement—"my grandfather warned us not to have anything to do with it"[23]—and thus numbered among those assimilated Jews who viewed themselves as Germans of Mosaic faith, for Mendelsohn the legitimacy of Zionism was beyond question. This attitude represented the result of his essentially positive view of the idea of the nation in general. For Mendelsohn, social and religious as well as regional aspects of national identity constituted important prerequisites for the healthy development of a sense of belonging. Already in his earliest lectures, he pointed to these connections and warned against internationalist tendencies: "Internationalism signifies the nationless aestheticism of a decaying world. Transnationality, however, encompasses national boundaries as a precondition; it is a free humanity that only a comprehensive culture can rebuild."[24]

Developments in Germany led him to the following political conclusion: "We Jews are caught between the national passions and—as is now apparent to all—can find our reckoning, our right to live, only as a nation, an independent, upright people."[25] Mendelsohn's conclusion coincides exactly with the political credo of the Zionist movement and its efforts to establish a national Jewish homeland in Palestine, in Eretz Israel. This view corresponds as well to the later argument that adduced the Holocaust as final proof of the necessity for the creation of the state of Israel. As early as 1896, Theodor Herzl, the founder of modern political Zionism, had propagated the Jewish state as the necessary, consistent reaction to the increasing national consciousness of the peoples of Europe and the anti-Semitism associated with it. Yet while Herzl sought to build a Jewish state based on Western European models, Mendelsohn adopted the approach of the so-called cultural Zionists. Led by figures such as Achad Haam and Martin Buber, they sharply criticized the "Europe in Asia" propagated by Herzl and his circle. They saw Zionism less as a purely political solution of the Jewish question than as a powerful opportunity to bring about a cultural renaissance of Judaism, hoping to achieve this inner strengthening by bringing the people into contact with their ancestral land of Israel. The preeminence of Western culture was to give way to a stronger emphasis on regional, Semitic-oriental traditions and forms of expression.

Like his philosophical and ideological model Buber, Mendelsohn saw the affirmation of regional Semitic culture as a great challenge and an opportunity to rediscover true Jewish identity and its roots. This eastward orientation, moreover, was now more than ever confirmed by a political reality in which the supposedly civilized, highly cultivated West revealed itself to be a primitive monster, a wolf in sheep's clothing. To recognize this development, it was no longer even necessary to espouse pessimistic prophecies of the fall of the West such as those of Oswald Spengler.

Illustration accompanying Theodor Herzl's essay "Judenstaat" ("The Jewish State") in his *Zionistische Schriften*.

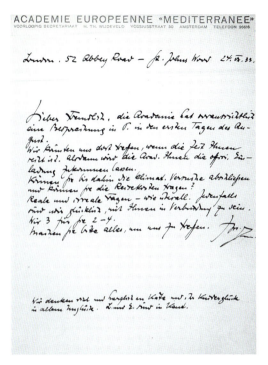

ACADEMIE EUROPEENNE «MEDITERRANEE»
VOORLOOPIG SECRETARIAAT H. TH. WIJDEVELD VOSSIUSSTRAAT 50 AMSTERDAM TELEFOON 26616

Letter from Mendelsohn to Finlay-Freundlich, inviting him to attend a meeting to discuss the Mediterranean Academy, July 24, 1933. The letter is among the first that Mendelsohn wrote in Latin script.

Mendelsohn's Zionist utopia called for an independent Jewish nation on the soil of Israel, a nation that, however, understood itself politically and culturally as an integral element of a Semitic commonwealth.[26] Since his student days, Mendelsohn had supported the Zionist movement and sought contact with its leaders.[27] Shortly after World War I, he added his name to a "Directory of Engineers Willing to Go to Palestine" compiled by the Jewish Agency.[28] The year 1923 brought with it the first contact to Palestine and the prospect of active participation in the development of the land. The trip made a tremendous impression on Mendelsohn, and from then on Eretz Israel was included in his list of countries for potential emigration.[29]

Against the background of this brief excursus, we now return to the chronology. From Cavalière, Mendelsohn traveled extensively to obtain the necessary financing for the academy, journeying to Brussels, Paris, and in summer 1933 to London as well. The social reception he enjoyed there, however, as well as his reputation as an architect, opened up new professional opportunities in prominent social circles, prospects that caused the Mediterranean and all of the projects (Mediterranean Academy) and emotions (Zionism) associated with it to recede relatively quickly into the background, or at least to be postponed indefinitely.

In late August, he informed Wijdeveld of his decision to settle in England.[30] Although this move did not automatically put an end to his active participation in the academy, it sealed the fate of the promising project. Without doubt, Mendelsohn had been the motor and switchboard of the entire program. Without him, even Ozenfant lost his nerve, and a few potential financiers withdrew their offers. Wijdeveld attempted to execute the project on a more modest scale,[31] yet without Mendelsohn's ambition and standards, this version was doomed to insignificance from the beginning.

"Why not Palestine immediately?" Mendelsohn was often asked in Zionist circles. A letter to Kurt Blumenfeld, a longtime friend from the Zionist organization, gives a clear answer to this question: "Here you touch a sore point. You know all my attempts, wanted and unwanted, to work for our land. All have failed. It is my only great disappointment, because I love Eretz Israel and call myself its true child. What I have produced—especially my explosions of imagination in sketches and preliminary projects—derives its best power from this biblical simplicity, which fulfills itself and at the same time comprehends the entire world. I know that the inimitability of my first constructions is of Jewish origin—an early insight that caused me, already as a young man, to spontaneously see the necessity of Zionism, the only way to find oneself and be truly creative. . . . All those years I envisioned Palestine built up by my hand, the entirety of its architecture brought into a unified form through my activity, its intellectual structure ordered by my organizational ability and striving toward a goal. But Palestine did not call me."[32]

Mendelsohn at first decided in favor of England, stating that "here the ground seems to be well enough prepared" that "it promises a good harvest."[33]

Notes p. 271.

"Enough mistakes and experience behind me—enough strength and future before me"
Buildings in England and the Partnership with Serge Chermayeff 1933–1941

In the early 1930s Mendelsohn, in early middle age, was at the height of his creative powers and reputation. But with the accession to power of the Nazis he suddenly found himself marginalized. Fearing the worst, in March 1933 the Mendelsohns fled from Germany to Holland. Without either a domestic or a professional base and faced with the prospect of trying to reestablish his career outside Germany, Mendelsohn characteristically chose to downplay his earlier successes and to mask whatever fears he may have had about his future prospects with optimistic declarations.

In Holland the Mendelsohns stayed for a time with the Dutch architect Hendricus Theodorus Wijdeveld,[1] whom Mendelsohn had known since 1918/19. Mendelsohn and Wijdeveld now worked together on the elaboration of a project conceived the previous year: to establish a Mediterranean Academy of the Arts at Cavalière in the South of France,[2] together with the painter Amédée Ozenfant and others—including Serge Chermayeff, with whom Mendelsohn would later go into partnership. His subsequent decision to settle in England seems to have been a matter of chance rather than premeditation, since it was to promote and fund-raise for the Academy that the Mendelsohns initially arrived in England in June 1933.

At this time Mendelsohn seems to have been fully committed to the Academy project, since he was a director of the limited liability company formed in the Academy's name in Paris on June 27, 1933; he was also a stakeholder in the property acquired for the Academy at Cavalière. And in the Academy's printed brochure he outlined the course on architecture that he proposed to teach.[3] In subsequent months, however, doubts about the viability of the project (given disagreements between the main protagonists—Mendelsohn, Ozenfant, and Wijdeveld) and about the future security of France (given France's political instability and the worsening situation in Germany) served to undermine Mendelsohn's confidence. These worries, combined with hopes of establishing himself in practice in England, which seem to have been encouraged by both Serge Chermayeff and Charles Reilly (a member of the Academy's "Comité d'honneur"), created a dilemma. Thus, on August 24, 1933, Mendelsohn wrote to Louise: "I am wavering between a house on the Côte d'Azur with you, with flowers and surrounded by nature and London."[4] A week later he had evidently decided on the latter, since he reported: "Wijdeveld and I have discussed . . . my position, talking over everything . . . my situation as it has developed demands settling down in England and . . . I have to make it dependent on . . . further developments in England how much I can be further involved and dedicate myself to the Academy. . . ."[5]

So it came about that, although he would continue to take an interest in plans for the academy, Mendelsohn began to make plans to settle permanently in England. With the encouragement of English friends and colleagues, he initiated moves to obtain a long-term residence permit, which would allow him to apply for British citizenship after five years. And, sometime in the autumn of 1933, he acquired a 55 percent stake in Serge Chermayeff's recently established architectural practice.

At the start, the Mendelsohns were fortunate; unlike many refugees they had both personal and professional support in England. During the early months they received unstinting hospitality

Eric and Louise Mendelsohn in exile in the 1930s.

De La Warr Pavilion, Bexhill-on-Sea, Sussex, sketch of entrance front.

De La Warr Pavilion, Bexhill-on-Sea, Sussex, view of model showing seaward side of pavilion with pergola and unbuilt swimming pool.

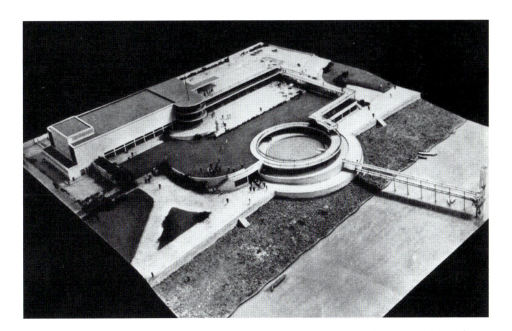

from Lady Swaythling.[6] And, largely because his work was already widely known and admired,[7] Mendelsohn received a warm welcome from a number of influential architects. Prompted by Charles Reilly,[8] Iain Macalister, the secretary of the Royal Institute of British Architects (RIBA), interrupted the summer holiday of the Institute's president, Sir Giles Gilbert Scott, on Mendelsohn's behalf, and efforts were made to see whether the Institute's membership regulations could be stretched to accommodate him.[9] As a consequence of the backing of such heavyweights,[10] Mendelsohn's application for a residence permit was successful.

Partly to thank Reilly for interceding with the RIBA and the British Home Office, Mendelsohn lectured at the Liverpool School of Architecture in November 1933. Here he received a rapturous reception, as Louise recorded: "This became an unforgettable event. After a big dinner, toasts, and an atmosphere of warmth and appreciation, Eric delivered his lecture, after which doors opened to a large sort of ballroom where a band played the then modern dances, such as foxtrot and tango. But the climax . . . was that all the walls were covered by paintings representing Eric's buildings, populated with angels. One of the walls was covered by a most humorous painting representing the architects Sir Edwin Lutyens and Sir Arthur Blomfield and Sir Giles G.

Scott trying to teach their students conservative architecture. The students were depicted sitting in a circle . . . drawn as little devils listening with one ear to Eric, who was represented as a devil showing them his buildings and sketches and those by the . . . conservative architects crossed out. We laughed and felt at home with all these young people. . . ."[11]

Despite such support, the Mendelsohns' decision to stay in England cannot have been taken lightly. For a start, in announcing the decision, Mendelsohn forfeited such of his fortune as he otherwise might have been able to salvage from Nazi Germany and which would have helped support him and his family in England.[12] Reilly records that Mendelsohn had agreed that the occasion of his Liverpool lecture should be used to announce his decision to stay and his intention of applying for naturalization. Just before the lecture, however, Reilly notes: "Mendelsohn's nerves seemed to give way. He said 'Reilly, do not make that announcement. My solicitors in Berlin say there is a chance yet of saving a portion of my fortune, about £70,000.' Of course I agreed. An architect who still might have £70,000! Who was I to risk it? Then the stately Louise spoke. She said, 'Erich, we have determined to be English at whatever cost. Professor Reilly, please make your announcement.' With that we trooped into the lecture room. . . . The press filled the front rows, beyond which was a packed, seething mass of students, soon to be swept away with Mendelsohn's enthusiasm and his lively sketches on the screen. At the end I got up to propose a vote of thanks and make my announcement. I said the great man was to become an Englishman and that it was like adding a Continent to the Empire. . . . The deed was done. The chance of saving £70,000 was thrown away."[13]

There were other problems, too. Although Louise records the personal generosity with which the Mendelsohns were received and the ways in which their social transition into a new world was eased,[14] there were practical obstacles to Mendelsohn establishing himself in professional practice. Not only did he have to improve his English[15] and familiarize himself with the Imperial system of measurement, but he had to form a partnership and adjust to a different kind of architectural culture.

Mendelsohn's earlier success had been built on independent practice, thus the priority given by the British Home Office and Ministry of Labour[16]—on the advice of the RIBA—to the admission of those foreign architects who were "in a position to establish themselves in independent practice"[17] presented no difficulty in principle. But the insistence that such architects should find British nationals with whom to form partnerships presented a problem. For one thing potential modernist partners were few and far between. For another, Mendelsohn's earlier practice had been, emphatically, a solo one—despite his close working relationship with some of his assistants.[18] He had neither any real experience of partnership nor was he temperamentally disposed toward the kind of sharing of responsibilities involved in such a relationship.[19] As Louise Mendelsohn observed, "Eric had never been in a partnership and was not the type to have a partner and I believe he [would] rather [have] had a young person who admired Eric Mendelsohn's work as a partner than enter a partnership with an architect of his generation."[20] The choice thus fell on Serge Chermayeff,[21] who was a self-taught modernist designer/architect and admirer of Mendelsohn's work,[22] several years his junior, whom Mendelsohn had met on a trip to England in 1930 and who had subsequently visited the Mendelsohns in Berlin.

For both partners the arrangement was, at least at the outset, opportune. For Chermayeff, in independent practice since 1930 but still attempting to consolidate a reputation as an architect (rather than as an interior and furniture designer), the partnership offered the kudos of association with one of the best-known and most admired names in European modernism and the opportunity to attract and undertake more ambitious architectural commissions than hitherto

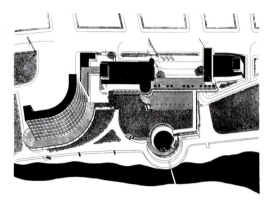

De La Warr Pavilion, Bexhill-on-Sea, Sussex, axonometric projection by H. J. Whitfield Lewis of a project by Mendelsohn and Chermayeff for a larger scheme with attached hotel and cinema.

De La Warr Pavilion, Bexhill-on-Sea, Sussex, construction of welded steel frame designed by engineer Felix Samuely, 1934.

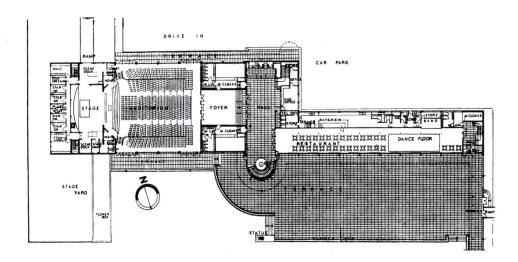

De La Warr Pavilion, Bexhill-on-Sea, Sussex, ground floor plan showing separation of main functions around the central circulation spine.

De La Warr Pavilion, Bexhill-on-Sea, Sussex, view of north facade, showing the cantilevered staircase next to the main entrance.

possible.[23] And, as he later recalled: "Eric Mendelsohn . . . was invaluable to me. I learnt architectural organization of some complexity, including both schematic presentation and meticulous detailing."[24] For Mendelsohn, the partnership fulfilled the practical need for an association with an English partner and had the added bonus that Chermayeff, despite his relative lack of building experience, appeared to have sufficient architectural work in hand to share.[25]

English approaches to building design and construction in 1933 were markedly conservative compared with those of Weimar Germany, despite regular coverage of recent European modernist developments in some of the leading British architectural journals.[26] Thus nearly a decade after the construction of some of the most accomplished early modernist buildings elsewhere in Europe, there was very little built evidence of the "Neues Bauen" in England. Ernst Freud—another immigrant from Berlin—commented: "it is most surprising to a continental observer how very few modern buildings are to be found and that on the whole the idea of modern architecture has not yet begun to influence the features of English towns."[27] The point was underlined by the English architect and writer F. R. S. Yorke, who noted that in 1934, when he published the first edition of his international survey, *The Modern House*, "it was difficult to find material to fill the fourteen pages of the book given to English examples."[28] Furthermore, the spread of the new architecture in Weimar Germany had been dependent both on a body of clients who were "inclined to accept and appreciate the principles of modern architecture" and on the appointment of modern architects to important executive posts—as city architects or teachers in the Technische Hochschulen.[29] In England such sympathetic conditions were largely conspicuous by their absence. As a result, modernist designs were frequently opposed and either refused planning permission or granted permission only with the proviso that compromises were made. Such circumstances may, in part, account for the fact that, during his six years in England, Mendelsohn would build very little.[30]

These were not the only kinds of problems Mendelsohn had to face. In December 1933 a potentially major setback threatened when Mendelsohn attempted to bring his former assistant Johannes Schreiner to London. Mendelsohn's loss of an eye some years earlier meant that he was particularly reliant on Schreiner's ability to interpret and develop his ideas from preliminary sketches to site drawings. He therefore applied for a work permit for Schreiner, writing to the Ministry of Labour: "Mr Schreiner has been my assistant for eight years, and has taken part in the preparation of all drawings in connection with the biggest projects of my practice, because his particular knowledge of modern steel and concrete constructions and his great practical experience and ability have specially recommended him for this position. For that reason he is essential to my work."[31] As Mendelsohn further noted, Schreiner's presence would help develop the practice—an important consideration at a time of economic depression and widespread unemployment amongst architects: "His work in the office will also contribute to the training of the English collaborators and will permit my office to undertake special work which, in its turn, will enable me to engage further English collaborators."[32] Despite this apparently persuasive case, however, the RIBA's Practice Standing Committee, to which the Ministry of Labour referred the application, resolved that "Mr Mendelsohn be informed that the Committee were not prepared to support his application. . . . Mr Mendelsohn should not have any undue difficulty in obtaining the services of an English architectural assistant who would readily be able to learn his methods."[33] Fortunately, Mendelsohn succeeded, by some means, in obtaining permission for Schreiner to work in London,[34] where, although he was not universally liked by those in the Mendelsohn/Chermayeff office, his skills were readily acknowledged. As Colin Crickmay, one of Mendelsohn and Chermayeff's assistants, recalled, Schreiner "was a brilliant draughtsman, and had a very clear idea as to how everything on any building on which he was working should be constructed."[35]

Within the partnership Mendelsohn appears to have taken the lead in initiating designs and overseeing design development, largely through the intermediary of Schreiner. Chermayeff, by contrast, seems to have borne much of the responsibility for dealing with—if not always attracting—clients,[36] working out the logistics of commissions, and conceiving and detailing the interiors.[37] Birkin Haward, a former assistant, remembered: "Eric Mendelsohn was obviously dominant on architectural issues (look at their respective backgrounds), so that Serge Chermayeff tended to be mainly involved in directing the interior designs and fittings within the architectural context—which conformed with his previous experience anyway."[38] Nevertheless, the division of responsibility was not altogether clear-cut. And, after the latter part of 1934—when Mendelsohn began working on projects for Palestine—overall responsibility for the running of the London

De La Warr Pavilion, Bexhill-on-Sea, Sussex, south facade showing auditorium block and glazed south staircase.

De La Warr Pavilion, Bexhill-on-Sea, Sussex, interior of south staircase with view of restaurant terrace.

Illustration right:
De La Warr Pavilion, Bexhill-on-Sea, Sussex. As in many of Mendelsohn's earlier buildings, the main staircases here play a pivotal role in the plan and lend drama to the elevations.

BALCONY ►
LOUNGE ►
SU...►

De La Warr Pavilion, Bexhill-on-Sea, Sussex. The first-floor library and reading room was furnished with Finmar occasional tables, upholstered chairs by Plan, and table and bookcases after designs by Mendelsohn and Chermayeff.

De La Warr Pavilion, Bexhill-on-Sea, Sussex. The first-floor lecture room was furnished with PEL tubular steel chairs.

Nimmo house (Shrub's Wood),
Buckinghamshire.

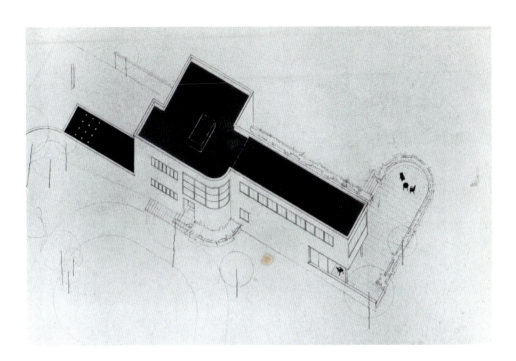

Nimmo house (Shrub's Wood),
Buckinghamshire, plans.

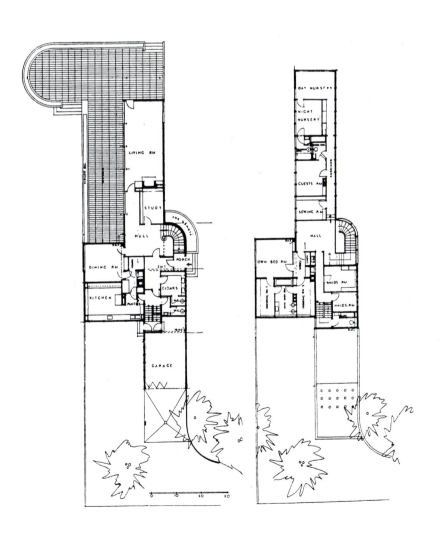

office, for design decisions and the supervision of projects in progress, increasingly devolved to Chermayeff. In consequence, he experienced a quantum leap in his knowledge of architectural practice, and his confidence in his own judgments and his ambitions seem to have increased. Mendelsohn's practice in England began auspiciously when, soon after it was established, the partnership won the competition for the De La Warr Pavilion at Bexhill-on-Sea, a small seaside resort on the South coast. In 1926, a general development plan for the town had recommended the building of a seafront entertainment center to help boost tourism. The recommendation was eventually endorsed by the town's socialist mayor, Earl De La Warr, and a competition was organized for the design of the new building. Unusually, the competition brief explicitly favoured modernist design and this, together with the presence of Thomas Tait—an architect sympathetic to modernism—as competition assessor, contributed to the success of Mendelsohn and Chermayeff's entry.[39] The results of the competition were not uncontested, however; both locally and in the professional press antimodernist and xenophobic sentiments were liberally aired.[40]

The site of the pavilion was relatively flat and uneventful, open to the sea to the south and bounded by a main road to the north. As both sketches and the finished building demonstrate, prominent staircases were deployed on both main fronts to dramatize the building. The staircases also acted as pivotal elements for the design in plan. Yet the plan was not sacrificed to formal effects; it was carefully considered in functional terms. Bar, restaurant, and cafeteria functions—with their common services—were grouped together to the east of the central foyer, with open views to the south. The auditorium was treated as a separate entity, placed to the west of the foyer, with its own services. Throughout the building, furniture and fittings underlined the modernity of the design as well as the careful attention to the integration of exterior envelope with interior volumes, and added to the impression of interior spaciousness and light, especially on the south side. Formally innovative for England at that time, the pavilion was also structurally innovative. Its all-welded steel skeleton was one of the first of its type in England and was designed by the

Nimmo house (Shrub's Wood), Buckinghamshire, north facade showing main entrance and curved wall generated by main staircase.

Nimmo house (Shrub's Wood), Buckinghamshire, view of south facade from terrace toward living room and hall on the ground floor and nursery and guest rooms on the first floor.

Nimmo house (Shrub's Wood), Buckinghamshire, view of entrance hall toward terrace and into living room.

engineer Felix Samuely, a fellow émigré, with whom Mendelsohn had worked in Germany and who now worked closely with the partnership on other projects. As built, the Bexhill pavilion was relatively modest and well scaled to fit with the surrounding buildings. An early variant of the scheme, however, was more ambitious—envisaging a multistory hotel on the southwest corner of the site and a cinema to the northeast. These additions, however, like the circular swimming pool (for which detail drawings were made) were abandoned, probably for reasons of cost.

Chronologically the first of the partnership's projects to be completed was the Nimmo house, Shrub's Wood, near Chalfont St Giles in Buckinghamshire. The commission was one that Chermayeff had received before the partnership was formed. It was already on the drawing board but, according to Geoffrey Bazeley, "When Mendelsohn arrived he took it over and Shrub's Wood as built was designed by him."[41] Colin Crickmay, too, recalled the design as executed as "90% Mendelsohn." Beautifully sited, in an old orchard, with commanding views to east and west, the house was composed of a long range running east-west, giving all the main rooms south light, with circulation and some services to the north. At the heart of the house, forming a kind of pivot in plan, was a spacious hall from which rose a curving staircase lit, across the whole of its upper part, by a curved window. As Bruno Zevi has pointed out, Shrub's Wood—like the Bexhill pavilion—in its horizontality and in the dialectic between rectangular and curved forms, derives much from Mendelsohn's earlier German work.[42]

The same was true, in certain respects, of the second of Mendelsohn's English houses, the Cohen house, although, with its constricted urban plot, the site had none of the picturesque potential that had characterized the sites of Shrub's Wood and Mendelsohn's Am Rupenhorn house. Here the limitations imposed by the site were compounded by the need to accommodate a squash court within the overall built volume of the house. Birkin Haward recalled that these constraints "gave Eric Mendelsohn a lot of design worry. He examined many forms and possible solutions for the house. He approached designs from the general to the particular having first got all the main factors into mind. . . . The problem of incorporating the large volume of the squash court within the house caused much concern. . . . [The] solution . . . was not discovered immediately. I think that the process went on longer than usual for a relatively small building. . . . Many roughs went into the wastepaper basket."[43] Mendelsohn's eventual solution was to group the services along the street front, providing a buffer for the private spaces of the house, and to sink the floor of the squash court below ground, so that the court's bulk was invisible from the exterior.

Between them these three buildings constitute the totality of Mendelsohn's built work in England. Two further executed schemes should be mentioned, however, in which he is known to have played a part; both were completed after the dissolution of the partnership and are usually attributed to Chermayeff alone. One is the British Dyestuffs (later ICI) Laboratories at Blackley, Manchester; the other is the Gilbey building in London. Little of Mendelsohn's contribution to the initial planning of the Blackley project remains evident in the scheme as built. The elevations of Gilbey's, on the other hand, are distinctly "Mendelsohnian" in character, and both Whitfield Lewis and Birkin Haward have confirmed that the initial designs for the scheme were made by Mendelsohn before the break-up of the partnership.[44] As Haward—who did the detail drawings for the project—observed, the completed building "has the stamp of Mendelsohn/Schreiner with Serge in attendance, making as much contribution as he was allowed."[45]

Although Mendelsohn completed few buildings during his six years in England, he made designs for several other—sometimes ambitious—schemes; they included a private house,[46] a large-scale housing scheme, and a range of commercial buildings. Two of these projects in particular are worth mentioning.

Cohen house, London, plans.

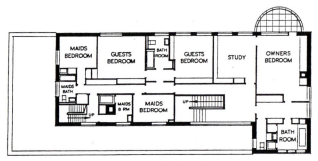

MAIDS BEDROOM | GUESTS BEDROOM | BATH ROOM | GUESTS BEDROOM | STUDY | OWNERS BEDROOM

MAIDS BATH | MAIDS B RM | MAIDS BEDROOM | UP | BATH ROOM

First Floor Plan

Scale of Feet

0 1 2 3 4 5   10   15   20   25   30   35

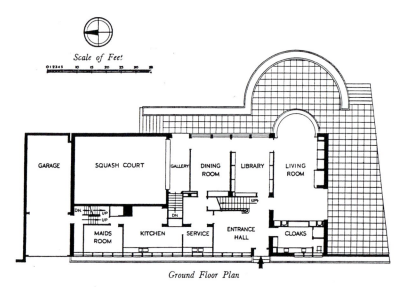

GARAGE | SQUASH COURT | GALLERY | DINING ROOM | LIBRARY | LIVING ROOM

DN. | UP | MAIDS ROOM | KITCHEN | SERVICE | ENTRANCE HALL | CLOAKS

Ground Floor Plan

Cohen house, London, street facade with Gropius and Fry's Levy house in the distance. The Cohen house is steel framed with rendered brick infill and sits on a plinth of blue bricks.

200

Cohen house, London, garden facade showing bay window of living room (with terrace above to master bedroom). To the right is the blank wall of the sunken squash court.

The first, for the White City, was prepared ca. 1935 while Mendelsohn was still in partnership and, had it been built, would have been one of the most ambitious projects ever undertaken by him. It involved the redevelopment of the White City Exhibition ground, a site of some eighty acres in West London. Two variants of the design are known. One envisaged a mixed development providing housing in high-rise and slab blocks, a commercial center including shops and a cinema, social facilities—such as tennis courts and a restaurant—and new exhibition buildings to the southeast of the site. The other used the same formula for the housing and commercial center to the north of the site, devoting the rest of the site to housing as well. In their overall formulation, both schemes—with their long curved ranges of repetitive eight-story *zeilenbau* elements counterpointed by a series of twelve-story point blocks set in greenery—owe a good deal to the typologies of German modernist social housing of the 1920s, although they have little direct precedent in Mendelsohn's own previous work. Had the project—which Mendelsohn and Chermayeff labeled "A scheme of national importance"[47]—been built it would have been one of the largest housing projects in Europe; but although the scheme aroused considerable interest among contemporary English town planners, nothing came of it.[48]

Gilbey building, London.

The second major project was for a large hotel, garage, and shops, in the center of Blackpool, designed by Mendelsohn in 1937, after the break with Chermayeff. Here two tall blocks (multistory garage and hotel), each about thirty-five meters high, were bound together at the lower level by shops, which encircled the perimeter of the site. Here, too, although some of the sketches suggest echoes of earlier Mendelsohn work, neither the scale (fifteen stories) nor the approach to the individuation and the integration of the component parts has any real precedent in Mendelsohn's earlier work.

Little is known about the clients for Mendelsohn's unexecuted commissions in England; and the reasons why they were not built must, in the absence of evidence, remain a matter of speculation.[49] Several factors may need to be taken into account here. For one thing, Mendelsohn's frequent absences in Palestine after 1934 may have made it difficult for him to convince clients that work could be adequately developed and supervised in his absence. For another, Mendelsohn may have encountered practical obstacles to translating projects from drawing board to site after the split with Chermayeff at the end of 1936 and before his naturalization in

1938, given the requirement to be in partnership with a British national. The necessary planning permissions may not have been forthcoming. And, since several of the schemes were for mixed programs of ambitious scale, it seems likely that—in the uncertain economic and political climate of the period—it would have been difficult to raise funding.[50]

As this account has indicated, Mendelsohn's early hopes for a new beginning in England were not realized to any great extent. Some of the reasons why have been identified; others can be guessed at. Some are attributable to external factors of the type which have been mentioned already; others to Mendelsohn himself. From an early stage there were tensions in the partnership. And already from the latter part of 1934, barely a year after his arrival in England, Mendelsohn was involved in work in Palestine. His initial intention was to combine this with work in England;[51] but this was not to be. In fact, in order to make a start in Palestine, he bought himself free from the partnership for a year and a half, establishing an office in Jerusalem early in 1935. From then on, the work in Palestine would increasingly displace that in England. Effectively, the partnership would not be reestablished, and disagreements about Chermayeff's supervision of English projects in progress during Mendelsohn's absences in Palestine, together with Chermayeff's claim for a share in the Palestine work, precipitated the formal dissolution of the practice toward the end of 1936.[52] For a time Mendelsohn continued to run an office from his London flat, but doubts about the practicality of maintaining two offices had emerged by 1937, when he wrote: "I do not believe both offices can be maintained in the long run, simply because I cannot do the work and suffer the travelling, the readjustments, the acclimatization and the uninterrupted tension with only a minimum of relaxation."[53] Despite the increased workload in Palestine and his commitment to the building of a Jewish homeland, however, he seems to have wanted to keep his options open. Yet his attitudes to England, too, were ambivalent. For obvious reasons he had cultivated influential establishment architects on his arrival, but he made little attempt thereafter to make common cause with those English architects who were most sympathetic to his work; thus he eschewed membership of the modernist MARS (Modern Architectural Re-Search) Group, although his work was represented in its exhibition in 1938.[54] That Mendelsohn never really felt settled in England is clear. He was all too aware of not "knowing what will happen in Europe during the next few years" and that England was "not far enough" away from Germany for comfort.[55] In addition, he found English culture too complacent to provide the necessary stimulus to his creative energies. As he wrote to Lewis Mumford: "I do not feel very happy in England.

Scheme for White City exhibition site, London, ca. 1935. Perspective drawing of public square, shopping center, and cinema, with multistory apartment blocks in the distance.

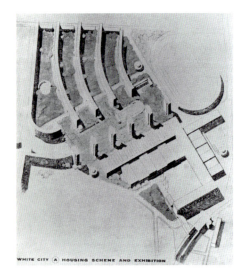

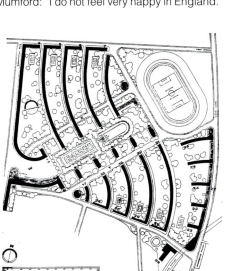

White City, Scheme A. The layout plan shows the site redeveloped with housing and shopping to the northwest and new exhibition buildings to the southeast.

White City, Scheme C. The bulk of the site was devoted to housing with a shopping center and cinema to the west of the site as in Scheme A.

Perspective drawing of project for hotel, multistory car park, and shops, Blackpool, ca. 1937.

I cannot breathe in a country without spiritual tension. I cannot work where creative fight is taken as an attack against the 'common sense' and where modern architecture has to dress with the arabesques of superficiality or highbrowisms. That is the reason why—soon after we had left Germany—I have concentrated my work on Palestine."[56] Yet although Palestine, for a time, seemed to offer more potential to both his practical skills and his temperament, Mendelsohn was aware both of the lack of permanent openings for himself and of the many difficulties facing the Jewish project in Palestine. As a result, he was unwilling to commit himself; in 1938, he applied, successfully, for British citizenship and was elected a Fellow of the Royal Institute of British Architects. But, in 1939, with no work available in London, unable to afford to continue to maintain a base there, with war in Europe a certainty, and with unfinished projects in Palestine, Mendelsohn wound up his affairs and moved to Palestine. His initial intention seems to have been to return to England after the war,[57] a theme to which he returned on a number of occasions. As early as 1941 he wrote to Norman Bel Geddes: "as the prospect of rebuilding in Britain is brighter than ever before I shall return as soon as possible in order not to miss the opportunity of adding my small work to that great undertaking."[58] And toward the end of the war he made an appointment to see the British Consul in New York, with a view to discussing his return to England.[59] In the event, however, he remained in the United States.

Mendelsohn's executed work in England was formally visibly of a piece with his earlier work in Germany; indeed, the architectural historian Henry-Russell Hitchcock even described it as "distinctly superior aesthetically to most of his German work."[60] Although small in quantity, its qualitative contribution to the evolution of English modernism was unmistakable; as Hitchcock aptly observed: "his pavilion at Bexhill is . . . recognized as about the most conspicuous and successful modern building in England."[61] Had some of Mendelsohn's other English projects— such as those for the White City and Blackpool—been realized, the course of his later career might have been very different. As things transpired, however, whether Mendelsohn could have adapted successfully to the changed conditions and challenges of architectural practice in England had he returned after the Second World War must be a matter for debate.

Notes p. 271.

"I am a free builder"
Architecture in Palestine 1934–1941

Ita Heinze-Greenberg

A New Chapter

In summer 1934, Vera and Chaim Weizmann paid a visit to Mendelsohn's office in London, approaching him with a commission that would mark the beginning of a new chapter in the architect's life. Mendelsohn had known Chaim Weizmann since his first visit to Palestine in 1923. Already in those days, Weizmann—who was to become the first president of Israel in 1948—had numbered among the most important figures in the Zionist movement. A chemist by profession, he was president of the World Zionist Organization between 1920 and 1930 and later from 1935 to 1946; beginning in 1929, he also served as president of the Jewish Agency.[1]

Although the Weizmanns lived in London, they had long planned to settle in Palestine. In spring 1934, Vera Weizmann bought a plot in Rehovot for a new family residence, whose planning was to be entrusted to Mendelsohn.[2] In fall 1934, Mendelsohn traveled to Rehovot together with Chaim Weizmann to engage in firsthand study of the site as well as other aspects connected with the planning and to prepare the initial sketches. Unlike his first business trip to Palestine in 1923, this journey was to initiate a period of creative work in Palestine that would continue for approximately seven years.

This time, Mendelsohn arrived as a self-made man, a cosmopolitan, internationally renowned architect. His already well-established office in London provided him with the material independence necessary for a self-assured demeanor in Palestine, and his debut in the Jewish "Altneuland" was correspondingly successful. In spring 1935, he rented an old Arab windmill in the Rehavia district of Jerusalem, where he opened his second office. In the years that followed, he traveled at regular intervals between his offices in London and Jerusalem, with the emphasis gradually shifting to the latter. Between 1939 and 1941, he transferred all his professional and private activities to Jerusalem. During his seven years of work there, Mendelsohn built about a dozen projects, numbering among the most ambitious in the land.

Chaim Weizmann on the voyage to Palestine in fall 1934, photographed by Erich Mendelsohn.

"Neues Bauen" in Palestine

Palestine had undergone decisive developments during the eleven years since Mendelsohn's first visit in 1923. The Jewish population had increased from 160,000 in the mid-1920s to 400,000 by the mid-1930s, growing from 18 to 30 percent of the total population of Palestine. Between 1924 and 1931, around 80,000 Jewish immigrants came to Palestine in the fourth *Aliyah* (wave of immigration). By 1932, and above all after 1933, the stream of immigrants had become a flood whose effects were clearly felt by 1934. The fifth *Aliyah* between 1932 and the outbreak of World War II brought a total of 247,000 immigrants; of the two-thirds that came from central Europe, around 50,000 of them came from Germany.

During the 1930s, the Jewish population of Palestine developed into the dominant economic force in the British Mandate territory. Most of the investments were made in the industrial development of the land, and to a lesser extent in agriculture. Half of the total capital, however, went to the construction industry. The fifth wave of immigration contributed decisively to the

Alexander Baerwald's "Technikum" building in Haifa with the Reali School in the foreground, 1920s.

growth of the cities. The Jewish population of Jerusalem doubled, while the population of the first entirely Jewish city, Tel Aviv, tripled to 150,000.[3]

The tremendous construction boom had already borne its first fruit when Mendelsohn arrived in 1934. The architects of the Zionist project were seeking an appropriate architectural language for the new Jewish homeland of Palestine; finding it, however, proved to be much more difficult than had been the case with language and writing, where modern Hebrew or *Ivrit* could still be based on ancient, living Jewish traditions. The revival of a Hebrew style of architecture would certainly have represented the ideal solution or at least a good place to start—except that such a thing never existed. Archaeological excavations from the Solomonic period uncovered local historical styles, but no specifically Hebrew form of expression. Thus the question revolved fundamentally around the opposition between occidental and oriental architecture, between West and East.[4] Each of these solutions was associated with different strains of Zionist ideology.

As a rule, the architecture of Tel Aviv and the Jewish quarters of Jerusalem and Haifa reflected the European origin of their inhabitants. To this extent it corresponded to the generally Western orientation of political Zionism, which sought to establish the new Jewish Palestine *expressis verbis* as "a piece of Europe in Asia." Early on, however, voices were heard calling for the adoption of Eastern architectural modes. Chief among them was the Jewish architect Alexander Baerwald, a native of Berlin who oversaw projects in Palestine beginning in 1910.[5] He investigated regional modes of construction, local working methods, and the stylistic details of indigenous architecture with scientific meticulousness and studied the composition of local materials and climatic conditions. He saw the local Arab architecture not least of all as a possible point of contact to the Jewish past in the Holy Land. But the connection between land and people could not be established on an *ad hoc* basis. As expressively earth-bound as Baerwald's architecture of the first two decades of the century may seem today, in the end it tells the story of a conflict of identity. Like its eclectic, Europeanizing counterparts, it bears witness to a disharmony between the land and a people returning from a two-thousand-year Diaspora. At times, his architecture adapts itself to the local Arab culture, but remains alien to its European Jewish inhabitants and users. At other times, it sympathizes with the immigrants' European roots—at the price of harmony with the land. This discrepancy could also not have been overcome by the definition of immigration as a return home or *Aliyah* (Hebrew for "going up"). Architecture narrates the tragic chapter of the first generation of immigrants for whom "culture shock" meant the lack or loss of identity.[6]

The great wave of immigration in the 1930s brought young architects to Palestine, graduates of the technical academies of Europe, including the Bauhaus.[7] They set about making Tel Aviv into an international metropolis. On the one hand, their pragmatic functionalism—informed by the motto "quick, cheap, but still good"—was the appropriate response to the increasing demand for housing for the refugees fleeing Hitler's henchmen. On the other hand, it corresponded with a Zionist-socialist ideology aimed at the creation of a new man—in this case a new Israeli—out of the multicultural mass of Diaspora Jews. Here, traditional Jewish culture had no role to play, and in fact was rejected. The preexisting identities of the immigrants—whether traditional Jewish or European bourgeois in character—were to be dissolved. The Neues Bauen, without history or tradition and ostensibly culturally neutral, rejected the dominant, eclectic Shtetl nostalgia as well as Baerwald's pan-Semitic "oriental enchantment" of the 1920s and set a new didactic course for the construction of Israeli society. An architecture oriented solely to functionality was to mark the beginning of a new development ensuring the equality of all participants and creating the basis for a new social identity.[8]

What the leading European planners of Eretz Israel failed to see, however, was that the Neues Bauen, despite a few Mediterranean borrowings, was the product of Western culture and technical knowledge and had sprung from its ideological soil. Thus it could neither express the equality of all Israelis nor successfully achieve that equality. In the final analysis, the Neues Bauen demonstrated only the West's hegemony over the East.

Mendelsohn's East-West Synthesis

Mendelsohn warned against precipitate, one-sided adherence to Western standards. He had personal reasons for this concern: the many doubles of his German masterpieces that he encountered in Tel Aviv's new districts embarrassed him, since they demonstrated that copies were possible, that his vocabulary could be degraded to the level of fashion.[9] Even apart from this phenomenon, however, he never tired of criticizing the Western tendencies of his architect colleagues against a social and cultural background: "As far as this land is concerned, its dwellings are much too strongly oriented to European patterns. Too much imitation exists and too little independent spirit of invention. The climate of Palestine and the lifestyle of its inhabitants, closely bound to nature, require us to free ourselves from the normal ground plan in order to achieve coolness and a larger scale for the interior. This purpose is fulfilled by the hall as the refreshing center of the Arab town house and the one-room stone tent of the sedentary Bedouins in Es-Salt. Open balconies, for example, serve no function in a subtropical climate, while trees next to the facade are more effective for producing shade and more pleasant in appearance. Thus much remains to be done."[10]

As a teacher, Mendelsohn recommended the study of the land itself—its earth, its sky, its landscape, its light and colors, the indigenous flora and fauna, the topography and its stone formations—in short, the dialogue with the *genius loci*. In this context he made reference again and again to the local Arab culture and architecture. The traditional Arab village in its magnificent synthesis with the Palestinian landscape was a constant leitmotiv for him. Martin Buber, in whose writings Mendelsohn often found support for his own intellectual attitude, had made this same point in 1929 in Berlin in a lecture on Palestinian national policy. He invoked the local culture of the Arabs to counter the widespread image of Palestine as a cultural and social tabula rasa: "We must never lose sight of the fact that with them, a rooted connection with the land has taken on a vital, even organic self-evidence that we do not even come close to possessing. They, not we, have something that can be called Palestinian form. The clay huts of the *fellahin* villages have sprung up from the ground; the houses of Tel Aviv are set on top of it."[11]

Like Buber, Mendelsohn saw Arab culture as far more than simply "anticultural, wild Asianness." His national efforts integrated the Arab population, which he viewed as a related tribe. Using their culture as a point of departure, he sought his own Semitic roots, which drew their power from the soil of the land. Mendelsohn, however, never went so far as to ignore two thousand years of Western development. He attempted to build a bridge between the biblical Palestine and the modern Western world. He described this process as finding a new platform whose foundations consisted of Western knowledge and Eastern wisdom, advocating an East-West synthesis on the basis of a national, Jewish-Semitic renaissance.

His ideas of an old-new, East-Western Jewish Palestine, which he conceived as part of a pan-Semitic commonwealth, were published in 1940 in a political pamphlet entitled *Palestine and the World of Tomorrow*. Here Mendelsohn presented his personal view of the nation: "Palestine is not an uninhabited land. On the contrary it forms a part of the Arabian world. The problem that confronts the Jew in Palestine is how to reach equal rank among his neighbors; how to

Typical Tel Aviv apartment house by Ben Ami Shoulman from the first half of the 1930s. "Corbusier and I" was Mendelsohn's commentary on buildings of this sort.

become a cell of the future Semitic commonwealth, to which they in fact belong by their race, tongue, and character. . . . Formerly the image of an uncreative provincial art Palestine of today is symbolizing the union between the most modern civilization and the most antique culture. It is the place where intellect and vision—matter and spirit meet. In the arrangement commanded by this union both Arabs and Jews, both members of the Semitic family, should be equally interested. On its solution depends the fate of Palestine to become a part of the New World which is going to replace the world that has gone. Genesis repeats itself."[12]

It was against this ideological background that Mendelsohn erected his buildings in Palestine. He understood them as the expression of a political confession. The first architectural manifesto of this East-West synthesis was the villa for Chaim and Vera Weizmann.

The Weizmann House in Rehovot, 1934–1936

After arriving in Rehovot with Chaim Weizmann, Mendelsohn inspected the site, sketching his first ideas then and there. In late 1934, he gave Weizmann a choice of two different designs. Vera and Chaim Weizmann decided in favor of the "original plan with inner courtyard" and an exposed central stairwell.[13] This plan became the basis of all further developments; it already shows the essential elements of the later, realized version can already be discerned. Once the design had been decided upon, "Vera's special mission" began, which Weizmann's biographer Norman Rose describes as follows: "For the next two-and-a-half years she waged a war of attrition with Mendelsohn on practically every aspect of the house."[14] The size of the house, for example, changed a number of times; at various stages in the negotiations, it ranged from 660 to 1028 square meters, depending on Vera Weizmann's changing desires and Chaim Weizmann's

Weizmann house, Rehovot, ground plan and perspective sketches, dated 1934.

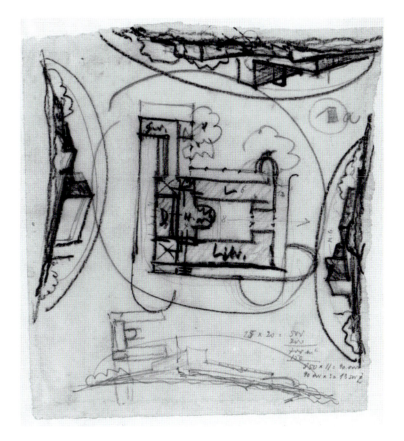

willingness to pay big money for architectural escapades. Mendelsohn fought for the best possible execution in terms of materials and technology as well as quality of craftsmanship. He supported these demands with an appeal to Weizmann's moral responsibility to the Jewish people: "Your position obligates you to build a house that is open and attractive to all segments of the population. . . . Important men, especially outside of Jewish circles, are waiting for the dignity of our people to finally come to expression in its architecture. They cannot get past it."[15] Weizmann, however, replied: "Even if I could permit myself this kind of expenditure, I would not do it, for moral reasons. It really should not be done in Pal[estine]. I want a decent house, but not a luxury building."[16]

All in all, Weizmann's position in the ambitious house project was not an easy one. He had to deal with—and pay for—the conceptions of two strong but diverging personalities. Vera Weizmann's and Mendelsohn's opposing ideas of beauty probably came to most flagrant expression in the interior furnishings. After the built-in furnishings such as wall closets and shelves, sanitary facilities, fireplaces, and doors had been executed by Mendelsohn, Vera Weizmann opted for furniture in the British Edwardian Style, hiring for this purpose the architect Robert Lutyens—son of the famous Sir Edwin Lutyens—who had married the Weizmanns' niece.[17] Mendelsohn was deeply hurt.

In late 1936, the Weizmanns moved into their new house.[18] The Weizmann house is located on a gentle slope planted with orange groves. In the 1930s, the view to the west extended to the Mediterranean, while the hill country of Judea was visible to the east. The only other buildings in the immediate vicinity were the first laboratories of the Daniel Sieff Institute, where Weizmann worked as director. By virtue of its exposed position on the highest point of the site, the residence is visible from afar. Its clear architectural composition is easily comprehensible. The complex consists of four interlocking blocks arranged symmetrically along an east-west axis around an open inner courtyard. Two essential elements violate the strict symmetry: a service tract attached to the northeast corner, and the entrance to the house, shifted out of axis to the south front. In this solution, we recognize the bravura typical above all of Mendelsohn's early work: the transformation of a symmetrical composition into an asymmetrical experience.

Weizmann house, Rehovot, sketch of entrance, dated October 3, 1935.

Weizmann house, Rehovot, northwest corner with garden after Mendelsohn's planting scheme. According to the architect, an integral element of the garden was Palestinian deer.

Weizmann house, Rehovot, plans and schematic site plan indicating the design of the garden.

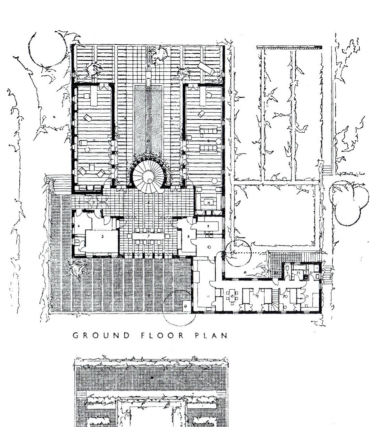

GROUND FLOOR PLAN

FIRST FLOOR PLAN

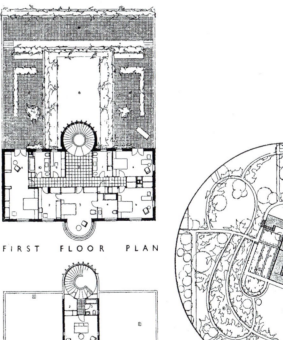

SECOND FLOOR PLAN

The three-story, semicircular stair tower, visible from afar, marks the center of the complex. It is inserted into a lower, two-story block with flat, one-story wings adjoining perpendicularly at either end. The U-shaped plan is thus traced by a clearly defined hierarchy of blocks of varying height. The open west side is defined by a broad terrace roof that connects the side wings with one another, thus enclosing the inner courtyard. The patio area, open to the sky, is occupied by a swimming pool. Flanked by covered walkways on either side, it forms the cooling centerpiece of the architectural composition.

While the building seems closed toward the outside, large glass doors open from the interior onto the inner courtyard. The low south wing accommodates Weizmann's study and library, the north wing a spacious living room. The ground floor of the two-story block to the east houses a spacious entrance hall with an adjacent dining room. The bedrooms of the Weizmann family and the guest rooms—each with its own bath—are located in the upper story. The stair tower represents the only connection between the floors; it towers over the east wing by an additional story, which accommodated a small bedroom for the family's private nurse.

As the home and reception office of the future president of the future State of Israel, the generous scale of the house prefigured things to come. Mendelsohn made use of a number of architectural means to emphasize the patron's public stature. The first was the stair tower, which lent the Weizmann house a monumental character. Numerous elements mark it unmistakably as the center of the building. A semicircular projecting oriel on the opposite east side balances it as a counterweight. The reflection of the tower in the water of the pool invites a contemplative mood. Mendelsohn's preference for exposed stair towers is familiar from earlier projects; the Weizmann house, however, represents the first and only example in which Mendelsohn exposed the stairwell on the exterior of a private house. In public buildings and large apartment blocks, exterior stair towers reveal the presence of a circulation network throughout the building and thus function as signposts. In a private house such as the Weizmanns', however, the stair tower serves as

Weizmann house, Rehovot, view of
winding garden path leading to
entrance.

the connection between the public rooms on the ground floor and the private rooms of the upper
story. An exposed stair tower in this context clearly indicates that this is the house of a man who
stands in the public eye. As president of the Zionist Organization, Chaim Weizmann was always
acting on the political and social stage—even in his own house. Thus the architecture of his villa
could not be that of an ordinary private house, but rather of one "where the head of the Zionist
Organization could receive and entertain guests from all walks of life."[19] The building created a
setting that ensured the observance of a particular etiquette.

According to one of Mendelsohn's axioms, "good architecture is designed around the corner."[20] He defined the relation between the human being and architecture as a dynamic process,
as the tension between moved and moving energy. The element of motion can reside with either
the object or the viewer: either the object "moves" in front of a static viewer or the latter moves
around a static object. These are the two possibilities that were explored in futurism and cubism.
Mendelsohn's extroverted German architecture speaks the futurist language: there, his curved
concrete masses seem to swerve around corners with long ribbon windows floating horizontally.
The closed walls of the Weizmann house, on the other hand, evince a static character in their
introversion and geometric tranquillity. In order to nonetheless produce a sense of dynamic tension, Mendelsohn resorted to a device that recalled the perspectival tricks of the cubists: he
moved the viewer around his object, here in a literal, physical sense. Mendelsohn developed
a carefully calculated perspective program for the house; a number of sketches show him
exploring various views of the house from different angles.[21] After completing these studies,
Mendelsohn designed the approach to the house as a winding path presenting all sides of the
building to the visitor. Before entering the interior of the house through the main door, the visitor
had already been confronted with all the facades and corner views of the house. Only one perspective was exempted: the northeast corner, where the service tract was located.

In this play of changing perspectives, Mendelsohn appears to have been inspired by the
architecture of classical Greece. He had visited Greece for the first time three years before, in
spring 1931: "The Acropolis overwhelmed him. He was especially impressed by the manner of
approach and how it was integrated into the overall concept."[22] Thus in his first built project for

the "old-new" land, Mendelsohn—one of the prophets of the machine age in Germany—returned to the ancient roots of the Mediterranean. His recourse to classical Mediterranean and Levantine traditions was based on climatic, topographical, and cultural considerations. He himself described the Weizmann house as "absolutely of our time . . . and yet adopted as a residence in a subtropical climate. This, I feel, is a type of home which will again after two thousand years, become popular throughout the Orient, as it was when Judea was a Roman Province."[23]

Finally, attention should be drawn to the nautical symbolism of the Weizmann house. The clear, symmetrical hierarchy of the long, low blocks recalls the longitudinal section of the hull of a ship; the projecting, semicircular stair tower with its continuous ribbon window beneath the roofline suggests a captain's bridge, while the windows of the library and the living room resemble the portholes of a steamer. Allusions to shipbuilding in modern architecture are well known,[24] most of them based on a glorification of functionality and the machine aesthetic. In the Weizmann house, however, other meanings associated with the image of the ship come into play as well: departure and voyage to faraway destinations, escape and deliverance, movement toward a defined or an undefined utopian goal, hope for a "brave new world." The archetypal motif associated with these meanings is the ark of Noah. Almost all literary utopias use the ship motif in one form or another: Theodor Herzl's utopian novel *Altneuland,* for example, begins with a voyage that leads, via many detours, to the Promised Land. The Weizmann house likewise symbolizes a Noah's ark that has alighted on Mount Ararat, laden with hopes for a better society in a new homeland.

Analysis of the house as a mere dwelling may reveal its well planned organism. Still, essential aspects that compensate for a number of functional shortcomings[25] remain unnoticed. The multiple layers of the architectural statement become apparent only when we accept it as a bearer of meaning, an *architecture parlante*. In this sense, it stands out from Mendelsohn's other projects in Palestine and occupies a place comparable to that of the Einstein Tower at the beginning of his career in Germany. The Weizmann house manifests the optimistic concept of Mendelsohn's East-West synthesis, the architect's political, social, and cultural imperative. Today the house is preserved in relatively good condition and is open to the public as a museum to the first president of Israel.

Mendelsohn's Office in Jerusalem

Mendelsohn's first projects in Palestine were still supervised out of his London office. Already his second trip to Palestine in the spring of 1935, however, was devoted to the establishment of a branch office in Jerusalem. It appears that he consciously chose the Holy City as his location and not the Jewish metropolis of Tel Aviv. He wanted to maintain direct contact with the living roots of the Semitic-oriental tradition, using it to create something new. Mendelsohn rented an old Arab windmill from the eighteenth century, a picturesque structure of powerful unworked stone in the wildly romantic ambience of an overgrown garden with a giant fig tree. While the broad octagonal tower of the windmill, narrowing toward the top, no longer possessed its blades, it was otherwise preserved in its original condition, including the wooden cupola.

Attached to the tower was a spacious, two-story wing built in a manner typical of rural Arab architecture: meter-thick masonry to ward off the heat of the day, punctuated by small, usually round-arched windows and an exterior staircase leading to the recessed upper story with its shallow domes and roof terrace.

Mendelsohn's office was on the ground floor, while the upper story and narrow tower spaces served him and his wife as a private dwelling. The tower room, just large enough for a desk, was chosen by Mendelsohn as his private study. In addition to pencils and sketch paper, the phonograph and record collection of classical music were the most important objects in this cloister. Living conditions in the mill were relatively rustic, not to say primitive. To what extent the memories of Am Rupenhorn, his established career, and Germany were only suppressed is hard to determine. In Palestine, at any rate, Mendelsohn clearly sought a new beginning oriented to simple structures, sublime in their primitive character.

Until 1939, Mendelsohn traveled regularly between London and Jerusalem, a situation that necessitated perfect organization in his Jerusalem office and a trustworthy representative in Palestine. Already in 1934 he contracted with Erich Kempinski, an experienced civil engineer who had worked for a large construction firm in Germany until 1933. His area of expertise was construction in reinforced steel.[26]

Kempinski hired additional assistants, whose number varied according to the commission situation and the amount of work in the office. From 1935 on, the permanent staff consisted of four architects (Wolfgang [Ze'ev] Bruckz, Gunther [Gad] Ascher, Jarost Javecz, and Hans Schiller), another engineer (Naftali Rostowsky), and a secretary (Dr. Wolfgang Ehrlich). When the work load became extreme, other assistants were hired on a short-term basis. Aside from Erich Kempinski, who received a five-year contract, Mendelsohn's uncertain political, financial, and personal situation made it inadvisable for him to make long-term contracts with any of his other assistants. The salaries they earned, however, were relatively high, resulting not least of all from the high fees Mendelsohn himself charged his clients: 9 to 10 percent of the total building cost for private commissions, 8 percent for public buildings. This scale of fees corresponded to that of the Royal Institute of British Architects (RIBA), although Mendelsohn did not become a member of RIBA until 1938 when he became a British subject. For local architects in Palestine, fees of around 3 to 5 percent of the total building cost were usual at that time.[27] Since the entire office profited from the relatively high wages, an extraordinarily good working climate prevailed with a high level of motivation, which Mendelsohn certainly appreciated: "No day goes by without twelve to fourteen hours at the drawing board with all my assistants, whose absolute devotion continues to touch me deeply. I have never, not even with C. [probably Charles Du Vinage], been able to work as I can with this group of people, who were simply tossed together. . . ."[28]

House and Library for Salman Schocken in Jerusalem, 1934–1936

Only a few meters away from Mendelsohn's mill, several plots had been acquired by Salman Schocken, who had emigrated to Palestine in 1933. Shortly after Mendelsohn arrived in Jerusalem, Schocken commissioned him to plan and build a house and a large private library on two of these building sites. Both buildings still stand; while the library has remained nearly unaltered, the house has unfortunately been subjected to repeated remodeling over the course of the years.

We have already encountered Schocken as a successful businessman and Mendelsohn's most important client in Germany. Schocken was characterized by German discipline and organizational ability as well as by the intellectual tradition of the land of his birth; at the same time, however, he also identified himself with a post-assimilatory generation of Jews. He became involved in the Zionist movement early on, and in 1910 joined the organization as an active member. From 1916 on, he was director of the Zionist cultural committee and promoted the publication of Jewish authors. This involvement climaxed in 1931 in the founding of the publishing house Schocken-Verlag in Berlin. From 1921 on, he served on the financial and economic advisory board of the World Zionist Organization and on the board of directors of the Jewish National Fund. In Schocken, we recognize a man with diverse interests and a passion not only for business, but above all for literature.[29]

Salman Schocken, Mendelsohn's most important client and supporter in Germany and Palestine.

Schocken house, Jerusalem, view of
north side with entrance and
pergola-covered terrace.

Schocken house, Jerusalem,
southwest view with projecting south
terrace and terraced garden planned
by Mendelsohn.

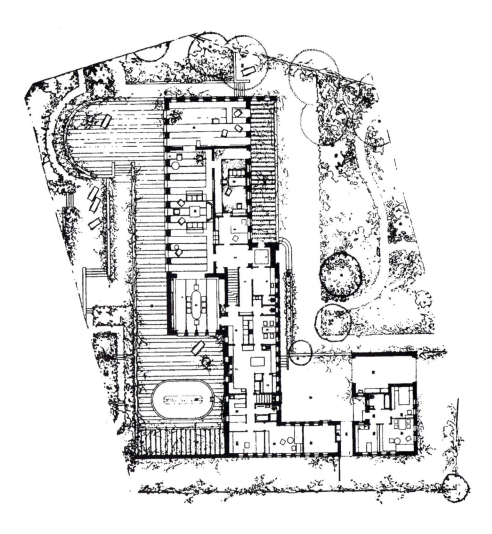

Schocken house, Jerusalem, ground floor plan. To the east are the adjoining servants' quarters.

From late 1934 to 1936, therefore, Mendelsohn designed private houses for two of the most important men in Jewish circles in Palestine. Despite the typological similarity of the two buildings, however, the results could not have been more different. Even the relatively smooth planning of the Schocken villa contrasted starkly with the complicated negotiations that marked Mendelsohn's dealings with the Weizmanns. On December 6, 1934, he wrote to his wife: "The Schocken sketches have been born. From noon on we will see if they are viable."[30] They were in fact "viable," for already a week later he wrote to her again: "I have just come from Schocken. I am already lying in bed, I only wanted to briefly tell you that both Schockens were delighted with the new plans. The house will only be reduced in size. . . ."[31] In late December came the final push for the submission of the plans to the building office: "Schocken has accepted all the plans and is very pleased and friendly. . . . The house is becoming very beautiful—a first shot. It is quite different from Weizmann's. We are working like madmen to finish the plans for submission."[32]

The Schocken residence is located in the northeast part of Rehavia, a district of Jerusalem planned as a garden city in the early 1920s by Richard Kauffmann.[33] In the 1930s, it developed into a villa suburb primarily occupied by well-situated inhabitants from Germany. The Schocken building site slopes downward toward the south and offers an expansive view of the hilly country around Jerusalem. The garden is strongly terraced. The house itself lies on a piled-up section of the terrain; like the Weizmann house, it is situated at the highest point of the site. In contrast to

Schocken house, Jerusalem, view of southeast corner with pergola and small swimming pool. Of particular note is Mendelsohn's flawless handling of the Jerusalem stone.

Living room of the Schocken house during a reception in honor of the inauguration of the Hadassah University Medical Center on May 9, 1939. In the foreground, Salman Schocken appears with members of the Women's Zionist Organization, with Henrietta Szold, after whom the medical center's Henrietta Szold Nursing School was named, at the far left.

the country-house character of the latter, however, the Schocken residence presents itself as a typical town house integrated into the structure of a villa suburb.

The main characteristic of the Weizmann house had been a clearly articulated composition designed to be seen from a distance, marked by symmetry and hierarchy with a dominant stair tower. With the Schocken house, however, Mendelsohn appears to have reverted to exactly the opposite. Each house is the portrait of its patron and his role in society. Mendelsohn reacted with psychological sensitivity to the position each of these personalities occupied in public life. Chaim Weizmann was the politician who represented the Zionist movement; accordingly, his house was laden with symbols representing a public political mission. Salman Schocken, on the other hand, avoided the public eye; despite his numerous activities and involvements within the Zionist movement, he represented the organizing power in the background. He was best and most comfortable planning from his desk.[34] His residence was thus free of symbolic superstructure, a private house designed from the inside out. A comfortable and refined interior arrangement defined the asymmetrical exterior of the building, on which the stairwell was not visible. The asymmetrical building is subjected to a graduated rhythm of vertical glass doors and horizontal bands of loggias, consolidated into a homogeneous composition by the repetition of motifs such as round projecting forms (terrace, balcony, swimming pool) and pergolas (east side of the south terrace, north terrace, porch of roof garden). While the Weizmann house is centered around an inner courtyard, in the Schocken house Mendelsohn emphasized the direct confrontation between interior and exterior, experienced directly by the inhabitants in the numerous glass doors throughout the entire ground floor. The long, narrow structure with rooms arranged in a row sequence—a building type also represented by the Nimmo house in Chalfont St. Giles in England from about the same time—recalls Mendelsohn's prototypical villa Am Rupenhorn, a house that had embedded itself in the consciousness of many visitors and clients. Mendelsohn's variations on this theme were built at his clients' request. Of Schocken's wife, for example, he reported that "she [measures] all the dimensions according to Rupenhorn, which is more unforgettable to her than to me. . . ."[35]

Like all of Mendelsohn's subsequent buildings in Jerusalem, the house is a concrete construction with stone facing on the exterior. The almost forty-centimeter thick masonry was produced using a method customary in Jerusalem at that time: two layers of stone were built up and then filled with cement or concrete. At important bearing points, the construction was reinforced with iron girders.[36] Mendelsohn's masterful handling of the yellowish-gold Jerusalem stone is especially striking in the careful treatment of the door and window frames. In calculating the cut of the stone, he placed greatest emphasis on the continuation of the primary lines around the building at the same height. In his use of natural stone, Mendelsohn followed the old Jerusalem building tradition, on which both the Ottoman and the British building codes had been based.[37]

The composition of the interior spaces was inspired by the furnishings of Am Rupenhorn as well as by Schocken's valuable art collection, which included significant impressionist works as well as a few special pieces of local provenance. Mendelsohn's holistic approach always also found expression in the design of his gardens, which constituted an integral element of his plans. For him, to be an architect was to create a microcosm encompassing all aspects of life. For the garden of the Schocken estate, he designed among other things a small bird bath. A wonderful letter from Mendelsohn to Schocken's secretaries, preserved in the Schocken Archive, shows the care taken by the creator of this small paradise garden: "Dear Sirs, Yesterday I visited the garden of the Schocken house and found that it had completely dried out. . . . . All the freshly planted trees must be carefully watered for three years, so that they survive the initial planting period. This has not occurred, and the results are already visible. In addition, there is a bird bath in the garden. This bird bath is without water. The bird bath is intended not only to nourish the birds, but above all to draw them and make them feel at home. Thus it is necessary to fill the bird bath, even when the Schocken family is out of the country."[38]

In the 1930s, the garden with its semicircular projecting terrace afforded a view of the Schocken library which stands less than a hundred meters away.[39] Seen from this vantage point, a semicircular glazed oriel set into the otherwise simple, almost archaic stone structure of the library answered on the opposite side. It was precisely this perspective that Mendelsohn represented in his sketches of the library. This corner view, however, which emphasizes the building's three-dimensional qualities and bears Mendelsohn's signature in the expressive glass oriel, is hardly noticed from the street. Toward the public, Schocken's private library presents a closed front.

Salman Schocken had brought his valuable library—comprising 60,000 volumes and a large collection of rare manuscripts, incunabula, and first editions—with him from Germany to Jerusalem. It formed the basis for his research institute for Hebrew poetry founded in 1930 in Germany, to which an institute for Cabala studies was added in 1939 in Jerusalem. Over the course of time, the private library had developed into a research institute open to various scholars.[40]

The library building was planned at the same time as the house. On December 7, 1934, Mendelsohn wrote to his wife: "Today I sketched the plan of the library with the lecture room and research institute for Jewish literature. The site is absurd, but the plan has spirit and something of Palladio."[41] The building did in fact radiate a contemplative tranquillity and noble reserve that recalled classical models. At this point in time, the Renaissance may have seemed to Mendelsohn an interesting lesson in the revitalization of a two-thousand-year-old culture. Just as Palladio's Teatro Olimpico conjured up the spirit of Rome and the classical principles of Vitruvius, Mendelsohn was seeking to awaken the Semitic culture of the People of the Book.

Like the house, the library was covered with a worked stone facing of yellowish-gold Jerusalem stone. The east side of the building, facing the street, appears simple and inconspicuous in the context of the villa district. Two rows of windows and an asymmetrical entrance artic-

Aerial photograph of Rehavia, Balfour Street. In the upper right is the Schocken house, at the lower left the library. Between them is Richard Kauffmann's Aghion house, now the official residence of the Israeli prime minister.

ulate the wall area. The windows of the upper and lower stories differ from one another in number and size and are not axially related to each other. Behind them in the lower story are the administrative spaces, in the upper story Schocken's private study. The windows of the upper story occupy a noticeably low position in comparison to the total height of the building. There are technical reasons for this strange proportional disharmony: the upper story possesses a double ceiling with an intermediate space corresponding to about four courses of stone. This space accommodated a built-in air conditioning system with ventilation and heating, facilities extremely modern for the time. The disproportion, however, also has an aesthetic justification, producing a sense of top-heaviness already observed in earlier projects such as the Rudolf Mosse publishing house and the Double Villa at Karolinger Platz and which for Mendelsohn was always an indication of spatial extent. The viewer is challenged to grasp the facade in its three-dimensional context and is, as it were, led "around the corner." Thus Mendelsohn used a subtle surface disharmony to call the viewer's attention to the three-dimensionality of the form.

The north side of the library received a special accent in the vertical windows extending over both stories and illuminating the interior of the spacious stairwell. The entire west part of the library is articulated only by three rows of small windows, marking the location of the book repositories on three floors. As already mentioned, the south facade is the most interesting, in typical Mendelsohnian fashion. Here he worked with abruptly opposing elements: glass against stone, round forms against blocks, opening against closure, dynamics against statics, high-tech against Jerusalem. He called the exciting glass oriel his "Rembrandt window": as the sole light source for the interior space behind it, it recalls the famous raking light in Rembrandt's pictures. The room in question is the most splendid in the library, the large reading room between the study of Schocken on the east side and the book repositories in the west. Mendelsohn devoted particular attention to the design of this room and its furnishings, which include built-in cabinets with multifunctional, technical conveniences. Ceiling-high wall cabinets of fine, golden-yellow lemon wood, in which valuable pieces from the Schocken collection were protected from the

Schocken library, Jerusalem, sketch, 1936.

light, line the entire room. The only exception is the north wall with its glazed bookshelves framed in bronze and windows above, allowing the indirect north light to enter the room. The projecting, semicircular shelf posts, extending from floor to ceiling in fine lemon wood, echo the form of the glass oriel on the opposite south side, the only source of direct sunlight.[42] The rounded form of the oriel serves to focus the light on the interior, suggesting to Mendelsohn the association with Rembrandt. In winter when the sun is low, the rays of light entering through the oriel behave like a sundial, wandering through the reading room from west to east over the course of the day, lending it an almost mystical atmosphere.

The Hebrew University on Mount Scopus in Jerusalem, 1934–1940
In 1902 at a time when it was not even certain there woud be land for the Jewish immigration—the "Uganda Congress" still lay ahead—Martin Buber, Berthold Feiwel, and Chaim Weizmann authored a publication in Berlin entitled *Eine Jüdische Hochschule* (*A Jewish University*). In it, they presented their program for the establishment of a cultural and intellectual center in Palestine as the basis of a national movement. Not until after the eleventh Zionist Congress of 1913, however, were the fund-raising efforts begun that made possible the purchase of a plot on Mount Scopus the following year.

Schocken library, Jerusalem, large reading and lecture hall in upper story.

The cornerstone of the university was laid in summer 1918 in a ceremonial act marked by a heroic spirit. Those attending heard the shots of the last conflicts in the background as Weizmann gave his solemn speech: "At first it may seem paradoxical that we should begin with the creation of a center for spiritual and intellectual development in a land with such a small population, a land in which everything remains to be done, a land that calls for such simple things as plows, streets, and harbors. But for those who know the Jewish soul, it can be no paradox."[43]

A year later, Sir Patrick Geddes developed the first architectural master plan, whose hexagonal form was based on the Star of David and whose center he interpreted as an overarching temple of life.[44] His son-in-law, the British architect Frank C. Mears, transformed this concept stylistically into a Romantic-oriental vision of *A Thousand and One Nights*.

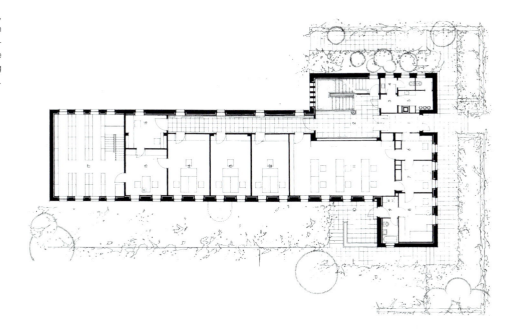

Schocken library, Jerusalem, plan of ground floor with narrow entrance area, projecting stairwell, administrative spaces, study and reading rooms, and book repositories.

The design was sent on a propaganda tour through America and managed to raise enough money to erect the first buildings after the Geddes-Mears plan. The construction of these first university institutes coincided with Mendelsohn's first trip to Palestine in 1923. A year later, his name appeared in the official correspondence related to the university for the first time when Kurt Blumenfeld[45] suggested him as the architect of the project. In letters to Zionist friends, Berthold Feiwel complained about the "artistically absolutely disastrous design by Geddes." He justified the choice of Mendelsohn among other things by an appeal to a feeling of national responsibility—"I think, however, that it is our task to allow monumental, national buildings to be realized by those few major Jewish artists"[46]—and suggested promoting Mendelsohn. Mendelsohn did not become directly involved in the project until 1934; already shortly thereafter, however, he occupied a key position on Mount Scopus. In early December 1934, he conjectured: "The University is already waiting and wants me to make an offertory. I write nothing and say nothing about architecture—I wait and see".[47] In mid-December, he began writing to his wife about the first negotiations and site inspections. In his letters he praised the unique building site on Mount Scopus with its magnificent view of the old city of Jerusalem with the Temple Mount to the southwest and the bare mountaintops of the Judean Desert to the east, extending down to the Dead Sea in the southeast. His disappointment over the first institute buildings, on the other hand, knew no bounds: "A God-given piece of country between the Dead Sea and the Mediterranean has been violated by devils' hands. A wretched, botched fruit of incompetence and self-complacency. I feel like Jeremiah—deeply depressed and wounded in my soul."[48]

In the early 1930s, the university consisted of four institute buildings and a few insignificant auxiliary structures. Three of the four institute buildings had been erected by the British-Jewish architect Benjamin Chaikin,[49] a resident of Jerusalem, after the Geddes-Mears plan. Chaikin employed an oriental formal vocabulary with a European-colonial accent. In 1934, the time was ripe for a new master plan, which was to include additional research and teaching institutes for various departments, a large university hospital, student housing, and not least of all new access streets.[50]

Since both Weizmann and Schocken—both important decision-makers in the affairs of the university—were involved in projects with Mendelsohn at the time, it was clear that he would be the

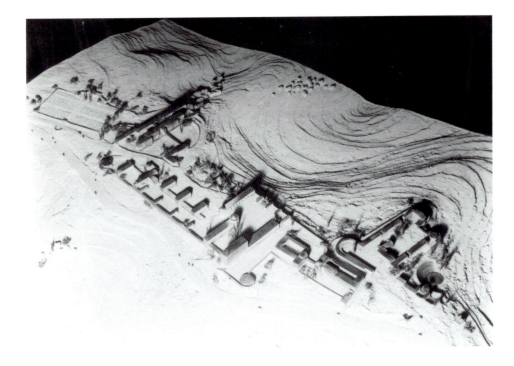

Hebrew University on Mount Scopus, Jerusalem. This model of the master plan was shown at the world exposition in Paris in 1937.

university's new man. An initial version of his master plan was presented to the local commission already in October 1935 and underwent repeated alterations throughout the following year.

In 1937, Mendelsohn had a model made of his Scopus plan. It showed the disposition of the buildings on the crest of the hill, which ascends from the northwest to the southeast. On both sides of the ridge, the terrain slopes downward, relatively steeply to the east toward the Dead Sea and in gentle terraces to the west toward the Kidron Valley. The difference in altitude to the Dead Sea amounts to nearly 1,100 meters, to the Temple Mount only about 45 meters. The character of the site forced Mendelsohn to plan a very compact campus. He positioned the axes of his buildings running east-west at a right angle to the ridge of the mountain, so that in winter they "would [counter] the direct force of the cold northeast wind, but capture the pleasant, warming sun; and in the summer, exclude the hot sun, but capture the cooling west wind."[51] Mendelsohn graduated the heights of his buildings, adapting them to the rise of the mountain ridge to the southeast. Echoing the natural form of the terrain, they culminate in a higher central group at the southeast of the campus, the highest point. Mendelsohn's plan integrated the existing buildings into a new overall context, using connecting wings and walls to counter their originally isolated character. U- and L-shape forms create charming plazas and shady, inviting inner courtyards.

The model of the Hebrew University in Jerusalem was shown in 1937 at the famous world exposition in Paris—the same one where the works of Albert Speer and Boris Iofan confronted each other with the claims of Hitler's Germany and Stalin's Russia, and where Picasso's *Guernica* in the Spanish pavilion sounded a lamentation against war and fascism. In this context, Mendelsohn's model represented the most important witness of the Jewish old-new homeland and its intellectual and cultural renaissance. Here, against the background of an approaching inferno, the concept of learning and erudition—deeply anchored in the Jewish tradition—brought the only glimmer of hope for a better future.

With this project, Mendelsohn had hoped to be able to realize a longtime dream, that of creating a large-scale urbanistic master plan. Mendelsohn's design, however, was gradually

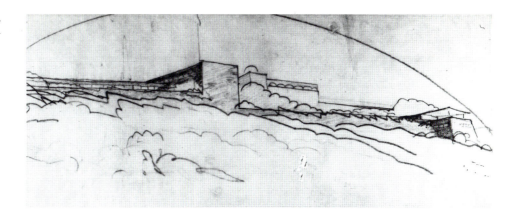

rubbed away between the bureaucratic demands of the British Mandate government, the pragmatism of the university administration, and the egotistical wishes of American donors. The only structures realized under Mendelsohn's direction were the Hadassah University Medical Center and two modest buildings as well as a garden.

In the spring of 1935, Mendelsohn busied himself with the planning of a University Clubhouse, which was erected in 1936 and inaugurated in January 1937. The one-and-a-half to two-story building, a simple, rectangular block with a flat roof, lies on the southwest tip of the mountain ridge. On the west side, the sharply sloping terrain permits two full stories; here, Mendelsohn took advantage of the splendid view of the old city to open the upper story onto a narrow, covered terrace. The interior spaces—lecture and assembly hall, smoking rooms, professors' rooms, and others—were likewise furnished by Mendelsohn.[52]

In the planning for the Museum of Jewish Antiquity and Institute for Archaeological Research, immediately adjacent to the clubhouse, the concerted protest of the association of architects and engineers prevented the commission from going to Mendelsohn. They demanded public competitions, in which Mendelsohn served on a three-member jury. The first prize and the award of the commission went to two of his former assistants: Jarost Javecz and Carl Rubin.[53]

In May 1939, Mendelsohn built a gymnasium with an adjacent sports field.[54] The hall itself was a very modest construction, with nine concrete pillars on each long side supporting a flat roof. The form Mendelsohn chose for the concrete supports is interesting; their cross sections form right triangles whose broad sides bear the roof, while the narrow points rest on the ground. In this way, the overhead windows could be optimally shaded.

Ultimately, however, Mendelsohn's master plan experienced the same fate that had befallen the Geddes-Mears plan: it remained fragmentary. When Mendelsohn left Palestine in 1941, Richard Kauffmann took over the architectural direction of the university, but his new concept remained unrealized as well. The war of independence after the founding of the State of Israel turned Jerusalem into a divided city. While the site on Mount Scopus officially remained Israeli territory, it stood under Jordanian military control. After a number of bloody incidents, university activities were abandoned and a new campus was erected in the west part of Jerusalem. After the Six-Day War in 1967, which reunified the city under Israeli control, the university campus on Mount Scopus acquired new political significance. It was restored, expanded, and gradually became again the center of university activities in Jerusalem.[55]

The Hadassah University Medical Center on Mount Scopus in Jerusalem, 1934–1939

With its breathtaking view of the Dead Sea desert and the old city of Jerusalem, the *Har Hazofim*, as it is called in Hebrew, presents an incomparable natural spectacle. Mendelsohn, always sensitive to the metaphysical, was overwhelmed by this landscape:

Har Hazofim

The divide between a world that we know

and a world that we sense

between the earthly demand

of all or nothing

and the divine fulfillment

that embraces All in the mysterious Nothing.

The place of creation, where heaven and earth

seem to touch one another,

where heaven and earth are often divided by worlds.[56]

At the height of his creative powers, Mendelsohn felt ready to meet the challenge of such a place, to engage in a dialogue with the divine creation. The Hadassah University Medical Center built on this site is arguably his largest project in Palestine.

The new medical complex, planned in connection with the university, consisted of three units: the Hadassah University Hospital, the Henrietta Szold Nursing School, and the Nathan Ratnoff School for medical research and education. The project appears in Mendelsohn's letters to his wife beginning in early December 1934.[57] Through skilled diplomacy, he succeeded in averting the open competition originally planned and gaining the commission for himself.[58] His first sketches for the hospital project date from February 1935. The large number of surviving sketches enable us to follow the course of the planning in detail; in addition, three models document the most important phases of the development.[59]

Model A from fall 1935 shows a composition of four long, parallel blocks, oriented from west to east and united by connecting wings and pergolas into a complex that integrates all three functions—hospital, research institute, and nursing school. Characteristic of this extremely dynamic design is the semicircular wing of the building, projecting to the east.

Model B, probably created in 1936, reflects fundamental changes in the arrangement of the buildings.[60] This design, too, shows longitudinal blocks; now, however, each of the three insti-

Hadassah University Medical Center, Jerusalem. Model A presents the first phase of planning.

Hadassah University Medical Center, Jerusalem. Model C represents the final version, composed of the Hadassah University Hospital, the Henrietta Szold Nursing School, and the Nathan Ratnoff School for medical research and education.

tutions appears as a self-contained unit with its own identity. These independent parts are only loosely connected into an overall complex. On the whole, Model B evinces a quieter, more static effect. The buildings seem to *stand* in their surroundings, an impression that is strengthened by the vertical windows. While the latter lend a sense of rhythm to the facade, the powerful dynamic of the ribbon windows is missing, and the sweeping curves of the building masses give way to more modest semicircular terraces. The mortuary, however—a projecting half-cylinder with a view of the boundless desert—remains a dramatically effective element. "The view is timeless. He who dies here has not far to travel," Mendelsohn commented.[61] Model B probably represents the version submitted for realization, while Model C documents the final version. It differs from its predecessor only in a few significant, but not fundamental, details. Each of the two wings of the hospital, for example, received an additional story as well as an impressive entrance with three domes.

These domes became the architectural logo of the hospital. To his friends, Mendelsohn called them the "breasts of the building," since the entrance led to the maternity ward.[62] With critics, he adopted a more serious tone and stated: "We are on Mount Scopus in Jerusalem looking down to villages 3 thousand years old or is it 6 thousand, who knows? Everywhere little domed stone houses. So I adopted the form of the dome. . . ."[63] His domes doubtless represent an

Hadassah University Medical Center on Mount Scopus against the spectacular backdrop of the Judean hill country and the expansive desert sky over the Dead Sea.

Aerial photograph of the Hadassah University Medical Center on Mount Scopus. In the foreground is the Nathan Ratnoff School for medical research and education; on the other side of the street is the Henrietta Szold Nursing School, connected to the Hadassah Hospital by a long pergola.

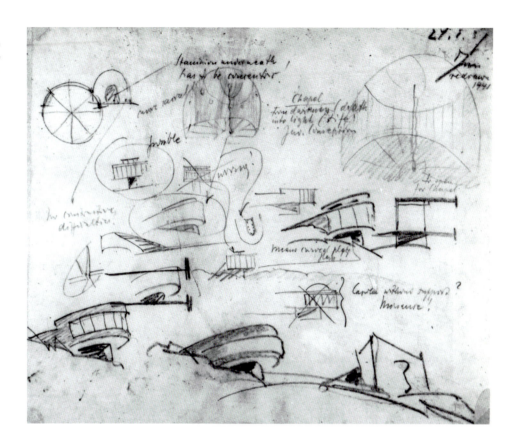

homage to the Arab architecture he repeatedly praised for its native sense of harmony. Closer examination, however, shows that Mendelsohn did not simply imitate the Arab motif, but approached it in a very differentiated, intellectual manner. Rather than copying, he quoted—and since the quotation was torn from its original context, he felt free to play with it uninhibitedly, translating the traditional masonry dome into concrete, relieving it of its function as a space-enclosing element by positioning it over an open passageway, and finally tripling it. The cornerstone of the entire complex was laid in a ceremony on October 20, 1936.[64] The construction period coincided with the great uprisings between 1936 and 1939, causing months-long delays due to continuing strikes by the Arab population.[65] The official inauguration took place on May 9, 1939.[66]

Mendelsohn devoted much time and special attention to the Hadassah project. Not infrequently, a night spent celebrating with friends would conclude with a trip to the Hadassah Hospital to see the structure gleaming in the first rays of the morning sun.[67] The project also occupied a special place in letters to his wife. Describing it, his words were like those of a lover: "I have today wandered for the entire morning through the Hadassah buildings, around them, into them, onto them, with the critical eye of the guardian, with the anxious care of the begetter, with the lover's eavesdropping caress. Always views—straight through; alignments. Intersections outside and in; built space and landscape; man's handiwork and God's; this marriage of our productive idea with the organic creative power of nature."[68]

Apart from a few dynamic reminiscences, the three buildings of the Hadassah complex stand as hard, rectilinear forms amid the barren, softly formed hills of Mount Scopus, producing an engaging contrast between organic nature and built architecture. The Jerusalem stone panels covering the reinforced concrete construction of the individual buildings both produce and reinforce their heavy, blocklike character as well as their sense of the indigenous, sprung up from

the natural soil. In a departure from the method employed in the two buildings for Schocken, Mendelsohn used stone panels cut and polished on both sides and "hung" in front of the facade. Each stone was anchored into the concrete surface with an iron pin.[69] In other words, the natural stone facing performed no static function whatsoever, but served merely for beautification—a function revealed in the vertical staggering of the individual panels. While the width of the panels remains constant, their length varies, creating continuous lines only in the vertical direction, with varying horizontal joints between them. In this way, the surface structure of the wall achieves a stronger sense of verticality, balancing the horizontal extension of the building masses.[70]

The interior of the entire complex—the furnishings of the foyer, reception, and waiting rooms as well as the director's rooms—was likewise designed by Mendelsohn. From the design of the furniture to the extravagant floors and ceilings, from the lighting system with its sophisticated fixtures to the necessary accessories such as flower dishes and ashtrays, all were designed by Mendelsohn's Jerusalem office. As in the Schocken house and library, prototypes from Am Rupenhorn served as models. For Mendelsohn's colleagues and assistants in the office, his elaborate publication on the Rupenhorn villa, *Neues Haus—Neue Welt*, functioned as a "Bible" of modern interior design.[71]

The buildings served their original purpose for eight years. Then, from 1947 to 1967, the site on Mount Scopus became a no-man's land-between the Israeli and Jordanian front. After 1967, the now-ruined buildings were renovated under the direction of the Israeli architect Ya'acov Rechter. Through various remodelings and expansions, the buildings were adapted to current technical standards, but were also considerably altered.

The Government Hospital in Haifa, 1937–1938
Mendelsohn built a second hospital in Palestine: the Government Hospital in Haifa, which differed completely from the Hadassah Hospital. As always with Mendelsohn, it was the site itself—its topography, atmosphere, and climatic conditions, but also its geo- and sociopolitical potential—that provided the decisive impetus for his first design sketches.

Illustration right:
Plans of basement, ground floor, and first and second floors of the Hadassah University Hospital. The inner courtyards provide lighting and ventilation for the interior spaces.

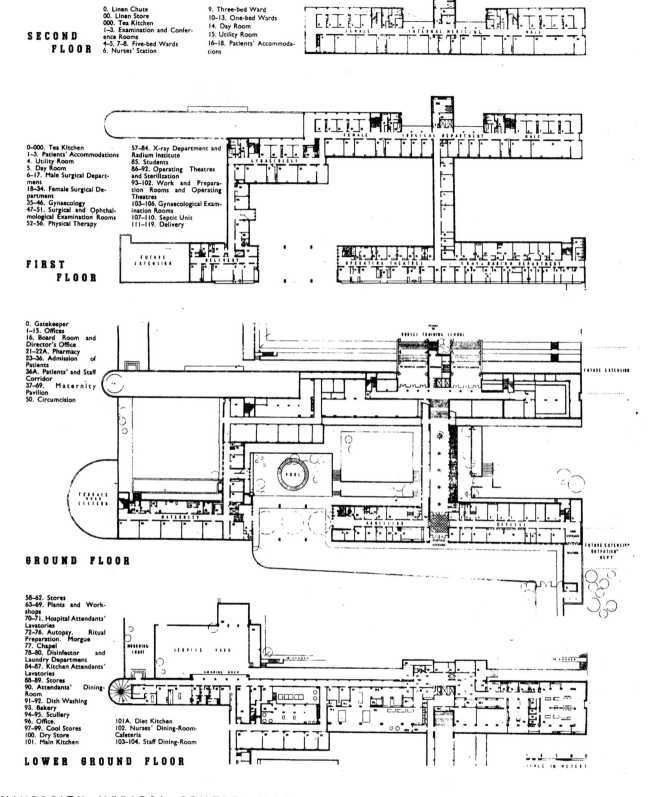

SECOND FLOOR

0. Linen Chute
00. Linen Store
000. Tea Kitchen
1–3. Examination and Conference Rooms
4–5, 7–8. Five-bed Wards
6. Nurses' Station
9. Three-bed Ward
10–13. One-bed Wards
14. Day Room
15. Utility Room
16–18. Patients' Accommodations

0-000. Tea Kitchen
1–3. Patients' Accommodations
4. Utility Room
5. Day Room
6–17. Male Surgical Department
18–34. Female Surgical Department
35–46. Gynaecology
47–51. Surgical and Ophthalmological Examination Rooms
52–56. Physical Therapy
57–84. X-ray Department and Radium Institute
85. Students
86–92. Operating Theatres and Sterilization
93–102. Work and Preparation Rooms and Operating Theatres
103–106. Gynaecological Examination Rooms
107–110. Septic Unit
111–119. Delivery

FIRST FLOOR

0. Gatekeeper
1–15. Offices
16. Board Room and Director's Office
21–22A. Pharmacy
23–36. Admission of Patients
36A. Patients' and Staff Corridor
37–69. Maternity Pavilion
50. Circumcision

GROUND FLOOR

58–62. Stores
63–69. Plants and Workshops
70–71. Hospital Attendants' Lavatories
72–76. Autopsy. Ritual Preparation. Morgue
77. Chapel
78–80. Disinfector and Laundry Department
84–87. Kitchen Attendants' Lavatories
88–89. Stores
90. Attendants' Dining-Room
91–92. Dish Washing
93. Bakery
94–95. Scullery
96. Office
97–99. Cool Stores
100. Dry Store
101. Main Kitchen
101A. Diet Kitchen
102. Nurses' Dining-Room-Cafeteria
103–104. Staff Dining-Room

LOWER GROUND FLOOR

UNIVERSITY MEDICAL CENTRE, MOUNT SCOPUS

Henrietta Szold Nursing School with connecting pergola to the Hadassah University Hospital. The Nathan Ratnoff School appears in the right background.

Foyer of Hadassah University Hospital.

Illustration left:
Hadassah University Hospital, Jerusalem, entrance area with inner courtyard.

Haifa was the city in Palestine with the greatest potential for technical progress, industrial development, and international trade.[72] In contrast to Jerusalem, Haifa was more closely oriented to Western ways and values. Accordingly, Mendelsohn responded with an architecture more closely related to his German buildings than any of his other projects in Palestine.

The construction of the Government Hospital was a part of a new urbanistic scheme devised by the British, calling for the development of the peninsula called Bat Galim (Daughter of the Waves) into an upscale quarter for British army personnel and their families. The district was to include a hospital, apartment blocks, a beach hotel, and a Government Swimming Club. Although Mendelsohn prepared a development plan that included all of these functions,[73] only the Government Hospital was realized. The patron of the hospital was the British Mandate government itself, represented by its High Commissioner in Palestine, Sir Arthur Wauchope. Mendelsohn knew Wauchope from London and enjoyed a friendly relationship with him. Common interests, including a passion for the music of Bach, bound the two together on a private level as well.[74] Mendelsohn expected great things from his relationship with the High Commissioner, hopes that were certainly not unfounded. In a letter to his wife, for example, he described an important meeting with Wauchope: "He said the National Home will exist as long as England exists and he wishes me to guide it architecturally—to build, as he said, all the important buildings."[75] Mendelsohn's great dream of becoming architect and chief planner of British Mandate Palestine was based not least of all on such statements by Wauchope. Yet in the end, the Government Hospital—a commission Wauchope had personally secured for Mendelsohn from the British colonial authorities—remained the only one he was to execute for the British in Palestine.

The authoritarian British style of leadership as well as the secure financial basis of the project caused it to progress quickly.[76] A model of efficiency in planning and execution, the hospital was much praised in the local media. Mendelsohn received the commission in August 1936; by December, his designs had been accepted by the building commission and began their usual route through

Construction sign for Government Hospital in Haifa with information in English, Hebrew, and Arabic.

Mendelsohn (left) with the British High Commissioner Sir Arthur Wauchope (second from right) and members of the local building commission during a tour of the building site of the Government Hospital in Haifa.

the building authorities for approval. Six months later, in July 1937, the foundation was laid. The construction took only fourteen months, and the hospital was able to accept its first patients already before the planned opening date. The official inauguration took place in December 1938.[77]

With a total of 250 beds, the hospital's capacity corresponded to that of the Hadassah Hospital, with a floor area of around 11,500 square meters on a plot of around 55,000 square meters. Mendelsohn designed the open spaces on the exterior as parks into which he incorporated the wide range of existing trees. Thus even the rough shell structure was surrounded by green, emphasizing the attractive interrelationship of nature and architecture.

In the spatial disposition of the hospital, Mendelsohn abandoned a compact layout in favor of good ventilation in the interior spaces. He divided the complex into loosely connected wings and rejected the usual arrangement of a corridor lined with patients' rooms on either side. In the main hospital wing, the rooms are located on only one side of the corridor and face the cooling sea breezes to the northwest. All the rooms have large glass doors and broad balconies; the latter are positioned like a grid in front of the exterior wall to provide shade from even the last rays of the hot afternoon sun. Windows above the doors to the patients' rooms provide cross ventilation through the narrow ribbon windows of the corridors.

With its six stories, the main hospital block extending from southwest to northeast is the highest in the complex. Adjoining it at a right angle are two lower wings, each of which follows the contour of the coast in a slight curve. The somewhat longer, narrower tract to the southwest accommodated shops, a laundry, and a chapel; to the south, it adjoined the quarters for the medical and service personnel at a right angle. The broader, shorter wing to the east housed the reception and emergency rooms and functioned as a connecting bridge to a three-story block with outpatient services, X-ray department, and operating room. At some distance to the west stood three blocks with rows of doctors' and nurses' quarters. In the northern area of the hospital grounds, directly along the Mediterranean coast, five pavilions for patients with infectious diseases and prison inmates were connected to the main building by a pergola.

Government Hospital, Haifa. The balconies on the main wing were to provide shade for the large windows in the patients' rooms.

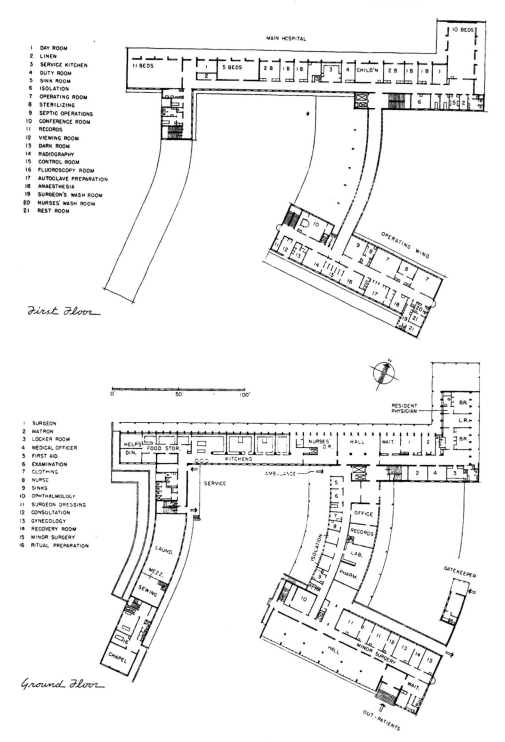

1 DAY ROOM
2 LINEN
3 SERVICE KITCHEN
4 DUTY ROOM
5 SINK ROOM
6 ISOLATION
7 OPERATING ROOM
8 STERILIZING
9 SEPTIC OPERATIONS
10 CONFERENCE ROOM
11 RECORDS
12 VIEWING ROOM
13 DARK ROOM
14 RADIOGRAPHY
15 CONTROL ROOM
16 FLUOROSCOPY ROOM
17 AUTOCLAVE PREPARATION
18 ANAESTHESIA
19 SURGEON'S WASH ROOM
20 NURSES' WASH ROOM
21 REST ROOM

First Floor

1 SURGEON
2 MATRON
3 LOCKER ROOM
4 MEDICAL OFFICER
5 FIRST AID
6 EXAMINATION
7 CLOTHING
8 NURSE
9 SINKS
10 OPHTHALMOLOGY
11 SURGEON DRESSING
12 CONSULTATION
13 GYNECOLOGY
14 RECOVERY ROOM
15 MINOR SURGERY
16 RITUAL PREPARATION

Ground Floor

Government Hospital, Haifa, typical corridor in main wing. Round windows above the doors to the patients' rooms provide cross ventilation.

Although the round supports on the ground floor of the main building at first suggest steel skeleton construction, the building was in fact executed in solid reinforced concrete. Thus both the exterior walls and most of the interior walls perform a load-bearing function.[78] The resulting rigidity of the interior disposition proved disadvantageous in later years, and later generations of architects were not especially careful to preserve the original fabric of Mendelsohn's building. After the hospital was ceded to the State of Israel in 1948, it underwent extensive remodeling, expansion, and modernization without regard for the existing architecture. For the Jewish population of Palestine, the British Government Hospital was a thorn in the side from the very beginning, a symbol of the British colonial mentality. From 1938 to 1948, the hospital was occupied only by British and Arab patients. The Jewish boycott resulted first of all from the strained relations between the British Mandate government and the Jewish population, which deteriorated increasingly throughout the 1930s as a result of the two white papers, the government reports of 1930 and 1939, and the limits on immigration. The hospital building itself, however, offered reason enough for a Jewish boycott. The British building commission had insisted on a strict division into a "British section" and a section for the "natives." In practice, this "racial segregation" manifested itself in such things as the accommodation of Arab and Jewish patients on the two lower floors of the main block. In subtle details such as the furnishings of the sanitary facilities, the discrimination became apparent. Although Mendelsohn criticized these stipulations, he realized them against his better judgment. He later attempted to redeem himself through public criticism of the British regulations: "Some planning elements that seem wrong to us, with our present knowledge of hospital routines may be traced to the fact that the program follows policy laid down by the British Colonial Office. For instance, there is a strict segregation of white people (English citizens and army personnel) from the natives: a policy which does not seem to be producing amity in Haifa at the moment."[79]

The Anglo-Palestine Bank in Jerusalem, 1936–1939

In the 1930s, the Anglo-Palestine Bank with its headquarters in Tel Aviv was the largest bank in Palestine. It was institutionalized at the beginning of the British Mandate and from then on represented the most important financial institution in Jewish Palestine. With the founding of the State of Israel, it was renamed Bank Leumi le Israel (National Bank of Israel). Bound up with this bank were many immigrants' hopes for a new, secure livelihood.

A general description of Mendelsohn's Jerusalem bank building reads like a successful "corporate design" intended to satisfy the client's expectations: a solid, serious appearance conveying reserved, controlled progressiveness, adherence to proven tradition, solid materials, trustworthy mass, power, and above all security. It is no coincidence that in his own description of the bank building, Mendelsohn himself invoked the monumental Florentine palazzi and therewith one of the most famous early banking families, the Medici.[80]

The site for the new Jerusalem bank building lay on Jaffa Street, a road leading northwest out of the old city from the gate of the same name. Jaffa Street was and is the most important business street outside the walls of the old city. Mendelsohn's first design sketches, dating to February 1935, called for an office building with a total of four to five stories, arranged in a U shape around a one-story bank hall. The point of departure for this concept was the neighboring four-story post office building, to which Mendelsohn sought to attune the height and distribution of the building masses.[81]

The building commission in charge—which did not officially award the commission to Mendelsohn until July 1936—nonetheless requested considerably more office space. Such an expansion could have been effected by the addition of another story; therewith, however, the

Anglo-Palestine Bank, Jerusalem, sketch, 1935.

project would have violated local Jerusalem building statutes. According to the building code, the height of a building was to be no more than five-fourths the width of the adjacent street. Exceptions were granted, if at all, only for public buildings, not for private institutions such as banks. This meant that on the north side of the plot along Jaffa Street, Mendelsohn could add several stories to his bank up to a height of around twenty-five meters without violating municipal regulations. Storrs Avenue in the south, however, was relatively narrow, and stood five meters below the level of Jaffa Street. As the building at this point could not exceed a height of thirteen meters, no additional stories could be added.[82] Mendelsohn's new design, realized between 1937 and 1939, shows a strict division of the complex into two parts. The sharp separation of the building masses corresponds exactly to the building code. In the south, along the narrow Storrs Avenue, the building is only three stories tall; in the north on Jaffa Street, it rises to become Jerusalem's first "skyscraper" with a total of seven stories, towering over the neighboring post office by a full three stories. Paradoxically, this modification of the skyline was based not on a lack of consideration on the part of client or architect, but rather on the very building code that was intended to preserve the homogeneity of the city, as Mendelsohn himself noted in an article.[83]

Only frontally, from Jaffa Street, does the building appear as a unified block. Its two-part division, visible from all other sides and at first somewhat disconcerting, loses its strangeness upon closer examination of the interior division. Here, it immediately becomes apparent that the separation on the exterior corresponds to the various functions served by the interior. The horizontal complex extending from Storrs Avenue to the first two stories on Jaffa Street accommodates the large bank hall and all the additional functions belonging to the bank. The stories above, from the third to the seventh floor, are occupied by offices leased by the bank and accessible through a separate entrance and stairwell. The stairwell, located in a wing set back from Jaffa Street on the northeast corner of the building, conveys the impression of a tower attached to the core building. In a building otherwise marked by static, quiet forms, the stepped configuration of this northeast corner forms a dynamic component corresponding to the course of the streets and their patterns of motion. Here, at an important traffic node, the connecting street runs into Jaffa Street at a sharp angle while another street branches off toward the north. It was from this vantage point that Alfred Bernheim[84] photographed his famous view of the bank with two trotting camels (see p. 240). A number of comparable photographs exist from the 1930s, particularly in the architectural circle of Tel Aviv.[85] All of them seek to capture the charming contrast

Anglo-Palestine Bank, Jerusalem, southeast view. The vertical strip is a shaft enclosed by iron grates and containing all the utility conduits in the building.

Anglo-Palestine Bank, Jerusalem,
"Lion Portal."

between Western modernity and the picturesque, but clearly inferior, orientalism. Modernism is clearly given preeminence; it represents the power of the future as manifested in its achievements. In the Mendelsohn/Bernheim photograph,[86] however, the situation is fundamentally different. Here, the camels are meant neither as a contrast nor as a Romantic attribute, but rather, like the stone wall cut off at an angle in the right half of the picture, simply represent the key to understanding Mendelsohn's bank building, its materials and its rhythm. The stone wall—reminiscent of the Wailing Wall, the stones of Solomon's Temple—symbolizes the Eternal Jerusalem. Mendelsohn pays tribute to the eloquent stones of Jerusalem; his use of Jerusalem stone as a building material is his homage to the Holy City: "The exterior of the Anglo-Palestine Bank reflects the eternal austerity of the Holy City."[87] The camels, in turn, represent its rhythm, echoed in the articulation of the facade. At Mendelsohn's request, the photographs by Arthur Köster of his office and commercial buildings in Berlin had included automobiles, an explicit reference to the rapid tempo of modern life in general and the motorized viewer in particular. Mendelsohn's architectural response to this viewer was the horizontal ribbon windows of his buildings. The "ships of the desert" photographed by Alfred Bernheim in front of Mendelsohn's bank building, on the other hand, symbolize the wave-shaped motion of the orient, characterized by a brief pause between each step.

The two camels in Bernheim's photo frame the main entrance of the bank hall. Mendelsohn himself designed the bronze cladding of the double oak doors.[88] Pointed conical bronze knobs and tapered cornice strips with small blocks below them and round moldings suggest the gates of a fortress, assuring potential customers that their money is safe here. The idea of power and strength is embodied in the two lions that appear on the door; at eye level with the visitor, one forepaw resting on each door handle, they appear to guard the entrance.

The lion portal as a symbolic expression of power, strength, and security was Mendelsohn's most direct aesthetic expression of the significance of the bank building and its most clearly articulated statement to its customers. Other elements such as the convex, Italianate window grilles on the ground floor underline this tendency. Between the windows, bronze ornaments reminiscent of torches contain small light tubes that illuminate the facade by night. Yet unlike the German department stores, this night illumination is not intended to promote transparency, but rather to emphasize closure in an aesthetic exaggeration of the wall. The form of the bronze torches recurs once again in the flag mast to the left of the entrance.

Anglo-Palestine Bank, Jerusalem,
main hall, 1939.

The interior of the bank, which unfortunately has undergone considerable alteration over the course of time,[89] is surprising for its light, serene elegance, contrasting with the severity of the exterior. Mendelsohn used various types of marble for the floors and wall facing, and fine woods for the built-in and freestanding furniture, combining all these materials into a striking unity. A sophisticated lighting system supplies the main hall with indirect sunlight from the roof, harmoniously blending it with indirect artificial light. A visit to the bank thus becomes an aesthetic experience.

Other Small Projects in Palestine

In addition to the major projects described in the preceding sections, Mendelsohn worked on a handful of other commissions in Palestine, at least four of which were realized. These represent his less well-known and less outstanding works.

First of all, it is interesting to note that there are "Mendelsohns" that still remain to be discovered. It is not unheard of for an attentive student or city archivist to come across the plans of a heretofore unknown building by Mendelsohn in the dusty drawer of a city planning office.

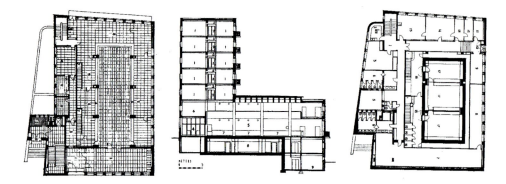

Mendelsohn by no means included every one of his buildings in his official list of works; like many other architects, he was selective. The first project to be discussed here is a "Mendelsohn" that has only recently been discovered. It was "found" in 1994 when the plans were discovered in the municipal building files in the context of an imminent renovation. The building was a vocational school for boys in southeast Tel Aviv: the Max Pine Boys' Trade School on Petach Tikwa Street. The plans submitted for approval by the building authorities in May 1935 bear the names of Mendelsohn and Chermayeff. We are thus dealing with a relatively early building, maybe even Mendelsohn's first finished building in Palestine. The three-and-a-half-story school building was conceived for about a hundred vocational students.[90] In addition to offices, storage spaces, and sanitary facilities, each floor accommodated a large workroom and a classroom. The stairwell is exceptionally spacious; with its windows, relatively large for the climatic conditions, and projecting platforms, it distantly recalls the famous Bauhaus staircase in Dessau. On the exterior, the school building conveys a quiet, almost static impression. The blocklike structure acquires a sense of rhythm only through the sequence of various window forms. The projecting stair block in the central axis intensifies the strict symmetrical arrangement of the building, interrupted only by an annex on the rear side.

The school is Mendelsohn's only known building in Tel Aviv. In its simplicity and introversion, it stands in almost provocative contrast to the other Tel Aviv architecture of the same period, for which Mendelsohn had only sharp criticism. His school building shows once more how much he loathed the misunderstood copies of his German architecture that many of his young Tel Aviv colleagues produced. He stubbornly distanced himself from them—with a building that, though of high quality, at first glance seems completely unspectacular.

Shortly thereafter, a second school building was erected by Mendelsohn between 1936 and 1937 in the Yagur kibbutz southeast of Haifa. The building in question was a craftsmen's school with attached boarding facilities for 60 to 80 students, immigrants from Germany who had come with the Youth Aliyah movement.[91] Mendelsohn himself viewed this commission, officially awarded to him in late 1935, as a "very simple, but attractive job," which "succeeded marvelously in two days."[92] Neither sketches nor plans exist of his designs from early 1936,[93] nor are the buildings themselves preserved for the most part. As far as can be reconstructed, the project as it was realized consisted of two separate units, a school building with attached workshops and a boarding house. A second phase of planning after 1937 called for a considerable expansion of the building to accommodate a student body of 250. This plan, which resembled a small campus, was only partially realized, and the school was closed in the 1940s.

In 1938, another promising project was entrusted to Mendelsohn, one that in the long term could have been expanded into a campus design for Weizmann's renowned institute in

Daniel Wolf Research Laboratory, Rehovot, partial view of laboratory and work spaces grouped around a courtyard, 1938.

Daniel Wolf Research Laboratory, Rehovot, interior view of machine hall, 1938.

Rehovot.[94] At first, however, the project was limited to the design of a research laboratory, which consisted of a machine hall, a number of testing laboratories, a fermentation complex, and a few storage and utility spaces. Mendelsohn received the commission for the Daniel Wolf Research Laboratory directly from his important patron and client Chaim Weizmann, the director of the institute. The design was finished in 1938; due to personal and financial difficulties, however, its realization was delayed until 1940–41. The completed building is an interesting, if contradictory, work by Mendelsohn. If it had been built in Germany in the 1920s, there might have been reason to include Mendelsohn in the recent, controversial discussion of "silent" modernism.[95] Aside from flat roofs and an interesting parabolic concrete shell structure for the machine hall, Mendelsohn used a traditional formal vocabulary in this project, visible for example in the formal layout of the overall complex. The buildings are arranged around an inner courtyard whose entrance is marked by two symmetrically arranged main blocks, which lend a sense of monumentality to the rather modest complex. The details, as well, speak an almost conservative language: beige-brown sprayed plaster, vertical windows with emphatic sills, and pilaster-like decoration between the windows.

Mendelsohn's last project in Palestine, the building for the Agricultural College in 1940, also in Rehovot, likewise raises questions of stylistic categorization. The project consists of three simple, L-shaped buildings placed in a staggered row, resulting in a climatically advantageous, loose sequence of open interior courtyards. The buildings accommodate two classrooms, a teachers' room, various smaller workspaces, a biological and a chemical laboratory as well as corresponding storage rooms and warehouses—in short, all the facilities necessary for the two-year, practically oriented course of study in agriculture. The entire complex, now part of the extensive campus of the Israeli agricultural school, makes a thoroughly simple, rural impression. Its rough, brown-toned plaster, white sash windows, and wooden roof trusses over covered walkways express its function in a language peculiarly rustic for Mendelsohn. Finally, the pitched, red-tiled roof—in modernist Germany the corpus delicti of reactionary architecture—stands as a great question mark in Mendelsohn's oeuvre to this day. In Germany some years before, Mendelsohn had brusquely turned down a commission because a steep pitched roof was required;[96] now, however, in a Levantine context, he chose to build it of his own accord. In so doing he doubtless confused his fans and critics and misled them to various speculations and attempts at explanation. Julius Posener interpreted the red roof as an act of pure spite against his Tel Aviv colleagues;[97] Bruno Zevi, on the other hand, sees the rural character of this project as evidence of an ideological turn toward to the Jewish pioneer spirit of the early years in Palestine, the "true Zionist dream."[98] If nothing else, these two extreme interpretations of a strange pitched roof show that with his last building in Palestine, Mendelsohn succeeded in leaving behind an irritation, a question mark, but perhaps also an exclamation point after a text written in architecture, one with continuing relevance for current discussions of regionalism.

Mendelsohn's Letter to Mumford

In early 1941, Mendelsohn dissolved his office in Jerusalem and set out for America with his wife. A number of considerations may have played a role in his emigration from Palestine; the appearance of Rommel as the Desert Fox was a cause of terror and consternation for many Jews in Palestine, while contacts had already been made between Hitler and the Grand Mufti of Jerusalem. Even in Palestine, the Second World War brought virtually all construction to a halt. Like many of his architect colleagues, Mendelsohn received no new commissions to enable him

Greeting card from the Mendelsohns, sent from America to their friends in Palestine, 1941.

to provide for himself and his family or to financially support a number of relatives who had fled empty-handed from Germany. The primitive nationalism he encountered in many of his contemporaries in Palestine may also have disturbed and distressed him. His emphatic call for an East-West synthesis in a future Semitic Commonwealth remained a solitary voice in the wilderness. The modern, Western city of Tel Aviv, the embryo of the later State of Israel, gained the upper hand. The message of Jerusalem, the Holy City, went unheard, a legacy that was to remain for the generations that followed.

And so it happened, as Julius Posener recalls, that Mendelsohn, although he loved Palestine like almost no other, felt marginalized, condemned to agitation on a side stage.[99] In any case, his decision to turn his back on the "Promised Land" and depart for the "Land of Unlimited Opportunity" was not a sudden or arbitrary one. For a number of years, Mendelsohn had been playing with the idea of starting over again in America; yet even this decision was not intended as a final, sharp caesura, but rather as an exploration of new possibilities on another continent.[100]

On April 12, 1939, Mendelsohn wrote from Palestine to his old American friend Lewis Mumford. In a letter that marks the introduction to the next chapter, he states: "I think that Palestine must necessarily be a center for the Jews, and I think that we can resolutely maintain our position here against the resistance of the unjustly incited Arab world and against England's self-centered ambiguity. For me personally, the difficulties come from another quarter. The scale of the land is very small, and its population is divided into two camps—politically and intellectually. There is no opportunity for me as architect to propagate the ideal values of my work. . . . And so I often wonder whether America could not be my field of activity. . . ."[101] Two years later, Mendelsohn left Eretz Israel. His affidavit was signed by Lewis Mumford.[102]

Notes p. 272.

Illustration left:
Anglo-Palestine Bank, Jerusalem,
view from Jaffa Street.

"It will be hard for us to find a home"
Projects in the United States 1941–1953

Hans R. Morgenthaler

Eric Mendelsohn flew from Palestine to Bombay, India, on March 13, 1941, and from there sailed by way of the southern tip of Africa to New York, arriving on April 28. The Mendelsohns spent summer on a trip through the United States that took them from New York to Los Angeles and New Orleans. For the remainder of 1941 Mendelsohn was busy with preparations for an exhibition of his work titled "Architecture by Eric Mendelsohn 1914–1940" scheduled for December at the Museum of Modern Art in New York.[1] In 1942, he lectured at various American universities.[2] During 1942 and 1943 he worked as a consultant to the American War Department. The air force conducted research tests for the planned bombing raids on German cities. Mendelsohn was among the architects who provided information on building styles, wartime housing, urban development, and construction details in Germany.[3] From 1943 to 1945, he lived at Finney Farm, an artist colony in upstate New York. He supported himself primarily through a Guggenheim fellowship granted to write a book titled *Architecture in a Changing World*.[4] In June 1943, he created sketches of his future architectural visions for *Fortune* magazine. In fall 1945, Mendelsohn moved to San Francisco and opened a new practice with two young partners, to which he brought the project for a synagogue in St. Louis.[5]

Project for a metropolitan airport, 1943.

B'nai Amoona Synagogue and
Community Center, St. Louis,
preliminary design, 1945.

In December 1945, he published the *Fortune* magazine sketches accompanied by a short essay on his vision for the postwar development of America. His architectural concepts were on a global scale and ranged from a world university to a metropolitan airport and a transportation system that integrated international air travel with suburban commuting, as well as an urban proposal for Pittsburgh. He incorporated rural features from the nineteenth-century garden city with urban characteristics of the radiant metropolis promoted by modernist planners in the 1920s, which he updated for the postwar American automobile age. Mendelsohn aimed to express the contextual function of buildings. He saw them as fixed poles in the dynamics of their environment. Through the design of the buildings, he expressed the function of streets as connectors.

Mendelsohn also laid out the design method necessary to generate such a global utopia. For him, creative acts were based on visions, which he called "the intuitive recognition of positive facts and potential consequences." This demanded that the architect consider the nature of the problem to be dealt with, to be practical, and to present an intellectual expression of the visionary conditions under which the design was created.[6]

Mendelsohn used this method of design in his synagogue projects. In summer 1945 negotiations with the Congregation B'nai Amoona of St. Louis entered their final stage. The congregation needed a larger synagogue closer to where their members lived.[7] Mendelsohn had been recommended to them[8] as the architect of the Hadassah Hospital in Jerusalem, which had attracted much financial support from American Jews. Moreover, the exhibition of Mendelsohn's work had traveled to the City Art Museum in St. Louis during March and April 1944. In a letter of

July 10, 1945, to his former assistant Julius Posener, Mendelsohn mentioned that he was already working on the design of this synagogue.[9] Dynamically drawn with broad pencil strokes, the building looks like a submarine emerging from water.

The congregation knew with whom it was dealing. In their *Bulletin,* Mendelsohn was introduced as someone for whom architecture must simultaneously address revolutionary political phenomena and changes in human relations in economics, science, religion, and art. "Mr. Mendelsohn is known all over the world for his fine vision and understanding of dignity and beauty in architectural design." He was praised for having attempted to create a new spatial sense in architecture.[10]

In February 1946, Mendelsohn presented his first project with a cylindrical temple protruding from a broad expanse of low structures.[11] The temple was topped by an overhanging roof capped by a Star of David. This high volume is placed in a corner of the square site, adjoining an existing building that was already used by the congregation for classrooms, offices, a temporary synagogue, and an auditorium.[12] Additional structures follow the perimeter of the site, forming a U-shaped complex enclosing a courtyard. Mendelsohn was primarily concerned with the temple. The Star of David contained in a circle seems to have generated its cylindrical form. The relative simplicity of the Jewish service requires similarly simple spatial solutions. Usually, the Bimah is placed together with the Ark on a platform in the main axis of the building. This layout emphasizes that the synagogue is a meeting hall more than a sanctuary.[13]

Subsequently, Mendelsohn changed the shape of the temple. A few sketches continue the earlier cylindrical form, but the majority of the sheets depict a cubical space containing an oblong rectangle with a central aisle covered by a parabolic roof overhanging at one end.[14] He continued the perimeter arrangement of the buildings and filled the resulting courtyard either with a cross-shaped building or one that divided it into two halves. A light monitor runs in the center along the entire roof. A slice of the roof is pushed farther out from the ceiling, with windows closing the gap between the two planes. This channel in the roof begins as a niche on the Bimah, which contains the Torah Ark. Light enters from both sides and illuminated from behind the Tablets of the Law that were placed on top of the Ark. It appears as if a light beam emanates from the tablets and divides the ceiling vault above.[15]

In December 1946, contractors' bids came in at about double what the congregation intended to spend.[16] After additional fundraising, construction began in September 1948. The entire complex was dedicated September 1–3, 1950. Between 1956 and 1957, an additional extension, which projected into the courtyard, was added to the classroom wing.[17] The temple roof, as well as all other roofs, is of reinforced concrete and supported on massive curved steel beams. The rest of the building is constructed of concrete blocks with brick surfaces.

Mendelsohn called this one of his best buildings.[18] In many aspects it culminates his previous creative efforts. The shape and structure of the temple in particular have a long genealogy in his oeuvre. The parabolic roof had already preoccupied Mendelsohn in his first creative period, when he had attempted to find a new architectural style based on the structural possibilities of new building materials like steel and reinforced concrete.[19] The round windows and the semicircular termination of the retaining wall for the little garden in front of the entrance facade are details that come from Mendelsohn's work in the 1920s. Rachel Wischnitzer saw Mendelsohn's synagogues as a "going back" home for him, using a comparison between his project for Dallas and the Einstein Tower to make her case.[20]

There is evidence indicating that, apart from formal similarities, his earlier work was also a theoretical frame of reference for Temple B'nai Amoona. Various statements published through-

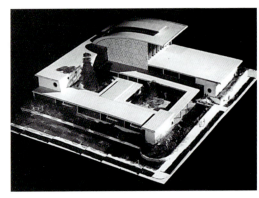

B'nai Amoona Synagogue and Community Center, St. Louis, execution model.

B'nai Amoona Synagogue and Community Center, view from inner courtyard.

out Mendelsohn's career corroborate a steadfast adherence to a number of clearly articulated positions. This was also the case in April 1942, when he gave three lectures at the University of California in Berkeley. These presentations summarized his own thoughts about his work and time and were intended to be his directives for future architecture. The first lecture, "Architecture in a World Crisis," dealt with his architectural beginnings during the First World War. In a truly modernist frame of mind, Mendelsohn promoted architecture as the expression of the "political, economic, and social situation" of the time. He continued with an analysis of prewar society and culture, commenting on the urge to experiment and discover new things, e.g., in architecture the use of new building materials and the new needs introduced by traffic and industry.[21]

This lecture quite openly reaffirmed his own design philosophy formulated during the previous twenty-two years. It is a shortened version of a lecture Mendelsohn gave in 1932, titled "Der schöpferische Sinn der Krise."[22] Therefore, one might conclude that he simply advocated his earlier visionary designs as the basis for post–World War II architecture.

However, Mendelsohn did not advocate a literal return to his modernist work. In the second lecture, "Architecture Today," Mendelsohn criticized International Style architects for adhering too closely to scientific and technical innovations, for being either purely functional or too overtly dynamic. For Mendelsohn, architecture needed to integrate human and social needs. Architecture had to leave material and functional efficiency behind and "transcend again into pure acts of creation."[23] This is what distinguishes his 1942 position from his earlier one. In 1923 he had also criticized functionalists and expressionists and advocated a combination of these two positions, which he called "function and dynamics."[24] In America, he demanded their complete fusion into his "act of creation."

A similar readjustment can also be found in his designs. Compared to the early sketches, the synagogue is pure architecture: it has shed symbolic references to forms outside of architecture and is instead assembled from inherently architectural elements. The building speaks in essences: flat and curved, horizontal and vertical, broken and solid planes enclose the interior spaces. The perception of space is strongly visual, as one's eyes follow the outlines created by edges and corners.[25]

In St. Louis, the elevations are fused into units, so that the facades appear to have been pulled over everything. Consequently, the skeleton cedes its importance to the (facade) skin and the elevations express surface tension.[26] This visualization differs from traditional modernism, where the exterior is either determined by the interior arrangement of spaces, expresses organic spatial continuity, or exhibits a predilection for transparency.

The time and place seemed indeed right for a renewed focus on modernist principles. Mendelsohn sensed this zeitgeist when he mentioned his "early sketches and their sense, which is only apparent today."[27] As the necessary building technology was at hand in 1950, Mendelsohn could return with full creative elan to the kind of architecture his early sketches visualized. Within a few years of Mendelsohn's St. Louis design, there would be a number of buildings using similar curved and dynamic forms by architects like Eero Saarinen, Pier Luigi Nervi, and Felix Candela.[28] After the Second World War, functional form became the universally accepted design language not only in industrial design, but also in architecture.[29]

The commission for a synagogue lent itself well to the application of earlier design modes. The term synagogue does not primarily identify a building but rather the ten men that form it in its fundamental sense, as a "house of congregants."[30] The institution synagogue began during the Babylonian exile in the sixth century B.C.E. as a temporary tabernacle not tied to a specific location.[31] Synagogues are oriented to the east, where the Ark with the Torah scrolls was placed, facing the entrance to the west.[32] The focus of the building is on the inside; the outside may resemble other buildings.[33] Indeed, most American congregations required only that the synagogue express the essence of Judaism, that it be of the soil and the soul, as well as aesthetically pleasing and functionally satisfying.[34] The modern synagogue is actually three buildings in one: a sanctuary, a school, and a social center.[35] Percival Goodman defined the synagogue tradition as a fourfold combination of the traditions of the service, of the sacred objects and furniture, of the iconography, and of the congregational function. Hence, he saw the need to design a building the uses of which were secular, while the reasons for its existence were sacred.[36] "Functionalism," in the sense of providing structurally expressive forms, appeared to be simply the most unalienating style for a synagogue, and was even seen as offering the possibility of developing a distinctly Jewish style of religious architecture.[37] This definition brought novel "suburban synagogue centers" with flexible plan, absence of (women's) galleries, and provision of extended social services.[38]

Mendelsohn had always been interested in the expressive quality of architectural form.[39] By aligning his present approach with earlier methods, Mendelsohn conveyed a particular meaning in his synagogue. His curving roof and sweeping horizontal lines add an expression of movement to his building. This encourages the users to grasp its meaning through inherently human capacities. The main design intention was to lead the congregation intuitively to become a community, not just an audience.[40] By exploiting intuition to generate the design of a spiritual building, Mendelsohn helped redefine form and typology of Jewish religious architecture in the United States. His design method did not produce architectural forms as metaphors, but forms that appealed to innate human perceptual capabilities, namely human notions of order and unity. Just as we are organisms in space, so is Mendelsohn's synagogue.[41] Hence, he did not represent Jewish dogma and liturgy, but interpreted religion through forms that each individual can comprehend through "the identity of ourselves with the surrounding world."[42] Cleveland Rabbi Armond Cohen called this ability "to be co-creator with God and to imitate only the Holy One."[43] Sacral buildings for the Jewish faith must attempt to present architecture as thought, not as artifact. Mendelsohn's building works along the concept of empathy. The user interprets the architectural forms by transposing his/her feelings into the structure, and thereby understanding subconsciously the forces at work.[44]

The flexibility of Mendelsohn's plan proved a valuable asset. By separating the temple from the adjacent foyer and assembly hall through movable partition walls, the space could be expanded for the larger congregations during the high holy days.[45] This was one of the most noted innovations of postwar synagogues in the United States.[46] The need to increase attendance by women and children through a greater offering of recreational, social, and educational activities was primarily responsible for the demand of ancillary space additions to the synagogue, thus turning it from a Sabbath-only to an all-week place, a community center. Elstein calls the period of 1920 to 1945 the age of the "synagogue center."[47]

The emphasis on meaning subsided when Mendelsohn dealt with more pragmatic commissions, such as the Maimonides Hospital in San Francisco. This was a hospice for the chronically ill and did not require extensive diagnostic and treatment spaces. Mendelsohn conceived of the complex as assembled from a tall ward block in the center of the narrow building lot, flanked in front and back by gardens and shielded from the streets by lower structures for administration and patient treatment. The southern facade of the ward block was to be articulated as a series of superimposed balconies with deeply inset walls. He tried a number of different versions for the balconies: flat with windows, or open with rhythmically placed protrusions, which

Maimonides Hospital, San Francisco, execution model, 1948.

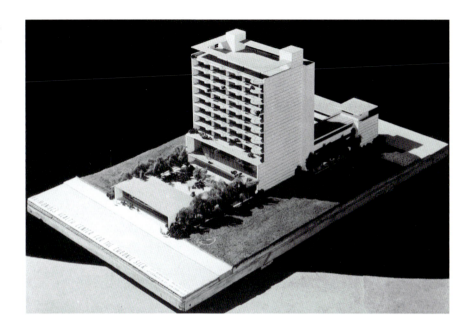

Maimonides Hospital, San Francisco, cross section, April 1948.

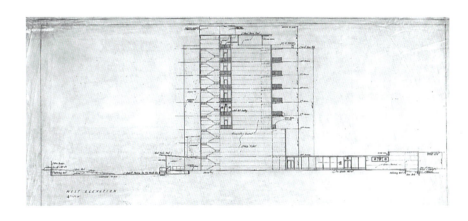

Maimonides Hospital, San Francisco, patient's room.

were either rectangular or curved. Finally, his modernist dynamism, with rhythmic semicircular projections, of which the rightmost one protruded farther than the others, won out. Administrative, treatment, and utility rooms are housed on the lower two floors and in the two buildings that shield the gardens from the streets. The lower floors of the ward building are protected from the sun by boxlike frames. The entire nine-story building is of reinforced concrete construction. The wall along the center of the ward block and its two narrow end walls form an H in plan, from which the floor slabs are cantilevered. Construction of the Maimonides Hospital began in 1948, and was completed in April 1950.[48]

In 1952 another architect extended the glass walls out to fill in the balconies. This intervention severely limited the contrast between the deep dark reveals of the balconies and the sharp lines created by the two-inch taper of the protruding floor slabs, which had created an uncanny, lithe effect. The original articulation had been intended to allow the patient rooms to face the winter sun directly, while providing shade from the harder summer sun and glare.[49] Consequently, the alteration affected the environmental and salubrious quality of the interiors.

In June 1946, Mendelsohn began working on the design of Park Synagogue in Cleveland. This project took shape as a low elongated building from which a cupola emerged, a shape that reflected the topography of the site.[50] Rabbi Cohen remembers that Mendelsohn presented the building committee with a drawing of "the outlines of the Park Synagogue, virtually as it stands today," on the day he was in Cleveland to be interviewed about becoming the architect for this project.[51] By 1948, the final wedge-shaped design had evolved.[52] An extensive classroom wing continuing from the curved end of the wedge was part of the building. Since this project would have cost more than the congregation wanted to spend, they asked Mendelsohn to change his design. He obliged the congregation by shrinking foyer and assembly hall and eliminating the classroom wing. Offices and classrooms were placed in structures that surround a trapezoidal patio behind the cupola. In February 1949, the final design was ready, and in May 1953, the building was dedicated.

Park Synagogue, Cleveland, model of first design, 1948.

Park Synagogue, Cleveland, aerial view. The scheme was realized without the curved classroom wing for lack of funds.

Park Synagogue, Cleveland, ground floor plan, September 1948.

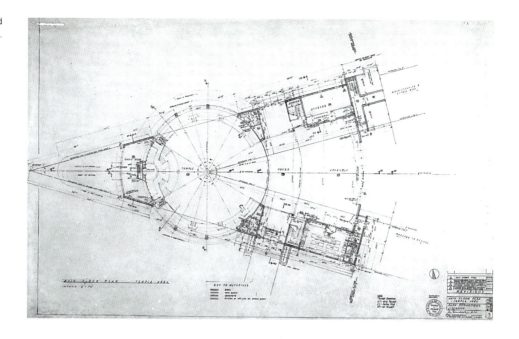

Park Synagogue, Cleveland. On high holy days the temple can be expanded to include the foyer by means of movable partition walls.

Park Synagogue in Cleveland stands on an undulating site outside the city, which gave Mendelsohn greater freedom than the urban environment in St. Louis. A number of concepts that were hinted at in St. Louis came to full bloom in Cleveland. The dominant metaphor of this synagogue is a vehicle. The image of a ship is the primary impression one gets from looking at Park Synagogue. The wedge-shaped circumference, curved lines, and a number of round porthole windows complement literally the impression from the massing of this building. The chapel at the tip of the wedge has been described as "cantilevered out over the end of the promontory like the prow of a ship."[53] Both functionally and symbolically, this building may be seen as a virtually moving, uniting container. The concrete-shell cupola over the main temple in particular shows such dynamic movement. This is a low cupola that comes down directly on the tops of the windows. The building's form reacts to its particular setting. Mendelsohn said on this subject: "Thank God, the building rises with the contour of the land and doesn't . . . shake its fist at God."[54] It overlooks its sloping site from the strategic position on top, by occupying the edge of the triangular ridge framed by two ravines. This site choice seems to respond to the only architectural requirements on synagogues contained in the Talmud and later codifiers, namely that it be built on the highest point of a city and have windows.[55] Mendelsohn's design is a composition in counterpoint, where the building's silhouette plays a variation on the dominant lines of the landscape on which it sits.[56] The low dome symbolizes the closeness of heaven and earth, and increases the intimacy of the large building mass. Whereas in St. Louis the entire sanctuary referred to the tabernacle of Moses in the wilderness, at Cleveland, there is a canopy over the Bimah that refers to this motif.[57] The main construction is entirely of reinforced concrete. The dome is of four-inch-thick gunnite sprayed on wooden forms. The copper roof is laid on a layer of felt.

Using a circular layout and a vault gave emphasis to the center of the space, even though the Bimah and Ark were actually at the front of the temple. The dome combined formal purity, the expression of unity, and was a symbol of universality. It makes the interior "a single, undivided room in which everyone can hear and see easily . . . and have a sense of congregational unity."[58] Such interpretations are reinforced by the physiognomic analogy of these same forms.

Park Synagogue is indeed a full tectonic shell that can be interpreted as the "muscles that are connected to the bones."[59] The focus on the smooth exterior skin is supported by the lack of deep reveals. Light and shadow are completely in the service of presenting the unified form of this temple.[60]

Mendelsohn had earlier promoted such a human kind of design for the postwar era. In the third of his lectures at Berkeley, "Architecture in a Rebuilt World," he interpreted architecture's and mankind's long history, and called for architects to deal with such themes as "physical and psychological protection (and) emotional values." The combination of human and technological requirements should be complemented by an outlook on architecture that deals with both buildings and open space. Architects should conceive "with reason and imagination" and change from "living for material ends" to "living for vital standards," comprising physical, spiritual, and social activity.[61]

As he was involved in the design and construction of these synagogues, Mendelsohn continued to amend his design philosophy. In 1947, in an article for the issue of *Commentary* that dealt extensively with postwar synagogue design, he explained his program for a contemporary synagogue. He demanded that the architect bring the various functions of a synagogue— worship, assembly, and education—into an organic planned relationship and express their material and mental unification. Contemporary temples should be built to human scale, and use contemporary building styles, architectural conceptions, and materials. "Layout and structural system (should be used as) the principal expression of technical and artistic ingenuity." He declared this style similar to the Greek temple and the Gothic cathedral, thus establishing the structural principle not only the basis of his, but of all architecture. He took issue with the conviction that religious buildings needed to express their dignity and emotional significance through historical association. Instead, he asked that the temple "make its vital functions conform with the life we have to live."[62]

Once more, the adaptability of Mendelsohn's architectural theory emerges. It is free of strict dogmas and simply demands practical ground plans, solid structure, and integration of all design requirements into a unified organism. In addition, Mendelsohn leaves room for the expressive

Park Synagogue, Cleveland, temple interior with baldachin over podium and lower part of dome.

Beth-El Synagogue and Community Center, Baltimore, model, 1947.

Russell house, San Francisco,
view of garden facade.

quality of architecture. Can this approach produce a sacred building that is a work of art? Stephen Kayser proposed that using "an organic stylistic principle" in designing a synagogue made it into a work of art. To build a work of "modern architecture," was for Kayser merely "a new technique, and not yet a new 'style.'"[63]

In 1947, Mendelsohn began working on synagogue projects in Baltimore and Washington, D.C., and was in consideration for one in Providence.[64] The analysis of these projects offers a chance to determine how Mendelsohn's approach to designing this building type evolved. In the unrealized projects for Baltimore and Washington there is a pronounced similarity to the characteristics of St. Louis and Cleveland. In both cases, the complex consists of a low, broad base from which a highly articulated building form emerges. This part is used for the main temple and is usually composed of shapes that refer to characteristic Jewish religious symbolism. The Washington temple exploited its site topography in a magnificent manner. The tall sanctuary was to be mostly of glass. However, in November 1947, the congregation began to turn away from supporting this attempt by a modernist architect and settled on a historicist design.

The sanctuary of the Baltimore synagogue has the same shape as the Washington synagogue, but is topped by three barrel vaults cantilevered out over the narrow ends. Mendelsohn experimented with a U-shaped arrangement of temple, administration, and classroom wings before finally settling on the T-shaped plan. The vertical bar of the T contains the temple, which sits on the promontory. Mendelsohn created once more a dramatic setting. The roof forms are similar to tents. Ultimately, the congregation only built the classroom wing.

It seems clear that by 1947 Mendelsohn had worked out a basic arrangement of the building volumes and a formal scheme for his synagogues that centered on shapes expressive of dynamism or referring to the first Jewish temple after the flight from Egypt.[65] He combined modernist forms, Jewish symbolism, and site interpretation in a manner that let the modernist characteristics increasingly recede into the background.

In 1947, Mendelsohn also received the commission for the Russell house in San Francisco. This project started out as two wings arranged in an L-shaped formation, one placed parallel to the street, the other behind it lining a yard. This had become Mendelsohn's favorite residential plan, and was used for other projects, such as the Walter Heller and the Walter Haas houses, both in San Francisco, as well as a house in Palo Alto, California. All of these projects feature widely glazed exteriors and flat roofs. Construction of the Russell house started in 1950. The layout was reversed, with a wing laid perpendicular to the street leading back to the main house placed across the site. The entrance floor is opened into a patio, as the main wing is raised on steel posts to preserve the view into San Francisco Bay. There are two upper floors, the top one cantilevered out over the lower one. A circular space protrudes from one of the overhanging corners. The building rests on a combination steel and wood frame and is covered in redwood siding. The Russell house presents a fine blend of Bay Region vernacular and International Style, with a bit of streamlining in its rounded corner bay.

That Mendelsohn increasingly used Jewish symbols in his synagogues is corroborated in his third built example. In June 1948, he was among the architects interviewed for Temple Emanu-El, Grand Rapids. The building committee visited Cleveland in August, which confirmed their view on Mendelsohn. By March 1949, Mendelsohn had worked out preliminary sketches. The design was presented and accepted in October 1949. Opposition to this project appears to have persisted, as Mendelsohn related in a letter of January 1950 that he had to address the congregation after Friday services to marshal support. He talked about the theory of relativity and general field theory as equivalents of the One God: "This became my theme. Einstein's

Russell house, San Francisco, view of
entrance terrace, 1951.

Russell house, San Francisco. The
round oriel on the seaward side offers
a spectacular view of San Francisco
Bay and the Golden Gate Bridge.
The furniture was designed by
Mendelsohn.

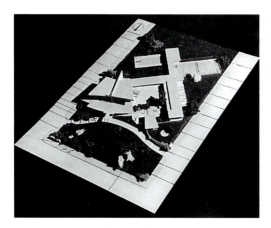

Emanu-El Synagogue and Community Center, Grand Rapids, model.

Emanu-El Synagogue and Community Center, Grand Rapids, 1951.

Emanu-El Synagogue and Community Center, Grand Rapids, design sketch on a concert program from a performance of Vivaldi's *Concerto Grosso*, 1948.

general field theory, the one law which regulates everything, the cosmic union between matter and energy."[66] After attempts to contain costs, the decision was made to go ahead only with parts of the entire complex: temple, auditorium, kitchen, lounge, library, and administrative wing. Ground breaking took place in December 1950, and after many postponements, the building was dedicated in May 1954. The school wing was finally added during the 1960s.

From the beginning, the buildings were arranged in a U-shaped plan, with the wedge-shaped temple occupying one of the arms of the U. Classrooms, administrative, and utilitarian rooms are arranged in four wings forming a cross. The building is held up by a steel frame; the exterior is of brick. The interior walls of the class rooms were of concrete block; otherwise brick was used. More ceremonial spaces had wood paneling or stucco finishes. The temple consists of the sanctuary and the auditorium, with a moveable wall in between. On the outside, this becomes a highly visible spine for the building similar to the one Mendelsohn had used on his Universum Cinema in Berlin.

The roof of the Grand Rapids synagogue, while devoid of curving features, nevertheless resembles the roof of St. Louis, but may also have been influenced by the work of Frank Lloyd Wright. Mendelsohn and Wright had met previously and kept in contact over the years. Indeed, in 1947 Mendelsohn noted that there was a similarity between his own early sketches and Wright's latest work.[67] Through the reverse pitch of the Grand Rapids temple roof, the containing quality of Mendelsohn's earlier buildings is absent here. Nevertheless, there is still a dynamic impression present. The exterior form of the building has been interpreted as a bird resting with wings spread.[68]

During August 1949, Mendelsohn finalized his entry to the competition for a monument to commemorate the six million Jews killed in the Holocaust. A memorial committee had been formed in 1947 and a site on Riverside Drive between Eighty-third and Eighty-fourth streets dedicated. Mendelsohn's earliest sketches for this project focus either on the tablets of the law or on a menorah as the main sculptural part of this monument. In addition, there were a small courtyard and a building. In October 1949, the committee chose Goodman's entry. However, the New York Park Commission rejected this design because it would have used too

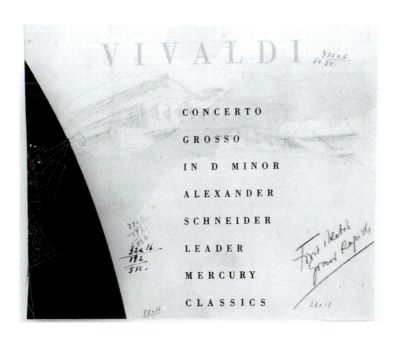

much of Riverside Park. In March 1950, Mendelsohn was commissioned for the project. By then, his design had become simpler. Mendelsohn made the commandment "Thou shalt not kill" the main theme of his memorial. The final version consisted of a terraced courtyard carved into the side of a small promontory, and the tablets of the law. The wall along the southern side of the courtyard was decorated with inscriptions and sculptures by Ivan Mestrovic, which depicted man's struggle to obey the commandments. This design was approved by the city art commission in July 1951. In 1952, the government of Yugoslavia offered the granite needed to build the monument. This offer was repeated in 1953, but ultimately the project was not executed.[69]

Mendelsohn was commissioned once more for a synagogue. The congregation of Mt. Zion in St. Paul had begun thinking about a new synagogue as early as April 1945. Above all, they needed better school facilities and increased seating for the high holy days. Mendelsohn had visited St. Paul in 1946 and had since then corresponded with the congregation. In December 1949, this congregation visited the Cleveland synagogue to get an idea of Mendelsohn's work. In February 1950, Mendelsohn was chosen as architect. This project seems to have begun with a horseshoe-shaped temple/assembly space. Two wings of different length extend from the side of the horseshoe, close to its turn. Subsequent plans, dated May 20, 1950, changed the temple to a rectangular circumference. The smaller wing, terminating in the chapel, extends from the foyer between temple and assembly. The longer wing, containing small rooms off either side of a hallway starts from the far corner of the temple and terminates in a semicircular end. The wings are connected along the temple wall by administrative offices. The entire complex is flat-roofed; the temple/assembly part is higher than the other wings. Sanctuary and chapel roofs protrude from this base and are formed of a series of external ribs, tapering toward the top and terminating in gables. The reference to tents cannot be missed.

Monument to the six million Jews killed by the Nazis in the Second World War, Riverside Park, New York, model of first design, 1949.

Monument to the six million Jews killed by the Nazis in the Second World War, Riverside Park, New York, model of final design, 1950.

Mount Zion Synagogue and Community Center, St. Paul, model of first project, 1950.

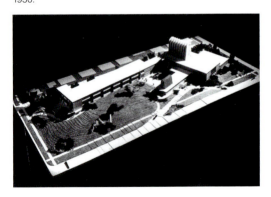

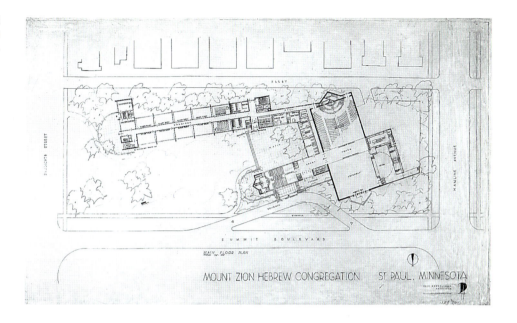

Mount Zion Synagogue and Community Center, St. Paul, site plan with ground floor plan.

Ground breaking took place in April 1951. However, after the contractors' bids had been evaluated, they were rejected by the board, and Mendelsohn was asked to change his design. Above all, he was to eliminate expensive items and submit a cheaper plan. In February 1952, the revised plans were tentatively approved by the congregation. This project is smaller and simpler. The two protruding roofs are now square in section.[70] In October 1952, it was decided that available funds allowed only the construction of the temple and school parts, a development that is corroborated by a few sketches depicting a project with only one part protruding from the roof plane. Construction began in November 1952. The building was finished in December 1954. Harris Chapel was begun in November 1953, after a sizeable donation was received, and dedicated with the entire building.[71] The foyer and the lounge were enlarged later. A library lounge is placed in front of Harris Chapel. A folding wall is between these two rooms, so that the chapel can be enlarged.

The building occupies its site with a bold sweep.[72] The forms are austere and the articulation simple, consisting of glass and brick outside, wood on the inside. The towers of the sanctuary and the chapel form a point/counterpoint motif. Their chief function is to articulate the axis of ascension. Both are built on the theme of "ten" and resemble phylacteries. The preliminary scheme for the roofs was described as "a series of hands folded in prayer."[73]

All the arts used in the synagogue must become an inseparable unit to create an organic style. Judaism is particular in that it does not have symbols, but motifs. Proper ornament may use Hebrew letters and be in the form of stained glass, murals, or ornamental structures.[74] In the early twentieth century, synagogues had shed excessive ornamentation characteristic of nineteenth-century historicist examples. However, undecorated forms were criticized for their inability to provide emotional inspiration. A modernist building's meaning is revealed through its forms, which is a rather demanding reading.[75]

For Mendelsohn, the Ark and its backdrop were the main decorative elements. In St. Louis, the Ark is a separate object, topped by a Decalogue, and set into the recess of the light monitor. The four doors of the Ark are of open metal grillwork, and a curtain is hung inside them.[76] At either end of the Bimah, which extends the width of the front, are two menorahs. At Park Synagogue, there is a three-stepped Bimah, which is covered by a copper canopy set into the dome.

Mount Zion Synagogue and Community Center, St. Paul, after 1954.

Representing staves and cloth, this canopy refers to the Tabernacle in the Wilderness. Twelve seats for the Torah readers are set into the compartments framed by the staves. The central panels of the canopy bear the four Crowns of the Torah. The Ark is of wood and decorated as the Decalogue, using the Hebrew letter shin for each commandment. The eternal light hangs from the top of the canopy. At Temple Emanu-El in Grand Rapids, the Bimah stretches the entire front of the sanctuary. On either side is a lectern and a door decorated with the tablets of the laws. A number of niches provide storage spaces for the Torahs. Lucienne Bloch Dimitroff created a silk screen mural that covers the entire front wall. Divided into small squares, it combines a number of significant motifs: grapes and wheat symbolize joy and work; there is also the letter shin, and the four crowns of the Torah.[77] In St. Paul, the wall behind the Bimah is decorated as the Tablets of the Law. Wooden slats create an additional layer on this wall. They are doubled in the center creating the illusion of two fluted pilasters, on which the Ten Commandments appear in Hebrew letters. Between these pilasters, the Ark is recessed and sits on a base in the form of a menorah. Its doors are of metal grillwork structured in the shape of the letter shin, and it is topped by a crown.[78]

The four synagogues Mendelsohn built in the United States present a telescoped evolution of this building type in the United States after the Second World War. He began with what was for him typical, namely two Expressionist/Functionalist buildings in St. Louis and Cleveland. Both already alluded to what would become the major symbolic attribute of synagogues, namely the reference to the Tabernacle in the Wilderness. At Grand Rapids and St. Paul, the roof forms refer literally to this motif. The final version for St. Paul changed this to a purely Jewish motif. This evolution makes Mendelsohn an important figure in the postwar history of this building type.[79]

The evolution of his synagogue designs as sketched out above seems to be corroborated by his last project, in Dallas, Texas. Here, the temple is laid out in the shape of a horseshoe. Its walls taper upwards, and it is covered by a flat roof over a circle of clerestory windows. At its back is a fan-shaped building housing foyer and auditorium. In front of this complex is a circular plaza lined by a covered walkway. A small chapel continues the axis of temple/auditorium, and terminates a circular walkway. This walkway continues straight on the other end with four classrooms and administration wings added at right angles. Here, the tent symbolism is beautifully merged with Mendelsohn's typical modernist dynamism. A sculpture of the tablets of the law articulates the center of the circular forecourt. Inside, the eternal light hangs from the center of the ceiling, while the triangular decoration of the front refers once more to the tabernacle in the wilderness.

Late in 1950, Eric Mendelsohn began work on the commission to design the headquarters for Varian Associates in Palo Alto, California. The Varian brothers had invented the klystron tube during the war, and were now ready to start peacetime production. They needed administrative offices, as well as research and development laboratories. Mendelsohn was to provide flexible interiors for large machinery that needed a dust-free atmosphere. He tried a number of grid plans, with all buildings having shed roofs. The final design consisted of three main buildings arranged in a pinwheel plan. Two office wings form a right angle around the driveway with the research and development laboratories continuing one of these wings in the shape of a T. A boiler house is located in the resulting U-shaped yard. All buildings have shallow, wide-pitched roofs that are held up on concrete posts. This allows the interiors to be loft structures free of any support functions, and provides for shaded loggias around all buildings. All mechanical equipment is housed in the roofs. Apart from the concrete columns, the buildings are of wood

Emanu-El Synagogue and Community
Center, Dallas, sketch of temple
interior, June 1951.

Emanu-El Synagogue and Community Center, Grand Rapids.

B'nai Amoona Synagogue and Community Center, St. Louis, interior.

Mount Zion Synagogue and Community Center, St. Paul.

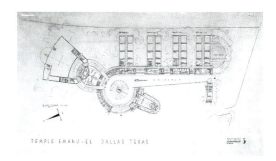

TEMPLE EMANU-EL DALLAS TEXAS

Emanu-El Synagogue and Community
Center, Dallas, plan, June 25, 1951.

Emanu-El Synagogue and Community
Center, Dallas, model, 1951.

construction. The facades give the impression of delicacy. Construction of this design was completed in 1954.[80]

In 1952, Mendelsohn began his last built commission, an office and research building for the Atomic Energy Commission and the University of California Radiation Laboratory in the Berkeley hills. Once again, strict requirements were placed on the interior arrangement. Mendelsohn had to separate areas where work with penetrating radiation was done from normal spaces. Structurally, provisions for the heavy loads of the radiation shielding were necessary. These materials also needed to be easily replaceable. The "cold" part of the interior is located near the entrance on the northern side, the only facade with windows. The second floor houses laboratories and workshops. The "hot" spaces are placed at the rear end of the first floor and are covered by earth, which forms a grassy terrace giving access to the cafeteria in the back. Mendelsohn designed the exterior of this box in a typically modernist fashion. A cubical building block with vertical and horizontal window strips was terraced into the steep topography.[81]

Throughout his life journey through different places and times, the belief in his own creativity and steadfast adherence to his beliefs are among the most remarkable qualities of Eric Mendelsohn's career. In his American period, he managed to emerge from the modernist concern with universal characteristics, and began to humanize the abstract shapes of the 1920s. His contributions to this renewal of modernism were spread through the many lectures he gave at schools of architecture. He taught a master class at the University of California, Berkeley, once a week, and was a frequent guest at the Universities of Oregon and Oklahoma. In his studio presentations, he did not emphasize technical aspects, but rather used analogies to the human body to explain a point. He was emphatic about always combining aspects of function with those of vision. The projects he assigned his students were either of interest to the future of San Francisco or the Bay Area, or for entirely new building projects. They might have included the replanning of San Francisco's Civic Center or the design of a rural center for the atomic age.[82] Among the most important concepts he communicated to his students were his capacity to express his time through architecture and his concern for the sociocultural setting and ethical aims of architecture. His contributions to the shape of the American postwar synagogue are even more significant if one considers how important this period was for Jews. Nineteen forty-five marks the melding of American Jewry, the destruction of European Jews, and the eve of the creation of the state of Israel.[83]

Mendelsohn's rejection of pure functionalism was mirrored in contemporary criticism. Reyner Banham noted with amazement in 1954 that Mendelsohn was not a "vulgarian," but a "nonconformist,"[84] and this was not only the beginning of renewed interest in Mendelsohn, but also of a reevaluation of functionalism resulting ultimately in its dismissal. In 1962, Columbia University held a symposium on modern architecture in which Mendelsohn was discussed as belonging neither to the Functionalist nor to the Expressionist wing.[85] In 1967, Nikolaus Pevsner interpreted Mendelsohn's American work as "a wonderfully humanized and eased 1930, not the great return to the stormy urges of 1914."[86]

In April 1953, a cancerous tumor was discovered in Mendelsohn. An operation and radiation therapy brought a short respite, but by August his condition had become irreversible. He died peacefully in a hospital bed on September 15, 1953. His ashes were scattered in an unrecorded place.

Notes p. 275.

B'nai Amoona Synagogue and
Community Center, St. Louis,
sketch of interior view toward
rear wall, 1946.

Park Synagogue, Cleveland, design
sketch of temple, 1946.

"Why should we be laymen with respect to art?"
The Formative Years 1910–1918

1 Allenstein is today called Olsztyn and is located in eastern Poland, approximately sixty miles south of Kaliningrad. *Ritters Geographisches-Statistisches Lexikon,* 9th ed. (Leipzig, 1910), 48. Hugo Bonk, *Darstellung der Geschichte Allensteins* (Allenstein, 1930), 187–88; Sigrid Achenbach, "Biographie mit Verzeichnis der wichtigsten Werke 1887–1953," in *Erich Mendelsohn. Ideen, Bauten, Projekte* (Berlin, 1987), 15–24.

2 Louise Mendelsohn, "Biographical Notes on Eric," *L'architettura* 95 (September, 1963), 304.

3 Arnold Whittick, *Eric Mendelsohn,* 2nd ed., (London, 1956), 34.

4 "Verzeichnis der von Erich Mendelsohn belegten Vorlesungen," Archive, Ludwig-Maximilians-Universität, Munich.

5 *Personalverzeichnis der Königlich Technischen Hochschule zu Berlin fürs Sommer-Halbjahr 1908* (Berlin, 1908).

6 Eric Mendelsohn, "Background to Design," *Architectural Forum* 98 (April 1953), 106; idem, "My Own Contribution to the Development of Contemporary Architecture," in Oskar Beyer, *Eric Mendelsohn: Letters of an Architect,* trans. by Geoffrey Strachen (London, 1967) (hereafter cited as Beyer, 1967), 162.

7 Joan Campbell, *Der Deutsche Werkbund 1907–1934* (Stuttgart, 1981), 14.

8 Mendelsohn claimed to have written a review of this show. Eric Mendelsohn, "Speech to the Artists' Equity Association," San Francisco (February 24, 1952), 2nd Ms., Mendelsohn Archive, Kunstbibliothek, Staatliche Museen zu Berlin—Preussischer Kulturbesitz (hereafter cited as KB, E. M. Archive), Folder IV/3. No trace of this review has been found yet.

9 Louise Mendelsohn (as note 2), 304.

10 Johannes Mendelsohn, "Über die Jugend von Erich Mendelsohn," from the Resource Collections of the Getty Center for the History of Art and the Humanities, Mendelsohn Papers (hereafter cited as GC, M. P.), Series XI, Folder 101.

11 Eric Mendelsohn, "Personal Data and Work of Eric Mendelsohn, October 1950," KB, E. M. Archive, Folder IV/1.

12 "Faschingsfest der Münchner Presse," in *Münchner Neueste Nachrichten* (February 9, 1912), 3.

13 See reports in *Münchner Neueste Nachrichten* (February 12, 1912), 2; (February 13, 1912), 5; (February 14, 1912), 3; (February 17, 1912), 3. I have been unable to find photographs of these decorations.

14 For information regarding this ball consult the following: "Ariadne auf Naxos," *Münchner Neueste Nachrichten* (January 4, 1913), 3; "Das Pressefest" (January 20, 1913), 2; H. R., "Vom Pressefest" (January 21, 1913), 3; and "Pressefest Nachfeier" (January 25, 1913), 4.

15 H., "Der Walhall-Ball," *Münchner Neueste Nachrichten* (February 10, 1914), 4.

16 "Walhallaball—Pressefest 1914," *Münchner Neueste Nachrichten* (February 4, 1914), 3.

17 These designs have been adequately described as "bodies draped in clothes." Kendra S. Smith, "Architectural Sketches and the Power of Caricature," *Journal of Architectural Education* 44 (November 1990), 54.

18 Mendelsohn also designed costumes for a pantomime based on E. T. A. Hoffmann's *Doge and Dogaressa.* Beyer 1967, 32.

19 "Münchner Künstlertheater," *Münchner Neueste Nachrichten* (April 14, 1914), 1–2. A proclamation was signed by, among others: Hugo Ball, Heinz Braune, Wilhelm Hausenstein, Franz Marc, Erich Mendelsohn, Franz von Stuck, and Albert Weisgerber. Hugo Ball, "Das Münchener Künstlertheater (Eine prinzipielle Beleuchtung)," *Phöbus* 2 (May 1914), 72.

20 Hugo Ball, "Künstlertheater," *Phöbus* (as note 19), 74; idem, *Die Flucht aus der Zeit* (Luzern, 1946), 13; *Der Blaue Reiter,* ed. by Wassily Kandinsky and Franz Marc, documentary edition by Klaus Lankheit (Munich, 1979), 283. "Münchner Künstlertheater," *Münchner Neueste Nachrichten* (April 22, 1914), 2. See also Walter Grohmann, *Das Münchner Künstlertheater in der Bewegung der Szenen- und Theaterreformen* (Berlin, 1935), 124–26.

21 Mendelsohn had met the cellist Luise Maas (1894–1980) in spring 1910. Eric Mendelsohn "Personal Data" (as note 11), 1, KB E. M. Archive.

22 Erich Mendelsohn, letter of August 16, 1910, in Beyer 1967, 23, and transcript of letter of September 12, 1910, GC, M. P., Series I, Folder 1.

23 Wassily Kandinsky, *Über das Geistige in der Kunst,* 10th ed. (Bern, 1952), 69, 80. Mendelsohn owned a copy of this book, which he had signed and dated 1911. "Catalog of Books from the Library of Eric Mendelsohn," compiled by Susan King, July 1972, GC, M. P., Series XI.

24 Erich Mendelsohn, transcript of letter of October 8, 1911, GC, M. P., Series I, Folder 2.

25 Siegfried Wichmann, "Die Dynamische Kraft des Gegenstandes," in Hermann Obrist, *Wegbereiter der Moderne* (Munich, 1968).

26 Erich Mendelsohn, transcript of letter of October 29, 1910, GC, M. P., Series I, Folder 1.

27 Erich Mendelsohn, transcript of letter of August 27, 1910, GC, M. P., Series I, Folder 1.

28 Peg Weiss, "Kandinsky in Munich: Encounters and Transformations," in *Kandinsky in Munich: 1896–1914* (New York, 1982), 62.

29 Kinesthetic ideas are formed by movements executed either with the eyes or the hands. Adolf Hildebrand, *Das Problem der Form in der Bildenden Kunst* (Strasbourg, 1901).

30 Erich Mendelsohn, transcript of letter of December 14, 1910, GC, M. P., Series I, Folder 1.

31 Erich Mendelsohn, " My Own Contribution," (as note 6), 162.

32 "Eine neue Friedhofanlage," *Münchner Neueste Nachrichten* (November 19, 1913), 2. The chapel is mentioned in Carl Wünsch, *Die Bauten und Kunstdenkmäler der Stadt Allenstein* (Königsberg an der Pregel, 1933), 118; and in Susan King, "Interview with Mrs. Eric Mendelsohn," in *The Drawings of Eric Mendelsohn* (Berkeley, 1969), 28. I have not been able to ascertain whether this chapel is still standing. For illustrations consult *L'Architettura* 95 (September 1963), 294; and Bruno Zevi, *Erich Mendelsohn. Opera Completa* (Milan, 1970), 6.

33 Carol Herselle Krinsky, *Synagogues of Europe* (New York/Cambridge/London, 1985), 48, 81–85; Brian de Breffny, *The Synagogue* (New York, 1978), 159.

34 Erich Mendelsohn, letter of March 16, 1913, in Oskar Beyer, *Erich Mendelsohn. Briefe eines Architekten* (Munich, 1961; reprint, Basel/Berlin/Boston, 1991), 19–20.

35 Worringer called this concept the "will to form" (Wilhelm Worringer, *Abstraktion und Einfühlung,* 2nd ed. [Munich, 1981], 42). In a letter of May 15, 1914, Mendelsohn had the highest praise for Worringer's ability to explain complex concepts in the most simple and clear terms. Transcripts of letters, GC, M. P., Series I, Folder 5.

36 Erich Mendelsohn, letter of August 16, 1910, in Beyer 1967, 23.

37 Mendelsohn praised this book in a letter of May 18, 1914. Beyer 1967, 32.

38 Reyner Banham, *Theory and Design in the First Machine Age* (Cambridge, Mass., 1980), 81, compared the Century Hall to buildings by Auguste Perret and called it "the most brilliant use of (concrete) achieved by anybody in its period."

39 Erich Mendelsohn, transcripts of letters of December 26, 1910, March 22, 1913, and March 14, 1914, GC, M. P., Series I, Folders 2, 3, and 5.

40 Erich Mendelsohn, transcript of letter of November 16, 1910, GC, M. P., Series I, Folder 1. The similarity of Mendelsohn's ideas with those expressed by Kandinsky in *Über das Geistige in der Kunst* (see note 23) is striking.

41 If Mendelsohn dated his sketches at all, he generally provided only the year. Additional information on dates and on the formal development of his work is contained in lectures on his own work that he gave at various occasions.

42 Oskar Beyer, "Sonderausstellung Erich Mendelsohn," *Magnum* 30 (June 1960), 51.

43 Susan King, "Eric Mendelsohn: The Germination of a Style," (as note 32), 20.

44 Nehama Guralnik, "Eric Mendelsohn: Drawings of an Architect," in *Eric Mendelsohn: Drawings of an Architect* (Tel Aviv, 1979), 70.

45 The Jugendstil origin of Mendelsohn's work has been noted from the beginning of critical review of his career in the 1920s: Karl Scheffler "Kunstausstellungen: Berlin," in *Kunst und Künstler* 18 (January 1920), 183; idem, "Erich Mendelsohn," *Kunst und Künstler* 26 (June 1928), 355; Paul F. Schmidt, "Erich Mendelsohn," *Cicerone* 12 (1930), 220; Ivo Pannagi, "Erich Mendelsohn," *Casabella* 9 (September 1931), 11.

46 Gustav Platz, *Die Baukunst der neuesten Zeit* (Berlin, 1930), 31–32. See also August Endell, "Formenschönheit und dekorative Kunst," *Dekorative Kunst* 1, 2 (1898), 75–77, 119–25.

47 Erich Mendelsohn, "Eigene Arbeit, 1923–1924," 1, KB, E. M. Archive, Folder V/1.

48 Oskar Beyer, "Architectuur in ijzer en beton," *Wendingen* 3 (October 1920), 10. This drawing technique is almost identical to that used by Frank Lloyd Wright in his two Wasmuth publications: *Ausgeführte Bauten und Entwürfe von Frank Lloyd Wright* (Berlin, 1910), and *Ausgeführte Bauten* (Berlin, 1911). Mendelsohn may have seen these by 1912. See Oskar Beyer (as note 34), 120.

49 Adolf Hildebrand, *The Problem of Form in Painting and Sculpture,* trans. Max Meyer and Robert Morris Ogden (New York/Leipzig/London/Paris, 1907), 71.

50 Wassily Kandinsky (as note 23), chapter 7, passim.

51 Julius Posener, "Mendelsohn," *L'Architecture d'aujourd'hui* 2 (May 1932), 11. See also idem, "Erich Mendelsohn," *Der Architekt* 17 (February 1968), 96; and idem, "Erich Mendelsohn," in *Aufsätze und Vorträge 1931–1980* (Braunschweig/Wiesbaden, 1981), 176–77.

52 Erich Mendelsohn, "Das Problem einer neuen Baukunst," in *Das Gesamtschaffen des Architekten. Skizzen, Entwürfe, Bauten* (Berlin, 1930; reprint, Braunschweig/Wiesbaden, 1988) (hereafter cited as Mendelsohn 1930), 8.

53 Hermann Muthesius, "Die ästhetische Ausbildung der Ingenieurbauten," *Zeitschrift des Vereins deutscher Ingenieure* 53 (July 31, 1909), 1212, 1215.

54 Walter Gropius, "Der stilbildende Wert industrieller Bauformen," in *Der Verkehr. Jahrbuch des Deutschen Werkbundes* (Jena, 1914). According to an article in *Münchner Neueste Nachrichten* (November 16, 1914), 2, this yearbook was published in mid-June 1914. See also Göran Lindahl, "Von der Zukunftskathedrale bis zur Wohnmaschine," *Figura* 1 (1959), 230–32.

55 Erich Mendelsohn, "The International Consensus of the New Architectural Concept, or Dynamics and Function", in: Erich Mendelsohn: *Complete Works of the Architect,* New York, 1992.

56 This interpretation was also held by Herman George Scheffauer, "Dynamic Architecture: New Forms of the Future," *Dial* 70 (March 1921), 326.

57 Erich Mendelsohn, "Eigene Arbeit," 2–3, KB, E. M. Archive.

58 Ibid., 3.

59 Erich Mendelsohn, letter of September 17, 1914, in Beyer 1967, 34.

60 Erich Mendelsohn, letter of December 22, 1914, in Beyer 1967, 35.

61 Hermann Muthesius, "Stilarchitektur und Baukunst," in Julius Posener, *Anfänge des Funktionalismus* (Berlin/Frankfurt/Vienna, 1964). The similarity of Muthesius's ideas to those expressed by Mendelsohn in "Das Problem einer neuen Baukunst," in Mendelsohn 1930, must be noted.

62 Hermann Muthesius, "Das Formproblem im Ingenieurbau," in *Die Kunst in Industrie und Handel* (Jena, 1913), 23–32; Walter Gropius, "Die Entwicklung moderner Industriebaukunst," ibid., 17–22.

63 See note 54.

64 Erich Mendelsohn, "Eigene Arbeit," 3, KB, E. M. Archive. See also Erich Mendelsohn, "Die internationale Übereinstimmung des neuen Baugedankens oder Dynamik und Funktion," in Mendelsohn 1930, 29; and idem, "My Own Contribution," (as note 6), 164.

65 Family book of Mendelsohn, GC, M. P., Series XI, Folder 101.

66 Martin Buber condemned the advent of the concept of evolution and lamented its effect on human will. Whereas once the "Maker" was present to change the face of the earth with his heroic deed, now one could only hope to be the exponent of a small progress. Martin Buber, *Drei Reden über das Judentum* (Frankfurt, 1920).

67 Erich Mendelsohn, letter of April 7, 1915, in Beyer 1967, 36.

68 Erich Mendelsohn, letter of May 28, 1917, ibid., 37–38.

69 This interpretation is also held by Cornelis van de Ven, *Space in Architecture* (Amsterdam, 1978), 168–69.

70 This was his first theoretical manifesto, although it was not published until 1924. Erich Mendelsohn, "Gedanken zur neuen Architektur (Im Felde 1914–1917)," *Wasmuths Monatshefte für Baukunst* 8 (1924), 3.

71 Hendrik Petrus Berlage, *Grundlagen und Entwicklung der Architektur* (Berlin, 1908), here quoted after Reyner Banham (as note 38), 140. Similar ideas are included in idem, *Gedanken über den Stil in der Baukunst* (Leipzig, 1905), 23–24. See also Cornelis van de Ven (as note 69), 168.

72 Beyer 1967, 41.

73 Oskar Beyer, "Eine neue Monumental-Architektur," *Feuer* 2 (1920), 114.

74 Kendra S. Smith (as note 17), 53–54.

75 For the use of this term in politics, see Barbara D. Wright, "Sublime Ambition: Art, Politics and Ethical Idealism in the Cultural Journals of German Expressionism," in *Passion and Rebellion: The Expressionist Heritage,* eds. Stephen E. Bronner and Douglas Kellner (New York, 1988), 91–97.

76 The opening of the exhibition was announced in "Aus der Kunstwelt," *Berliner Tageblatt* 1 (December 1919), 3: and Oskar Beyer, "Die Kunst in Berlin," *Feuer* 1 (February 1920), 393. See also Erich Mendelsohn, "Das Problem einer neuen Baukunst," in Mendelsohn 1930, 7–21.

77 Norbert Huse, "Erich Mendelsohn. Zeichnungen und Bauten 1914–1922," in *Neues Bauen 1918–1933* (Munich, 1975), 18–29.

"Organic!"
Einstein, Finlay-Freundlich, Mendelsohn,
and the Einstein Tower in Potsdam

1 Erich Mendelsohn, "The Work of Erich Mendelsohn," typescript of a lecture delivered in Pittsburgh in 1924, 7, Mendelsohn Archive, Kunstbibliothek, Staatliche Museen zu Berlin—Preussischer Kulturbesitz (hereafter cited as KB, E. M. Archive).

2 Klaus Hentschel, *Der Einstein-Turm* (Heidelberg, 1992), 23–29; idem, "Physik, Astronomie und Architektur—Der Einsteinturm als Resultat des Zusammenwirkens von Einstein, Freundlich und Mendelsohn," in *Der Einsteinturm in Potsdam. Architektur und Astrophysik* (Berlin, 1995), 35–40.

3 Erwin Finlay-Freundlich, *The Foundations of Einstein's Theory of Gravitation,* trans. Henry L. Brose (1916; reprint, New York, 1920).

4 Erich Mendelsohn, letter to Luise Mendelsohn, June 17, 1917, collection of Ita Heinze-Greenberg (hereafter cited as coll. I. H.-G.).

5 Klaus Hentschel 1992 (as note 2), 51–58; Erwin Finlay-Freundlich, "Wie es dazu kam, dass ich den Einsteinturm errichtete," *Physikalische Blätter* 25 (1969), 538–41.

6 Erwin Finlay-Freundlich, letter to Erich Mendelsohn, July 2, 1918, in Sigrid Achenbach, *Erich Mendelsohn 1887–1953. Ideen, Bauten, Projekte* (Berlin, 1987), 61–62.

7 Erwin Finlay-Freundlich, *Das Turmteleskop der Einstein Stiftung* (Berlin, 1927) (hereafter cited as Finlay-Freundlich 1927), 4; *Annual Report of the Director,* ed. Mount Wilson Solar Observatory of the Carnegie Institution of Washington (1907), 139, 149, pl. 8; idem (1909), 178–79; idem (1910), 175–176, pl. 2; idem (1912), 177–78; *The Legacy of George Ellery Hale,* eds. Helen Wilson, Joan Warnow, and Charles Weiner (Cambridge, Mass., 1972), 21, 42–45, 67–69, 75, 239; Rolf Riekher, *Fernrohe und ihre Meister* (Berlin, 1990), 256–59.

8 Joachim Krausse, "Gebaute Weltbilder von Boullée bis Buckminster Fuller," *Arch⁺* 116 (1993), 32–33.

9 Jörg Limberg, "Entwürfe, Ausführung und Erweiterungsbau," in *Erich Mendelsohns Einsteinturm in Potsdam* (Potsdam, 1994) (hereafter cited as Limberg 1994), 8–13.

10 Erwin Finlay-Freundlich, letter to Erich Mendelsohn, 7.2.1918, in: Sigrid Achenbach (as note 6), 64.

11 Albert Einstein, "Meine Antwort," in *Berliner Tageblatt,* August 27, 1920. Fritz Stern, *Dreams and Delusions, The Drama of German History,* New York 1987, 25–50.

12 *Albert Einstein in Berlin, 1913–1933,* vol. 1, eds. Christa Kirsten and Hans-Jürgen Treder (Berlin, 1979), 177–79; idem, vol. 2, 91–93; Barbara Eggers, "Der Einsteinturm—die Geschichte eines Monumentes der Wissenschaft," in *Der Einsteinturm in Potsdam,* 76–79.

13 Erich Mendelsohn, letter to Luise Mendelsohn, December 5, 1920, Erich Mendelsohn, *Briefe eines Architekten,* ed. Oskar Beyer (Munich, 1961; reprint, Basel/Berlin/Boston, 1991), 53–54.

14 Iain Boyd Whyte, *Bruno Taut and the Architecture of Activism* (Cambridge, 1982); *Expressionist Utopias: Paradise—Metropolis—Architectural Fantasy,* ed. Timothy. O. Benson (Los Angeles, 1993).

15 "Das Problem einer neuen Baukunst," *Berliner Tageblatt* (January 29, 1920), for the date of this lecture, which Mendelsohn later gave as 1919.

16 Erich Mendelsohn, "Das Problem einer neuer Baukunst," in *Erich Mendelsohn: The Complete Works* (1930), trans. Antje Frisch (New York, 1992) (hereafter cited as Mendelsohn 1930), 18–19.

17 Limberg 1994, 53.

18 Erich Mendelsohn, letters to Luise Mendelsohn, May 14, 1920; June 9, 1920; and June 18, 1920; copies, I. H.-G. collection.

19 Erich Mendelsohn, letters to Luise Maas, August 20, 1913; September 14, 1914; in Oskar Beyer, *Eric Mendelsohn: Letters of an Architect,* trans. Geoffrey Strachen (London, 1967) (hereafter cited as Beyer 1967), 26, 33.

20 Erich Mendelsohn, letter to Luise Mendelsohn, June 30, 1920, copy, coll. I. H.-G.

21 Limberg 1994, 20–22; "Bautenachweise," *Bauwelt* 11 (1920), 392.

22 Erich Mendelsohn, letters to Luise Mendelsohn, June 14, 1920; June 21, 1920; June 24, 1920; June 26, 1920; July 3, 1920; copies, coll. I. H.-G., partially published in Beyer 1967, 53–54, and Limberg 1994, 23, 33–34.

23 Limberg 1994, 23–37, 51–55.

24 Mendelsohn, "Beschreibung des Baues für den Turmspektrographen auf dem Gelände des Astrophysikalischen Observatoriums," Geheimes Staats-

archiv Preussischer Kulturbesitz Merseburg, Ministerium für Wissenschaft, Kunst und Volksbildung, Rep. 76 V c, Sekt. 1, Tit. 11, Teil II, Nr. 6, i Bd. I, Bl. 7.

25 Finlay-Freundlich 1927, 6.

26 Gustav Adolf Platz, *Die Baukunst der Neuen Zeit* (Berlin, 1927; reprint, Berlin, 1930), pls. 204, 254.

27 Erich Mendelsohn, letter to Arnold Whittick, March 20, 1950, KB, E. M. Archive.

28 Hochbauamt Potsdam, Report to the Prussian Kultusministerium, October 28, 1920, Geheimes Staatsarchiv Preussischer Kulturbesitz Merseburg, Ministerium für Wissenschaft, Kunst und Volksbildung, Rep. 76 V c, Sekt. 1, Tit. 11, Teil II, Nr. 6, Bd. 1, Bl. 28.

29 Karl Bernhard, "Hochhäuser oder Skelett," *Zentralblatt der Bauverwaltung* 41 (1921), 44, who declared that the price of concrete was fifteen times higher than its prewar cost. See also *Bauwelt* 11 (1920), for reports on the cost and availability of materials.

30 Erich Mendelsohn, letter to Luise Mendelsohn, June 15, 1920, in Beyer 1967, 53.

31 Erich Mendelsohn, letters to Luise Mendelsohn, May 27, 1917; July 8, 1918; July 31, 1918; August 9, 1918; copies, coll. I. H.-G., document his consultations with an engineer named Salomonsen, who later collaborated with him on the Red Flag factory in Leningrad (Mendelsohn 1930, 118). Finlay-Freundlich 1927, 6, writes that two engineers from Carl Zeiss named Meyer and Villiger, and a third from the Siemens & Halske company named Böttcher, collaborated with Mendelsohn in the tower's design.

32 Limberg 1994, 38.

33 Ibid., 39–46.

34 Finlay-Freundlich 1927, 6.

35 Ibid., 11–19.

36 Richard Neutra, letter to Dione Niedermann, December 1921, in Dione Neutra, *Richard Neutra: Promise and Fulfillment, 1919–1932, Selections from the letters and diaries of Richard and Dione Neutra* (Carbondale/Edwardsville, 1986), 54, and a photograph of the completed workroom appeared in the *Berliner Illustrite Zeitung* (June 30, 1922), 586, establish that the furnishings were designed and built between December 1921 and July 1922.

37 Erich Mendelsohn, "The International Consensus on the New Architectural Concept, or Dynamics and Function," in Erich Mendelsohn 1930, 24.

38 Peter Hutter, *Die feinste Barbarei. Das Völkerschlachtdenkmal bei Leipzig* (Mainz am Rhine, 1990).

39 Paul Westheim, "Mendelsohn," *Das Kunstblatt* 4 (1923), 307.

40 The exception is Fritz Hellwag, "Der Einsteinturm," *Dekorative Kunst* 29 (1926), 157–60, based on his visit to the tower, through which he was probably guided by Freundlich.

41 The most notable such publications of the building, and the first in Germany, were the cover of *Die Berliner Illustrite Zeitung* (September 4, 1921), and "Der neue Einstein-Turm auf dem Telegraphenberg in Potsdam," *Berliner Tageblatt, Der Welt-Spiegel* (September 4, 1921), 3. Pictures of it could also be found in many of Berlin's cigar stores according to Richard Neutra, letter to Dione Niedermann, October 1921, in Dione Neutra (as note 36), 49.

42 Jan Frederick Staal, "Naar Anleiding van Erich Mendelsohn's Ontwerpen," *Wendingen* 3, 10 (1920), 3.

43 Adolf Behne, *Der Moderne Zweckbau* (Munich, 1926), 38–39; Thomas P. Bennett, *Architectural Design in Concrete* (London, 1927), 11, LXII, LXIII; Sheldon Cheney, *The New World Architecture* (London, 1930), 319; Walter Müller-Wulckow, *Architektur der Zwanziger Jahre in Deutschland*, vol. 1 (Königstein im Taunus, 1975), pl. 58; Francis S. Onderdonk, *The Ferro-Concrete Style* (New York, 1928), 239–21; Gustav Adolf Platz (as note 26), 70; Julius Vischer and Ludwig Hilberseimer, *Beton als Gestalter* (Stuttgart, 1928), 17; J. G. Wattjes, *Moderne Architectuur* (Amsterdam, 1927), pl. 124.

44 Herman George Scheffauer, "Erich Mendelsohn," *Architectural Review* 53 (1923), 158.

45 Paul Westheim (as note 39), 307.

46 Peter Meyer, *Moderne Architektur und Tradition* (Zurich, 1928), 8.

47 Paul Fred Schmidt, "Erich Mendelsohn," *Der Cicerone* 12 (1930), 220.

48 For contemporary recognition of Mendelsohn's debt to the Jugendstil see Adolf Behne (as note 43), 38; Platz (as note 26), 70; and E. M. Hajos, "Berliner Architektur und Architektur von Heute," *Die Kunstwanderer* (1929), 493–97.

"Thinking from day to day, where history takes great turns, leaving hundreds of thousands unsatisfied"
Early Expressionist Buildings in Luckenwalde, Berlin, and Gleiwitz

1 Kunstbibliothek, Staatliche Museen zu Berlin–Preussischer Kulturbesitz, Erich Mendelsohn Archive (hereafter cited as KB, E. M. Archive), V 27a, invitation to lectures in January and February 1919. In the same letter, "25 Mk." is specified as the "honorarium for the lecture series."

2 Luise and Molly Philippson met in 1913 in Berlin, where they lived in the same pension in Westend. Philippson arranged the lecture series in order to promulgate Erich Mendelsohn's ideas on a new architecture. See Louise Mendelsohn, *My Life in a Changing World*, unpublished memoirs (San Francisco, n.d.) (hereafter cited as Louise Mendelsohn n.d.), 85. The manuscript is found in the Kunstbibliothek, Staatliche Museen zu Berlin–Preussischer Kulturbesitz; the Museum of Modern Art, New York; and the collection of Ita Heinze-Greenberg (hereafter cited as coll. I. H.-G.).

3 KB, E. M. Archive, V 27a, unpublished ms.: "I. Abend. Entwicklungsgesetze der Kunst," 4.

4 Ibid., "Vortrag des Herrn Mendelsohn am 5.2.1919."

5 My discussion here is based on a number of recent studies on the hat factory in Luckenwalde: Susanne Schmitt, *Die Hutfabrik in Luckenwalde von Erich Mendelsohn*, M.A. thesis (Hamburg, 1992) (kindly made available to me by the author); Karin Carmen Jung and Dietrich Worbs, "Funktionelle Dynamik. Die Hutfabrik Steinberg – Hermann [sic] & Co. in Luckenwalde von Erich Mendelsohn," *Bauwelt* 83 (1992), 116–21; Thomas Drachenberg, "Luckenwalde – Ein unbekanntes Werk Erich Mendelsohns," in *Brandenburgische Denkmalpflege*, (1996), 71–78; Kathleen James, *Erich Mendelsohn and the Architecture of German Modernism* (Cambridge, Mass., 1997) (hereafter cited as James 1997), 78–88.

6 Oskar Beyer, *Erich Mendelsohn. Briefe eines Architekten* (Munich, 1961; reprint, Basel/Berlin/Boston, 1991), 9.

7 Oskar Beyer, "Architectuur in ijzer en beton," *Wendingen* (October 1920), 4–14.

8 See Louise Mendelsohn, *Biographical Notes: Eric Mendelsohn*, unpublished ms., 17, and Ita Heinze-Greenberg in this volume, 60.

9 Only the foundations of the pavilion have survived. Cf. Thomas Drachenberg (as note 5), p. 78.

10 Illustrated in *Erich Mendelsohn 1887–1953. Ideen, Bauten, Projekte*, ed. Sigrid Achenbach, exh. cat. Staatliche Museen Preussischer Kulturbesitz (Berlin, 1987), 9.

11 See Regina Stephan in this volume, 153.

12 Letter from Erich Mendelsohn to Luise, early May 1920, coll. I. H.-G.

13 Ibid., June 24, 1920; June 5, 1920. The three rooms occupied by the Mendelsohns in the Westend pension were likewise decorated with colored paint or wallpaper: "Our home consisted of a dark blue music-living room with a glassed-in, quite large square veranda. . . . Next door was Esther's room, which was all in light grey of fabrics with vertical stripes in gay colors on light grey. . . . Then our bedroom, all in yellow with dark brown wall-to-wall carpeting!" In Louise Mendelsohn n.d., p. 115.

14 Letter from Erich Mendelsohn to Luise, June 12, 1920, coll. I. H.-G.

15 Published by Erich Mendelsohn in *Das Gesamtschaffen des Architekten. Skizzen, Entwürfe, Bauten* (Berlin, 1930; reprint, Braunschweig/Wiesbaden: 1988) (hereafter cited as Mendelsohn 1930), 40 f.

16 First published by Thomas Drachenberg (as note 5).

17 Letter from Erich Mendelsohn to Luise, May 14, 1920, coll. I. H.-G.

18 The site, bounded on the north by the railroad and on the south by a highway, was optimally situated for the transport of goods.

19 Mendelsohn 1930, p. 62.

20 All ground plans, elevations, sections, and site plan are illustrated in ibid., 63–65.

21 Quoted in Susanne Schmitt (as note 5), 11.

22 Kathleen James, *Erich Mendelsohn. The Berlin Years 1918–1933*, Ph.D. diss., University of Pennsylvania (Philadelphia, 1990), 115.

23 See James 1997, 79–88.

24 The roof frame was constructed of wood and faced on the interior with boards, on the exterior with rubberoid panels.

25 See Kathleen James (as note 24), 116 ff. On Mendelsohn's lecture to the Arbeitsrat für Kunst in 1919, cf. "Das Problem einer neuen Baukunst," in Mendelsohn 1930, 7–21.

26 On the subsequent fate of the hat factory, see above all Susanne Schmitt (as note 5).

27 See the extensive discussion in Regina Stephan, *Studien zu Waren- und Geschäftshäusern Erich Mendelsohns in Deutschland* (Munich, 1992), 172–75.

28 James 1997, 91. We have neither building files, plans, nor letters from Mendelsohn from 1921.

29 See 92–94, 110–19 in this volume.

30 James 1997, 91.

31 Letter from Erich Mendelsohn to Luise, June 22, 1922, coll. I. H.-G.

32 Ibid., August 6, 1922.

33 Regina Stephan (as note 29), 66.

34 Erich Mendelsohn, "Die internationale Übereinstimmung des neuen Baugedankens oder Dynamik und Funktion 1923," in Mendelsohn 1930, esp. 24.

35 James 1997, 95–97.

36 Ibid., 96. Kathleen James studied Neutra's literary remains in Los Angeles and there found numerous designs and working plans for the Lachmann-Mosse office.

37 The Rudolf Mosse publishing house used views of the building for advertising purposes and gifts.

38 Mendelsohn 1930, 27 f.

39 Ibid.

40 Dione Neutra, *Richard Neutra: Promise and Fulfillment 1919–1932* (Carbondale/Edwardsville, 1986), 59: "Today the client from Silesia came again. I was in my element, spoke like a waterfall. For the time being he thinks I am his man. He trembles that Mendelsohn might change my design sketches. This, however, he has no intention of doing. . . ." Letter from Neutra to his future mother-in-law, March 1922.

41 Letter from Erich Mendelsohn to Luise, August 25, 1922, coll. I. H.-G.

42 Hermann Schildberger, "Das Seidenhaus Weichmann," in Erwin Stein, ed., *Monographien deutscher Städte,* vol. 13 (Gleiwitz/Berlin, 1925), 257–62.

43 KB, E. M. Archive, V 32. Erich Mendelsohn, *Das neuzeitliche Geschäftshaus* (1929), 14.

"Around noon land in sight"
Travels to Holland, Palestine, the United States, and Russia

1 Jan Frederik Staal, "Naar Anleidung," and Oskar Beyer, "Architectuur in ijzer en beton," *Wendingen* 3 (October 1920), 2 f., 4 ff. German ms. in the Mendelsohn Archive, Kunstbibliothek, Staatliche Museen zu Berlin–Preussischer Kulturbesitz (hereafter cited as KB, E. M. Archive).

2 Kathleen James has already made this point in her remarkable study *Erich Mendelsohn and the Architecture of German Modernism* (Cambridge, Mass., 1997) (hereafter cited as James 1997), 48 ff.

3 Cf. Suzanne S. Frank, *Michel de Klerk (1884–1923): An Architect of the Amsterdamer School* (Ann Arbor, Mich., 1984).

4 Jan Frederick Staal and Oskar Beyer, in *Wendingen* (as note 1).

5 Erich Mendelsohn, "Das Problem einer neuen Baukunst," in idem, *Das Gesamtschaffen des Architekten* (Berlin, 1930), 7 ff.

6 Letter from Erich Mendelsohn to Luise, Herrlingen, August 19, 1923, in Oskar Beyer, *Eric Mendelsohn: Letters of an Architect* (London/New York/Toronto, 1967) (hereafter cited as Beyer 1967), 60.

7 Erich Mendelsohn, "Die internationale Übereinstimmung des neuen Baugedankens oder Dynamik and Funktion," in idem, *Das Gesamtschaffen des Architekten* (as note 5), 22 ff.

8 Copies of this correspondence are found in KB, E. M. Archive, IV 7/96. The original letters are in the Nederlands Architectuur Instituut, Rotterdam.

9 Cf. James 1997, 50 ff., for a discussion of the exchange between Oud and Mendelsohn in contradistinction to Gropius's concept of the standardization of architecture.

10 Letter from Erich Mendelsohn to Oud, Charlottenburg, March 4, 1928. The subject of Hegemann appears in the correspondence beginning in 1926 (cf. note 8).

11 Suzanne S. Frank (as note 3), 31 ff.

12 Letter from Erich Mendelsohn to Richard Kauffmann, Charlottenburg, December 1, 1923, Kauffmann Archive, Central Zionist Archives, Jerusalem, A 175/226. Richard Kauffmann (1887–1958) studied with Theodor Fischer in Munich at the same time as Mendelsohn. He worked in Palestine beginning in 1921, above all as a settlement planner.

13 Louise Mendelsohn, *My Life in a Changing World,* unpublished memoirs (San Francisco, 1960), 253. Copies of the ms. are found in the Kunstbibliothek, Staatliche Museen zu Berlin–Preussischer Kulturbesitz; the Museum of Modern Art, New York; and the collection of Ita Heinze-Greenberg (hereafter cited as coll. I. H.-G.).

14 Cf. Nic. H. M. Tummers, "Over het werk van H. Th. Wijdeveld, bij diens 80ste verjaardag," *Overdruk uit het Bouwkundig Weekblad* (September 24, 1965).

15 Cf. my discussion of the project for the Académie Européenne Méditerranée in this volume, 184–86.

16 Telegram from Hendricus Theodorus Wijdeveld to Erich Mendelsohn, Amsterdam, February 14, 1923, KB, E. M. Archive, IV 7 (2).

17 Letter from Erich Mendelsohn to Hendricus Theodorus Wijdeveld, Charlottenburg, February 2, 1923, KB, E. M. Archive, B IV 7.

18 For a detailed discussion see Gilbert Herbert and Ita Heinze-Greenberg, *The Beginnings of Modern Architecture in Israel: The First Power Stations 1921–1932* (Haifa, 1996). On Mendelsohn's connections to the Zionist organization, cf. my discussion in this volume, 188–89.

19 Charles Robert Ashbee, *Palestine Notebook 1918–1923* (London, 1923), 211.

20 Whether and to what extent Wijdeveld was involved in the design as well cannot be determined.

21 Mendelsohn's stay in Palestine and his projects there were discussed in Zionist circles in Germany. It was through a letter of recommendation intended to strengthen his position in Palestine that Mendelsohn met the man who was to be his most important client, Salmann Schocken. At first, however, Schocken engaged him for projects in Germany.

22 Letter from Erich Mendelsohn to Oskar Beyer, Jerusalem, March 9, 1923, coll. Ralph Beyer, Teddington.

23 Lecture ms.: KB, E. M. Archive, IV 5a.

24 Mendelsohn, "Own Work," lecture in Liverpool 1933 and in Cambridge 1934. Lecture ms.: KB, E. M. Archive, B IV 1.

25 The Kauffmann-Mendelsohn correspondence on this project is found in the Kauffmann Archive (as note 12), A 175/233, A 175/141 E.

26 Letter from Erich Mendelsohn to Kauffmann, Berlin, July 17, 1923, Kauffmann Archive (as note 12), A175/141 E.

27 In a letter written from Berlin on October 8, 1923, Mendelsohn writes to Kauffmann: "This is the first time I have worked with a contractor, but it has already been enough to cure me of it." In a letter from Berlin on January 22, 1924, he indicated to Kauffmann that he had resigned from the affair with considerable financial loss. Both letters are in the Kauffmann Archive (as note 12), A175/141E. Cf. also Gilbert Herbert and Silvina Sosnovsky, *Bauhaus on the Carmel and the Crossroads of Empire* (Jerusalem, 1993), 98 ff. Herbert and Sosnovsky discuss the project in detail.

28 *Jüdische Rundschau* (March 6, 1923). For more detailed information on this project, cf. Gilbert Herbert and Silvina Sosnovsky (as note 27), 110 ff.

29 Erich Mendelsohn, lecture ms. of 1924 without further designation, KB, E. M. Archive, B IV 1.

30 Third prize was awarded to the Berlin architectural office of Arthur Korn and Siegfried Weitzmann. See Gilbert Herbert and Silvina Sosnovsky (as note 27), 117.

31 In his essay, "The Divided Heart: Erich Mendelsohn and the Zionist Dream," in *Erich Mendelsohn in Palestine,* ed. Architectural Heritage Research Centre (Haifa, 1994), 11, Gilbert Herbert points to the conflict Mendelsohn experienced between his Zionist persuasions and the available opportunities for professional advancement.

32 Richard Neutra, *Auftrag für Morgen* (Schleswig, 1962), 175.

33 James 1997, 58. Cf. the anthology *Zukunft aus Amerika. Fordismus in der Zwischenkriegszeit,* ed. Stiftung Bauhaus Dessau and Rheinisch-Westfälische Technische Hochschule Aachen (Berlin, 1995).

34 In two letters to his wife, for example, Mendelsohn mentions the possibility of organizing a trip to America: letter from Erich Mendelsohn to Luise, Charlottenburg, June 26, 1920, coll. I. H.-G., and letter from Erich Mendelsohn to Luise, Charlottenburg, June 4, 1922, coll. I. H.-G., in Beyer 1967, 56 f.

35 Letter from Erich Mendelsohn to Luise, Charlottenburg, July 10, 1924, coll. I. H.-G.

36 Letter from Erich Mendelsohn to Luise, Charlottenburg, July 16, 1924, coll. I. H.-G.

37 Letter from Erich Mendelsohn to Luise, on board the *Deutschland,* October 3, 1924, coll. I. H.-G, and letter from Erich Mendelsohn to Luise, on board the *Deutschland,* October 9, 1924, in Oskar Beyer, *Erich Mendelsohn. Briefe eines Architekten* (Munich: 1961; reprint, Basel/Berlin/Boston, 1991) (hereafter cited as Beyer 1991), 55.

38 Letter from Erich Mendelsohn to Luise, on board the *Deutschland,* October 11, 1924, in Beyer 1991, 56.

39 Fritz Lang, "Was ich in Amerika sah," *Film-Kurier* 292 (December 11, 1924). In an interview with Peter Bogdanovich, Lang described the arrival in New York harbor as the birthplace of his film *Metropolis.* Peter Bogdanovich, *Fritz Lang in America* (London, 1967). Cf. also Jean-Louis Cohen, *Scenes of the World to Come: European Architecture and the American Challenge 1893–1960,* English ed. (Paris, 1995), 85 ff.

40 Herman George Scheffauer was a German-born architecture critic in America. He published the following articles on Mendelsohn: "Dynamic Architecture: New Forms of the Future," *Dial* 70 (March

1921), 323 ff.; "Erich Mendelsohn," *The Architectural Review* 53 (March 1923), 156 ff.; "Activist Architecture," *The New Vision in the German Arts* (New York, 1924).

41 Letter from Erich Mendelsohn to Luise, Detroit, October 24, 1924, coll. I. H.-G. Excerpts from the letter are printed in Beyer 1991, 66; the passage describing Kahn's office, however, is not included.

42 Letter from Erich Mendelsohn to Luise, Chicago, November 13, 1924, coll. I. H.-G.

43 Letter from Erich Mendelsohn to Luise, Chicago, November 5, 1924, in Beyer 1967, 71 ff. Neutra gave a less felicitous assessment of the meeting between Wright and Mendelsohn and characterized Wright's opinion of Mendelsohn as rather negative. Cf., for example, the letter from Richard Neutra to Frances Toplitz, Taliesin, November 1924, in *Richard Neutra: Promise and Fulfillment 1919–1932: Selections from the Letters and Diaries of Richard and Dione Neutra,* ed. Dione Neutra (Carbondale/Edwardsville, 1986), 130.

44 Letter from Erich Mendelsohn to Luise, Chicago, November 8, 1924, in Beyer 1967, 71 ff. Cf. also James 1997, 63, who draws particular attention to the traditional image of Chicago communicated to Mendelsohn by Byrne.

45 Letter from Erich Mendelsohn to Luise, Chicago, October 29, 1924, in Beyer 1991, 69.

46 Ibid., 67, as well as Beyer 1967, 70.

47 Letter from Erich Mendelsohn to Luise, Pittsburgh, October 22, 1924, coll. I. H.-G. This portion of the letter is not among the excerpts printed in Beyer 1991, 64 ff.

48 Erich Mendelsohn, "New York," *Berliner Tageblatt* (January 3, 1926), 5; Erich Mendelsohn, "Besuch bei Wright," *Baukunst* 2 (1926), 56; Erich Mendelsohn, "Frank Lloyd Wright," *Wasmuths Monatshefte* (1926), 244 ff.

49 Cf. James 1997, 66 ff.; Jean-Louis Cohen (as note 39), 85 ff.; and Herbert Molderings, "Mendelsohn, Amerika und der 'Amerikanismus,'" afterword to the reprint of *Erich Mendelsohn, Amerika. Bilderbuch eines Architekten* (Berlin, 1926; reprint, Braunschweig/Wiesbaden, 1991), 83 ff. Most recently, see Rolf Sachsse, "Bild und Bau. Zur Nutzung technischer Medien beim Entwerfen von Architektur," *Bauwelt Fundamente* 113 (1997), 125–33.

50 Not all of the photographs chosen by Mendelsohn for his book were taken by him; sixteen of them came from Knud Lonberg-Holm, another from Fritz Lang. In a new edition of 1928, Mendelsohn replaced a few of the original photographs with photographs by his assistant Erich Karweik, who had visited America in 1927. Cf. Jean-Louis Cohen (as note 39), 91.

51 Mendelsohn met Lewis Mumford in New York. Mumford aroused Mendelsohn's interest in the historical development of America and gave him a copy of his recently published book *Sticks and Stones* (New York, 1924). Mendelsohn read it on the return voyage from New York to Hamburg and planned with the help of his wife to translate the book into German. Cf. James 1997, 64 f. A translation, however, was already in progress and was published in 1926 by Cassirer in Berlin under the title *Vom Blockhaus zum Wolkenkratzer.* In the preface to the German

edition, Mumford mentions Mendelsohn's works as exemplary for their humane treatment of mechanical forms and methods. Mumford's regionalistic approach paralleled Mendelsohn's own efforts, and the two men cultivated a regular exchange of ideas into the 1950s. (Letters from Erich Mendelsohn to Mumford: KB, E. M. Archive, II/7.) Mumford personally supported Mendelsohn after his emigration to America by writing numerous letters of recommendation.

52 El Lissitzky, "Glaz Arhitektora," *Stoitelnaya promyshlennost* 2 (1926). English translation published in *Photography in the Modern Era,* ed. Christopher Phillips (New York, 1989), 221 ff.

53 Letter from El Lissitzky to Erich Mendelsohn, Moscow, January 12, 1926, KB, E. M. Archive, IV 7/90.

54 Cf. Kathleen James in this volume, 142–43.

55 The most recent major survey of the theme is *Berlin, Moskau 1900–1950,* eds. Irina Antonowa and Jörn Merkert, (Munich/New York, 1995).

56 Louise Mendelsohn (as note 13), 166 ff.

57 Erich Mendelsohn, *Russland, Europa, Amerika. Ein architektonischer Querschnitt* (Berlin, 1929).

58 Ibid.

"The merchandise is primary—all architectural means serve its praise"
Department Stores in Berlin, Breslau, Chemnitz, Duisburg, Nuremberg, and Stuttgart, 1924–1929

1 On January 25, 1936, Mendelsohn wrote to Oskar Beyer: "I never sold my soul to department store buildings. It is as close to God as the greatest heart of any artist." Kunstbibliothek, Staatliche Museen zu Berlin–Preussischer Kulturbesitz, Erich Mendelsohn Archive (hereafter cited as KB, E. M. Archive), Briefe 1936.

2 Erich Mendelsohn, "Das neuzeitliche Geschäftshaus," unpublished lecture ms., n.p., n.d. (ca. 1929), KB, E. M. Archive, M. V 32. Excerpts quoted in Regina Stephan, *Studien zu Waren- and Geschäftshäusern Erich Mendelsohns in Deutschland* (Munich, 1992) (hereafter cited as Stephan 1992), 199–201.

3 Erich Mendelsohn, *Amerika. Bilderbuch eines Architekten* (Berlin, 1926; reprint, Braunschweig/Wiesbaden, 1991), 45.

4 See the extensive discussion in Stephan 1992, 73–78.

5 See the essay by Regina Stephan in the German edition of this volume: "'Man kämpft mühsam um Centimeter, wo die Reaktion Meter besetzt hat.' Mendelsohns Mitwirken im Arbeitsrat für Kunst, in der Novembergruppe und im Ring," in *Erich Mendelsohn. Architekt 1887–1953. Gebaute Welten*, ed. Regina Stephan (Ostfildern-Ruit, 1998), 69–71.

6 KB, E. M. Archive, Bauten D, Archivmaterial 9, C. A. Herpich und Söhne 1924–29, Einzelhandelsführer II/d/25.

7 Letter from Erich Mendelsohn to Luise, August 15, 1925, collection of Ita Heinze-Greenberg (hereafter cited as coll. I. H.-G.), quoted in Oskar Beyer, *Eric Mendelsohn: Letters of an Architect* (London/New York/Toronto, 1967), 88.

8 Kathleen James, *Erich Mendelsohn and the Architecture of German Modernism* (Cambridge, Mass., 1997) (hereafter cited as James 1997), 115.

9 Ernst May, in Lotz and Halberfeld, *Licht and Beleuchtung* (1928), 46.

10 On the Schocken company, see Konrad Werner Fuchs, *Ein Konzern aus Sachsen* (Stuttgart, 1990).

11 Ibid., 100.

12 "Rede des Herrn Salmann Schocken beim Empfang für Erich Mendelsohn 15. März 1937 in der Schocken Bibliothek" ("Speech by Mr. Salmann Schocken at the Reception for Erich Mendelsohn on March 15, 1937, in the Schocken Library"), Ms., Schocken Archive, Jerusalem (hereafter cited as Sch/A), 71M/725.

13 Bauhof Nürnberg (Nuremberg Building Office), Aufsessplatz 18, building files, building application, January 30, 1926.

14 Stadtarchiv Nürnberg (Nuremberg City Archives), C 20/V.14865, January 12, 1926.

15 Bauhof Nürnberg (Nuremberg Building Office), Aufsessplatz 18, building files, February 15, 1926.

16 Ibid., February 23, 1926.

17 *Kaufhaus Schocken im Jahre 1926. Vorträge, Ansprachen and Leitsätze aus früheren Schocken-Hauszeitungen* (Nuremberg, 1952), 9–15.

18 Erich Mendelsohn, "Warum diese Architektur," published, e.g., in *Baukunst,* 5, 2, (1929), 7.

19 Justus Bier, "Der Kaufhausneubau am Aufsessplatz," *Nürnberger Zeitung und Korrespondent* (October 6, 1926), 5.

20 Konrad Werner Fuchs (as note 10), 141f.

21 James 1997, 178, was the first to note this fact. The Stuttgart Schocken store is better documented than almost any other project by Mendelsohn: not only are the files of the Stuttgart building authorities complete, but the letters and records of telephone conversations between client and architect are also preserved in the Schocken Archive in Jerusalem (as note 12). In addition, considerable information is contained in letters from Erich Mendelsohn to Luise.

22 According to the land register of the city of Stuttgart, the purchase contract was concluded on June 4, 1926; the conveyance followed on June 17 and the payment on June 19, 1926.

23 On the course of the planning and construction, see the extensive discussion in Stephan 1992, 108–15. At the recital, Luise played the cello sonata in D minor by Johann Sebastian Bach, KB, E. M. Archive, Hdz. 155, K 30.

24 Erich Mendelsohn, "Harmonische and kontrapunktische Führung in der Architektur," *Baukunst* 1 (1925), 179. In connection with the Stuttgart Schocken building, see James 1997, 179.

25 KB, E. M. Archive, Briefe 42, 1926, July 11, 1926.

26 Quoted in Oskar Beyer, *Erich Mendelsohn. Briefe eines Architekten* (Munich, 1961), 78f.

27 Pointed out most recently in James 1997, 182. See also the discussion by E. A. Karweik in Günter Meier, "Erinnerungen an Erich Mendelsohn," *Bauwelt* 3 (1968), 57, as well as Regina Stephan in this volume, 155.

28 Konrad Werner Schulze, *Der Stahlskelettbau* (Stuttgart, 1928), devoted most of his book to the Stuttgart Schocken building.

29 Stadtarchiv Stuttgart (Stuttgart City Archive), D 1500/3, Eberhardstr. 28, Fasz. 3 Rs.

30 See the extensive discussion in Stephan 1992, 33–38.

31 Gilbert Herbert, *International Dictionary of Architects* (1993), 317, views Mendelsohn's Schocken building as the further development of the entrance to Sullivan's Schlesinger and Mayer Department Store. See also James 1997, 186. In Chicago, the two side windows were generally double-hung rather than casements.

32 On the subsequent history of the Stuttgart Schocken store and the decision to demolish it, see Stephan 1992, 235–47.

33 Gilbert Herbert (as note 31), 318, describes the Stuttgart Schocken store as "The Scope of total architecture."

34 For the Breuninger company in Stuttgart, Eisenlohr and Pfennig built a department store derived entirely from Mendelsohn's formal repertoire (completed 1931). Plans for a new department store for the Hermann Tietz company at around the same time were abandoned due to poor economic conditions.

35 KB, E. M. Archive, Briefe, January 4, 1925; January 16, 1925. Later, Mendelsohn also met Dr. Epstein on vacation in St. Moritz, Chantarella. See the letter from Erich Mendelsohn to Luise, January 19, 1931, coll. I. H.-G.

36 The surviving building files and plans are found in the city archives in Duisburg. On the history of the planning and construction, see the extensive discussion in Stephan 1992, 96–107.

37 Report by local editor Karl Ludwig Zimmermann, "Ein Haus voll Ware," *Duisburger Generalanzeiger* 46 (November 29, 1927), 5654.

38 Building files for the renovation and expansion could not be located in the Breslau city archives.

39 Erich Mendelsohn, *Das Gesamtschaffen des Architekten* (Berlin, 1930; reprint, Braunschweig/ Wiesbaden, 1988), 201.

40 Erich Mendelsohn (as note 2), 21.

41 Emil Lange, "Ein Geschäftshaus von Erich Mendelsohn," *Schlesische Monatshefte* 5 (1928), 198f.

42 "Der Neubau Petersdorff," *Architektur und Schaufenster* 25 (May 1928), 1.

43 Emil Lange (as note 41), 199.

44 On the current state of the high-rise discussion in Breslau, see *Hochhäuser für Breslau 1919–1932,* eds. Jerzy Ilkosz and Beate Störtkuhl (Braunschweig, 1997).

45 Letters and records of telephone conversations are preserved in the Schocken Archive in Jerusalem (as note 12).

46 On the history of the planning and construction, see Stephan 1992, 132–35.

47 See James 1997, 199.

48 See Julius Posener, "Betrachtungen über Erich Mendelsohn," *Bauwelt* 10 (1988), 375–80, where this question is discussed for the first time. James 1997, 196, raised it again.

49 Unfortunately, in the 1980s gold-toned window panes were installed, completely destroying the effect of the clear window bands.

50 *Norgens Kunstnerleksikon,* vol. 2 (Oslo, n.d.).

51 KB, E. M. Archive, Briefe 48, 1932.

52 Erich Mendelsohn (as note 2), 6f.

53 Ibid., 15.

54 Ibid., 11.

"No stucco pastries for Potemkin and Scapa Flow"
Metropolitan Architecture in Berlin: The WOGA Complex and the Universum Cinema

1 George R. Collins and Christiane Crasemann Collins, *Camillo Sitte: The Birth of Modern City Planning* (New York, 1986).

2 Louise Mendelsohn, *My Life in a Changing World,* unpublished ms., Mendelsohn Archive, Kunstbibliothek, Staatliche Museen zu Berlin—Preussischer Kulturbesitz, 98; and collection of Ita Heinze-Greenberg (hereafter cited as coll. I. H.-G.).

3 Karl-Heinz Metzger and Ulrich Dunker, *Der Kurfürstendamm. Leben und Mythos des Boulevards in 100 Jahren deutscher Geschichte* (Berlin, 1986).

4 On the Kabarett, whose interiors Mendelsohn did not design, see Peter Jelavich, *Berlin Cabaret* (Cambridge, 1993), 198–201, 203, 246–48.

5 *Der Mendelsohn-Bau am Lehniner Platz. Erich Mendelsohn und Berlin,* ed. Schaubühne am Lehniner Platz (Berlin, 1981) (hereafter cited as *Der Mendelsohn-Bau am Lehniner Platz*), 26, for the complete mix of apartment sizes. Hans-Henning Joeres and Barbara Schulz, "Liste der Mehrfamilienhäuser 1918–1945," in *Berlin und seine Bauten,* vol. 4: *Wohnungsbau,* part B: "Die Wohngebäude—Einfamilienhäuser" (Berlin, 1975), 369–548, who incorrectly date the block to 1926 to 1928. The Cicerostrasse housing was first published, however, only in 1929, when a photograph of the balconies appeared in "Neue Berliner Perspektive," *Berliner Tageblatt, Der Welt-Spiegel* (May 12, 1929), 2.

6 *Der Mendelsohn-Bau am Lehniner Platz,* 40.

7 Erich Mendelsohn, letter to Luise Mendelsohn, July 2, 1925, copy, coll. I. H.-G.

8 Adolf Donath, "Das neue Kabarett der Komiker. Architektur und Stadtbild," *Berliner Tageblatt* (September 21, 1928), reprinted in *Der Mendelsohn-Bau am Lehniner Platz,* 68.

9 Peter Boeger, *Architektur der Lichtspieltheater in Berlin. Bauten und Projekte 1919–1930* (Berlin, 1993).

10 Erich Mendelsohn, "Zur Eröffnung des 'Universum,'" *Der Montag* (September 17, 1928), republished in *Der Mendelsohn-Bau am Lehniner Platz,* 49, and in translation in Dennis Sharp, *Modern Architecture and Expressionism* (New York, 1966), 126.

11 *Der Mendelsohn-Bau am Lehniner Platz,* 53–54, for Mendelsohn's account of the building, focusing on the safety of its escape routes, that accompanied his application for a building permit on April 28, 1928.

12 Theodor Böll, quoted in *Die Metropole. Industriekultur in Berlin am Anfang des 20. Jahrhunderts,* eds. Jochen Boberg, Tilmann Fichter, and Eckhardt Gillen (Munich, 1986), 100.

13 "Ein Lichtspieltheater," *Die Form* 4 (1929), 85–87.

14 Ibid., 85–87; H. Bauer, "Erich Mendelsohn. Lichtspielhaus 'Universum,'" *Das Kunstblatt* 14 (1930), 106–8; Adolph Donath, "Erich Mendelsohns Architektur," *Berliner Tageblatt* (September 17, 1928), reprinted in *Der Mendelsohn-Bau am Lehniner Platz,* 67; and Günter Herkt, "Probleme des Tonfilm Theaters," *Wasmuths Monatshefte für Baukunst* 13 (1929), 429–34.

15 A. Wedemeyer, "Die Moderne Künstliche Beleuchtung," *Deutsche Bauzeitung* 65 (1931), 80.

16 Erich Mendelsohn, "Zur Eröffnung," (as note 10), 49. For a direct view from the projection booth toward the screen see *Baumeister* 21 (1930), 10.

17 Erich Mendelsohn, *Das Gestamtschaffen des Architekten. Skizzen, Entwürfe, Bauten* (Berlin, 1930; reprint, Braunschweig/Wiesbaden, 1988), 232; idem, "Zur Eröffnung" (as note 10).

18 Howard Robertson and Frank R. Yerbury, "The Architecture of Tension," *The Architect and Builders' News* 122 (1929), 707.

19 William Gaunt, "A New Utopia? Berlin—The New Germany—The Modern Movement," *The Studio* 98 (1929), 859–65.

20 J. R. Leathart, "Modern Cinema Design," *Journal of the Royal Institute of British Architects* 38: 3 (1930), 68.

21 Dennis Sharp, *The Picture Palace and Other Buildings for the Movies* (London, 1969), 126–46.

"We believe in Berlin!"
The Metal Workers' Union Building, the Columbushaus, and Other Office Buildings in Berlin

1 In the debate over high-rise buildings, see Dietrich Neumann, *Deutsche Hochhäuser der zwanziger Jahre,* diss., Technische Universität (Munich, 1988); Florian Zimmermann, ed., *Der Schrei nach dem Turmhaus. Der Ideenwettbewerb Hochhaus am Bahnhof Friedrichstrasse Berlin 1921/22,* exh. cat. Bauhaus-Archiv, Technische Universität (Berlin, 1988); Rainer Stommer, *Hochhaus. Der Beginn in Deutschland* (Marburg, 1990); Jerzy Ilkosz and Beate Störtkuhl, eds., *Hochhäuser für Breslau 1919–1932,* exh. cat. (Braunschweig, 1997), esp. 17–30.

2 "Architektonische Lösung Ecke Bellevue- and Viktoriastrasse am Kemperplatz in Berlin," *Frühlicht* 3 (1921/22), 80–84.

3 Adolf Behne, "Neubauaufgaben," *Sozialistische Monatshefte* (1923), 644.

4 Dietrich Neumann (as note 1), 205, has presented convincing arguments in this regard.

5 Letter from Erich Mendelsohn to Luise, December 16, 1928, Kunstbibliothek, Staatliche Museen zu Berlin–Preussischer Kulturbesitz, Erich Mendelsohn Archive (hereafter cited as KB, E. M. Archive), Briefe 44.

6 Published by Mendelsohn in *Das Gesamtschaffen des Architekten* (Berlin, 1930; reprint, Braunschweig/ Wiesbaden, 1988), 190–93.

7 Letter from Erich Mendelsohn to Luise, July 24, 1927, KB, E. M. Archive, Briefe 43.

8 Quoted in *Fünfzig Jahre Metallarbeiterhaus. Eine Dokumentation,* compiled by Karl-Heinz Volck (Berlin, 1980), 7.

9 Norbert Huse, *Neues Bauen 1918–1933. Modernes Bauen in der Weimarer Republik* (Berlin, 1975), 142, n. 23, sees the advantage of Reichel's design (despite its "Teutonic style") in the plaza in front of the building, an element Mendelsohn adopted as well.

10 The chairman of the metal workers' union at the time of the commission was a man named Georg Reichel.

11 Sigrid Achenbach, *Erich Mendelsohn 1887–1953. Ideen, Bauten, Projekte,* exh. cat. Staatliche Museen Preussischer Kulturbesitz (Berlin, 1987), 82.

12 Letter from Erich Mendelsohn to Luise, July 22, 1928, KB, E. M. Archive, Briefe 44: "We are beginning the preliminary project for the *Vorwärts* expansion. . . ."

13 Quoted in Bruno Zevi, *Erich Mendelsohn* (Zurich, 1983), 111.

14 Letter from Erich Mendelsohn to Luise, January 14, 1929, KB, E. M. Archive, Briefe 45.

15 The building files and plans are held in Berlin in the archives of the Bezirksamt Kreuzberg, Bau- and Wohnungsaufsichtsamt (Kreuzberg district, Building and Housing Supervisory Office), files for Alte Jakobstrasse 148–55, vol. 6. On the history of the planning and construction of the building, see the extensive discussion in Regina Stephan, *Studien zu Waren- and Geschäftshäusern Erich Mendelsohns in Deutschland* (Munich, 1992) (hereafter cited as Stephan 1992), 144–57.

16 On Ernst Sagebiel, see Regina Stephan in this volume, 155–56, and 131-32 of this chapter.

17 *Fünfzig Jahre Metallarbeiterhaus* (as note 8), 36f.

18 Sigrid Achenbach (as note 11), 82.

19 Adolf Donath, "Neues Wahrzeichen Berlins. Das Haus des Deutschen Metallarbeiterverbands. Ein neues Werk Erich Mendelsohns," *Berliner Tageblatt* 1 (September 9, 1930). There are no known files or drawings to confirm this.

20 Werner Hegemann, "Wettbewerb für das Verwaltungsgebäude des Stickstoffsyndikats in Berlin," *Wasmuths Monatshefte für Baukunst and Städtebau* 13 (1929), 305–11.

21 Ibid., 307f.

22 See Florian Zimmermann (as note 1).

23 The competition is described in detail in Stephan 1992, pp. 191–93.

24 "Das Hochhaus am Bahnhof Friedrichstrasse," *Wasmuths Monatshefte für Baukunst and Städtebau* 14 (1930), 125–28.

25 *Martin Wagner 1885–1957. Wohnungsbau and Weltstadtplanung. Die Rationalisierung des Glücks,* exh. cat. Akademie der Künste (Berlin, 1985). A list of Wagner's publications is found on 179–87.

26 Erich Mendelsohn, "Das Columbushaus in Berlin," *Wasmuths Monatshefte für Baukunst and Städtebau* 19 (1933), 81–88, esp. 82.

27 See the extensive discussion in Kathleen James, *Erich Mendelsohn and the Architecture of German Modernism* (Cambridge, Mass., 1997), 131f.

28 Letter from Erich Mendelsohn to Luise, January 29, 1929, collection of Ita Heinze-Greenberg.

29 Letter from Erich Mendelsohn to Luise, January 12, 1929, KB, E. M. Archive, Briefe 45.

30 Erich Mendelsohn (as note 6), 236.

31 Ernst Sagebiel, "Die Konstruktion des Columbus-Hauses," *Zentralblatt der Bauverwaltung* 52: 46 (1932), 543–48, esp. 543.

32 Beginning in 1928, Mendelsohn's letters regularly report on the increasingly radical political climate and its effects on daily life in Berlin.

33 Ernst Sagebiel (as note 31), 543.

34 Ibid., 547.

35 See Werner Durth and Niels Gutschow, *Architektur und Städtebau der fünfziger Jahre,* Schriftenreihe des deutschen Nationalkomitees für Denkmalschutz (Bonn, 1987).

36 Erich Mendelsohn (as note 26), 84–86.

37 Ibid.

38 A. Bock, "Das Stahlskelett des Columbus-Hauses am Potsdamer Platz in Berlin," *Der Stahlbau* 4: 22 (October 30, 1931), 255f.

39 On the construction of the building, see Dietrich Worbs, "Das Columbshaus am Potsdamer Platz von Erich Mendelsohn, 1931/32," in Sonja Günther and Dietrich Worbs, *Architektur-Experimente in Berlin und anderswo für Julius Posener* (Berlin, 1989), esp. 84–89; Stephan 1992, 165–69.

40 On the subsequent fate of the Columbushaus, see Stephan 1992, 248–51.

41 There is no documentary evidence for the existence of a Gestapo post or prison in the Columbushaus, as is often maintained in the literature.

42 The reasons for the Politburo's decision remain unclear.

"Russia—a miracle in the past and in the present"
Soviet Buildings and Projects

1 Albert Sigrist (Alexander Schwab), *Das Buch vom Bauen* (Berlin, 1930), 65.

2 Erich Mendelsohn, letters to Luise Mendelsohn, August 7, 1925; August 11, 1925; August 15, 1925; August 19, 1925; and August 25, 1925 in Oskar Beyer, *Eric Mendelsohn: Letters of an Architect,* trans. Geoffrey Strachen (London, 1967) (hereafter cited as Beyer 1967), 86–88.

3 Erich Mendelsohn, letter to Luise Mendelsohn, July 31, 1925, Beyer 1967, 92, and *Erich Mendelsohn: The Complete Works* (1930), trans. Antje Frisch (New York, 1992), 118–26. Maria L. Makagonova, "The 'Red Banner' factory in Leningrad—the work of E. Mendelsohn," in *Docomomo Conference Proceedings,* ed. by Wolfgang Paul, 2nd international conference, September 1992, 224–26, gives the fullest account of the commission, including what was actually built. Leonie Pilawski, "Neue Bauaufgaben in der Sowjet-Union," *Die Form* 5 (1930), 234, published a photograph of the powerhouse. See also Peter Knoch, "Nieder mit dem Eklektizmus! Industrie-architektur in Leningrad 1917–1939," *Bauwelt* 83 (1992), 106–15.

4 Erich Mendelsohn (as note 3), 118, 126.

5 Louise Mendelsohn, "Biographical Note on Erich," *L'architettura. Cronache e storia* 9 (1963), 322.

6 El Lissitzky, letter to his mother, undated, Sophie Lissitzky-Küppers, *El Lissitzky: Life, Letters, Texts,* trans. Helene Aldwinckle and Mary Whittall (London, 1980), 71; Louise Mendelsohn, *My Life in a Changing World,* Mendelsohn Archive, Kunstbibliothek, Staatliche Museen zu Berlin—Preussischer Kulturbesitz, 79; S. Frederick Starr, *Melnikov: Solo Architect in a Mass Society* (Princeton, 1978), 135–36.

7 Erich Mendelsohn, letter to Luise Mendelsohn, August 4, 1926, Beyer 1967, 93.

8 Erich Mendelsohn, letter to Luise Mendelsohn, August 1, 1926, copy, collection of Ita Heinze-Greenberg. Louise Mendelsohn (as note 6), 73, remembers that on their first trip they were appalled by the shortages of food and by the censorship.

9 Mendelsohn, *Russland—Amerika—Europa. Ein Architektonischer Querschnitt* (Berlin, 1929), 138, 152, 158.

10 Bruno Zevi, *Erich Mendelsohn. Opera Completa* (Milan, 1970), 185; Alberto Samona, *Il Palazzo del Soviet, 1931-33* (Rome, 1976); Jean-Louis Cohen, *Le Corbusier and the Mystique of the USSR: Theories and Projects for Moscow 1928–1936* (Princeton, 1992), 166–98.

"Even if the Berlin buildings had been well underway, I would have kept on fighting"
Small Buildings for the Jewish Communities in Tilsit, Königsberg, and Essen

1 Otto Bartning, *Vom neuen Kirchenbau* (Berlin, 1919), and *Dominikus Böhm,* introduction by His Eminence Joseph Cardinal Frings, with essays by August Hoff, Herbert Muck, and Raimund Thoma (Munich, 1962).

2 Harold Hammer-Scheuk, *Synagogen in Deutschland. Geschichte einer Baugattung im 19. und 20. Jahrhundert (1780–1933)* (Hamburg, 1981), 506–12, 528–41.

3 Sigrid Achenbach, *Erich Mendelsohn 1887–1953. Ideen, Bauten, Projekte* (Berlin, 1987), 75, for the dates of the Königsberg Cemetery; drawings in the collection of the Alte Synagogue, Essen, photographs of which are also in the Mendelsohn Archive (Kunstbibliothek, Staatliche Museen zu Berlin – Preussischer Kulturbesitz, V/e/1–9), establish that Mendelsohn's plans for the Jewish Youth Center in Essen date from October 1930 through July 1931.

4 *Erich Mendelsohn: The Complete Works* (1930), trans. Antje Frisch (New York, 1992), 127–31.

5 Carol Herselle Krinsky, *Synagogues of Europe: Architecture, Design, Meaning* (New York, 1985), 285–88, 291–94, 302–9.

6 The street names are taken from the caption to fig. 90 published in Peter Joost and Ingolf Koehler, *Tilsit—wie es war. Bilder einer deutscher Stadt* (Kiel, n. d).

7 Fritz Gause, *Die Geschichte der Stadt Königsberg in Preussen,* vol. 3 (Cologne, 1971), 59, 146.

8 As illustrated in a 1931 map of the city reproduced as an endpaper in Willi Scharloff, *Königsberg—damals und heute. Bilder aus ein verbotener Stadt* (Leer, 1982).

9 Erich Mendelsohn (as note 4), 170.

10 Curt Horn, "Das Praktische Ergebnis der Kirchenbautheorie," *Kunst und Kirche* 6 (1929/30), 88.

11 *Die Form* 5 (1930), 569.

12 Fritz Gause (as note 7), 149; Edna Brocke and Michael Zimmermann, *Stationen jüdischen Lebens. Von der Emanzipation bis zur Gegenwart* (Bonn, 1990), 165–73.

13 Michael Zimmermann, "Zur Geschichte der Essener Juden im 19. und im ersten Drittel des 20. Jahrhunderts. Ein Überblick," in *Jüdisches Leben in Essen 1800–1933,* eds. Michael Zimmermann and Claudia Konieczek (Essen, 1993), 54–57.

"One of the most lovable people and at the same time one of the most unpleasant"
Mendelsohn and His Assistants in the 1920s and Early 1930s

1   Susan King, "Interview with Mrs. Louise Mendelsohn," in *The Drawings of Eric Mendelsohn* (Berkeley, 1969), 28–30.
2   Ibid., 28.
3   Mendelsohn's methods of design have been described elsewhere and will not be dealt with at length here. For a summary and additional bibliography, see Regina Stephan, *Studien zu Waren- and Geschäftshäusern Erich Mendelsohns in Deutschland* (Munich, 1992), 33–38.
4   Susan King (as note 1), 28.
5   This phenomenon has yet to be studied in detail.
6   Louise Mendelsohn, *My Life in a Changing World*, unpublished memoirs (San Francisco, n.d.) (hereafter cited as Louise Mendelsohn n.d.), 227. The manuscript is found in the Kunstbibliothek, Staatliche Museen zu Berlin–Preussischer Kulturbesitz; in the Museum of Modern Art, New York; and in the collection of Ita Heinze-Greenberg (hereafter cited as coll. I. H.-G.).
7   Julius Posener in a letter to the author, April 19, 1990.
8   Julius Posener, in Günther Meier, "Erinnerungen an Erich Mendelsohn," *Bauwelt* 3 (1968) (hereafter cited as Meier 1968), 57.
9   Hans Bernhard Reichow, ibid., p. 58.
10 See Regina Stephan in this volume, 38–40.
11 Letters from Erich Mendelsohn to Luise, June 12, 1919, and June 12, 1920, Kunstbibliothek, Staatliche Museen zu Berlin–Preussischer Kulturbesitz, Erich Mendelsohn Archive (hereafter cited as KB, E. M. Archive), Briefe 33, Briefe 34.
12 Quoted in Charlotte Benton, *A Different World: Emigre Architects in Britain 1928–1958,* exh. cat. RIBA, Heinz Gallery (London, 199, 176). Benton also describes the later career of Arthur Korn and cites the most important literature.
13 Paul Westheim, "Hinweis auf Arthur Korn," *Das Kunstblatt* 8 (1924), 334 f. Korn left Germany in 1934 and went to England, where he died in 1978.
14 Letter from Erich Mendelsohn to Luise, June 12, 1919, KB, E. M. Archive, Briefe 33.
15 Letter from Erich Mendelsohn to Luise, August 14, 1922, coll. I. H.-G.
16 Heinrich Kosina's airport is illustrated in Karl-Heinz-Hüter, *Architektur in Berlin 1900–1933,* 266, fig. 492; a photo of Arthur Korn is found in Will Grohmann, *Zehn Jahre Novembergruppe,* special issue of the journal *Kunst der Zeit. Zeitschrift für Kunst and Literatur* 3 (1928), 86.
17 Heinrich Kosina in Meier 1968, 57.
18 His residential architecture included the Mariengarten development in 1930 and the Holdheim house in 1931.
19 Kathleen James, *Erich Mendelsohn and the Architecture of German Modernism* (Cambridge, Mass., 1997), was the first to intensively research the collaboration between Mendelsohn and Neutra. In Neutra's literary remains, now in the collection of the University of California, Los Angeles, James found numerous preliminary and construction drawings for the Rudolf Mosse publishing house. In this regard, see esp. 95–99, chapter 3, notes 47–58.

20 Letter from Erich Mendelsohn to Luise, August 4, 1922, KB, E. M. Archive, Briefe 36.
21 Letter from Erich Mendelsohn to Luise, August 9, 1922, coll. I. H.-G.
22 Kathleen James (as note 20), 97.
23 Quoted in Thomas S. Hines, *Richard Neutra and the Search for Modern Architecture* (New York, 1982), 36 f.
24 Letter from Erich Mendelsohn to Luise, August 14, 1922, coll. I. H.-G.
25 E. A. Karweik in Meier 1968, 56.
26 Letter from Erich Mendelsohn to Luise, July 12, 1925, coll. I. H.-G.
27 Letter from Erich Mendelsohn to Luise, January 16, 1926, coll. I. H.-G.
28 Letter from Erich Mendelsohn to Luise, August 22, 1923, KB, E. M. Archive, Briefe 38.
29 Quoted in Charlotte Benton (as note 13), 48.
30 *Erich Mendelsohn 1887–1953. Ideen, Bauten, Projekte,* ed. Sigrid Achenbach, exh. cat. Kunstbibliothek, Staatliche Museen Preussischer Kulturbesitz (Berlin, 1987), 9.
31 Louise Mendelsohn n.d., 30.
32 Julius Posener in a letter to the author, April 19, 1990. Ernst Sagebiel likewise confirmed Du Vinage's special relationship to Mendelsohn, in Meier 1968, 57.
33 Ernst Sagebiel, ibid., 57.
34 Louise Mendelsohn n.d., 179.
35 In the Westend district of Berlin the office was located at Ahornallee 25, Ebereschenallee 29, and Nussbaumallee 2–4.
36 Louise Mendelsohn, *Biographical Notes,* unpublished manuscript (n.d.), 30, collection of Jürgen Holstein.
37 Louise Mendelsohn n.d., 249–50.

"The same means, the same end"
Private Houses in Berlin and the Influence of Frank Lloyd Wright

1   Christian Schröder was the first to extensively research the villas in "Studien zur Villen- and Wohnhausarchitektur Erich Mendelsohns in Berlin," unpublished master's thesis, Freie Universität Berlin, 1994 (hereafter cited as Schröder 1994). I am grateful to the Institut für Kunstgeschichte of the Freie Universität Berlin for making the thesis available to me. My discussion of Mendelsohn's Berlin villas is based on Schröder's investigation of the structure and building history.
2   Until now the project, documented only in letters to Luise, has found no mention in the literature.
3   Letter from Erich Mendelsohn to Luise, May 7, 1920, collection of Ita Heinze-Greenberg (hereafter cited as coll. I. H.-G.).
4   Ibid., May 15, 1920.
5   Ibid., June 5, 1920.
6   In the first year after the currency reform of 1924, Erwin Gutkind built a low-lying residential development in Staaken, which may perhaps have been a successor project.
7   The Werkbund exhibition at Weissenhof is disregarded here, since it represented an experimental residential development with single- and multiple-

family houses. The records do not indicate which building type Mendelsohn was supposed to design. He backed out of the project before the detailed planning had been concluded. See Karin Kirsch, *Die Weissenhofsiedlung* (Stuttgart, 1987), 44–58.
8   Schröder 1994 evaluates the building files of all the Mendelsohn villas discussed in the following and describes their construction histories in detail. On the double villa see 9–23. Dr. Kurt Heymann was most likely a relative of Dr. Hans Heymann, who commissioned the Hausleben-Versicherung building (see 48 in this volume).
9   Letter from Erich Mendelsohn to Luise, June 26, 1922, coll. I. H.-G.
10 Ibid., July 1, 1922.
11 Erich Mendelsohn, *Das Gesamtschaffen des Architekten. Skizzen, Entwürfe, Bauten* (Berlin, 1930), 73.
12 This view is advanced by authors including Bruno Zevi, *Erich Mendelsohn. Opera completa* (Milan, 1970), 90, and Sigrid Achenbach, in *Erich Mendelsohn 1887–1953. Ideen, Bauten, Projekte,* exh. cat. Staatliche Museen Preussischer Kulturbesitz (Berlin, 1987), 67. Schröder 1994, 17, n. 57, on the other hand, expresses some doubt.
13 Hermann Muthesius, *Das englische Haus,* 3 vols. (Berlin, 1908–11).
14 See Ita Heinze-Greenberg in this volume, 58–60.
15 Holland and France, as well, boasted very few single-family houses of reinforced concrete. As late as 1928, Julius Vischer and Ludwig Hilberseimer wrote: "It is said that reinforced concrete is unsuitable for the construction of houses. Poor thermal insulation, above all, is mentioned as a quality that speaks against the use of reinforced concrete for these purposes. Following attempts to correct this deficiency with hollow spaces in the body of the wall, nowadays pumice concrete is used, which . . . in regard to thermal insulation possesses the same qualities as a brick wall. . . . Since, therefore, a strong objection has been answered, there are an extraordinary number of reasons in favor of the use of reinforced concrete in residential architecture." In "Beton als Gestalter. Bauten in Eisenbeton und ihre architektonische Gestaltung," in *Die Baubücher,* vol. 5 (Stuttgart, 1928), 73. In the pages that follow, these reasons are elaborated; with the exception of the "small dwelling as a [cheaply produced] mass article," the advantages mentioned were all used by Mendelsohn after 1922: large windows, balconies without consoles, all loads born by supports that could also be incorporated into the interior of the building, etc.
16 Mendelsohn Archive, Kunstbibliothek, Staatliche Museen zu Berlin–Preussischer Kulturbesitz (hereafter cited as KB, E. M. Archive), Briefe 95. Copy of a letter from Mendelsohn to J. J. P. Oud, January 9, 1923.
17 Schröder 1994, 26. The concerns of the building authorities doubtless also had to do with the catastrophe that had occurred on January 19, 1923, at the Mosse construction site. There, thirteen employees of the publisher were killed and eleven seriously injured when a section of floor from which the formwork had been prematurely removed collapsed and crashed to the ground. See the extensive discussion in Regina Stephan, *Studien zu Waren- and Geschäftshäusern Erich Mendelsohns in Deutschland* (Munich, 1992), 66.

18 Schröder 1994, 30.
19 Ibid., 26.
20 To name only one example, see the important study by Heidemarie Kief, *Der Einfluss Frank Lloyd Wrights auf die mitteleuropäische Einzelhausarchitektur. Ein Beitrag zum Verhältnis von Architektur und Natur im 20. Jahrhundert* (Stuttgart, 1978), 180.
21 See, e.g., "Erich Mendelsohn. Frank Lloyd Wright und seine historische Bedeutung," in *Das Neue Berlin. Grossstadtprobleme,* ed. Martin Wagner (Berlin, 1929), 180 f.; Erich Mendelsohn, "Eröffnungsrede bei der F. L. Wrightausstellung in der Akademie der Künste, Berlin 1929," unpublished ms., KB, E. M. Archive, Mss 12.
22 Erich Mendelsohn, "Frank Lloyd Wright," *Wendingen,* 1925, KB, E. M. Archive, Mss 6.
23 Schröder 1994, 43–56, investigated the building history for the first time and owes his knowledge of Mendelsohn's authorship to Dietrich Worbs. In 1872, the Villa Quistorp was built by the architect Piater for the banker and business manager of the Westend Gesellschaft; in 1905 it was renovated and expanded by Emil Schlüter for the manufacturer Max Schwarzlose.
24 Other renovation projects by Mendlesohn, on the other hand—the Rudolf Mosse publishing house, the Nuremberg Schocken store, the C. A. Herpich and Sons store, and the Rudolf Petersdorff department store in Breslau—attained great significance and were largely responsible for his fame.
25 Erich Mendelsohn (as note 11), 146.
26 Schröder 1994, 58.
27 On Am Rupenhorn, see the essay by Ita Heinze-Greenberg in this volume, 174–81.
28 Letter from Erich Mendelsohn to Luise, October 22, 1924, coll. I. H.-G.

"I often fear the envy of the gods"
Success, House, and Home

1 *Erich Mendelsohn 1887–1953. Ideen, Bauten, Projekte,* ed. Sigrid Achenbach, exh. cat. Kunstbibliothek, Staatliche Museen Preussischer Kulturbesitz (Berlin, 1987), 23.
2 On Mendelsohn's international reputation, cf. also Kathleen James, *Erich Mendelsohn and the Architecture of German Modernism* (Cambridge, Mass., 1997), esp. the chapter "At Home and Abroad. The Architect's Growing Reputation," 219 ff.
3 Quoted in Angelika Kindermann, "Max Liebermann," *Art* 7 (July 1997), 25.
4 Mendelsohn's name does appear, however, in the earliest lists of the architects participating in the project; cf. the detailed study by Karin Kirsch, *Die Weissenhofsiedlung* (Stuttgart, 1987), 53 ff.
5 Letter from Erich Mendelsohn to Luise, P. L., July 28, 1918, collection of Ita Heinze-Greenberg (hereafter cited as coll. I. H.-G.).
6 Letter from Erich Mendelsohn to Luise, Berlin, November 10, 1931, coll. I. H.-G.
7 Ibid.
8 Letter from Erich Mendelsohn to Luise, P. L., July 13–14, 1918, coll. I. H.-G.

9 Letter from Erich Mendelsohn to Luise, Charlottenburg, July 2, 1920, coll. I. H.-G.
10 The original letters from Mendelsohn to his wife are preserved in the Erich Mendelsohn Archive of the Kunstbibliothek, Staatliche Museen zu Berlin–Preussischer Kulturbesitz. Typed copies of these letters are found in the collection of the present writer as well as in the Getty Center for the History of Art and the Humanities in Los Angeles, where the original letters from Luise Mendelsohn to her husband are also held.
11 Letter from Erich Mendelsohn to Luise, Charlottenburg, August 15, 1922, coll. I. H.-G.
12 Letter from Erich Mendelsohn to Luise, Charlottenburg, August 15, 1925, coll. I. H.-G., quoted in Oskar Beyer, *Eric Mendelsohn. Letters of an Architect* (London/New York/Toronto, 1967) (hereafter cited as Beyer 1967), 88.
13 Letter from Erich Mendelsohn to Luise, St. Moritz, December 28, 1929, coll. I. H.-G., quoted in Beyer 1967, 107.
14 Letter from Erich Mendelsohn to Luise, Herrlingen, August 19, 1923, quoted in Oskar Beyer, *Erich Mendelsohn. Briefe eines Architekten* (Munich, 1961; reprint, Basel/Berlin/Boston, 1991) (hereafter cited as Beyer 1991), 53 f.
15 Letter from Erich Mendelsohn to Luise, Darmstadt, June 19, 1922, coll. I. H.-G., quoted in Beyer 1967, 55.
16 Letter from Erich Mendelsohn to Luise, St. Alban, July 10, 1922, coll. I. H.-G.
17 Letter from Erich Mendelsohn to Luise, Charlottenburg, June 25, 1922, quoted in Beyer 1991, 52.
18 Letter from Erich Mendelsohn to Luise, Charlottenburg, March 4, 1930, coll. I. H.-G.
19 Cf. esp. Martin Buber's main philosophical work *Ich und Du* of 1923, 13th ed., (Gerlingen, 1995). Published in English as *I and Thou* (1937).
20 Probably the most famous portrait of Luise Mendelsohn is by Max Pechstein. Cf. the illustration in Arnold Whittick, *Eric Mendelsohn,* 2nd ed. (London, 1956), between pages 192 and 193.
21 Letter from Erich Mendelsohn to Luise, Zurich, June 2, 1932, coll. I. H.-G.
22 Letter from Erich Mendelsohn to Luise, Berlin, November 10, 1931, coll. I. H.-G., quoted in Beyer 1967, 120.
23 Louise Mendelsohn, *My Life in a Changing World,* unpublished memoirs (San Francisco, n.d.) (hereafter cited as Louise Mendelsohn n.d.), 181. The manuscript is found in the Kunstbibliothek, Staatliche Museen zu Berlin–Preussischer Kulturbesitz; in the Museum of Modern Art, New York; and in the coll. I. H.-G.
24 Letter from Erich Mendelsohn to Luise, Stellung Ilipau, September 14–15, 1917, coll. I. H.-G.
25 Letter from Erich Mendelsohn to Luise, Charlottenburg, June 3, 1920, coll. I. H.-G.
26 For many years the Mendelsohn office was located in the house in Westend, Nussbaumallee 2–4, a structure built in the 1870s. The plot in Babelsberg was soon rejected as the site for Mendelsohn's own villa, as he explains in a letter to his wife: "Babelsberg itself is strongly characterized by the impression of fat prosperity and thus inhibits freedom, especially in this part." Letter from Erich Mendelsohn to Luise, Charlottenburg, July 20, 1926, coll. I. H.-G.

27 Letter from Erich Mendelsohn to Luise, Charlottenburg, July 24, 1927, coll. I. H.-G.
28 A letter of July 1927, for example, describes a potential site in Geltow as one "which . . . could be designed as a farm like Wright's Taliesin." Letter from Erich Mendelsohn to Luise, Charlottenburg, July 24, 1927, coll. I. H.-G.
29 Letter from Erich Mendelsohn to Luise, Charlottenburg, July 12, 1928, coll. I. H.-G.
30 Documented in two letters from Erich Mendelsohn to Luise, Charlottenburg, July 20 and July 22, 1928, coll. I. H.-G. Both letters are quoted in Beyer 1967, 100 f.
31 "The Rupenhorn inspection yesterday was completely harmless—Petzold did a splendid job of the thing and sent me home after I had already said too much on the first question. If that is the only inspection, we will have one less obstacle." Letter from Erich Mendelsohn to Luise, Charlottenburg, March 4, 1930, coll. I. H.-G.
32 Louise Mendelsohn n.d., 229.
33 Letter from Erich Mendelsohn to Luise, St. Moritz, December 16, 1928, quoted in Beyer 1991, 81.
34 Letter from Erich Mendelsohn to Luise, St. Moritz, December 28, 1929, coll. I. H.-G.
35 Letter from Erich Mendelsohn to Luise, Charlottenburg, June 20, 1915, quoted in Beyer 1991, 32.
36 Erich Mendelsohn, *Neues Haus—Neue Welt,* with essays by Amédée Ozenfant and Edwin [Erwin] Redslob (Berlin, 1932; reprint [with an afterword by Bruno Zevi], Berlin, 1997).
37 Amédée Ozenfant, "Für Erich Mendelsohn," in *Neues Haus—Neue Welt* (as note 36).
38 Ibid.
39 In her work on Ozenfant, Susan L. Ball describes the painting *Musik and die plastischen Künste* as Ozenfant's last purist work. Cf. Susan L. Ball, *Ozenfant and Purism: The Evolution of a Style 1915–1930* (Ann Arbor, Mich., 1981), 148.
40 Erich Mendelsohn (as note 36).
41 Amédée Ozenfant, report on the symposium "on how to combine architecture, painting, sculpture, Mr. Philip C. Johnson presiding," in *Interiors* (May 1951), 104. Likewise cited in Susan L. Ball (as note 39), 187, n. 25.
42 *Von Arp zu Warhol. Sammlung Daimler-Benz,* ed. Karin v. Maur (Stuttgart, 1992), 236, ill. p. 237.
43 Mendelsohn was personally acquainted with Edwin Redslob through Einstein's assistant Erwin Finlay-Freundlich. Cf. Edwin Redslob, *Von Weimar nach Europa. Erlebtes and Durchdachtes* (Berlin, 1972), 235 f.
44 Amédée Ozenfant (as note 36). We may assume that the comparison was Mendelsohn's own. Mendelsohn wrote to his wife in great detail concerning a visit to Weimar and was enthusiastic about Goethe's house. Letter from Erich Mendelsohn to Luise, Charlottenburg, May 12, 1920, coll. I. H.-G., quoted in Beyer 1967, 51. Mendelsohn's companion in Weimar was Erwin Finlay-Freundlich, who commented on a birthday sketch just drawn for Luise: "Your husband is engaging in mimicry. Your house will be an image of Goethe's garden house." Commentary by Freundlich, attached to a letter from Erich Mendelsohn to Luise, Weimar, May 8, 1920, coll. I. H.-G.

45 Werner Hegemann, "Mendelsohn-Haus and Goethe-Haus," *Wasmuths Monatshefte für Baukunst* (May 1932), 221.

46 Mies van der Rohe's Tugendhat house gave rise to a similar discussion. Cf. Justus Bier, "Kann man in Haus Tugendhat wohnen?" *Die Form* 6: 10 (October 15, 1931), 324 f.

47 See Ita Heinze-Greenberg in this volume, 184–86.

48 Letter from Erich Mendelsohn to Luise, Berlin, February 3, 1933, coll. I. H.-G.

49 Louise Mendelsohn n.d., 225 ff.

"We'll leave it to the Schultzes from Naumburg to ignore the Mediterranean as the father of the international art of composition"
The Mediterranean Academy Project and Mendelsohn's Emigration

1 Letter from Erich Mendelsohn to Luise, on board the *Patria* on the Mediterranean, January 13, 1936, collection of Ita Heinze-Greenberg (hereafter cited as coll. I. H.-G.).

2 Letter from Eric Mendelsohn to Richard Döcker, San Francisco, November 28, 1947, Kunstbibliothek, Staatliche Museen zu Berlin–Preussischer Kulturbesitz, Erich Mendelsohn Archive (hereafter cited as KB, E. M. Archive), B IV 9. Beginning in late 1938, Erich Mendelsohn used the Anglicized spelling of his first name, "Eric," a change presumably associated directly with the Mendelsohns' acquisition of British citizenship in August 1938. A short time later, Luise Mendelsohn too began using the English spelling "Louise."

3 Letter from Eric Mendelsohn to the municipal administration of Darmstadt, San Francisco, July 1, 1951, KB, E. M. Archive, B IV 6.

4 Letter from Erich Mendelsohn to Luise, Jerusalem, December 10, 1934, in Oskar Beyer, *Eric Mendelsohn: Letters of an Architect* (London/New York/Toronto, 1967) (hereafter cited as Beyer 1967), 137.

5 Letter from Erich Mendelsohn to Luise, Herrlingen, August 26, 1923, in Beyer 1991, 54.

6 Interview of the author with Ilse Goldenzweig, Mendelsohn's niece, Tel Aviv, July 1997.

7 Letter from Eric Mendelsohn to Charles Du Vinage, December 31, 1948, KB, E. M. Archive, B IV 5.

8 Letter from Erich Mendelsohn to Luise, between Brindisi and Venice, July 1, 1935, coll. I. H.-G.

9 Letter from Erich Mendelsohn to Luise, Allenstein, August 16, 1910, coll. I. H.-G.

10 Louise Mendelsohn, *My Life in a Changing World*, unpublished memoirs (San Francisco, n.d.) (hereafter cited as Louise Mendelsohn n.d.), 568. The manuscript is held in the Kunstbibliothek, Staatliche Museen zu Berlin–Preussischer Kulturbesitz; the Museum of Modern Art in New York; and in the coll. I. H.-G.

11 Letter from Erich Mendelsohn to Luise, Corsica, October 29, 1931, coll. I. H.-G.

12 Eric Mendelsohn, *Palestine and the World of Tomorrow* (Jerusalem, 1940), 5.

13 In a letter to Luise, Erich Mendelsohn describes Wijdeveld as the "father of this two- or three-year-old

idea." Letter from Erich Mendelsohn to Luise, Cavalière, August 13, 1932, coll. I. H.-G.

14 Letter from Erich Mendelsohn to Luise, Paris, January 2, 1931, coll. I. H.-G.

15 Letters from Erich Mendelsohn to Luise, Hyères, August 11, 1932, and August 18, 1932, coll. I. H.-G.

16 Letters from Mendelsohn to Luise, Hyères, August 12, 1932; Cavalière, August 13, 1932; and Comologno, August 18, 1932, all from the coll. I. H.-G. The first is also printed in Oskar Beyer, *Erich Mendelsohn. Briefe eines Architekten* (Munich, 1961; reprinted, Basel/Berlin/Boston, 1991) (hereafter cited as Beyer 1991), 85.

17 Letter from Erich Mendelsohn to Luise, Amsterdam, April 23, 1933, coll. I. H.-G.

18 Copies of English and French versions of the statutes, application forms, and brochure are found in the KB, E. M. Archive (unmarked, unnumbered file).

19 Regarding Paul Hindemith, Erich Mendelsohn wrote to his wife: "I have heard that Hindemith has been dismissed on account of his Jewish wife. So he is safe for the Academy." Letter from Erich Mendelsohn to Luise, Cavalière, September 1, 1933, in Beyer 1967, 136.

20 As note 18.

21 Letter from Erich Mendelsohn to Luise, Cavalière, June 6, 1933, coll. I. H.-G.

22 Letter from Erich Mendelsohn to Luise, Cavalière, May 30, 1933, in Beyer 1967, 135 f.

23 Louise Mendelsohn n.d., 120.

24 Erich Mendelsohn, "Das Problem einer neuen Baukunst," in *Programme and Manifeste zur Architektur des 20. Jahrhunderts*, ed. Ulrich Conrads (Braunschweig, 1975), 52.

25 Letter from Erich Mendelsohn to Luise, Berlin, February 11, 1933, in Beyer 1991, 89.

26 Mendelsohn addressed this theme a number of times in letters, lectures, and manuscripts, but most unequivocally in his pamphlet *Palestine and the World of Tomorrow* (Jerusalem, 1940).

27 Louise Mendelsohn n.d., 121.

28 Jewish Agency, *Verzeichnis derjenigen, welche bereit sind, nach Palästina zu gehen* (Jerusalem, 1919), Central Zionist Archives, Jerusalem, L3/608.

29 See Ita Heinze-Greenberg in this volume, 60–65.

30 Letter from Erich Mendelsohn to Luise, Paris, August 30, 1933, coll. I. H.-G.

31 Louise Mendelsohn n.d., 281.

32 Letter from Erich Mendelsohn to Kurt Blumenfeld, London, July 11, 1933, Blumenfeld Archive, Central Zionist Archives, Jerusalem.

33 Letter from Erich Mendelsohn to Salmann Schocken, London, May 20, 1934, Schocken Archive, Jerusalem 844/182.

"Enough mistakes and experience behind me—enough strength and future before me"
Buildings in England and the Partnership with Serge Chermayeff 1933–1941

1 Born in 1885, Hendricus Theodorus Wijdeveld had been a pupil of Petrus Josephus Hubertus Cuypers and J. van Straaten and had worked in England and

France. He was a founder and editor of the Dutch architectural journal *Wendingen*, which began publication in 1918. He was sympathetic to Mendelsohn, publishing some of the earliest articles on his work in a special issue (*Wendingen* 3: 10 [October 1920]).

2 No detailed account of the Academy project exists. Others involved in its initial program included the sculptors Pablo Gargallo and Eric Gill and the composer Paul Hindemith. Members of the Academy's "Comité d'honneur" included Hélène de Mandrot and the architects Auguste Perret, Charles Reilly, Raymond Unwin, and Henry van de Velde.

3 See *Projekt: Académie Européenne Mediterrannée*, Mendelsohn Archive, Kunstbibliothek, Staatliche Museen zu Berlin—Preussischer Kulturbesitz (hereafter cited as KB, E. M. Archive).

4 Extract from a letter quoted in Louise Mendelsohn, *My Life in a Changing World*, unpublished ms. (San Francisco, n. d.), copies are in Mendelsohn Archive, Kunstbibliothek, Staatliche Museen zu Berlin—Preussischer Kulturbesitz (hereafter cited as Louise Mendelsohn n. d.), 280.

5 Ibid.

6 Gladys Swaythling, widow of Louis Samuel Montagu (d. 1927), second Baron Swaythling and head of the Samuel Montagu banking firm. The Mendelsohns probably made her acquaintance in 1930, and she subsequently visited them in Berlin. Through Lady Swaythling the Mendelsohns (in particular Louise, since Erich was often absent in the early months on trips to Holland and France in connection with the projected Academy) made a number of contacts in English high society, some of whom may have been helpful in later commissions and projects.

7 Through its extensive coverage in British architectural periodicals and the publication of *Erich Mendelsohn: Structures and Sketches* (London, 1923) and the English edition of *Neues Haus—Neues Welt* (Berlin, 1932). An exhibition of Mendelsohn's work was shown in London 1930, when he lectured at the Architectural Association. Yet although Mendelsohn was much admired, he was not universally liked. The architectural critic J. M. Richards found him "friendly only to those he thought could be useful to him" (J. M. Richards, *Memoirs of an Unjust Fella* [London, 1980], 134), and Colin Penn, who worked as an assistant in the Mendelsohn/Chermayeff office, did not remember Mendelsohn with affection (interview with the author, 1977).

8 A Beaux-Arts architect, who was then head of the Liverpool School of Architecture—which was considered to be one of the more progressive of the English architectural schools.

9 The RIBA's membership rules excluded those who were not British nationals.

10 However, by no means all of the architects who sympathized with Mendelsohn's plight as a professional were sympathetic to modernism.

11 Louise Mendelsohn n. d., 289–90.

12 Given that Mendelsohn may have already had—or later assumed—financial responsibility for guaranteeing several relatives from Germany. See his letter to Arnold Whittick of May 12, 1939, KB, E. M. Archive.

13 See Charles Herbert Reilly, *Scaffolding in the Sky* (London, 1938), 293.

14 Louise Mendelsohn n. d., 276–78, 282–84.

15 Louise Mendelsohn records the joke that—even when Mendelsohn was familiar with the language—there was "real English, American English, and Mendelsohn English." See Bruno Zevi, *Erich Mendelsohn. Opera completa* (Milan, 1970), 207.

16 Responsible, respectively, for granting residence and work permits.

17 Effectively non-nationals were confined to self-employment; they were excluded from posts with public bodies (e.g., as assistants in local authority housing departments or teachers in schools of architecture).

18 In particular Johannes Schreiner, of whom Mendelsohn often said that without him he "couldn't have built a thing."

19 Kathleen James, in *Erich Mendelsohn and the Architecture of German Modernism* (Cambridge, 1997), has pointed to the difficulties Mendelsohn experienced in accommodating the ambitions of some of his assistants in the 1920s, notably Richard Neutra. Arthur Korn, who claimed to have been in partnership with Mendelsohn in the early 1920s, also recalled the difficulties of working with him.

20 Letter to the author, July 3, 1976.

21 On Chermayeff, see Richard Plunz, *Design and the Public Good: Selected Writings 1930–1980* (Cambrige, Mass., 1982); and Barbara Tilson, *The Architecture and Design of Serge Chermayeff, 1928 to 1939,* unpublished MA dissertation (Birmingham, 1984) (hereafter cited as Tilson 1984).

22 See Chermayeff's "Film shots in Germany," *Architectural Review,* (November 1931), 131–33. The stills included the Universum cinema complex, the Stuttgart and Chemnitz Schocken stores, and the Metalworkers' Union building. In his captions Chermayeff described Mendelsohn's work as representing a "new classicism."

23 His only completed building to date was a small house in Rugby.

24 Tilson 1984, ix.

25 Chermayeff had recently received a commission for a house at Chalfont St. Giles in Buckinghamshire.

26 Such as *Architect and Building News, Architectural Review,* and *Architects' Journal.*

27 *Design for To-day* (October, 1934), 394–95.

28 In his introduction to *The Modern House in England* (London, 1937).

29 See note 27.

30 Although other factors have to be taken into account as well.

31 Minutes of the RIBA's Practice Standing Committee, January 2, 1934.

32 Ibid.

33 Ibid.

34 The Ministry of Labour may have been persuaded by Mendelsohn's arguments and used its own discretion to issue a permit.

35 Quoted in Tilson 1984, 57–58. Relatively little is known about Schreiner. He worked with Mendelsohn on some of the Palestinian projects and helped establish the office in Palestine but did not stay there. After the dissolution of the Mendelsohn/-Chermayeff partnership he worked for Mendelsohn in London. In 1939 lack of work compelled Mendelsohn to dismiss him. Schreiner was interned as an "enemy alien" in the early part of the war, an experience that, reportedly, devastated him. Afterwards he worked for a time, on William Holford's recommendation, on the design of hostels for munition workers. He collaborated with Arnold Whittick on *The Small House: Today and Tomorrow* (1947), in which he is recorded as a former pupil of Behrens and as a Fellow of the RIBA. Had Mendelsohn been unable to obtain permission for Schreiner to work in London, it is perhaps doubtful whether Mendelsohn's English works would have been so successful in preserving the qualities of his earlier work.

36 It is probable, for example, that Mendelsohn's presence in the practice was the key factor in attracting the commission for the Cohen house in Chelsea, since the clients for this and the neighboring house (designed by Gropius and Fry) were both active in refugee relief work.

37 See Tilson 1984. Birkin Haward remembers Chermayeff's input on the design of the interiors of the De La Warr Pavilion and the Cohen house as "considerable" although "within an already established framework" (interview with the author, April 1998). However, Whitfield Lewis remembers that when he was detailing fitments for the Chelsea house, Mendelsohn was very precise about his requirements (interview with the author, January 1998).

38 Quoted in Tilson 1984, 61.

39 Which was, like the other 200+ entries, anonymous.

40 Underpinned in some cases by anti-Semitism. For discussion of the pavilion see Timothy Benton, "The De La Warr Pavilion. A type for the 1930s," in *Leisure in the Twentieth Century* (London, 1977), 72–80; R. Stevens and P. Willis, "Earl De La Warr and the competition for the Bexhill Pavilion 1933/34," *Architectural History,* vol. 33 (1990), 135–66.

41 Quoted in Tilson 1984, 63. Bazeley was then an assistant in the office and the commission was from a friend of his.

42 Bruno Zevi (as note 15), 210.

43 Tilson 1984, 92. Haward confirmed these points in an interview with the author, April 1998.

44 Interview with the author, April 1998. See also Tilson 1984, 101.

45 Interview with the author, April 1998.

46 Designed in 1934 or 1935, probably for Earl De La Warr. The site was at Beaulieu in Hampshire. Birkin Haward still possesses a photocopy of a drawing for the scheme, although he does not recall any details of the scheme or, indeed, whether it was developed any further. (An illustration of the drawing appears in Tilson 1984, pl. 35.) With a vast, double-height "studio"-type window on its main front, the house seems to represent something of a new departure in Mendelsohn's domestic design.

47 Extracts from which were published in the architectural press.

48 The site was later developed for housing by the London County Council, whose scheme has been described as "dismally monotonous five storey balcony access brick blocks, laid out on a dull rectangular grid."

49 These are not the kinds of matters with which the surviving assistants from the Mendelsohn and Chermayeff office would have been involved.

50 This last seems to have been the case with the White City scheme, since the extracts from Mendelsohn and Chermayeff's prospectus for the scheme that were published in the architectural press at the time seem to suggest that although the project was privately initiated it would be more suitable as a public sector undertaking.

51 See his letter of March 30, 1935, in Oskar Beyer, *Eric Mendelsohn: Letters of an Architect* (New York, 1967), 140.

52 Whitfield Lewis attributes the main causes to Chermayeff's claims for equal status and a share of the Palestinian work.

53 Letter of May 19, 1937, in Oskar Beyer (as note 51), 150.

54 The MARS Group was the British offshoot of the Congrès Internationaux d'Architecture Modern (CIAM). Chermayeff was a member, as were Gropius and Samuely.

55 Letter to Erwin Finlay-Freundlich, January 23, 1934, KB, E. M. Archive.

56 Letter of April 12, 1939, KB, E. M. Archive.

57 For an account of the period 1939–1945 see Louise Mendelsohn in Bruno Zevi (as note 15).

58 Letter, January 14, 1941, KB, E. M. Archive.

59 Simultaneously, however, he was sounding out the possibilities of work in the U.S.

60 Henry-Russell Hitchcock, "An American critic in England," *Architect and Building News*, January 15, 1937, 67–70. In the same year, Hitchcock mounted his exhibition "Modern Architecture in England" at the Museum of Modern Art in New York. His rather effusive praise for Mendelsohn's English work may be connected with an underlying agenda of that exhibition—the association of modernism with democracy.

61 Ibid.

"I am a free builder"
Architecture in Palestine 1934–1941

1 Of the numerous biographies of Chaim Weizmann, one of the most extensive is Norman Rose, *Chaim Weizmann: A Biography* (New York, 1986). The present discussion of Mendelsohn's architectural activity in Palestine is based on the corresponding chapters in the author's dissertation, Ita Heinze-Mühleib, *Erich Mendelsohn. Bauten and Projekte in Palästina, 1934–1941,* diss. (Bonn, 1984; published Munich, 1986). This study will no longer be specifically cited in the following notes.

2 At first, in the mid-1920s, the Weizmanns bought a plot in Jerusalem on Mount Scopus next to the grounds of the Hebrew University, a site for which plans were prepared by the architect Alexander Baerwald. On the history of the Weizmann villa, cf. Ita Heinze-Greenberg, "'The Impossible Takes Longer': Facts and Notes about the Weizmann Residence in Rehovot," *Cathedra* 72 (June 1994), 99 ff. (in Hebrew).

3 The statistics are drawn from the *Neues Lexikon des Judentums,* ed. Julius Schoeps (Gütersloh and Munich, 1992), 28. An older, but still outstanding

account of the immigration of Jews from Germany and their contribution to the development of Palestine/Israel is Gerda Luft, *Heimkehr ins Unbekannte* (Wuppertal, 1977).

4 The new Israeli "indigenous style" was extensively discussed in the local media. A special issue of the magazine *Mischar Wetaasia Land-of-Israel Economic Magazine* 3–4 (February 15, 1925), entitled "Building in Palestine," made an important contribution to the theme. Here a number of architects active in Palestine at the time, including Alexander Baerwald, Josef Minor, Josef Berlin, and Alexander Levy, made statements and offered differing suggestions and opinions.

5 Alexander Baerwald (1877–1930) was born in Berlin. He studied at the technical universities in Berlin and Munich and participated in numerous projects as the Prussian government architect. From 1910 on, he received commissions in the context of Zionist development work in Palestine. In 1924, he accepted a position as the first professor of architecture at the newly opened "Technikum" in Haifa. He died in Haifa in 1930. Cf. also Liane Richter, ed., *Alexander Baerwald 1877–1930. Architect and Artist,* exh. cat. The National Museum of Science, Planning and Technology (Haifa, 1990).

6 Cf. also Ita Heinze-Greenberg, "Immigration and Culture Shock: On the Question of Architectural Identity in Altneuland," in *Tel Aviv. Modern Architecture 1930–1939,* ed. Winfried Nerdinger (Tübingen and Berlin, 1994), pp. 36 ff.

7 Cf. also Gilbert Herbert and Ita Heinze-Greenberg, "The Anatomy of a Profession: Architecture in Palestine during the British Mandate," *Computers and the History of Art* 4 (January 1993), 75–85. A survey of architects emigrating to Palestine from German-speaking Europe is also found in Myra Warhaftig, *Sie legten den Grundstein. Leben und Wirken deutschsprachiger jüdischer Architekten in Palästina 1918–1948* (Tübingen and Berlin, 1996).

8 On Mendelsohn's relation to the Tel Aviv Chug, cf. Alona Nitzan-Shiftan, "Contested Zionism–Alternative Modernism: Eric Mendelsohn and the Tel Aviv Chug in Mandate Palestine," *Architectural History* 39 (1996), 147–80.

9 Already in his 1969 lecture on Mendelsohn, Julius Posener pointed to the many copies of Mendelsohn's German buildings that greeted the architect when he came to Palestine. Julius Posener, "Erich Mendelsohn," in idem, *Aufsätze and Vorträge 1931–1980,* ed. Ulrich Conrads (Braunschweig, 1981), 181.

10 Eric Mendelsohn, *Twenty Years of Building in Tel Aviv* (1940), manuscript of an (unpublished?) review, Kunstbibliothek, Staatliche Museen zu Berlin–Preussischer Kulturbesitz, Erich Mendelsohn Archive (hereafter cited as KB, E. M. Archive), B IV 5a/1.

11 Martin Buber, "Jüdisches Nationalheim and nationale Politik in Palästina" (lecture from October 31, 1929), in idem, *Der Jude and sein Judentum. Gesammelte Aufsätze and Reden* (Cologne, 1963), 339 ff.

12 Eric Mendelsohn, *Palestine and the World of Tomorrow* (Jerusalem, 1940).

13 Letter from Erich Mendelsohn to Luise, Jerusalem, December 7, 1934, in Oskar Beyer, *Eric Mendelsohn: Letters of an Architect* (London/New York/Toronto, 1967) (hereafter cited as Beyer 1967), 136.

14 Norman Rose (as note 1), 299.

15 Letter from Erich Mendelsohn to Chaim Weizmann, Jerusalem, May 26, 1935, Weizmann Archive, Rehovot.

16 Letter from Chaim Weizmann to Dr. Bergmann, June 1, 1935, Weizmann Archive, Rehovot.

17 Vera Weizmann, *The Impossible Takes Longer* (London, 1967), 139.

18 Letter from Erich Mendelsohn to Chaim Weizmann, Jerusalem, July 22, 1936, Weizmann Archive, Rehovot. The letter names November 1936 as the moving-in date.

19 Louise Mendelsohn, *My Life in a Changing World,* unpublished memoirs (San Francisco, n.d.) (hereafter cited as Louise Mendelsohn n.d.), 298.

20 As recalled by Hans Schiller, a former Mendelsohn assistant in Jerusalem and San Francisco, in a short paragraph on Mendelsohn's working method quoted in Louise Mendelsohn n.d., 604.

21 Sketches in the Mendelsohn Archive of the Kunstbibliothek Berlin, here above all KB E. M.-Archiv, Hdz. 41/52.

22 Susan King, "Interview with Mrs. Eric Mendelsohn," in *The Drawings of Eric Mendelsohn,* exh. cat. University Art Museum, University of California, Berkeley (Berkeley, 1969), 26. Mendelsohn described his impressions of Greece in a column for the *Berliner Tageblatt,* May 1931. Portions published in Beyer 1967, 110 ff.

23 "Interview with Eric Mendelsohn," *Evening Standard* (July 31, 1937), 12.

24 Cf. Gert Kähler, *Architektur als Symbolverfall. Das Dampfermotiv in der Baukunst* (Braunschweig, 1981).

25 A single stairway connecting the two floors, for example, seems inadequate, while the living room and library appear disproportionately long; in addition, the direct juxtaposition of swimming pool and reception hall seems less than functional.

26 Cf. "Engineer and Organizer. Dr. E. Kempinski at 50," *Palestine Post* (January 16, 1938), 4.

27 Interview of the author with Naftali Rostowsky, Tel Aviv, winter 1979–80.

28 Letter from Erich Mendelsohn to Luise, Jerusalem, September 5, 1937. In Oskar Beyer, *Erich Mendelsohn. Briefe eines Architekten* (Munich, 1961; reprint, Basel/Berlin/Boston, 1991) (hereafter cited as Beyer 1991), 101.

29 Quoted in Siegfried Moses, "Salman Schocken. Wirtschaftsführer and Zionist," in idem, *Deutsches Judentum. Aufstieg and Krise* (Stuttgart, 1982), 152. On Schocken's involvement in publishing, see, e.g., Saskia Schreuder and Claude Weber, *Der Schocken Verlag / Berlin. Jüdische Selbstbehauptung in Deutschland 1931–1938* (Berlin, 1994); and Volker Dahm, *Das Jüdische Buch im Dritten Reich* (Munich, 1993).

30 Letter from Erich Mendelsohn to Luise, Jerusalem, December 6, 1934, collection of Ita Heinze-Greenberg (hereafter cited as coll. I. H.-G.).

31 Letter from Erich Mendelsohn to Luise, Jerusalem, December 15, 1934, coll. I. H.-G.

32 Letter from Erich Mendelsohn to Luise, Jerusalem, December 27, 1934, coll. I. H.-G. English translation published in Beyer 1967, 139. The surviving sketches for the Schocken house are not very extensive. Since Mendelsohn himself described the house as "sort of a lucky strike," it may be assumed that he prepared only a few sketches. The actual construction period, however, was fairly long, since most of the building materials were imported from Germany in the context of the so-called Ha'avara Agreement of 1933 between the German government and a Palestine trust company. On the Ha'avara Agreement, cf. Werner Feilchenfeld, Dolf Michaelis, and Ludwig Pinner, *Ha'avara-Transfer nach Palästina and Einwanderung deutscher Juden 1933–1939* (Tübingen, 1972).

33 Richard Kauffmann (1887–1958) was a former fellow student with Mendelsohn and a pupil of Theodor Fischer at the Technische Hochschule in Munich. In 1921, he emigrated to Palestine and was hired by the Palestine Land Development Company. In the 1920s, 1930s, and 1940s, he was the most important settlement planner and architect in Palestine, with projects including around 150 *moshavim* and *kibbutzim.*

34 In a letter of May 9, 1944, to his brother Hermann, Salman Schocken wrote: "I am not actually a politically oriented person; I have never really seen myself directly or immediately involved in political work. If I have often appeared in the public eye, it always resulted from an orientation whose focus did not lie in the political, but grew out of my work in two areas of interest: business and culture." Quoted in Siegfried Moses (as note 29), 158.

35 Letter from Erich Mendelsohn to Luise, Jerusalem, December 17, 1934, coll. I. H.-G.

36 Interview of the author with Naftali Rostowsky, Tel Aviv, winter 1979–80.

37 Cf. also Michael Levin, "The Stones of Jerusalem," *Journal of Jewish Art* 2 (1975), 72 ff.

38 Letter from Eric Mendelsohn to Schocken's secretaries, Jerusalem, October 2, 1938, Schocken Archive (hereafter cited as Sch/A) 823/126.

39 Between the Schocken residence and the library, the residence of the Aghion family was erected a short time later by Richard Kauffmann. Today the house belongs to the State of Israel and is used as the official residence of the prime minister. For a short time, the Aghions considered hiring Mendelsohn as the architect of their house. In a letter to his wife on September 14, 1935, Mendelsohn wrote: "Yesterday immediately after my arrival meetings from 9–12 in the evening. With the Aghions, who are enthusiastic about our house, but are too careful to immediately award the commission. I rejected the idea of sketches without payment or obligation." Coll. I. H.-G.

40 Today, the Jewish Theological Seminary of America is located in the library building. Schocken's collection and library as well as his archives form the basis of this research institute.

41 Letter from Erich Mendelsohn to Luise, Jerusalem, December 7, 1934, coll. I. H.-G. English translation published in Beyer 1967, 136.

42 Both in summer and on sunny winter days, however, the light is so intense that the oriel has to be darkened with the venetian blinds and a curtain.

43 From Chaim Weizmann's speech at the cornerstone-laying of the Hebrew University on Mount Scopus near Jerusalem on June 24, 1918. Translated into German and published in *Jüdische Rundschau* (Berlin, September 13, 1918); *Chaim Weizmann. Reden and Aufsätze 1901–1936,* ed. Gustav Krojanker (Tel Aviv, 1937), 48 ff. Information on the development of the Hebrew University is taken from *The Hebrew University, Jerusalem: Its History and Development,* ed. Hebrew University (Jerusalem, 1939); Lotta Levensohn, *Vision and Fulfillment: The First Twenty-Five Years of the Hebrew University 1925–1950* (New York, 1950).

44 A detailed discussion of the design by Patrick Geddes would exceed the scope of this article. Among other studies on Geddes, special mention should be made of the 1997 dissertation by Volker Welter of the University of Edinburgh, currently one of the most knowledgeable scholars on Geddes: *BIOPOLIS – Patrick Geddes, Edinburgh, and the City of Life,* diss. (Edinburgh, 1997). Other important works on Geddes include Benjamin Hyman, *British Planners in Palestine, 1918–1936,* diss. (London, 1994); Helen Meller, *Patrick Geddes: Social Revolutionist and City Planner* (London/New York, 1990); and Philip Boardman, *The Worlds of Patrick Geddes* (London, 1978).

45 Kurt Blumenfeld (1884–1963) was born in Treuberg in East Prussia and studied law in Berlin, Freiburg, and Königsberg. He was already an active member of the Zionist Organization by 1904. From 1910 to 1914, he directed the information office of the Zionist Organization in Berlin and served as editor of the Zionist weekly *Die Welt*. From 1923 to 1933, he was president of the German Zionist Organization. In 1933 he emigrated to Palestine and served in important capacities within the Zionist development work in Palestine. Kurt Blumenfeld described his activities in his autobiography *Erlebte Judenfrage. Ein Vierteljahrhundert deutscher Zionismus* (Stuttgart, 1962). A portion of his correspondence is published in Joseph Ginat and Miriam Samburky, eds., *Kurt Blumenfeld. Im Kampf um den Zionismus. Briefe aus 5 Jahrzehnten* (Stuttgart, 1976).

46 Letter from Kurt Blumenfeld to Berthold Feiwel, Berlin, July 2, 1924, Weizmann Archive, Rehovot. Patrick Geddes was not Jewish. Berthold Feiwel (1875–1937) was a writer and Zionist politician and a close assistant to Chaim Weizmann. Together with Kurt Blumenfeld, he was one of the first directors of the Zionist fund Keren Hayessod. Letter from Kurt Blumenfeld to Salman Schocken, Berlin, September 3, 1924, in Joseph Ginat and Miriam Samburky (as note 45), 86.

47 Letter from Erich Mendelsohn to Luise, Jerusalem, December 7, 1934, coll. I. H.-G. English translation published in Beyer 1967, 136.

48 Letter from Erich Mendelsohn to Luise, Jerusalem, December 27, 1934, coll. I. H.-G. English translation published in Beyer 1967, 139.

49 Benjamin Chaikin (1885–1950) studied architecture in London and worked in Palestine beginning in 1920. He built mainly in Jerusalem and Haifa.

50 The "Extract of Minutes of the 1st Meeting of the Jerusalem District Town Planning Commission" (Sch/A 042/61) indicates that the commission for the master plan was awarded to Mendelsohn in the context of plans for a "Ring Road" that had become necessary.

51 Eric Mendelsohn, "Town Planning on Mount Scopus and the Hadassah Medical Centre as Part thereof," *Palestine Post* (May 9, 1939). Retranslation from original German version by Mendelsohn in KB, E. M. Archive, B IV 5a.

52 Mendelsohn never published this building and did not include it in his list of works. His authorship as well as the building and planning history, however, can be reconstructed from the plans and photographs in the archives of the Hebrew University, Jerusalem, as well as from correspondence on the project preserved in the Schocken Archive, Jerusalem. In a report on the official inauguration of the clubhouse in the *Palestine Post* on January 28, 1937, 5, Mendelsohn is named as the architect.

53 Mendelsohn's role in the competition for the Museum of Jewish Antiquity and Institute for Archaeological Research can be reconstructed from correspondence between Mendelsohn and Schocken in the Schocken Archive, Jerusalem. The *Palestine Post* devoted two articles to this project, on October 16, 1939, 3, and December 21, 1939, 6.

54 This modest project was likewise omitted from Mendelsohn's list of works. As the building is no longer preserved, the description of the building here is based on plans and photographs from the archives of the Hebrew University, Jerusalem. Mendelsohn's authorship is clearly documented in correspondence preserved in the Schocken Archive in Jerusalem.

55 The modest buildings from the planning phase prior to the founding of the State of Israel were either destroyed or integrated into the new planning of the campus. Of Mendelsohn's buildings, only the clubhouse has survived as a part of the department of archaeology.

56 Personal notes by Mendelsohn, May 16, 1939, KB, E. M. Archive, B IV 5a.

57 A letter from Erich Mendelsohn to Luise, Jerusalem, December 7, 1934, reads: ". . . is supposed to be a big commission—250-bed hospital as well as a medical university." Coll. I. H.-G. English translation published in Beyer 1967, 136.

58 Letters from Erich Mendelsohn to Luise, Jerusalem, December 12, 1934; December 19, 1934; December 23, 1934; coll. I. H.-G. English translation published in Beyer 1967, 137 f. See also the letter from Salman Schocken to Erich Mendelsohn, Jerusalem, March 1, 1935, Sch/A 433.

59 Sketches for the Hadassah University Hospital project are held in the hospital archives, in the graphic collection of the Tel Aviv Museum, and the Erich Mendelsohn Archive of the Kunstbibliothek Berlin. Although the whereabouts of the original models are unknown, they are well-documented in numerous illustrations.

60 The change in plans is documented in letters from Mendelsohn to his wife; the reasons, however, remain unclear. Letters from Erich Mendelsohn to Luise, Jerusalem, January 18, 1936; January 25, 1936, coll. I. H.-G.

61 Letter from Erich Mendelsohn to Luise, Jerusalem, July 27, 1936, coll. I. H.-G. English translation published in Beyer 1967, 144.

62 Interview of the author with Naftali Rostowsky, Tel Aviv, winter 1979–80.

63 Manuscript of an interview by Prof. J. Murphy (Washington University School of Architecture) with Eric Mendelsohn in the City Art Museum of St. Louis, March 13, 1944, KB, E. M. Archive, B IV 4.

64 "First Earth Broken for Hadassah Medical Centre," *Palestine Post* (October 21, 1936), 1.

65 Because of the strike, Mendelsohn had to resort to artificial stone panels for the facing of the building.

66 On this occasion, the *Palestine Post* published a special supplement with a number of articles on various aspects of the new university hospital on Mount Scopus.

67 Interview of the author with Naftali Rostowsky, Tel Aviv, winter 1979–80, and with Louise Mendelsohn, San Francisco, May 1980.

68 Letter from Erich Mendelsohn to Luise, Jerusalem, August 10, 1937, in Beyer 1991, 102. English translation in Beyer 1967, 151.

69 Interview of the author with Naftali Rostowsky, Tel Aviv, winter 1979–80.

70 Mendelsohn had already used a similar stone facing for the front wing of the main administrative building of the Metal Workers' Union building in Berlin.

71 Interview of the author with Naftali Rostowsky, Tel Aviv, winter 1979–80.

72 On the history of Haifa, cf. the outstanding study by Gilbert Herbert and Silvina Sosnovski, *Bauhaus-on-the-Carmel and the Crossroads of Empire. Architecture and Planning during the British Mandate* (Jerusalem, 1993).

73 See Arnold Whittick, *Eric Mendelsohn,* 1st ed. (London, 1940), 2nd expanded ed. (London, 1956), 141. Arnold Whittick also published his own article on the project, "New Government Hospital Haifa," *Building* (February 1939), 70 ff.

74 In her memoirs, Louise Mendelsohn writes: "We met the High Commissioneer of Palestine at a dinner party in London and at once felt very drawn to each other. Sir Arthur Wauchope asked us to see him whenever we were in residence in Jerusalem. During our different visits, when we lived in the windmill no week passed by when we were not asked to dinner at Government House. Sir Arthur Wauchope was a bachelor, a Scot, a general of the Black Watch, and very civilized and interested in all arts, with architecture and music his favorites. Very frequently his aide-de-camp would phone in the morning and ask us to come for an informal dinner alone with him and, if possible, to bring some Bach records. . . . We passed unforgettable evenings with Sir Arthur—one evening in profound conversation with Eric about the development of contemporary architecture and about architecture in general, another listening to the Bach 'Art of Fugue.'" In Louise Mendelsohn n.d., 323 f.

75 Letter from Erich Mendelsohn to Luise, Jerusalem, August 7, 1936, coll. I. H.-G. English translation published in Beyer 1967, 147.

76 From the very beginning, for example, no move was made to announce a public competition. With all the public buildings for the socialistically oriented Jewish community in Palestine, Mendelsohn constantly had to struggle against the demands of the architects' association for public competitions, which among other things always caused long delays in the beginning of construction.

77 "The New Haifa Hospital. A Record of Speed and Efficiency," *Palestine Post* (December 25, 1938), 12.

78 Interview of the author with Naftali Rostowsky, Tel Aviv, winter 1979–80.

79 Eric Mendelsohn, "General Hospital Haifa, Palestine," *Pencil Points* (November 1946), 71.

80 Eric Mendelsohn, "The Anglo-Palestine Bank Building. Site and Town Planning" *Palestine Post* (June 18, 1939), 10.

81 KB, E. M. Archive, Hdz. 729/54, Hdz. 731/54. Mendelsohn discussed his first design in his article for the *Palestine Post* (as note 80). The post office building was designed by the British architect Austen St. Barbe Harrison. Cf. also Aharon Ron Fuchs, *Austen St. Barbe Harrison. A British Architect in the Holy Land,* diss., Haifa 1992.

82 Eric Mendelsohn, "Bank Building at Jerusalem," *Architectural Review* 89 (May 1941), 120.

83 Eric Mendelsohn (as note 80).

84 On the life and work of Alfred Bernheim, cf. the exhibition catalogue *Panim, chasitot wa-od. Zilumei Alfred Bernheim* (*Faces, Facades, and Other Things: Photographs by Alfred Bernheim*), ed. Israel Museum (Jerusalem, 1992).

85 In the estate of the Tel Aviv architectural photographer Itzhak Kalter are a number of photographs showing camels in front of modern Tel Aviv architecture. Kalter Archive, Tel Aviv Museum.

86 Mendelsohn accompanied the photographer Alfred Bernheim to the buildings he was to photograph, giving him precise instructions on particular vantage points, alignments, and perspectives. Interview of the author with Riccarda Schwerin, Bauhaus student and longtime assistant of Alfred Bernheim, Jerusalem, winter 1980–81.

87 Eric Mendelsohn, "My Own Contribution to the Development of Contemporary Architecture" (lecture of 1948), in Beyer 1967, 170 ff.

88 Letter from Eric Mendelsohn to Louise, Jerusalem, October 6, 1938. In Beyer 1991, 111.

89 The original furnishings no longer exist. In addition, the ceilings were lowered to accommodate air conditioning in the bank hall, completely destroying the proportions of the hall as well as the lighting scheme.

90 An evaluation of the meager building files was performed by Adi Weinberg in the context of a seminar paper at the school of architecture at the Technion in Haifa.

91 For detailed discussion of the Youth Aliyah movement from Germany, cf. Gerda Luft 1977 (as note 3).

92 Letters from Erich Mendelsohn to Luise, Jerusalem, January 21, 1936, and January 25, 1936, coll. I. H.-G.

93 The only surviving sketch (KB, E. M. Archive, Hdz. 834/57) as well as elevation drawings, layouts, and photographs of the model show a considerably expanded version which was planned beginning in late 1937 and probably never realized.

94 Mendelsohn was involved with the expansion of the research institute even into the 1940s, when he was already in America. Many of the sketches for this project preserved in the Mendelsohn Archive come from this late phase. Since they required Mendelsohn's presence in the country, however, they were never realized.

95 The controversy on "silent" modernism came to a head in the 1992 exhibition "Tradition und Moderne" at the Deutsches Architektur-Museum in Frankfurt and the publication accompanying it (Vittorio Magnago Lampugnani and Romana Schneider, eds., *Moderne Architektur in Deutschland 1900 bis 1950. Reform und Tradition* [Stuttgart, 1992]). A critical response followed in Gerhard Fehl, *Kleinstadt, Steildach, Volksgemeinschaft. Zum 'reaktionären Modernismus' in Bau- und Stadtbaukunst* (Braunschweig/Wiesbaden, 1995).

96 In a letter from Erich Mendelsohn to Luise, Berlin, May 10, 1924, coll. I. H.-G., we read: "The building commissioner of Allenstein is a folk architect. He wants the 'indigenous' high roof and by this he means that the flat roof is Oriental. . . . Against this, even my tenacity fails. I will not make the roof, because this house does not need an attic and because—I don't like it. Therewith, the commission is returned."

97 Julius Posener, "Vorwort," in idem, *Aufsätze und Vorträge 1931–1980*, ed. Ulrich Conrads (Braunschweig, 1981), 10.

98 Cf. Bruno Zevi, *Erich Mendelsohn. Opera completa* (Milan, 1970), 275; idem, *Eric Mendelsohn* (New York, 1985), 166.

99 Julius Posener, "Erich Mendelsohn" (lecture at the Mendelsohn exhibition at the Akademie der Künste, Berlin, 1968), in *Der Architekt*, special issue (March 1968), 8.

100 Numerous letters from Mendelsohn to friends and potential clients in the mid-1940s show that he kept open the possibility of a return to Palestine/Israel (KB, E. M. Archive).

101 Letter from Eric Mendelsohn to Lewis Mumford, Jerusalem, April 12, 1939, KB, E. M. Archive, B IV 5 a 1/2.

102 Louise Mendelsohn n.d., 390.

"It will be hard for us to find a home"
Projects in the United States 1941–1953

1 Arnold Whittick, *Eric Mendelsohn* (London, 1956) (hereafter cited as Whittick 1956), 135.

2 Among the schools he visited were the University of California at Berkeley, Yale, Harvard, Cornell, Princeton, and Columbia Universities, the University of Michigan in Ann Arbor, the University of Oklahoma, as well as schools in Chicago and Detroit.

3 Mendelsohn's work for the War Department is mentioned in practically every relevant publication on his work. Most probably, his consultancy began in spring 1942, and ended in the latter half of 1943. During this time, target selection for the combined bomber offensive was conducted. This offensive prepared the way for the invasion of 1944 (See *The Army Air Forces in World War II*, ed. by W. F. Craven and J. L. Cate [Washington, D. C., 1983], 2 vols.). I am also grateful to Dr. Wolfgang Voigt of the Deutsches Architektur-Museum, Frankfurt, for sharing some findings of his own research with me.

4 An outline of this book exists, which consists mainly of lists of works and buildings. Mendelsohn only

managed to finish the first three chapters before he began designing again in 1945. Some of the ideas of this book are contained in his *Three Lectures on Architecture* (Berkeley/Los Angeles, 1944) (hereafter cited as Mendelsohn 1944), especially in the lecture titled "Architecture in a Rebuilt World." Excerpts are also contained in his talk "The Three Dimensions of Architecture—Their Symbolic Significance," presented at the 1953 Symposium of the Conference on Science, Philosophy, and Religion.

5 Louise Mendelsohn, "Biographical Notes on Eric," *L'architettura* 95 (September 1963), 405–8.

6 Eric Mendelsohn, "Visions of an Architect," *Magazine of Art* 48 (December 1945), 307–10.

7 The congregation had bought the site in 1944 and was raising a building fund (Congregation B'Nai Amoona, *Bulletin,* March 3, 1945).

8 René Fülöp-Miller, a writer of books on Russian history and culture, introduced Mendelsohn to a rabbi from St. Louis (Louise Mendelsohn, *My Life in a Changing World,* unpublished ms. [San Francisco n. d.], copies are in Mendelsohn Archive, Kunstbibliothek, Staatliche Museen zu Berlin—Preussischer Kulturbesitz, 182). See also George M. Goodwin, "The Design of a Modern Synagogue: Percival Goodman's Beth-El in Providence, Rhode Island," *American Jewish Archives* 45 (spring/summer 1993), 40.

9 Oskar Beyer, *Eric Mendelsohn: Letters of an Architect,* trans. by Geoffrey Strachen (London, 1967) (hereafter cited as Beyer 1967), 157. The congregation reports that they engaged him by December 28, 1945 (B'Nai Amoona, *Bulletin,* December 28, 1945). Sigrid Achenbach dates a perspective of the new synagogue to 1945 and calls it the first version (*Erich Mendelsohn 1887–1953. Ideen Bauten Projekte* [Berlin ,1987], 102, 104).

10 This information was contained in a reprint from the Universal Jewish Encyclopaedia (B'Nai Amoona, *Bulletin,* December 28, 1945; January 25, 1946).

11 Eric Mendelsohn, letter to Julius Posener, February 24, 1946 (Oskar Beyer, *Erich Mendelsohn. Briefe eines Architekten* [Basel/Berlin/Boston, 1991], 112). In January 1946, stakes and pegs were in place, marking the outline of the new synagogue (B'Nai Amoona, *Bulletin,* January 25, 1946).

12 Rosalind Bronsen, *B'Nai Amoona for all Generations* (St. Louis, 1982), 143–44.

13 Carol H. Krinsky, *Synagogues of Europe* (Cambridge, 1985) (hereafter cited as Krinsky 1985), 12, 22–23, 63–66. The interior furnishing is determined by liturgy and consists of Torah, Ark, Bimah, and Eternal Light.

14 Bruno Zevi, *Erich Mendelsohn. Opera completa* (Milan, 1970) (hereafter cited as Zevi 1970), 303–4. All drawings show a cubical shape, only 305/8 has two versions with a cylindrical form. Mendelsohn had already proposed a parabolic roof for a synagogue project in Palestine, in 1934, which is included in the portfolio *Eric Mendelsohn 1887–1953* (San Francisco, 1955).

15 Bruno Zevi, *Erich Mendelsohn* (Zürich, 1983), 176. This could also be interpreted as a means to provide the eternal light necessary in a synagogue. Here, at least during the day, this light is produced naturally (Walter Leedy, "Eric Mendelsohn's Park

Synagogue," in *The Gamut. Cleveland's Sacred Landmarks* [1990] [hereafter cited as Leedy 1990], 51–52). Mendelsohn explained that through this lighting solution he wanted "to achieve additional glory from the afternoon sun. . . ." (Eric Mendelsohn, "Congregation B'Nai Amoona," in *An American Synagogue for Today and Tomorrow* [New York, 1954] [hereafter cited as *American Synagogue* 1954], 101).

16 Due to cost, the project was postponed in mid-1947 (B'Nai Amoona, *Bulletin,* June 20, 1947). In June 1947, substitute plans by Mendelsohn were rejected by the congregation (B'Nai Amoona, *Minutes,* June 2, 1947). At the annual meeting of the congregation in November, a new site further west was contemplated (B'Nai Amoona, *Bulletin,* November 21, 1947).

17 For information on the building campaign and other details, see Rosalind Bronsen (as note 12), 147–51; the *Bulletin* of the congregation; Whittick 1956, 149–50; Rachel Wischnitzer, *Synagogue Architecture in the United States* (Philadelphia, 1955) (hereafter cited as Wischnitzer 1955), 137; "Eric Mendelsohn," in *Architectural Forum* 98 (April 1953), 105–21.

18 Beyer 1967, 175.

19 Erich Mendelsohn, "Das Problem einer neuen Baukunst," in *Das Gesamtschaffen des Architekten. Skizzen, Entwürfe, Bauten* (Berlin, 1930; reprint, Braunschweig/Wiesbaden, 1988), esp. 8, 11.

20 Wischnitzer 1955, 146–48. See also Maria Federico Roggero, *Il contributo di Mendelsohn alla evoluzione dell'architettura moderna* (Milan, 1952) (hereafter cited as Roggero 1952), 52, 55.

21 Mendelsohn 1944, 3–18. Quotes taken from pages 3 and 4. See also the summary of the three lectures in Whittick 1956, 137–39.

22 Erich Mendelsohn, *Der schöpferische Sinn der Krise* (Berlin, 1932).

23 Mendelsohn 1944, 21–31, esp. 26, 31.

24 Erich Mendelsohn, "Die internationale Übereinstimmung des neuen Baugedankens oder Dynamik und Funktion," in *Erich Mendelsohn* (as note 19), 22–34.

25 Paul Frankl, *Principles of Architectural History* (Cambridge, 1968) (hereafter cited as Frankl 1968), 148. Roggero mentioned "the drama of spatial conquest affirmed in linear terms" in Roggero 1952, 26.

26 Frankl 1968, 121, 146, 148.

27 Eric Mendelsohn, letter to Louise Mendelsohn, January 7, 1953, in Beyer 1967, 176.

28 Wolf von Eckardt, *Eric Mendelsohn* (New York, 1960), 31.

29 Kathryn B. Hiesinger, "Introduction: Design Since 1945," in *Design Since 1945* (Philadelphia, 1983), ix–xxiv. Percival Goodman seconded this assessment by stating that synagogue designers needed to face the reality of the industrial climate in the United States (Percival Goodman, "The Character of the Modern Synagogue," in *American Synagogue 1954,* 88). See also the comparisons between Mendelsohn's German work and streamlining in Reyner Banham, "Mendelsohn," *The Architectural Review* 116 (August 1954), 84–93; Elizabeth Macmillian, "Erich Mendelsohn and his Influence on American Architecture and Design of the Thirties," Ph. D. Diss., University of Southern California, 1984.

30 Avram Kampf, *Contemporary Synagogue Art* (New York, 1966), 3; Krinsky 1985, 5.

31 *American Synagogue* 1954, viii, 5–7.

32 Julian Morgenstern, "The Temple and the Synagogue: To 70 C. E." in *American Synagogue* 1954, 16–26.

33 Krinsky 1985, 8, 13.

34 "Preface," in *American Synagogue* 1954, vii–viii.

35 Eugene Lipman, "Reform Judaism: Its Ritual Observances, its Education Practices, and its Social Activities," in *American Synagogue* 1954, 60.

36 Percival Goodman, "Modern Synagogue," in *American Synagogue* 1954, 88, 91; *Temple Emanuel, Open House* (8 pp. brochure for an open house at Temple Emanuel in Grand Rapids, May 23, 1954), 3.

37 Alexander S. Kline, "The Synagogue in America," in *American Synagogue* 1954, 44–45. When Rachel Wischnitzer mentioned in 1947 that Mendelsohn's synagogues for Cleveland and St. Louis may indicate the future of American synagogue architecture, she wrote that period pieces were no longer in demand, although even a twentieth-century building needed to harmonize with its surroundings (Rachel Wischnitzer-Bernstein, "The Problem of Synagogue Architecture," *Commentary* 3 [March 1947], 241).

38 Rachel Wischnitzer, *The Architecture of the European Synagogue* (Philadelphia, 1964), 244. Jewish immigration from Nazi-occupied countries in the 1930s and the Jewish flight from congested neighborhoods in the city to outlying areas after 1945 were mostly responsible for the building boom in synagogues (See Wischnitzer 1955, 135). See also Rochelle Elstein, *Synagogue Architecture in Michigan and the Midwest: Material Culture and the Dynamics of Jewish Accommodation, 1865–1945,* Ph. D. Diss., Michigan State University, 1986 (hereafter cited as Elstein 1986), 29.

39 Roggero called this a "romantic search for purity of expression" (Roggero 1952, 43).

40 Stephen Kayser, "Art in the Synagogue," in *American Synagogue* 1954, 163. Walter Leedy identified the concept of "community" as "central to the idea of a synagogue; this idea constitutes the synagogue in its most fundamental sense" (Leedy 1990, 50). Carol H. Krinsky states that unification and smoothness had been the design goals of early twentieth-century synagogues (Krinsky 1985, 91). Roggero interpreted Mendelsohn's sketches as depicting incommensurable buildings, scaleless, and with a perspective that reaches to infinity. Through such methods, the designs may suggest community (Roggero 1952, 25).

41 Whittick 1956, 186–87; Roggero 1952, 2–3.

42 Whittick 1956, 190. Zevi also mentions this correspondence between Expressionism and the organic (Zevi 1970, 182). Demetri Porphyrios called this capacity of Expressionism "physiognomic Expressionism." He posits that with regard to representation, Expressionist drawings are "based on figural onomatopoeia," which enables them to reveal their inner character through external form. These are understood through "correspondence, resemblance, similarity, or identity" to physiognomic likenesses. Through such operations, forms are endowed with significance (Demetri Porphyrios, *Sources of Modern Eclecticism: Studies on Alvar Aalto* [New York, 1982], 42).

43 Armond Cohen, "Eric Mendelsohn as a Man and Friend," *The Reconstructionist* 20 (October 29, 1954), 16.

44 Charles Reilly praised these designs for reaching "a sublimity in their architecture which few other modern buildings can even aim at." He qualified the interior of the St. Louis synagogue by quoting Mendelsohn's statement that this was "a serene and echoless place of worship" (I have been unable to trace the origin of this quote to Mendelsohn). Charles Reilly, "Mendelsohn in America," *Architecture and Building* (November 1947), 348–49. In a letter to the curator of the Jewish Museum in New York, Mendelsohn wrote: "The meaning of things . . . should be legible even to the illiterate, immediately and automatically" (quoted after Leedy 1990, p. 62).

45 This solution had already been proposed by Ben Bloch in 1944 (Ben Bloch, "Notes on Postwar Synagogue Design," *Architectural Record* 96 [September 1944], 104).

46 Flexible planning and moveable partitions were already used in late-nineteenth-century synagogues (Elstein 1986, 111). According to Rachel Wischnitzer, this idea was part of 1940s synagogue design theory, and derived from practices in modern industrial plans (Reference from Leedy 1990, 50, n. 28).

47 Elstein 1986, 29–30, 43, 53, 100–114.

48 On this building see "A Top Architect's Hospital," *Architectural Forum* 94 (February 1951), 92–99.

49 "Cost-dictated Remodeling Mars Beauty of San Francisco's Maimonides Hospital," *Architectural Forum* 97 (October 1952), 43–44.

50 Leedy 1990, 54–55.

51 Armond Cohen (as note 43), 17.

52 There is a correspondence disputing fees dating July 1948 (Cohen Papers, Western Reserve Historical Society, Cleveland).

53 "Eric Mendelsohn," *The Architectural Forum* 86 (May 1947), 74. Further examples of formal and material relationships between Mendelsohn's designs and transportation vehicles can be found in his early sketches and some of his buildings of the 1920s.

54 Cohen (as note 43), 18.

55 Elstein 1986, 58; Krinsky 1985, 36.

56 Beyer 1967, 165. Earlier examples of this union between site and building are: the Mendelsohn house, Berlin; the Weizmann house, Rehovot; and Hadassah Hospital on Mt. Scopus, Jerusalem. Roggero also commented on the landscape forming a romantic background for the rhythms of the building. He described the Hadassah Hospital in Jerusalem as an unwinding of compact masses down the hillside (Roggero 1952, 45, 48).

57 Eric Mendelsohn described it as "the idea of the tent—shielding the Ark" in Beyer 1967, 171. See also Wischnitzer 1955, 238.

58 Krinsky 1985, 92, 356, 401.

59 Frankl 1968, 112, 130, 146, 148.

60 For an inadequate evaluation of this building see William H. Jordy, "The Aftermath of the Bauhaus in America: Gropius, Mies, and Breuer," in *The Intellectual Migration: Europe and America, 1930–1960,* eds. Donald Fleming and Bernard Bailyn (Cambridge, 1969), 500–502, 521–22.

61 Mendelsohn 1944, 37, 40, 43–44.

62 Eric Mendelsohn, "In the Spirit of Our Age," *Commentary* (June 3, 1947), 541–42.

63 Stephen Kayser (as note 40), 155–56.

64 Eric Mendelsohn (as note 11), 112. For his involvement in the project for Providence, see George
M. Goodwin (as note 8), 38–43.

65 Such tent-like roof structures are a trademark of Percival Goodman's synagogues from his most productive decade, 1953–1963 (Evelyn Greenberg, "The
Tabernacle in the Wilderness: The Mishkan Theme
in Percival Goodman's Modern American Synagogues," *Journal of Jewish Art,* 20 [1993], 45–55).
See also the many illustrations in Kampf 1985.

66 Eric Mendelsohn, letter to Louise Mendelsohn,
January 27, 1950, in Beyer 1967, 174.

67 Eric Mendelsohn, letter to Julius Posener, 1947, in
Beyer 1967, 159. Mendelsohn visited Wright on his
1941 trip through the United States. He stayed at
Taliesin East and saw Wright's Johnson Wax Factory
in Racine. In the previous year, Mendelsohn had visited Wright at Taliesin West and conveyed to Posener his admiration for the elder colleague. He saw
himself as having an "inner affinity" with Wright,
mentioned his "singular greatness," and praised his
latest works as "the completion of all that . . . he
[Wright] has striven to resolve, to discover and to
create." Whittick 1956, 136.

68 Evaluation of the synagogue by Edith Weiss in *History of Temple Emanuel,* May 1954, Archives of Temple Emanuel, Grand Rapids.

69 See the various reports in the *New York Times,*
January 18, 1950; March 14, 1950; July 17, 1951;
May 23, 1951; February 17, 1953. It appears that this
monument was not built because at that time major
memorials to the Holocaust were erected in Israel.
Most probably, American Jews did not want to
compete for the funds needed for these efforts.

70 According to Zevi, there was an exhausting fight for
the pointed gables, but the committee wanted
square forms (Zevi 1970, 193).

71 The dates of the building campaign have been
reconstructed from the pertinent issues of Mt. Zion
Hebrew Congregation, Temple Bulletin. See also
W. Gunther Plaut, *Mount Zion 1856–1956: The First
Hundred Years* (St. Paul, 1956), 102–4.

72 On this building see "The Last Work of a Great
Architect," *Architectural Forum* 102 (February 1955),
106–15.

73 Kampf 1985, 32.

74 Stephen Kayser (as note 40), 156, 163, 166, 168,
171.

75 Krinsky 1985, 96. Mendelsohn certainly considered
architecture the most significant part of the building,
and treated art as "an organic part of the structure"
(Kampf 1985, 41).

76 Curtains and draperies may again point to the Tent
in the Wilderness. See Evelyn Greenberg 1993, 51.

77 Sylvia G. Krissoff, "Temple Emanuel, Grand Rapids,
Michigan," *Thesis* (1971).

78 For the interiors of St. Louis, Cleveland, and St. Paul
see Kampf 1985, 174–80. For Cleveland, see Leedy
1990, 61. For St. Paul, see W. Gunther Plaut (as note
71), 5–6.

79 *Recent American Synagogue Architecture* (New
York, 1963), 7.

80 "For Electronic Research and Development," *Architectural Record* 116 (July 1954), 156–61.

81 "Laboratory for Radioactive Research," *Architectural
Record* 121 (June 1957), 224–26.

82 Eric Mendelsohn, "Ideas in Action," *Seven Arts* 1
(Summer 1953), 7–11.

83 Elstein 1986, 5, 12.

84 Reyner Banham (as note 29), 93.

85 Modern Architecture Symposium, Columbia University, *Architecture 1918–28: From the Novembergruppe to the C.I.A.M. (Functionalism and Expressionism)* (New York, 1962).

86 Nikolaus Pevsner, "Introduction," in Beyer 1967, 20.

Eric Mendelsohn in his third and final exile in the United States of America. This undated photograph from the collection of his daughter, Esther, shows him sketching a high-rise, a building type for which he had found an exemplary solution in the 1920s in Germany with the Columbushaus, but which he no longer had opportunity to build in America.

March 21, 1887
Born in Allenstein, East Prussia, the fifth child of Emma Esther Mendelsohn, née Jaruslawsky, a milliner, and David Mendelsohn, a merchant.

1893–1907
Attends elementary school; secondary education completed at the Humanistisches Gymnasium, Allenstein.

1907
Studies political economy at the Ludwig-Maximilians-Universität, Munich.

1908–10
Studies architecture at the Technische Hochschule, Berlin-Charlottenburg.

1910–12
Completes studies in architecture under Theodor Fischer at the Technische Hochschule, Munich.

1911–13
First realized building: Jewish cemetery chapel in Allenstein.

1912–14
After finishing his studies, works as an independent architect, stage and costume designer, furniture designer, and decorator in Munich. Becomes involved in Expressionist theater through his friendship with the artists of the Blue Rider Group.

1914
Moves to Berlin.

1915
Called up for military service. Marries Luise Maas, whom he has known since 1910.

1916
Birth of daughter, Marie Luise Esther.

1917
Stationed on the Russian front. Sketches during his night watches.

1918
Transferred to the western front. On November 7, returns to Berlin and opens his own architectural office. Member of the Arbeitsrat für Kunst and the Novembergruppe.

1919
Gives lectures in the salon of Molly Philippson in Berlin and at the Arbeitsrat für Kunst. An exhibition of his sketches is shown in the gallery of Paul Cassirer, Berlin. Friendship with Oskar Beyer begins.

1920
Extensive works for Gustav Herrmann in Luckenwalde until 1923: residential development, garden house, and hat factory for Steinberg, Herrmann & Co. Commission for the planning of the Einstein Tower in Potsdam, realized 1920–24. Trip to Holland.

1921
Remodeling and expansion of the Rudolf Mosse publishing house in Berlin together with Richard Neutra and Paul Rudolf Henning; Double Villa at Karolinger Platz, completed 1922. Serious eye operation and removal of left eye due to cancer.

1922
Weichmann silk store in Gleiwitz and renovation of textile factory for Meyer-Kauffmann-Textilwerke AG in Wüstegiersdorf, both completed 1923.

1923
Travels to Palestine and Holland, followed by projects for Haifa and a lecture. Sternefeld villa, Berlin, completed 1924.

1924
C. A. Herpich & Sons store, completed 1929. Cofounder of Zehnerring (Ring of Ten), expanded in 1926 into the architects' union Der Ring. Trip to America.

1925
Travels in the USSR for the Krasnoje Snamja (Red Flag textile factory) project in Leningrad. Lodge of the Three Patriarchs, Tilsit. Schocken department store in Nuremberg, completed 1926. Plans for WOGA complex with Universum Cinema, executed 1927–1931. First project for remodeling and expansion of Cohen & Epstein department store, executed in reduced form 1926–27.

1926
Publication of *Amerika*. Planning begins for Schocken department store in Stuttgart, completed in 1928. Country house for Dr. Bejach, Steinstücken near Berlin, completed 1927.

1927
Petersdorff department store, Breslau, completed 1928. Planning begins for Schocken department store in Chemnitz, erected 1929–30.

1928
Rudolf Mosse pavilion for the "Pressa" trade fair in Cologne. Plans for the Galéries Lafayette at Potsdamer Platz in Berlin, realized in modified form as the Columbushaus in 1931–32. Plans his own house, Am Rupenhorn, near Berlin, executed 1929–30.

1929
Publication of *Russland–Europa–Amerika*. Travels to Spain.

1930
Travels to England. Becomes honorary member of the Art Club in London. Jewish youth center, Essen, completed 1931.

1931
Travels to Corsica and Greece. Becomes member of the Prussian Academy of the Arts.

1932
Travels to Paris and the Côte d'Azur to plan the Académie Européenne Méditerranée. Also travels to Norway, where he is commissioned to plan the Dobloug department store in Oslo, executed in 1932 by Rudolf Emanuel Jacobsen.

1933
Emigrates via Holland to England, where he founds an architectural office in partnership with Serge Chermayeff.

1934
Nimmo house, Chalfont St. Giles. Wins first prize in a competition for a resort at Bexhill-on-Sea, Sussex, largely completed by 1935. Planning begins for the Hebrew University on Mount Scopus, partially executed 1936–1939; planning begins for the Weizmann house in Rehovot and the house and library of Salman Schocken in Jerusalem, both realized 1935–36.

1935
Founds architectural office in Jerusalem. Private house for Dennis Cohen in London. Planning begins for the Anglo-Palestine Bank, Jerusalem, executed 1937–39.

1936
End of partnership with Chermayeff, who realizes the Gilbey building in Camden near London and a laboratory building for the Dyestuffs Group of Imperial Chemical Industries in Blackley near Manchester after plans by Mendelsohn.

1937
Government Hospital in Haifa, completed 1938.

1938
Becomes a British subject. Planning begins for the Daniel Wolf Research Laboratory, Rehovot, executed 1940–41.

1939
Becomes a fellow of the RIBA (Royal Institute of British Architects). Emigrates to Jerusalem.

1940
Agricultural College of the Hebrew University, Jerusalem, in Rehovot.

1941
Closes Jerusalem office and emigrates to the United States via Basra, Karachi, Bombay, Cape Town, and Trinidad. Two-and-a-half-month tour of the United States. Solo exhibition at the Museum of Modern Art in New York.

1942
Lectures at Yale and in Chicago, Detroit, and Berkeley.

1943
A scholarship from the John Simon Guggenheim Memorial Foundation enables him to gather material for his long-planned book *A Contemporary Philosophy of Architecture*, which he worked on until 1945. The Mendelsohns live in Croton-on-Hudson, New York. Becomes a member of the New American Society of Architects and Planners and the Sociedad de Arquitectos Mexicanos.

1945
Moves to San Francisco and opens his own architectural office (for a brief time together with John Ekin Dinwiddie and Albert Henry Hill). B'nai Amoona Synagogue and Community Center, St. Louis, Missouri, completed 1950.

1946
Receives American citizenship and official licensing as an architect in California. Plan of Park Synagogue in Cleveland, Ohio, erected 1952. Maimonides Hospital, San Francisco, executed 1948–50.

1947
Receives a teaching post at the University of California, Berkeley.

1948
Emanu-El Synagogue and Community Center, Grand Rapids, Michigan, executed 1952. Russell house, San Francisco, built 1950–51.

1949
Designs monument to the six million Jews killed in the Holocaust, Riverside Park, New York.

1950
Mount Zion Synagogue and Community Center, St. Paul, Minnesota, erected 1952–54. Electronic Research and Development Plant in Palo Alto for Varian Associates, executed 1952–53.

1951
Beginning of work on his uncompleted autobiography, *My Life in Sketches*.

1952
Laboratory building for the Atomic Energy Commission of the University of California at Berkeley, executed 1953.

1953
Mendelsohn dies of cancer on September 15, 1953. In accord with his wishes, his ashes are scattered on the sea.

Achenbach, Sigrid, ed. *Erich Mendelsohn 1887–1953. Ideen, Bauten, Projekte* exh. cat. Staatliche Museen Preussischer Kulturbesitz zu Berlin. Berlin, 1987.

Astrophysikalisches Institut Potsdam. *Der Einsteinturm in Potsdam. Architektur und Astrophysik.* Berlin, 1995.

Baacke, Rolf-Peter. *Lichtspielhausarchitektur in Deutschland von der Schaubühne bis zum Kinopalast.* Berlin, 1982.

Banham, Reyner. *Die Revolution der Architektur. Theorie und Gestaltung im Ersten Maschinenzeitalter.* Hamburg, 1964. Reprint, Braunschweig, 1990.

Behn, Helga. *Die Architektur des deutschen Warenhauses von ihren Anfängen bis 1933.* Cologne, 1984.

Benton, Charlotte. *A Different World: Emigre Architects in Britain 1928–1958.* Exh. cat. RIBA, Heinz Gallery. London, 1995.

———. "Mendelsohn and the City." In *Erich Mendelsohn 1887–1953.* Edited by Jeremy Brook and Nasser Golzari. Bexhill-on-Sea, Sussex, 1987.

Benton, Tim, and Charlotte Benton, eds. *Form and Function. A Source Book for the History of Architecture and Design 1890–1939.* London, 1975.

Berckenhagen, Ekhart. "Erich Mendelsohns Architekturzeichnungen in Berlin." In *Jahrbuch Preussischer Kulturbesitz.* Vol. XIII. Berlin, 1977.

Berg, Peter. *Deutschland und Amerika 1918–1929. Über das deutsche Amerikabild der zwanziger Jahre.* Lübeck, 1963.

Beseler, Hartwig, and Nils Gutschow. *Kriegsschicksale deutscher Architektur. Verluste—Schäden—Wiederaufbau. Eine Dokumentation für das Gebiet der Bundesrepublik Deutschland.* 2 vols. Neumünster, 1988.

Beyer, Oskar. "Architectuur in ijzer en beton." *Wendingen* (October 1920): 4–14.

———. *Erich Mendelsohn. Briefe eines Architekten.* Munich, 1961. Reprint, Basel/Berlin/Boston, 1991.

———. *Eric Mendelsohn: Letters of an Architect.* London/New York/Toronto, 1967.

———. "Eine neue Monumentalarchitektur." *Feuer* 2: 2/3. (November/December 1920): 111–17.

Frecot, Janos, and Helmut Geisert. *Berlin im Abriss.* Berlin, 1981.

Fuchs, Konrad. *Ein Konzern aus Sachsen. Das Kaufhaus Schocken als Spiegelbild deutscher Wirtschaft und Politik 1900–1953.* Stuttgart, 1992.

Grimm, Georg. *Kauf- und Warenhäuser.* Berlin, 1928.

Guralnik, Nehama. *Eric Mendelsohn: Drawings of an Architect.* Tel Aviv, 1979.

Heinze-Mühleib, Ita. *Erich Mendelsohn. Bauten und Projekte in Palästina 1934–1941.* Munich, 1986.

Hentschel, Klaus. *Der Einsteinturm.* Heidelberg, 1992.

Herbert, Gilbert, and Silvina Sosnovsky. *Bauhaus on the Carmel and the Crossroads of Empire: Architecture and Planning in Haifa during the British Mandate.* Jerusalem, 1993.

Hilberseimer, Ludwig. *Großstadtarchitektur.* Stuttgart, 1928.

Huse, Norbert. *Neues Bauen 1918–1933. Moderne Architektur in der Weimarer Republik.* Munich, 1975.

Hüter, Karl Heinz. *Architektur in Berlin 1900–1933.* Stuttgart, 1988.

Jelavich, Peter. *Munich and Theatrical Modernism: Politics, Playwriting, and Performance 1890–1914.* Cambridge, 1985.

Kähler, Gert. *Architektur als Symbolverfall. Das Dampfermotiv in der Baukunst.* Braunschweig, 1981.

King, Susan. *The Drawings of Eric Mendelsohn.* Exh. cat. University Art Museum, University of California, Berkeley. Berkeley, 1969.

Lampugnani, Vittorio Magnago, and Romana Schneider, eds. *Moderne Architektur in Deutschland 1900 bis 1950. Expressionismus und Neue Sachlichkeit.* Stuttgart, 1994.

Lane, Barbara Miller. *Architecture and Politics in Germany 1914–1945.* Cambridge, 1985.

Lotz, Wilhelm, and E. R. Haberfeld. *Licht und Beleuchtung. Lichttechnische Fragen unter Berücksichtigung der Bedürfnisse der Architektur.* Berlin, 1928.

Mendelsohn, Erich. *Amerika. Bilderbuch eines Architekten.* Berlin. 1926. Reprint, Braunschweig/Wiesbaden, 1991.

———. *Complete Works of the Architect: Sketches, Designs, Buildings.* New York, 1992.

———. *Das Gesamtschaffen des Architekten. Skizzen, Entwürfe, Bauten.* Berlin, 1930. Reprint, Braunschweig/Wiesbaden, 1988.

———. *Neues Haus—Neue Welt.* With contributions by Amédée Ozenfant and Edwin [Erwin] Redslob. Berlin, 1932. Reprint, Berlin, 1997.

———. *Russland–Europa–Amerika. Ein architektonischer Querschnitt.* Berlin, 1928. Reprint, Basel/Berlin/Boston, 1989.

———. *Der schöpferische Sinn der Krise.* Berlin, 1932. Reprint, Berlin, 1986.

Mendelsohn, Louise. "Biographical Note on Eric." *L'architettura. Cronache e storia* 9 (1963): 295 ff.

Morgenthaler, Hans R. *The Early Sketches of German Architect Erich Mendelsohn (1887–1953): No Compromise With Reality.* New York, 1992.

———. *Erich Mendelsohn 1887–1953: An Annotated Bibliography.* Monticello, Ill., 1987.

Müller-Wulckow, Walter. *Architektur der zwanziger Jahre in Deutschland.* Königstein/Taunus, 1975.

Nerdinger, Winfred. *Theodor Fischer. Architekt und Städtebauer 1862–1938.* Berlin, 1988.

Neumann, Dietrich. *"Die Wolkenkratzer kommen!" Deutsche Hochhäuser der zwanziger Jahre. Debatten, Projekte, Bauten.* Braunschweig, 1995.

Pehnt, Wolfgang. *Die Architektur des Expressionismus.* 1st ed. Stuttgart, 1973. 2nd ed. Stuttgart, 1981. 3rd ed., rev. Stuttgart, 1998.

———. *Architekturzeichnungen des Expressionismus.* Stuttgart, 1985.

Pfeifer, Hans-Georg. "Entstehung und Entwicklung der Kauf- und Warenhäuser von der Mitte des 19. Jahrhunderts bis in die 30er Jahre des 20. Jahrhunderts." In *Architektur für den Handel.* Basel/Boston/Berlin, 1996.

Posener, Julius, ed. *Erich Mendelsohn.* Exh. cat. Akademie der Künste. Berlin, 1968.

Brook, Jeremy, and Nasser Golzari, eds. *Erich Mendelsohn 1887–1953.* Bexhill-on-Sea, Sussex, 1987.

Posener, Julius. *Fast so alt wie das Jahrhundert.* Berlin, 1990.

Robinson, Cervin, and Joel Herschmann. *Architecture Transformed: A History of the Photography of Buildings from 1839 to the Present.* Cambridge, 1987.

Roggero, Mario Federico. *Il contributo di Mendelsohn alla evoluzione dell'architettura moderna.* Milan, 1952.

Sachsse, Rolf. *Zur Nutzung technischer Medien beim Entwerfen von Architektur.* Braunschweig, 1997.

Schiller, Lotte. *Eric Mendelsohn 1887–1953: Catalog of Sketches.* Mill Valley, Calif., 1970. (Twenty-five numbered copies of the manuscript, one of them in the Kunstbibliothek, Staatliche Museen zu Berlin, Preussischer Kulturbesitz.)

Schulze, Konrad Werner. *Glas in der Architektur der Gegenwart.* Stuttgart, 1928.

———. *Der Stahlskelettbau. Geschäfts- und Hochhäuser.* Stuttgart, 1928.

Stephan, Regina. *Studien zu Waren- und Geschäftshäusern Erich Mendelsohns in Deutschland.* Munich, 1992.

Stommer, Rainer. *Hochhaus. Der Beginn in Deutschland.* Marburg, 1990.

Von Eckardt, Wolf. *Grosse Meister der Architektur.* Vol. 8, *Erich Mendelsohn.* Ravensburg, 1962.

Wagner, Martin. *Das Neue Berlin. Großstadtprobleme.* Berlin, 1929.

Whittick, Arnold. *Eric Mendelsohn.* 2nd ed. London, 1956.

Zevi, Bruno. *Erich Mendelsohn.* Zürich, 1983.

———. *Erich Mendelsohn. Opera completa.*

First published in the United States of America in 1999 by

The Monacelli Press, Inc.
10 East 92nd Street, New York, New York 10128.

Copyright © 1998 Verlag Gerd Hatje, Ostfildern-Ruit,
Germany, and authors and photographers
English edition © 1999 The Monacelli Press, Inc., and
authors and photographers

Translated by Melissa Thorson Hause
(Ita Heinze-Greenberg, Regina Stephan)

Designed by Christine Müller
Production by Dr. Cantz'sche Druckerei, Ostfildern-Ruit,
Germany

Library of Congress Cataloging-in-Publication Data
Erich Mendelsohn. English.
Eric Mendelsohn : architect 1887–1953 / edited by
Regina Stephan ; with essays by Charlotte Benton . . .
[et al.].
p. cm.
Includes bibliographical references and index.
ISBN 1-58093-034-4
1. Mendelsohn, Erich, 1887–1953 Criticism and
interpretation. 2. Architecture, Modern—20th century.
I. Mendelsohn, Erich, 1887–1953. II. Stephan, Regina,
1963– . III. Benton, Charlotte. IV. Title.
NA1088.M57E7513   1999
720'.92—dc21   99-39551

Printed and bound in Germany

Photography Credits

The numbers refer to pages. With one exception
(p. 102 m.), all of the photographs reproduced here
show Mendelsohn's buildings immediately following
completion. The photographs from the 1920s and early
1930s were taken primarily by Arthur Köster, those of
Mendelsohn's buildings in Palestine primarily by Alfred
Bernheim.

Abbreviations: t. = top, m. = middle, b. = bottom, l. = left,
r. = right

Akademie der Künste Berlin, Sammlung Baukunst,
Photo: Arthur Köster: 130 b.
Alte Synagoge Essen: 151
Architectural Heritage Research Centre, Technion Haifa:
64 b., 206, 208 t., 210 b., 215, 217 t., 220 b., 225 b.,
232, 233, 235, 236 b., 237 t., 237 b., 240
Architectural Review, October 1937: 209
Architectural Review, February 1940: 229
Archives of the Hebrew University, Jerusalem: 217 b.,
223 b., 224, 226 b., 228, 230, 231 t.
Bauhaus-Archiv Berlin: 59
Bauhof, Nuremberg: 79 m., 79 b.
Charlotte Benton Archive: 193 b., 197 t., 197 b., 200 t.,
202 t.
Bernheim Collection, Israel Museum: 174, 214, 220 t.
Bezirksbauamt Berlin-Kreuzberg: 124
Bildstelle und Fotoarchiv, Nuremberg: 82 t.
Central Zionist Archives, Jerusalem: 188, 205
Gabriel Epstein, Paris: 99
Frühlicht, 3, 1921/22: 121
Ilse Goldenzweig, Tel Aviv: 184
Will Grohmann, Zehn Jahre Novembergruppe, special
issue of Kunst der Zeit, 3, 1928: 154
Jürgen Holstein, Berlin: 156 t., 170
Karl-Heinz Hüter, Architektur in Berlin 1900–1933,
Dresden/Stuttgart, 1988: 109, 122 t.
Landesbildstelle Württemberg: 87, 89 b.
Landeshauptstadt Stuttgart, Stadtarchiv: 83
Erich Mendelsohn, Bilderbuch eines Architekten, Berlin,
1926: 68 r.
Erich Mendelsohn, Das Gesamtschaffen des Architek-
ten, Berlin, 1930: 29, 30, 40 t., 42, 44, 50, 51, 54 m.,
63 b., 64 t., 75, 84, 86 l., 93 t., 97 t., 104, 100 m.,
105 b., 111, 114, 115 l., 132, 143, 146, 147 t., 168
Erich Mendelsohn, Neues Haus—Neue Welt, with essays
by Amédée Ozenfant and Edwin (Erwin) Redslob,
Berlin, 1931: 178 t.
Erich Mendelsohn, Russland—Europa—Amerika, Berlin,
1929: 68 l., 70, 71
Erich Mendelsohn 1887–1953, ed. by Jeremy Brook,
London, 1987: 191 b., 192, 193 t., 194 t.
Esther Mendelsohn-Joseph, San Francisco: 15 t., 23,
56, 60 b., 155 t., 155 b., 176, 183, 185, 190, 204, 241,
278
Moderne Bauformen, 29, 1930: 105 m.
National Monuments Record Centre, Swindon: 201 b.
Nürnberger Zeitung und Korrespondent, 10-9-1926:
82 b.
Wolfgang Pehnt, Die Architektur des Expressionismus,
Stuttgart, 1973: 58 t.
Pencil Points, November 1946: 234
Julius Posener, Fast so alt wie das Jahrhundert, Berlin,
1990: 158 t.

Schocken Archives Jerusalem: 221
Arieh Sharon, Kibbutz + Bauhaus. An Architect's Way in
a New Land, Stuttgart, 1976: 61
Staatliche Museen zu Berlin—Preussischer Kulturbesitz,
Kunstbibliothek. Reproduction photographs by Dietmar
Katz, Karl Paulmann-Jungblut and Knud Peter Petersen,
Berlin. For sketches, the inventory number from the
Erich Mendelsohn Archive of the Kunstbibliothek is
added in parantheses: 6, 12 (487), 13 (297), 14 (266,
504), 17 (213), 18 (956), 19 (257), 20 (695), 21 (1112),
22 (885), 24 l. (239), 24 r. (238), 25 (237), 27 l. (336),
27 r. (letter from Erwin Finlay-Freundlich to Erich
Mendelsohn), 28 (1137), 32 (145), 33 t. (144), 33 b.
(142), 34, 35, 36, 39 (5146r), 40 b., 41 (321), 43, 45 t.
(178), 45 b., 48 t. (36), 46 (203), 47 (5162/1), 48 t. (662),
49 t. (36), 49 b. (880), 52 t., 52 b., 55 (675), 54 b., 62
(1199), 63 t. (653/21), 63 m. (369/19), 66 t., 67, 72, 74,
76, 77, 78 t., 79 t. (115), 80, 81, 85 (155), 86 b., 88, 89 t.,
92, 93 b., 90 (156), 95 (154), 96 (165), 97 b., 100 t.
(173), 100 b. (166), 102 b., 101, 102 t., 103 (177), 105 t.
(472), 106, 107, 108, 112, 115 b., 116, 117, 119 t. (28),
119 b. (18), 122 b., 123 (Fol 2035), 125, 126, 127, 128 t.,
128 b. (123), 129, 130 t., 131 (894), 133, 135, 136, 138,
139, 140 (471), 141 (478), 142, 144, 147 b., 148, 149,
150, 153, 156 b., 157 t. (5219 recto), 157 b. (5219 ver-
so), 158 b., 159 (233), 161, 162, 163 (130), 164, 165,
166, 169, 171 (131), 173, 175 r. (1372), 175 l. (1351),
177, 178 m., 178 b., 179, 180, 181, 187, 189, 191 t. (741),
194 b., 195, 196, 198, 199, 200 b., 201 t., 202 b., 207
(40/52), 208 b., 210 t., 211 (41), 219 t., 219 b. (435/53a),
222, 223 t. (63/55), 226 t., 227, 231 b., 236 t. (728/54),
239, 242 (681), 243 (4098), 244 t., 244 b., 247 t., 247 m.
(4421), 247 b., 248, 249 t. (4384), 249 b., 250 t., 250 b.,
251, 252, 253 t., 253 m., 253 b. (1174), 254 t. l., 254 t. r.,
254 b., 255 (4949), 257 (584), 258 t., 258 b. l., 258 b. r.,
259 t. (4721), 259 b., 260 (1084), 261 (712)
Stadt Allenstein, Stadtkreisgemeinschaft in der Lands-
mannschaft Ostpreussen e. V., Allensteiner Heimat-
museum, Der Treudank, Gelsenkirchen: 16
Städtebau, 20, 1925: 73
Stadtverwaltung Potsdam, Amt für Denkmalpflege: 37
Der Stahlbau, supplement to the magazine Die Bautech-
nik, 4, 1931: 134 b.
Erwin Stein (Ed.), Monographien deutscher Städte,
vol. XII: Gleiwitz, Berlin, 1925: 54 t.
Regina Stephan, Stuttgart: 91, 102 m.
Carsten-Peter Warncke, The Ideal as Art De Stijl
1917–1931, Cologne, 1991: 58 b.
Wasmuths Monatshefte für Baukunst und Städtebau,
15, 1931: 134 t.
Wasmuths Monatshefte für Baukunst und Städtebau,
8, 1924: 120
Arnold Whittick, Eric Mendelsohn, London, 1956: 225 t.,
238
Archive Anne and Jürgen Wilde, Bonn: 78 b.
Wim de Witt, The Amsterdam School. Dutch Expressionist
Architecture 1915–1930, New York, 1983: 60 t.
Sibel Zaudi-Sayak: 113
Zentralblatt der Bauverwaltung, 52, 46, 1932: 137
Bruno Zevi, Erich Mendelsohn. Opera completa, Milan,
1970: 15 b., 66 b., 98, 110, 202 r., 203, 216

Every effort was made to give appropriate credit for
all the photographs in this book. Omissions will be
corrected in subsequent editions.